ADVANCE PRAISE FOR *TWENTY DOLLARS AND CHANGE*

"In this original and brilliantly conceived book, acclaimed political scientist Clarence Lusane offers an incisive analysis of how racism and inequality shaped—and continue to shape—American society. Timely and significant, *Twenty Dollars and Change* deftly draws upon the past to offer a road map for how we might work to build an inclusive democracy in the United States."

—Keisha N. Blain, coeditor, *Four Hundred Souls:
A Community History of African America, 1619–2019*

"*Twenty Dollars and Change* offers a metaphor about two Americas: one striving to live up to its promise of justice and liberty, and the other mired in the bloody legacy of white supremacy. The historical arc Lusane provides demonstrates that the freedom struggle changes its cast of characters over time, but never forsakes its hope for liberation. A great and refreshing read."

—Loretta Ross, author of *Calling In the Calling Out Culture*

"Thoughtfully balanced and nuanced, *Twenty Dollars and Change* explores the ways that American hero and national icon Harriet Tubman resonates across racial, gender, and political divides. Lusane captures not only the significance of historic symbols, but how winning the fight over representation and memory advances the ongoing struggles for racial justice and democracy right now."

—Janell Hobson, editor of *Ms. Magazine's* Harriet Tubman Bicentennial Project and author of *When God Lost Her Tongue: Historical Consciousness and the Black Feminist Imagination*

"*Twenty Dollars and Change* travels the back alleys of fear of racist white America. . . . Harriet Tubman's image on the money is an opportunity to establish the symbol of democracy she wanted, one where actions led by a conceived idea of being inferior or superior are crushed. Clarence Lusane has put it where the goats can get it. An extraordinary and wonderful book."

—Tina Wyatt, great great great grandniece of Harriet Tubman, co-founder of Harriet Tubman Day, Washington D.C.

"*Twenty Dollars and Change* is a book for our times. As challenges to racial justice, women's rights, and democracy itself intensify, Lusane's sober and historically rooted analysis provides much-needed clarity and insight. Tubman represents the best that this nation has produced, and her life experiences and unrelenting commitment to equality echo in today's struggle for reforming criminal justice, dismantling white supremacist symbols, protecting voting rights, and securing health equity. Lusane expertly links these campaigns and calls for the nation to implement the principles it claims to hold. As Lusane argues, yes, Andrew Jackson should be replaced by Harriet Tubman. And, yes, gender and racial inequalities and marginalization should be replaced by a genuine multi-racial, inclusive democracy. *Twenty Dollars and Change* is exactly the book we need at this moment."

—Congresswoman Karen Bass

"Clarence Lusane has been a respected scholar activist and keen observer of the Black Freedom Movement for many decades now. His new book, *Twenty Dollars and Change*, offers powerful analyses of race and U.S. history and our present crucible moment. Writing from what he terms a 'Tubman, liberationist, perspective' he delivers powerful and provocative insights that must be engaged seriously. A must read."

—Barbara Ransby, author of *Making All Black Lives Matter: Reimagining Freedom in the Twenty-First Century*

"Freedom and democracy are the core values the U.S. advertises when vaunting the rights to life, liberty, and the pursuit of happiness. *Twenty Dollars and Change* confronts the biases that privilege the few over the many in the supposed realization of these values. In this trailblazing study, Dr. Lusane builds an irrefutable case that justice in representation goes hand in hand with justice in policy. Replacing Andrew Jackson with Harriet Tubman on the twenty-dollar bill parallels intergenerational struggles to end racism and sexism in America. Urgent and inspiring, *Twenty Dollars and Change* should compel the U.S. Treasury to make real our core value of equality for all with currency images that honor the contributions and humanity of African Americans, Native Americans, women, and all marginalized people of this country. Dr. Lusane sees Tubman as a Founding Mother of American democracy yet to come, and offers a persuasive case how a new twenty and change can get us there sooner."

—Barbara Ortiz Howard, Founder, Women On 20s

"This brisk and intelligent study shows readers why the question of whether freedom fighter Harriet Tubman replaces oppression fighter Andrew Jackson on the twenty-dollar bill is a matter of great importance. Lusane teaches us of the starkly contrasting lives of Tubman and Jackson, and captures blow-by-blow the intricacies of the struggles over changing currency before connecting them to broader ones in the moment of Donald Trump and George Floyd. He brilliantly insists, with the great Stuart Hall, that struggles over identity and power never exist 'outside representation.'"

—David Roediger, author of *Working Toward Whiteness: How America's Immigrants Became White*

"Columbus lurched upon our shores with his men, rats, fleas, weapons of torture, disease, and death, launching generational waves of manifest destiny, white supremacy, and genocide in this red quarter of Mother Earth, ravaging her children and poisoning her waters, lands, and skies. Inquisition-era religious and 'discovery' doctrines, gold fever, land lust, and settler/slaver colonialism shaped the United States, defined its symbols, and drove its policies of privilege and exclusion. This history of foundational injustice is carefully analyzed in the courageous and unflinching *Twenty Dollars and Change*, which also joyfully celebrates ongoing resistance to all racism, sexism, and bigotry. By lifting up the life and legacy of the self-emancipated Harriet Tubman—who heroically freed scores of others from slavery through the Underground Railroad, despite her own conditions of illiteracy and disability, and who became an unstoppable liberator and warrior for equality—Clarence Lusane reminds us that we all can contribute enormously to a more perfect society based on the dignity, diversity, and democracy of the peoples. In that spirit, and with great clarity and integrity, Lusane calls on us to wake up, fight back, and never back down until justice prevails."

—Suzan Shown Harjo (Cheyenne & Hodulgee Muscogee), writer/editor, curator, Native & Indigenous Rights advocate, and recipient of the Presidential Medal of Freedom

TWENTY DOLLARS *and* **CHANGE**

TWENTY
DOLLARS
—— *and* ——
CHANGE

HARRIET TUBMAN AND THE ONGOING
FIGHT FOR RACIAL JUSTICE AND DEMOCRACY

CLARENCE LUSANE

City Lights Books | Open Media Series
San Francisco

Open Media Series Editor: Greg Ruggiero

Cover: Mingovits Design

Library of Congress Cataloging-in-Publication Data
Names: Lusane, Clarence, 1953– author.
Title: Twenty dollars and change : Harriet Tubman and the ongoing fight for
    racial justice and democracy / by Clarence Lusane.
Description: San Francisco, CA : City Lights Books, 2022. | Series: Open
    Media series | Includes bibliographical references.
Identifiers: LCCN 2021045826 | ISBN 9780872868854 (trade paperback) |
    ISBN 9780872868595 (epub)
Subjects: LCSH: Paper money design—United States—History. | Dollar,
    American—History. | African Americans in numismatics—United
    States. | Politics in numismatics—United States. | Racism—United States. |
    United States—Race relations.
Classification: LCC HG591 .L87 2022 | DDC 332.4/973—dc23/eng/20220414
LC record available at https://lccn.loc.gov/2021045826

City Lights Books are published at the City Lights Bookstore
261 Columbus Avenue, San Francisco, CA 94133
citylights.com

In memory of family, close friends, and mentors:
Naima Natalie Bayton, Saphronia S. Drake, Sandra F. Dulyx,
Joann Johnson, Eloise Greenfield, Keith Kamu Jennings,
Askia Muhammad, and Kimberley Washington

CONTENTS

Foreword   xv

Preface   xxiii

Introduction   1

I. TWENTY DOLLARS

ONE
Symbolism Matters   21

TWO
Harriet Tubman Represents Solidarity, Struggle,
and Genuine Democracy   43

THREE
Andrew Jackson's Face Is a Meme for White Supremacy   73

FOUR
The Movement to Transform the Faces on U.S. Currency   91

FIVE
The Tubman Twenty—Black Support and Opposition   105

SIX
Conservative Hostility to the Tubman Twenty   115

II. AND CHANGE

SEVEN
Fear of a Diverse America   127

EIGHT
From 1619 to Covid-19, Racism Is a Pre-existing Condition   157

NINE
The George Floyd Catalyst   191

TEN
Abolishing Symbols of White Supremacy   241

ELEVEN
Black Voters Matter   289

CONCLUSION
Good Trouble and a Harriet Tubman–Inspired Future   321

Acknowledgments   327

Endnotes   329

Index   381

About the Author   395

Bibliography   clarencelusane.com

"If Black women were free, it would mean that everyone else would have to be free."

—COMBAHEE RIVER COLLECTIVE STATEMENT

Images of Harriet Tubman, Frederick Douglass, George Floyd, and others were projected by Dustin Klein and Alex Criqui on the statue of Robert E. Lee in Richmond, Virginia, in solidarity with the Black Lives Matter protests of 2020. PHOTO BY ZACH FICHTER, "RECLAIMING THE MONUMENT," 2020.

FOREWORD

By Kali Holloway

One of America's most fervently held—and desperately clung to—myths is that our racial hierarchy is neither engineered nor rigorously enforced, but the natural and inevitable result of every group getting exactly what they deserve. At the core of this fictive theory is the belief that the innately civilized, law-abiding, industrious, and intelligent nature of whiteness justifies its position atop the racial order, just as the inherent pathology, criminality, ignorance, and self-defeating ways of blackness perpetually constrain it to the bottom. Of the myriad self-absolving and racist lies propagated by white supremacist culture, the notion that black folks have only themselves to blame for their oppression is perhaps the most insidious. It's a denialist view wholly divorced from both the consequences of American policy and the realities of our past, and its hegemony requires defensive maintenance of a national memory built on lies of historical omission.

This whitewashing happens not just symbolically, in textbooks, monuments, memorials, and markers, but materially, in policies that directly impact the life, death, and political power of black Americans. Affronted by black emancipation and enfranchisement after losing the Civil War, defeated Confederates developed the Lost Cause mythos, white supremacist propaganda with multiple aims. Relying heavily on public symbols, it sought to project a Southern antebellum innocence onto the past, while telegraphing absolute white power onto the future. To that end, Lost Cause mythologists portrayed Confederate leaders—men whose most notable contribution to history was armed defense of white folks' right to buy, sell, and enslave black human beings—as heroes. Anonymous Confederate combatants, cast in bronze and stone, stood sentry atop lofty pedestals that implicitly demanded public veneration. The Confederacy's dishonorable fight for black enslavement was tacitly rendered an honorable but lost cause. In town centers, along avenues, and in myriad other public spaces, these statues stood as constant signifiers of racial terror. On courthouse lawns and statehouse grounds, they were strategically erected to serve as reminders to black folks that those institutions had no regard for them.

Black folks, then as now, implicitly and empirically understood how white supremacist symbols are inextricably linked to white terror violence, imbuing the environment with harassment and intimidation, race-stamping public spaces as immutably white, and emboldening anti-black vigilantism. Civil rights activist, educator, and Charleston, South Carolina, native Mamie Garvin Fields grew up in the shadow of a statue that went up in 1887 depicting politician John C. Calhoun, a vocal and virulent racist who once called black enslavement a "positive good."

"Our white city fathers wanted to keep what [Calhoun] stood for alive," Fields stated in her memoirs nearly a century later. "Blacks took that statue personally. As you passed by, here was Calhoun looking you in the face and telling you, 'Nigger, you may not be a slave, but I am back to see you stay in your place.'"

Black folks protested white supremacist symbols littering the landscape, a brave risk under the often lethal threat of Jim Crow, which those same monuments monumentalized and made tangible. When the United Daughters of the Confederacy (UDC) in 1931 erected a "loyal slave monument"—a type of Confederate marker promoting the insane idea that black people were happiest being enslaved by white folks—near the West Virginia site of John Brown's rebellion at Harpers Ferry, the NAACP demanded a tablet be placed nearby to honor Brown, noting a counter was needed to the "nationally publicized tablet giving the Confederate point of view" and the rising movement of "Copperheadism," or Confederate sympathy and slavery apologism. W. E. B. Du Bois, who wrote that the dedication event for the UDC's monument had been a "pro-slavery celebration," drafted the proposed wording for the Brown memorial, which called the abolitionist's rebellion "a blow that woke a guilty nation." It was never erected, but the NAACP made its resistance known.

Mamie Garvin Fields described how she and other black children would "carry something with us, if we knew we would be passing that way, in order to deface" the Calhoun statue in Charleston, to "scratch up the coat, break the watch chain, try to knock off the nose—because he looked like he was telling you that there was a place for 'niggers' and 'niggers must stay there.'" Newspaper accounts catalog yet more protests using defacement, as in 1888 when a statue of the figure of Justice positioned at Calhoun's feet was found with "a tin kettle in her hand and a cigar in her mouth"; in 1892, when someone painted the face of the Justice statue "lily" white; or in 1894, when a young black boy named Andrew Haig shot at the figure of Justice with a tiny pistol. A park keeper was ultimately hired to stop "the nuisances and depredations now committed by goats, boys and night prowlers," but apparently failed in that mission. In 1895, the Calhoun statue was removed. A local newspaper article recounts how, as the statue was being lowered off its pedestal by a rope, a group of black boys watching nearby "skillfully pasted Mr. Calhoun in the eye with a lump of mud." The original Calhoun's plinth stood forty-five feet in the air. In 1896, a replacement Calhoun was erected on a pedestal some 115 feet off the ground. Officially, the first Calhoun statue was removed because of design flaws, but Fields contended that black "children and adults beat up John C. Calhoun so badly that the whites had to come back and put him way up high, so we couldn't get to him." The figure was finally removed for good on June 25, 2020.

Black protests against white supremacist symbols continued during the Civil Rights era, becoming even more overt. In 1966, after an all-white jury acquitted the white man who admitted to murdering Sammy Younge Jr., a black student activist attending Alabama's Tuskegee Institute, thousands of protesters congregated at the town's central Confederate marker, spray-painting its pedestal with Younge's name and the phrase "Black Power." Less than two years later, just after the April 1968 assassination of Martin Luther King Jr., black students at the University of North Carolina at Chapel Hill expressed their grief and rage by dousing a campus Confederate statue known as "Silent Sam" in red paint. After a young black man named James Cates was murdered by a white motorcycle gang in 1970, black students rallied at the foot of the monument. In a callback to those demonstrations, UNC–Chapel Hill student Maya Little would pour a mixture of her own blood and red ink on the statue in April 2018, in an action that presaged its toppling by protesters four months later, boldly and accurately stating that "the statue and all statues like it are already drenched in black blood."

In these and far too many examples to describe here, black folks have protested the iconography of white power from its earliest appearance, as part of a broader movement toward the dismantling of white supremacy, writ large. W. E. B. Du Bois, Mamie Garvin Fields, the early NAACP—all were involved in seeking rights for black folks in various spheres, in calling out white supremacist socio-politics of their day. But in tandem with those efforts to secure black folks' civil rights, they also noted the way those symbols attempted to write black folks out of American history, and how the net effect of symbols that conveyed anti-blackness and white terror added fuel to the prevalence of both.

This was never mere conjecture. In fact, a 2021 study by researchers at the University of Virginia confirmed that there is a direct correlation between Confederate monuments and white racial terror, concluding that "the number of lynching victims in a county is a positive and significant predictor of the number of Confederate memorializations in that county." Those markers, most of which still stand, continue to do the work of white supremacy. But there are hints of progress in acknowledging the damage they do, the hostile ambience they create, and the structural inequities their existence perpetuates. In late 2021, a Tennessee appeals court granted a new trial to a black man convicted by an all-white jury who deliberated in a room full of Confederate memorabilia—including a portrait of Confederate president Jefferson Davis, a framed Confederate flag, and a placard displaying the insignia of the United Daughters of the Confederacy. The appellate court's jurists agreed with the argument that white supremacist symbology had an "inherently prejudicial" impact on jurors. Just as the architects of the Lost Cause had hoped they would.

In *Twenty Dollars and Change*, scholar Clarence Lusane makes the same argument about the power of symbols and their impact on public consciousness, but in its inverse, suggesting that the "inherently prejudicial" effect of the images we choose can and should be used to augment larger struggles for real change. Using the debate around the U.S. Treasury's promise to replace Andrew Jackson with Harriet Tubman on the front of a twenty-dollar bill as a springboard, Lusane argues that "rolling out a Tubman twenty not only disrupts and diminishes the legacies of white supremacy that persist in official narratives, but that doing so is a necessary step toward diminishing and abolishing racist distortions of our political economy, health and medical institutions, and justice system."

"This is why the book is named *Twenty Dollars and Change*," writes Lusane: "it is an effort to address the connection between official narratives and power, and the urgent need to transform both."

What does it mean to have Tubman on the twenty, as well as poet Maya Angelou on the quarter, as white supremacist legislators and white parents work in tandem to ban Angelou's books and legally prohibit teaching about slavery using the mislabeled racist boogeyman of "critical race theory"? How do we reckon with the incongruity of putting Tubman and Angelou on money even as racial capitalism is directly responsible for black women, who have the highest labor force participation rate among women, being paid 36 percent less than white men and 20 percent less than white women, being three times as likely to live in poverty as white women, and suffering the greatest job losses and economic suffering among all American women amidst the coronavirus pandemic?

More broadly, Lusane elucidates how structural racism and the convulsive and circular political violence of white backlash—embedded in contemporary Republican politics, anti-black voting suppression, and resistance to legislation that would repair the Supreme Court's decimation of the Voting Rights Act; anti-protest laws, some allowing vicious attacks against demonstrators, passed at a fast clip after the anti-racist uprisings following the police murder of George Floyd; and statutes against "wokeness" that target public schools, libraries, and places of work—undermine the strides of black progress. "It is the quotidian violence of America's racial caste system," writes Lusane, "that poses the most critical threat to communities of color and democracy itself. Ultimately, it is that system, and the narratives that validate it, that must be overthrown." It is in the service of that goal that Lusane also carefully, and contemplatively, contextualizes Tubman's work and legacy as foundational to a tradition of resistance, including the fierce battle against the regressive anti-black racism of this moment. It is also in the service of that goal that he advocates we make the conscious "inherently prejudicial" choice to see an illiterate, disabled, self-emancipated, insurgent black woman for the thoroughly original American icon—and hero—she is.

This, Lusane notes, is exactly why figures such as Harriet Tubman and Maya Angelou, for all the valid concerns over empty efforts at racial inclusion, should be represented, centered, honored and celebrated. The exclusion of black folks, and particularly black women, from America's public-facing images of itself—monuments, money, and more—has always been a warped reflection of whiteness wholly incongruous with the actual face of this country. Honest narratives about black women and other folks who continue to fight for what this country purports to stand for, saving America from its own worst and most insidious tendencies, should be in our public spaces and on our shared objects. In tandem with the work of change on the ground and elsewhere, they are the totems of progress.

If representation didn't matter, the right wouldn't be fighting so hard to keep it all white.

Twenty Dollars and Change is a future-gazing guide to who we must be to become who we claim to be. And, as Lusane notes, we will only get there by changing, inside and out.

Kali Holloway is a monthly columnist for both The Nation *and* The Daily Beast. *She is the former director of the Make It Right Project, a national initiative dedicated to taking down Confederate monuments and telling the truth about history. She is lead vocalist for the band Easy Lover and is currently working on her first book,* The Secret Racist History of Everything.

PREFACE

On March 13, 2017, I and my then seven-year-old son, Ellington, woke at 5:00 a.m. for a bus trip to the much-anticipated grand opening of the Harriet Tubman Underground Railroad Visitor Center in Church Creek, Maryland. Thanks to my good friend, WPFW radio host and producer Joni Eisenberg, we were able to secure the last two tickets on a bus chartered by senior black women who were going to the event. The ladies—most of whom were in their seventies or older—were dignified and rowdy the whole ride there. It was a great experience for my son and me. On our way, we had lots of discussions about history, race, and what Harriet Tubman meant to African Americans and the nation as a whole. Although my son did engage in a few discussions and enjoyed being fawned over by the ladies, for much of the ninety-minute ride he quietly read his *Power Rangers* book.

Operated by the state of Maryland, the Center features exhibits, a theater, and a library dedicated to Harriet Tubman, the Underground Railroad, slavery, and abolitionism in Maryland. The main exhibit features lots of hands-on history about Tubman's life. For the opening, a large tent was set up and talks were presented on a range of subjects. For young people, there were history lessons and role-playing, entailing costumes and wigs that could be worn as the youth learned about the antebellum period and how enslaved people organized revolts and escapes to freedom.

Ellington enjoyed it all immensely. The inspiring moment to me came when we were on our way back and Ellington put away his *Power Rangers* book and read—and eventually fell asleep reading—his new book, *What Was the Underground Railroad*, by Yona Zeldis McDonough.

The timing of our trip was fortuitous. Months earlier, in April 2016, the Obama administration's Treasury Department had announced plans to redesign U.S. five-, ten-, and twenty-dollar bills. The purpose of the initiative was to better reflect the racial and gender diversity of the American people. The part of the announcement that drew the most response—both celebration and anger—was the declaration that Harriet Tubman would appear on the front of the redesigned twenty, pushing Andrew Jackson's image, long on the bill's front, to the back. Debate about Tubman, Jackson, and the future of the U.S. twenty was jolted to another level on November 8, 2016, when Donald Trump, the most overtly bigoted and misogynist presidential candidate in living memory, was announced winner of the election. Occurring less than two months after Trump's inauguration, our trip to the Center provided a needed injection of hope. Everything about Tubman's life resisted the pervasive racism, sexism, and classism of her time. She never backed down in the face of threats and peril that most of us will never have to experience. I especially wanted my son to know and embrace the black female leadership and agency that her life story embodies. The trip occurred as I was in the process of researching this present work, and inspired me to dive deeper into Tubman's life and legacy.

This book is an effort to link the struggles of the past with the challenges of the present. Whether or not one agrees about placing Tubman on the front of the twenty-dollar bill, the debate provides yet another opportunity to advance the nation's reckoning with white supremacy, patriarchy, and institutional injustice. Raising public consciousness about these issues is even more urgent today than when the announcement was first made in April 2016. Since then we have faced the emergence of a killer pandemic, an authoritarian presidency, and an attempt to overthrow the 2020 election with mob violence. At the same time, we have also seen the emergence of a powerful racial justice movement, organized largely by black women, challenging white supremacy and patriarchy in all their forms, particularly in the ways police target communities of color. More than ever, we need to clarify and elucidate the two competing political visions before us: one rooted in exclusion and domination, the other in diversity and liberation. The lessons and lifework of Harriet Tubman provide inspiring proof we can still achieve the latter.

Harriet Tubman, circa 1871–1876. PHOTOGRAPH BY HARVEY B. LINDSLEY. COURTESY OF THE LIBRARY OF CONGRESS.

INTRODUCTION

The Civil War had ended, and one of its most heroic figures was facing difficult financial times. She was caring for her elderly parents, Harriet "Rit" Green and Ben Ross, as well as trying to meet her own needs. By law, and certainly by any sense of justice, she deserved compensation for her wartime efforts, ones that had involved substantial risk to her life and liberty. Harriet Tubman, best known for personally guiding dozens of people out of slavery through the Underground Railroad, also worked for the Union Army under contract in numerous positions from roughly 1862 to 1865, becoming the first woman to lead an armed military operation during that war. In what would come to be known as the Combahee Ferry Raid, Tubman led a contingent of 150 black soldiers from the U.S. 2nd South Carolina Volunteers in an operation that liberated more than seven hundred people from their enslavers.[1] Despite her exceptional military service, she received little in return, a total of about $200 for a three-year period.[2] Then, as now, justice and fairness were rarely available for African Americans—particularly African American women—no matter how well deserved.

Tubman first sought additional compensation in the summer of 1865. She pursued help from her friends, longtime abolitionists Secretary of State William H. Seward and his wife, Frances Miller Seward. Tubman had become friends with the Sewards and bought one of their homes in Auburn, New York, where she and her family would spend much of the rest of her life. At the time Tubman first approached him, Seward was still recovering from wounds sustained during an attempted assassination targeting him, Vice President Johnson, and President Lincoln a few months earlier in April 1865.[3] Despite the challenges of his recuperation, Seward tried to help Tubman but was unsuccessful. This was the beginning of what would become a multi-decade effort.

Seward initially asked for assistance from Charles Woods. In 1865, Woods, a banker in Auburn who was a friend of Seward's, came to her aid.[4] Tubman informed Woods that she was owed $766 for her time serving in the Union Army from May 25, 1862, to January 31, 1865. Her accounting was based on a monthly fee of $30, minus $200 that she had been paid previously for other work done for the Union during that period.[5] Citing official papers she had in her possession, Woods wrote a nine-page document detailing Tubman's claims. He noted that she had used the $200 to help others. He wrote that "she immediately devoted that sum to the erection of a wash-house in which she spent a portion of her time in teaching the freed women to do washing—to aid in supporting themselves instead of depending wholly on Gov't aid."[6]

Receiving no positive response, she petitioned the U.S. government again in 1867. At this point, an impressive array of political figures, community leaders, feminists, and activists from around the nation began to coalesce around her cause. These included Sojourner Truth, Frances Seward, Frederick Douglass, Ralph Waldo Emerson, educator Horace Mann, and abolitionist William Lloyd Garrison, among others.

Her struggle for just compensation eventually went to the halls of Congress. Woods's report was later sent to Congressman Clinton Dugald MacDougall (R-NY), who served in the U.S. House of Representatives from 1873 to 1877. His congressional career seems undistinguished with the exception that on June 22, 1874, he and Wisconsin congressman Gerry W. Hazelton, both of the Committee on War Claims, issued a report that, if heeded, would have provided Tubman a lump payment of $2,000, about ten times what she had received earlier. The bill, titled Report No. 787, stated that "Harriet Tubman, a colored woman, and formerly a slave, was, in the month of May 1862, sent to Hilton Head, South Carolina, at the suggestion of Governor Andrew, of Massachusetts, upon the theory that she would be a valuable person to operate within the enemy's lines as a scout and spy. It appears from testimony submitted to the committee that she served in that capacity during most of the war and rendered valuable service, obtaining information which was of great value in military operations."

Report No. 787 goes on to cite military leaders who formally document the strategic importance of Tubman as a scout and spy. It also notes that she was "detained in Philadelphia" during her travels and was persuaded to render service as a nurse at James River Hospital in the city and later at a "colored hospital" in Fort Monroe, Virginia. Finally, the bill notes that she served as a teacher to emancipated black women under the Freedmen's Bureau after the war. It concludes by stating, "She should be paid for these services . . . appropriating the sum of $2,000 for services rendered by her to the Union Army as scout, nurse, and spy."[7]

The bill passed in the House but not in the Senate. When MacDougall left office in 1877, the campaign lost steam but never died. According to writer and biographer Beverly Lowry, congressional committees rejected her petitions for years because they were apparently unable to believe a black woman capable of the acts of heroism described in Tubman's requests and letters of support.[8]

Tragic circumstances intervened in 1888. That was the year that Tubman's second husband, Nelson Davis, an army veteran, passed away. According to scholar Kate Clifford Larson, Tubman finally received a lump payment of five hundred dollars in 1895 to cover the five years she spent trying to get the widow's pension. She then received eight dollars per month until 1899, when, after pressure on Congress, she was awarded an additional twelve dollars per month for her role as a Civil War nurse. The five hundred dollars she received in 1895, though, she donated to her local Thompson Memorial AMEZ church. She never stopped giving.[9]

On December 5, 1898, the U.S. Senate and House of Representatives passed an act "granting an increase of pension to Harriet Tubman Davis" to twenty-five dollars monthly, but only paid her twenty dollars a month until she passed away in 1913.[10] This was more than thirty years after she began her quest. It should be underscored that Tubman never received compensation for her work as a spy and soldier, only for her role as a scout, for which she maintained she was underpaid.[11] The act reads:

Be it enacted by the Senate and House of Representatives of the
United States of America in Congress assembled, That the Secretary
of the Interior be, and he is hereby, authorized and directed to place
on the pension roll, subject to the provisions and limitations of the
pension laws, the name of Harriet Tubman Davis, widow of Nelson
Davis, late a private in Company G, Eighth Regiment United States
Colored Infantry, and pay her a pension at the rate of twenty dollars
per month in lieu of that she is now receiving.[12]

In an irony of epic proportions, Harriet Tubman—the first
woman slated to appear on the U.S. twenty-dollar bill—eventually
received a lifelong monthly payment of twenty dollars. However,
she was not acknowledged as the black woman who heroically led
150 soldiers in the armed raid on Confederate positions and slave
plantations at Combahee Ferry. Instead, the compensation was in
recognition of her deceased husband, and her status as his widow.
"In 2003, the protests of grade school children who visited her
former home in Auburn, New York, led to a $11,750 congressional
appropriation to make up the difference," writes Mary Frances
Berry in *My Face Is Black Is True*.[13] According to Tubman's great-
great-great-grandniece Ernestine Tina Martin Wyatt, the pension
issue has reached an impasse, due in part to the government's con-
tention that pensions are tied to direct descendants and Tubman
did not have any children of her own.[14]

TWENTY DOLLARS AND CHANGE

On April 20, 2016, Treasury Secretary Jack Lew announced that
the image of Harriet Tubman would replace that of Andrew
Jackson on the twenty-dollar bill. Lew had taken advantage of the
need to make security improvements to the currency and a 2008
U.S. Court of Appeals for the District of Columbia ruling that U.S.
currency had to be more user-friendly for people who are blind or
visually impaired.[15] He initiated public discussion about changing
the images on U.S. paper currencies to better reflect the racial,

ethnic, and gender diversity of the nation. At the time of the debate, all paper currency had images of white men front and center. Reflecting on the yearlong period of public response regarding who should replace Jackson on the face of the twenty-dollar bill, Lew stated:

> The decision to put Harriet Tubman on the new $20 was driven by thousands of responses we received from Americans young and old. I have been particularly struck by the many comments and reactions from children for whom Harriet Tubman is not just a historical figure, but a role model for leadership and participation in our democracy. You shared your thoughts about her life and her works and how they changed our nation and represented our most cherished values. Looking back on her life, Tubman once said, "I would fight for liberty so long as my strength lasted." And she did fight, for the freedom of slaves and for the right of women to vote. Her incredible story of courage and commitment to equality embodies the ideals of democracy that our nation celebrates, and we will continue to value her legacy by honoring her on our currency. The reverse of the new $20 will continue to feature the White House as well as an image of President Andrew Jackson.[16]

In addition to the changes on the twenty, Lew endorsed images of the 1963 March on Washington and Marian Anderson's 1939 performance at the Lincoln Memorial to be placed on the back of the five-dollar bill; and images of Lucretia Mott, Sojourner Truth, Susan B. Anthony, Elizabeth Cady Stanton, Alice Paul, and the 1913 Woman Suffrage Procession to appear on the back of the ten-dollar bill.

It should be noted that Tubman was preceded by other women on U.S. paper money and coins. In 1865, as the Civil War ended, Native American Pocahontas was placed on the twenty-dollar bill, and in 1886, Martha Washington was placed on the one-dollar silver certificate. Women, both real and imagined, have appeared on U.S. coins, including Susan B. Anthony (one-dollar coin), disability activist Helen Keller (a quarter), and Native American field explorer Sacagawea (one-dollar coin) among others. In January 2022, the

U.S. Mint released a redesigned quarter bearing the image of George Washington on the front, and African American poet Maya Angelou on the back, with more to come featuring astronaut Sally Ride, Cherokee leader Wilma Mankiller, New Mexico suffrage leader Nina Otero-Warren, Chinese American film star Anna May Wong, and many other women.[17]

The U.S. Mint's American Women Quarters Program honors "the historic contributions of twenty trailblazing American women."

The announcement and gradual rollout of these changes has stoked wide-ranging discussions about the realities of sexism, racism, and inequality in American life, past and present. In 2016, a national movement of millions mobilized around the proposed changes as a step, however modest, toward more substantive social justice transformations. There was also considerable excitement among women and people of color that the redesigned money would signal another victory in the long struggle to abolish the influence of white supremacy and patriarchy in the official historical narratives of the United States.

At the time it was first announced, the plan for a Tubman twenty was viewed as one of several major acknowledgments made by the Obama administration of African Americans' long-overlooked contributions to U.S. history. On October 16, 2011, the Martin Luther King Jr. Memorial, the first monument to an African American on the National Mall, was unveiled in Washington, D.C., and dedicated by President Obama. The thirty-foot-tall statue of King includes quotes reflecting on justice, democracy, hope, and love—the core principles for which he fought. The memorial was first approved by Congress and then by President Bill Clinton in 1996, and work at the site began in 2006. The King memorial was designed and created by Chinese artist Lei Yixin and sculpted in China. While much of the media coverage of the memorial's dedication focused on the political figures and celebrities in attendance, tens of thousands of working-class people found their way to the event.[18] The dedication was originally scheduled for August 28, 2011, commemorating the forty-eighth anniversary of the March on Washington and King's famous "I Have a Dream" speech, but was postponed due to the threat of Hurricane Irene.

"We can't be discouraged by what is," said Obama at the dedication. "We've got to keep pushing for what ought to be, the America we ought to leave to our children, mindful that the hardships we face are nothing compared to those Dr. King and his fellow marchers faced fifty years ago, and that if we maintain our faith, in ourselves and in the possibilities of this nation, there is no challenge we cannot surmount."[19]

Five years later, on September 24, 2016, with only months left in office, Obama presided over the opening of the National Museum of African American History and Culture, also in Washington, D.C. According to the Smithsonian Institution, the nearly 400,000-square-foot building is "the nation's largest and most comprehensive cultural destination devoted exclusively to exploring, documenting, and showcasing the African American story and its impact on American and world history."[20]

At the dedication, attended by ex-presidents, politicians, civil rights leaders, social justice activists, and celebrities, Obama described the importance of the new building by stating, "This national museum helps tell a fuller, richer story of who we are. It helps us better understand the lives, yes of the President, but also the slave. The industrialist but also the porter. The keeper of the status quo but also the activist seeking to overthrow that status quo. The teacher, or the cook, alongside the statesman."[21]

The museum, which features items from the pre-slave era to the present, has attracted tens of millions of people. Its exhibits present an accurate counter-narrative to traditional versions of U.S. history where the legacies of white supremacy and settler colonialism are downplayed, white national leaders are lionized and sanitized, and black voices are diminished or muted. The museum's popularity belies the notion that interest in history has waned among non-scholars, the non-college-educated, and working people. Black historians and other scholars continue to play a key role in shaping the tone, quality, and historic rigor of the museum.

At the dedication, Obama also noted that the museum would not in and of itself bring about the change that was needed to address the issues facing African Americans and other marginalized communities:

> A museum alone will not alleviate poverty in every inner city, or every rural hamlet. It won't eliminate gun violence from all our neighborhoods, or immediately ensure that justice is always color-blind. It won't wipe away every instance of discrimination in a job interview, or a sentencing hearing, or folks trying to rent an apartment. Those things are up to us, the decisions and choices we make. It requires speaking out and organizing and voting, until our values are fully reflected in our laws and our policies and our communities.[22]

Although both the memorial and the museum were planned long before Obama became the nation's first black president, some felt it was historic justice that he was in office to preside over their dedication and official opening. These two new national fixtures continue to send a message of social inclusion and diversity that disrupts the legacies of white settler-colonialism that have depicted the nation's history and character in its own interests and image. The plan to update U.S. currency with images that celebrate movements for abolition, civil rights, and women's suffrage was an additional affront to those legacies and their domination of nearly all official public displays, symbols, and monuments since the nation's founding.

The abolitionist legacy of Harriet Tubman, at its core, represents solidarity and liberation. In the broadest and most inclusive sense, her mission to emancipate and empower others endures today through ongoing social movements against marginalization and injustice. Given her selfless dedication to freedom and liberation, it seems appropriate to dignify her legacy by having her become the first woman in over a century to be placed on U.S. paper currency, and the first woman ever to appear on the front of one of America's most commonly used bills.

On the other hand, Andrew Jackson's legacy represents white supremacy and self-interest in their most vulgar and repressive forms. He was a committed enemy of the First Nations, and led genocidal campaigns to take possession of their territories. Jackson's politics, lauded by his supporters and biographers, were of, by, and for white men who were opposed to expanding democracy to women and people of color. An unapologetic opponent of abolitionism, Jackson enslaved black people and championed an elitist political economy financed by slave labor. His face has been on the front of twenty-dollar bills since 1928, and the time has come to retire it.

Ironically, the only thing Tubman and Jackson have in common is that they may have both been born on March 15. Beyond that, no two individuals could have been more different. Tubman was a working black woman who struggled financially all her life as she fought for abolition, racial justice, gender equality, and expanded democracy. Jackson was a rich, highly privileged white man who accrued wealth and power through slavery and violence. The two visions of the nation that Tubman and Jackson represent have been at war for centuries and remain so today.

Despite this, numerous debates have emerged from conservatives—as well as from some African Americans and non-black progressives as well—attempting to prevent Tubman from appearing on the twenty. Conversely, support for adding Tubman and removing Jackson came from some unlikely conservative sources, such as Senators James Lankford (R-OK) and Mike Lee (R-UT), and Congressman John Katko (R-NY). The nature and contour of these conversations reveal much about the state of America today. Underlying much of the opposition are perspectives that should be publicly exposed, discussed, and dissected, particularly the thinly veiled racism and misogyny of white conservatives. However, some black progressives, as Brittney Cooper expressed in her January 2021 piece for *Time*, feel that "putting Tubman on legal tender, when slaves in the U.S. were treated as fungible commodities, is a supreme form of disrespect."[23]

The idea for *Twenty Dollars and Change* was sparked by those debates. Work on the book began as the nation's first black president was completing his second term, and the election of the nation's first woman president appeared imminent. As I started to research and write, I thought those historic markers would offer more than enough material to study in terms of themes related to Harriet Tubman, diversifying images on currency, and changing narratives about race, gender, and political power in the contemporary United States. But, as I wrote, I realized that official narratives and unjust material conditions are structurally connected. Changing one transforms the other, and it's never enough to simply address representation without addressing the lived realities of the people, families, and communities at stake—their everyday life, well-being, dignity, security, and civic agency. This is why the book is named *Twenty Dollars and Change*—it is an effort to address the connection between official narratives and power, and the urgent need to transform both.

INTRODUCTION

"TWO THEORIES OF THE FUTURE OF AMERICA"

Two centuries after her birth, Harriet Tubman's mission for gender, race, and economic equality continues to resonate among today's social justice movements, just as Andrew Jackson's white nationalism lives on today through much of the Republican Party. America is at war with itself, and has been before, during, and after the Civil War. During certain flash points, the war becomes more apparent than others, as was the case during the uprisings that followed the killing of George Floyd. But it would be a mistake to pin all the blame on racism and white supremacy. The profit-above-all-else ethos that defines the political economy of the United States and much of the world, elevating the wealthy few and marginalizing the rest, in many ways compounds the other forms of injustice endured by much of the population.

The controversy over the Tubman twenty provides a valuable opportunity to appraise the political possibilities her legacy represents today—a diverse and inclusive democracy that has yet to exist for tens of millions in the United States—and to examine the obstacles to that objective in the form of the contemporary racialized, gendered, and class-biased political economy. As an insurgent black woman living in defiance of a system governed for and by white men, Tubman challenged the core of an economy enriched by slavery. The capitalism of our era would not exist if not for hundreds of years of violence, land theft, chattel slavery, and marginalization of people of color and women.

In numerous studies, from Eric Williams's classic *Slavery and Capitalism* to Edward E. Baptist's *The Half Has Never Been Told: Slavery and the Making of American Capitalism*, historians and economists have documented how the U.S. economy from the pre–Revolutionary War period until the last days of slavery was built on the backs of enslaved African people and their descendants.[24] At the onset of the Civil War in 1861, white people enslaved 3.9 million (88 percent) of the 4.3 million black people in the United States. The abolition of slavery represented the victory of an industrial aristocracy over an agrarian one. The emancipatory politics of Tubman, Frederick Douglass, Sojourner Truth, Nat Turner, and others overlapped with the interests of wealthy Northerners who founded the Republican Party and created an inevitable clash that led to the Civil War. While the claim of Southern revisionists that the war was not about slavery has no credibility, neither does the Northern argument that it was solely for the liberation and full inclusion of black people in U.S. society.

Following the Civil War, "two theories of the future of America clashed and blended," writes W. E. B. Du Bois in *Black Reconstruction*, "the one for abolition-democracy based on freedom, intelligence, and power for all . . . the other was industry for private profit directed by an autocracy determined at any price to amass wealth and power. The uncomprehending resistance of the South, and the pressure of black folk, made these two thoughts uneasy and temporary allies."[25] Since that time, African Americans have continued to forge a politics of freedom, intelligence, and power for all—radical democracy. Such politics are rooted in notions that institutional structures and political systems serve the needs of society without marginalizing people or communities. In this sense, radical democracy means ensuring justice in all its forms. Such notions, in theory and in practice, existentially challenge the political economy of a nation skewed since the days of settler colonialism to advantage white people—racial capitalism—and the deeper codes that structurally shape it and society—white supremacy.

Between the agrarian capitalism of Tubman and Jackson's eras and the racial capitalism of the contemporary era, other variations evolved, including what economists term laissez-faire and Keynesianism. Each era shaped the nature and character of black life and resistance, and differentiated working-class experiences. The post-Reconstruction era, as Du Bois documents so well in *Black Reconstruction*, reinforced the second-class status of African Americans through state-sanctioned and state-encouraged lynching, segregation, and other means, exploiting black labor in ways that, like slavery, amassed great wealth for white elites, middle-class wealth for others, and minimum advantages for working-class whites. For decades, as noted by political scientist Ronald Walters, historian Douglas Blackmon, and other scholars, many African Americans in the South continued to be subjected to conditions that amounted to "slavery by another name."[26]

The unregulated tenure of laissez-faire capitalism in the first two decades of the twentieth century eventually led to the Great Depression. The crisis was resolved only through state intervention, a rescue operation called Keynesianism after the theories of economist John Maynard Keynes, who argued on behalf of regulation and social security, limited work hours, unemployment insurance, and other concessions. These benefits, overwhelmingly, excluded people of color, female and male. Thus, following the lead of other Western liberal governments, a hedged version of the welfare state emerged in the United States. While such developments were a response to pressure from organized labor and social movements, they were nevertheless a project of U.S. capitalism and not some experimental version of socialism gone bad.

Any forces that might reduce profit for the wealthy were always contested, and by the early 1970s, neoliberal policies—aka Chicago School economics—were replacing Keynesianism inside the United States and beyond. In her masterful work *The Shock Doctrine: The Rise of Disaster Capitalism*, Naomi Klein expertly lays out the history of the transition from a welfare-state ethos to the imposition of principles and policies that ushered in a new configuration of capitalist power.[27] Klein argues that the desperation generated by economic and political crises enables big business to impose policies that would be untenable in other circumstances. Rather than offer more protections for workers, communities, and the environment, corporations aim to reduce such protections by gutting the primary institution dedicated to forging them: government. The result of this phase of capitalism has been environmental destabilization, climate change, deindustrialization, job exportation, union destruction, democracy erosion, the commercialization of everything, and near total control of the two-party political system by corporate interests. Along the way, manipulating racial anxieties has emerged as a reliable strategy for those in power to attract less wealthy white people to act against their own economic interests. As a result, racialized attacks on the welfare state have been a successful method for getting white people to reject policies that would directly benefit them, such as the subsidized healthcare system known as "Obamacare." It is in this manner that white supremacy has been manipulated by corporate and political interests, which is why liberation movements must focus not just on the abolition of racial injustice, but also on freedom from the multiple ways power marginalizes people—particularly women of color—and denies them their full human agency.

A key theory and praxis that has emerged for doing this is intersectionality, a form of analysis created by legal scholar and activist Kimberlé Crenshaw. As Crenshaw explains:

> The conjoining of multiple systems of subordination has been variously described as compound discrimination, multiple burdens, or double or triple discrimination. Intersectionality is a conceptualization of the problem that attempts to capture both the structural and dynamic consequences of the interaction between two or more axes of subordination.[28]

"Intersectionality," writes Black Lives Matters co-founder Alicia Garza, "is a way to understand how power operates. It is also a way to ensure that no one, as Crenshaw states, is left behind. . . . It offers a road map for change by making visible those who are currently invisible. In doing so, we become better prepared to demand more, for the sake of winning more."[29]

Tubman's life story—as a conductor on the Underground Railroad, abolitionist soldier in the Civil War, and advocate for women's right to vote—offers such a road map for change. The compound forms of injustice that plagued her era persist to this day in new guises. It is the responsibility of each new generation to continue the fight for liberation from such injustices with the same verve and commitment that Tubman did over a century ago, and to do so with all the tools and resources their era provides.

TUBMAN VS. JACKSON, AND THE FUTURE OF AMERICA

It is difficult to think of a more contradictory political message than having an insurgent black woman who dedicated her life to abolishing slavery honored on the same national platform as a white man who led the effort for "Indian Removal" and bred, enslaved, and sold black people for profit. But that is the Treasury Department's current plan for the redesigned twenty-dollar bill: Harriet Tubman will appear on one side of the bill and Andrew Jackson will appear on the other.

That contradiction is unacceptable at every level. *Twenty Dollars and Change* makes the case that these conflicting legacies will only be reconciled when one path is officially chosen and implemented. In the pages ahead, I argue that rolling out a Tubman twenty not only disrupts and diminishes the legacies of white supremacy that persist in official narratives, but that doing so is a necessary step toward diminishing and abolishing racist distortions of our political economy, health and medical institutions, and justice system. As the upheaval over Critical Race Theory and the 1619 Project demonstrates, conservatives' efforts to control historical narratives are crucial to maintaining racial hierarchy and political control.[30] Thus, understanding and winning battles over memory and representation are part of the process of winning larger struggles over structural disparities in politics, policing, protest, voting, and democracy itself.

There are many informative and well-researched studies dedicated to both Harriet Tubman and Andrew Jackson. Both are iconic figures in U.S. history. Yet they are rarely discussed together, despite the fact that their lives overlapped. Tubman and Jackson represent two competing visions of America, and their legacies are unavoidably intertwined in the ongoing fight over the future of the twenty-dollar bill. This book, however, is not about Harriet Tubman and Andrew

Jackson; it is about connecting past struggles with the ongoing war between racial justice and white supremacy. The fight over the future of the twenty offers a lens on that the war, what's at stake, and why we need to win it. This is how the book came to be named *Twenty Dollars and Change* and why it is presented in two sections.

In Section One, Chapters 1–6, I examine the debate around the Tubman twenty from a racial justice perspective, and how white supremacy has been coded into the visual narratives on U.S. and Confederate money. In Section Two, Chapters 7–11, I extend the analysis to current trends and flashpoints, parsing the ways change is needed to structurally address the chronic intersection of injustices that continue to plague people of color in the United States, including the influence of white supremacy in U.S. politics, public health, policing, public symbolism, and suppression of protest and voting rights.

Chapter 1 argues that symbolism and public narratives matter. Images and words on national currency are carefully and deliberately chosen to formally convey a common narrative. Individuals who are selected, whether real or mythical, are subjects of contestation for broader concerns around justice and memory. This chapter challenges the white-dominated narrative that has, until recently, been advanced on paper currency and coins.

Chapter 2 focuses not only on Harriet Tubman as a legendary liberator of enslaved people and Civil War military leader, but also on her importance as a symbol of racial justice, gender equality, and democracy. While detailed records of her voiced position on these matters is scant, consisting mostly of interviews and contemporary press reports, her deeds and actions speak volumes. This chapter touches on known highlights of her achievements alongside other dimensions of her life and argues that America's political, social, and democratic future should be modeled after Tubman's legacy of liberation, inclusion, and solidarity.

In Chapter 3, I focus on the life and politics of Andrew Jackson. Given his record as a slaveholder, slave trader, and advocate and participant in genocide against Indigenous communities, he never should have been lionized nor had his image adorn multiple U.S. currencies. The conclusion here is unassailable: Jackson should be removed from the twenty-dollar bill and all other honorific national platforms.

The campaigns to place a woman, and specifically Tubman, on U.S. paper currency, and to remove Jackson, that existed before Lew made his announcement are the topics of Chapter 4. Thanks to the work of Women On 20s, a popular movement grew that bolstered Treasury Secretary Lew's decision to change the twenty and other denominations. While the process was slowed by the Trump administration, though not dismissed as he hoped, Biden's treasury secretary Janet Yellen confirmed in March 2022 that the Tubman bill will appear in 2030.

Chapters 5 and 6 assess the support and opposition to Lew's announcement for the Tubman twenty. In Chapter 5, black support and opposition are presented. While there is no disagreement in the black community on the importance and significance of Tubman, there is principled dispute regarding whether including her image on the twenty honors or exploits the integrity of her life and legacy. I present critical voices from multiple sides of this debate. Among conservatives, however, the same folks who decry so-called "cancel culture" have no hesitation in wanting to cancel the Tubman twenty. This is the subject of Chapter 6.

Chapter 7 examines the social science data that documents the white supremacist views, prejudices, and anti-democratic tendencies of the contemporary right, especially "Make America Great Again" (MAGA) Republicans—those who seem willing to act on anything Trump-aligned politicians and platforms say. I argue that current racial trends manifesting as white fear, anxiety, and rage have existed for generations, and will likely continue long after the Trumps become irrelevant. At the same time, Donald Trump's particular role in accelerating and amplifying today's white supremacists cannot be minimized, and fully implicates the party that gave rise to him, supported him, and continues to advance his disinformation and agenda.

Chapter 8 focuses on recent black resistance, protest, and movement building. Ironically, the chapter begins with an accusation concerning a fake twenty-dollar bill. That charge would lead to the tragic and unwarranted death of George Floyd and the explosive protests of 2020 demanding justice and police reform or abolition. The contours of these efforts are explored in detail.

The successful effort to remove public monuments honoring Confederates, segregationists, white nationalists, slavers, and other racists is discussed in Chapter 9. In addition to freeing public space of these menacing symbols, campaigns succeeded in renaming buildings, schools, sport teams, and other sites of racist narrative expression.

Chapter 10 looks at one of the most critical issues confronting black communities: Republican efforts to suppress black votes. The fact that fair and easy access to voting is still a challenge for African Americans underscores the persistence of racial hierarchies more than one hundred years after Tubman's death. The chapter discusses the importance of voting as well as its limits.

The final chapter brings it all together. In the words of the late civil rights leader and congressman John Lewis, "Speak up, speak out, get in the way. Get in good trouble, necessary trouble, and help redeem the soul of America."[31] Tubman created "good trouble" all her life, an enduring resistance that continues today by activists fighting for racial justice, gender equality, and a full democracy.

I. TWENTY DOLLARS

John Gast's 1872 painting *American Progress* depicts the deity Columbia—named after Christopher Columbus—as the white nationalist symbol of Manifest Destiny.

ONE

SYMBOLISM MATTERS

"It is not our differences that divide us. It is our inability to recognize, accept, and celebrate those differences."
—Audre Lorde, *Our Dead Behind Us*

"Symbols are powerful reminders of what we treasure and what we repudiate. It is not too much to say that symbols tell us who we are."
—Margaret Renkl, "America's Ugliest Confederate Statue Is Gone. Racism Isn't.," *New York Times*, January 17, 2022

THE LAST POETS were one of the earliest and most influential political rap groups in black music. Formed in 1968 in New York City, the group has had many different members over the years, including Alafia Pudim (aka Jalaluddin Mansur Nuriddin), Sulaiman El-Hadi, Umar Bin Hassan, and Abiodun Oyewole. In conga-backed poems they often performed in parks and on the street, The Last Poets exuded a sense of black power and revolutionary possibility.[32]

The band's 1972 *Chastisement* album features "E Pluribus Unum," a number that raps about the symbols on the U.S. one-dollar bill. The song begins with a critique of the Great Seal of the United States—the nation's official stamp or national coat of arms, created in 1782—which appears on the back of the bill:

Now the US mints on paper prints, millions every day
and use the eagle as their symbol 'cause it's a bird of prey
The laurels of peace and the arrows of wars
are clutched very tightly in the eagle's claws
filled with greed and lust,

and on the back of the dollar bill,
is the words IN GOD WE TRUST
But the dollar bill is their only God

The song also takes aim at the other major symbol on the back of the bill, including a thirteen-tier pyramid that has the Eye of Providence floating over it:

Then there's the pyramid, that stands by itself
created by Black people's knowledge and wealth
and over the pyramid hangs the devil's eye
that stole from the truth and created the lie

According to the State Department, the Latin phrases *Annuit Coeptis* and *Novus Ordo Seclorum*, which appear above and below the pyramid, mean God "favored our undertakings" and "a new order of the ages."[33] The Last Poets provide their own translation of the words:

Now ANNUIT means an endless amount stolen over the years
and COEPTIS means a new empire of vampire millionaires
And NOVUS is a Latin word meaning something new
an ORDO means a way of life chosen by a few
SECLORUM is a word that means to take from another
knowledge, wisdom and understanding stolen from the brother

Here they rap that, if properly understood and interpreted, the symbols openly justify the crimes of the nation. The super-rich are seen as self-interested bloodsuckers who dispossess others, especially black people, for their own benefit. The song then moves to describe the front of the bill.

The four words apart form the last parts of the secrets of the seal
and tells how they fooled the people into thinking paper money was real!
. . .

22

And so the power is in the hand of the ruling classes
playing god with the fate of all the masses
so the people don't get any in the land of the plenty
because E PLURIBUS UNUM means One Out of Many

Rather than interpret "One Out of Many" to mean a single nation of many states, as promoted by official narratives, the Last Poets
view the phrase as a description of how the interests of the powerful
few replace those of the many. For them, the U.S. dollar symbolizes
all the oppressive politics that have left millions of people marginalized, abused, and deceived.

Intriguingly, the song does not address the portrait of George
Washington and what his image on the front of the bill symbolizes to them. Certainly, they could have made the argument that
Washington, who fought a war for "life, liberty, and the pursuit of
happiness" while enslaving hundreds of black people, embodies all
the contradictions the song criticizes. In any case, it is important to
note that there have been voices in the black community who have
long recognized and rejected the official narratives exerting steady
influence from the money, monuments, and symbols of a system
that omits their political presence and power.

CASH NARRATIVES

Until recently, the story of symbolism on U.S. money has been one of
how white America has racialized the mythology of the nation in its
own image and interests. Unlike the Last Poets, however, most of us
rarely, if ever, spend time decoding the meaning of the symbols on
our money. Yet every single image staring back at us from U.S. paper
currency tells a story. Taken together, these images form a narrative
about the nation, its values, and its people. Currently, the images on
our paper money portray no women, no people of color, no Native
Americans, and no working-class people. The images on our money,
like our monuments, statues, street names, and geographical place
names are now all contested territory.

Census projections predict that the national non-Hispanic white population, as currently self-identified, will fall below 50 percent nationally by 2045 at the latest.[34] By mid-century, African Americans (currently 13.1 percent); Latinx people, many of whom will identify as white (24.6 percent); Asians (7.9 percent); and multiracial individuals (3.8 percent) collectively will constitute a slight majority.[35] In 2019, people of color made up a majority of the population in 372 out of 3,141 counties in the nation.[36] Birth rates among people of color, which are higher than that of whites, and immigration will continue to change the hue of the nation.

The 2020 Census, released on August 12, 2021, confirms these trends and shows the emergence of a more diverse population than at any other time in U.S. history. According to the *Washington Post*, the 2020 Census "marks the first time the absolute number of people who identify as White alone has shrunk since a census started being taken in 1790."[37] The report indicates that the country also passed another milestone: for the first time, the portion of white people "dipped below 60 percent, slipping from 63.7 percent in 2010 to 57.8 percent in 2020."[38]

In terms of gender, women continue to comprise over 50 percent of the population. In a nation where a majority of the population is female and the number of people of color will soon surpass that of white people, it is unacceptable that every single image on U.S. paper currency depicts a white man. These images tell a narrative, one that by exclusion elides the experience and contributions of those who were and are not white, privileged males. The absence of a woman on U.S. currency has stood out even more since the 2020 centennial anniversary of the passage of the 19th Amendment, which forced white men to finally extend electoral access to white women—and potentially women of color.

CURRENCY CHAOS

According to researcher and journalist Adam Clark Estes, the word "dollar" comes from the Dutch word *leeuwendalwer,* which means lion dollar.[39] In 1664, the *leeuwendaler* was the currency of choice in New Amsterdam—the Dutch colony that would eventually become Manhattan—when the settlement was captured by the British. The term "dollar" would become common throughout the colonies leading up to the time of the American Revolution.

In 1775, the Continental Congress issued the colonies' first paper currency.[40] Known as "continentals," the bills bore the image of a thirteen-tier pyramid to symbolize the thirteen colonies. Following the Revolution, however, states and private banks were allowed to print paper notes with little oversight. This led to a boom in counterfeiting, scams, inflations and devaluations, and confusion. While businesses and individuals could trade in the state- and bank-issued notes, they were not considered legal tender by the federal government, and the principal form of currency shifted to coins. As Estes notes, Congress passed the Coinage Act of 1792 in order to officially designate the "silver dollar as the primary unit of money in the United States."[41] Distrust of paper money dominated for generations, and was later aggressively politicized by Andrew Jackson during his presidency. But we are getting ahead of ourselves.

Prior to the establishment of the Federal Reserve system in 1913, there had been several attempts to launch a federal bank. On February 8, 1791, the House of Representatives passed a bill establishing the First Bank of the United States. Signed into law by President George Washington, the bill faced strong opposition from the likes of Thomas Jefferson and James Madison, but was championed by Treasury Secretary Alexander Hamilton, who argued that a national bank was "a political machine, of the greatest importance to the state."

The bank was tasked with many goals, including paying off war debts and establishing a common coin-based currency. The bank's biggest and most controversial job was to raise desperately needed funds through taxation. With Washington's support, one way Hamilton attempted to fundraise was by taxing whiskey. The effort did not go well. Small producers and farmers rebelled almost immediately. Opposition turned to violence and full-scale revolt, and by 1794, Washington and state officials were forced to send troops to western Pennsylvania to quell what became known as the Whiskey Rebellion. This uprising soured many on the idea of a national bank. The institution's charter was due to be renewed by Congress in 1811, but the vote to do so resulted in a tie in the U.S. Senate. Vice President George Clinton broke the tie, sending the bank to its grave.[42]

There were many others who detested the whole idea from the beginning. Future president Andrew Jackson was in alignment with Jefferson's and Madison's views that a national bank was unconstitutional. He voiced strong opposition to a federal bank and had the opportunity to do something about it during his time in office. Under Jackson's presidency (1829–1837), the Second Bank of the United States that had been chartered in 1816 was terminated, and national paper currency almost disappeared with it.

SLAVERY DOLLARS

With the advent of the Civil War, financial chaos ensued. The Confederacy, viewing itself as a sovereign political entity, began printing millions of "Greybacks" with the promise that they would be backed by gold or silver once the South won the Civil War. The visual narratives printed on Confederate money communicated the racial caste system the South fought to permanently preserve. As historian James Loewen and others have thoroughly shown, such imagery provides more evidence against the historical revisionism suggesting that the cause of the Civil War was anything other than the defense of slavery.[43] In critiquing the vast national array of Confederate statues and memorials, Loewen writes, "Across America, the landscape has commemorated those men and women who opposed each agonizing next step our nation took on the path toward freedom and justice, while the courageous who challenged the United States to live out the meaning of its principles have lain forgotten or even reviled."[44]

Confederate five-dollar bill portraying enslaver president George Washington in classical garb.

A Confederate five-dollar note was issued on September 2, 1861, by the Southern Bank Note Company. The center image on the front depicts five white women positioned right above the words "Confederate States of America." According to researcher Pierre Fricke, the women represent the fields of commerce, agriculture, justice, liberty, and industry.[45] To the left of the women appears Minerva, the Roman goddess of war, who is sometimes also viewed as the goddess of wisdom, arts, and trade. To the right of the women appears a Romanized image of George Washington standing on a pedestal wrapped in a robe. By evoking Washington on its money, the South signaled that the goals of the Confederacy and the Founding Father were the same: an economy minted on a political system designed to perpetuate the practice of white people enslaving black people.

The conditional value of the note is stated on the front of the bill. Written across the front are the words "Six Months after the Ratification of a Treaty of peace between the Confederate States and the United States," implying that the bill would be worth nothing if the Confederacy did not win the war.

The Confederate hundred-dollar bill portrays three enslaved black people above pro-slavery leader John C. Calhoun and white nationalist symbol Columbia.

The Confederacy printed more than 670,000 hundred-dollar notes conveying the visual message that whites' right to own black people was divinely guided and politically enforced. In the middle and near the top is an image of three black people slaving in a cotton field. Two black men are digging with hoes, and a black woman carries a bundle of cotton. To the degree that the men are shown toiling as instructed, the scene reinforces the trope of "happy slaves" that prevailed in the Southern imagination.

On the bill's lower left is an image of John C. Calhoun, the fervent pro-slavery leader who viewed slavery not as a necessary evil but as a positive good.[46] Calhoun served as secretary of state, secretary of war, and a U.S. senator, as well as two terms as vice president. He also established the Second Bank of the United States, which was fiercely opposed by Jackson, leading to a permanent rift between the two men. Calhoun also fought with Jackson over the issue of nullification, the view that states could choose to ignore federal laws if they felt they were against their interests, especially if such laws were related to the issue of slavery.[47] Calhoun died in 1850 before the Civil War erupted.

On the bill's lower right is an image of Columbia, the female personification of the United States as a white woman with long, flowing blond hair. The word Columbia derives from the name Christopher Columbus. In many ways, the creation of the Columbia myth and symbology crystalizes the settler-colonial ethos whose white nationalist legacies we continue to reckon with today. In 1697, Samuel Sewall, a prominent Puritan judge and merchant better known for his involvement in the Salem Witch Trials, published *Phaenomena Quaedam Apocalyptica*, in which he referred to the country of "Columbina." In his time, First Nations territories were referred to as America in honor of the Italian explorer Amerigo Vespucci. Sewall, however, advanced the notion that "men should rather call it Columbina from the magnanimous Heroe Christopher Columbus a Genuese, who was manifestly Appointed by God to be the Finder out of these lands."[48] And thus, the feminized name of a Genoese explorer working on behalf of the Spanish crown became associated with the British colonies. As it did, writes Jordan Baker, "the inhabitants of these colonies gained a collective identity as Americans, rather than Englishmen," and the name Columbia emerged as a powerful symbol representing them.[49]

The beta version of this symbol took form in the invention of a new goddess, America, which derived its imagery from a fleeting recognition that the settler-colonial project was foreign and secondary to an Indigenous civilization of color that preceded it. Fashioned in the image of the people populating that civilization, the American goddess first appeared as a woman of color. This symbol did not last long, and was soon replaced by the image of a white person, a variation of the Roman goddess Liberty. In the pivot from a person of color to a white person, the visual coding caught up with the racial caste system that was inherent from the start of the settler-colonial project. This shift takes place during the colonial insurrection against the British, in which First Nations sided with the Crown in an effort to repel further colonial invasion into Native land. In his 1990 study for the American Antiquarian Society, Johns Hopkins scholar John Higham writes:

By the end of the Revolution an attractive young goddess named America could be seen, on maps and in almanacs, proudly holding aloft her cap-topped staff while waving farewell to a blindfolded or weeping Britannia. This was the tableau that adorned the Wallis map published in London, 1783, on which the boundary of the United States drawn by the British and American peace commissioners was first recorded. At the beginning of the peace negotiations the year before, John Jay had used a famous North American map drawn by John Mitchell, which had retained the Indian princess as its cartouche. The change from one symbolic system to another could not have been more dramatically declared.[50]

The creation of Columbia drew from and merged with the goddess of Liberty to represent a new white nation. In creating a United States mint in 1792, writes Higham, Congress formalized this image as "the embodiment of national consciousness." Throughout the nation's first century of existence, the two terms—Columbia and Liberty—were used interchangeably. The first is rooted in place, the second in principle. Both established a visual narrative that projected whiteness as settler-colonial power consolidated into national and imperial forms.

The image of Columbia often appeared in early newspapers and elsewhere, and was the subject of song, including "the great patriotic song of the decade," "Hail Columbia," by Joseph Hopkinson.[51] The image of Columbia was so prevalent at the time that it appeared in one of the early poems of Phillis Wheatley, the nation's first well-known African American writer and poet. In 1775, she sent a letter and the poem to George Washington, as war loomed in the colonies. She evokes Columbia as a protector of sorts in her poem:

> Celestial choir! enthron'd in realms of light,
> Columbia's scenes of glorious toils I write.
> . . .
> One century scarce perform'd its destined round,
> When Gallic powers Columbia's fury found;
> And so may you, whoever dares disgrace

The land of freedom's heaven-defended race!
Fix'd are the eyes of nations on the scales,
For in their hopes Columbia's arm prevails.[52]

Wheatley does not critique the racial, gender, and colonializing narratives that Columbia represents, nor the slave-holding hypocrisy of Washington. Instead, she channels the imperialistic narratives that romanticize the emerging American project in which enslavement and genocide are as central as the anti-monarchy politics leading to colonial insurrection.

By the end of the 1800s, Columbia is seen in visual narratives depicting white nationalist acquisition of Native territory—Manifest Destiny—as is in the case of John Gast's 1872 painting *American Progress*. The painting depicts an oversize apparition-like Columbia floating over an unstoppable wave of white people as they surge westward. Indigenous people are depicted as fleeing the wave, rather than defending themselves and their land from the coming plunder. The unconquered West is presented as a dark and dangerous space to be saved by the white authority of Columbia as she hovers over the throngs of white people flooding the Indigenous off their land. As art critic Jake Colberg writes, the painting "portrays Western expansion by Americans as a glorious and righteous thing."[53] The book in Columbia's right hand emphasizes the essential role that narratives are to play in the process of conquest, indoctrination, and assimilation. The legacies of that process are seen in the naming of the institutions around us, from Columbia Pictures to Columbia University, where I once taught.

Other individuals who were included at various points on Confederate dollars included Andrew Jackson, Jefferson Davis, and Lucy Holcombe Pickens.[54] Though Jackson hated paper money, his fierce defense of whites' right to enslave black people earned him an honored place on Confederate currency. Pickens, who was popularly known as the "Queen of the Confederacy," enslaved hundreds of people in concert with her husband, Francis Wilkinson Pickens, governor of South Carolina when it seceded from the Union in 1861, the first state to do so.[55]

The Confederacy financially collapsed long before the Civil War ended, and the paper currency it had issued was worth nothing. According to James Stokesbury, "the Confederates had run up a national debt of more than $700,000,000, and had experienced inflation of 6,000 percent."[56] At the core of the Southern financial crisis was the loss of slave labor as African Americans fled the plantations and generally went on strike, successfully crashing the Confederate economic system.[57]

UNION MONEY

The Union also issued paper currency. Lincoln and the Union Congress sought to counter the Confederacy's currency gambit with several paper bills of its own. First, in the summer of 1861, the Union printed 50 million dollars in so-called "Demand Notes" that were backed by government bonds. When those quickly were spent financing the war, Congress passed the Legal Tender Act, which allowed for the printing of 150 million dollars in so-called "Greenbacks," a reference to the green ink used on the currency.[58] All the denominations initially featured white men, including Lincoln, with an occasional image of Liberty/Columbia.

Pocahontas was a teenager when she was abducted by white settlers. While in captivity she was raped, converted to Christianity, and married. The conversion is depicted on the back of an 1865 twenty-dollar bill.

Representations of actual women briefly appeared on U.S. currency after the Civil War. In 1865, an image of Pocahontas adorned the back of the national twenty-dollar bill. Portraying her conversion to the religion of the white settlers, it shows the Indigenous princess dressed in a gown and kneeling before a white priest. Native Americans flank her on one side, foreign colonists on the other. The image is based on John Gadsby Chapman's monumental, twelve-by-eighteen-foot mural in the Capitol Rotunda, and is one of several in the Rotunda depicting white domination of the Americas. The image of Pocahontas formalizes the nation's Disney-esque mythologizing of its relationship with Native America. In reality, Pocahontas, a teenager at the time, was abducted and used as leverage in negotiations.[59] According to Mattaponi oral history, white settlers killed Pocahontas's husband, Kocoum, and raped and impregnated her while she was in captivity.[60] She went through the ritual of conversion before being married off to a white invader, John Rolfe, and died in her early twenties.[61] As depicted by John Gadsby Chapman's painting and the image on the twenty-dollar note, her conversion was not just to the settlers' religion, but also to their whiteness. Thus, by omitting the preceding abduction and rape, the image falsely suggests voluntary surrender, and the racial supremacy of the colonizers. A more historically accurate representation might have depicted how Pocahontas was tricked, abducted, and used by the white invaders as a bargaining chip with the Indian communities who negotiated for her safe release, while the whites burned their villages, as shown in the 1618 illustration *The Abduction of Pocahontas*.

Also on display in the Capitol Rotunda is Constantino Brumidi's *Frieze of American History*, in which Hernando Cortés's conquest of the Aztecs is depicted alongside a portrayal of "American Army Entering Mexico." As Matthew Restall writes, "Each surrender— Montezuma's in 1519 and Santa Anna's in 1847—is used to legitimize the other."[62] Taken together, these representations formalize a visual narrative of white conquest, domination, and Manifest Destiny. The result is a blanched version of historical realities that purposely omits

A more accurate rendering of white invaders' attack on Pocahontas and her community is seen in this 1618 illustration from *DeBry, Americae, VII*.
COURTESY OF LIBRARY OF CONGRESS.

an understanding of the racialized destruction of whole cultures, traditions, and civilizational memory.

In 1886, a special and short-lived series of silver certificate notes was issued. These notes were redeemable for silver, and denominations ran from one dollar to one thousand dollars. Martha Washington appeared on the front of the one-dollar silver certificate.[63] As I discuss in my book *The Black History of the White House*, Martha, along with her husband, George, enslaved hundreds of people over the course of their lives together. When the First Lady's personal slave, Oney Judge, successfully escaped after being notified that she would be given to the Washington's granddaughter as a wedding gift, Martha demanded that Oney be pursued, captured, and re-enslaved. Oney, however, outwitted the Washingtons and the agents they employed, and lived freely, as did Harriet Tubman following her escape, for the rest of her life. For many, a depiction of Oney Judge becoming independent of her enslaver, Martha Washington, would be a more apt representation of "Life, Liberty, and the Pursuit of Happiness" in America than any image of colonists becoming independent of the British Crown.

Hunkpapa Lakota Sioux chief Running Antelope appeared on a U.S. five-dollar silver certificate in 1899.

In 1899, for reasons unknown, the U.S. minted a five-dollar silver certificate that featured Chief Running Antelope, leader of the Hunkpapa Lakota Sioux people. This rare currency had a very limited printing and distribution and has been offered for sale on eBay and other websites for as much as fifteen thousand dollars. Chief Running Antelope appears in the center of the bill, and there are no other images on the front or the back. The use of Chief Running Antelope was not without controversy. According to a report by Aura Bogado in *Colorlines*, there is conflict over whether the headdress he is wearing is Lakota, which was his native tribe, or Pawnee.[64]

Chief Running Antelope was friends with the more famous Lakota chief Sitting Bull, who, along with Crazy Horse, inspired and led the Lakota and Cheyenne to a historic victory over General George Custer at the Battle of the Little Big Horn (known as the Battle of the Greasy Grass by Indigenous communities) in Montana on June 25–26, 1876. Reportedly, Chief Running Antelope eventually distanced himself from Chief Sitting Bull, as the former sought a more conciliatory relationship with white settlers and the U.S. government, a position he later came to regret.[65] This may account for why U.S. authorities chose him to be on the five-dollar bill.

THE BIRTH OF THE JACKSON TWENTY

In 1863, during the Civil War, the United States established its first national banking system. One outcome of this was the creation of a common national paper currency to be used universally in all the states. Up until that point, each state issued its own currency. On the front of the first national twenty-dollar bill appeared the image of Columbia/Liberty armed with sword and shield. In 1880, her image was moved from the center to the right of the bill, to make room for Alexander Hamilton, the nation's first head of the U.S. Department of Treasury, whose likeness was printed to the left. In 1905, both Columbia/Liberty and Hamilton were replaced

The first national twenty-dollar bill that was legal tender, issued in 1862–63, featured Columbia armed with sword and shield.[66]

by George Washington in the center spot on the bill's front. More changes were to come.

The Federal Reserve System was established in 1913, the year that Harriet Tubman passed away. It was the third attempt to create a national bank, and one of its main functions was the distribution of a wide variety of banknotes to Federal Reserve banks around the nation. The bills issued by the Federal Reserve continued to present racialized, masculinized, and politically biased imagery. In 1914, the Federal Reserve issued a five-dollar bill that featured an image of Lincoln centered on the front and one of the Pilgrims landing at Plymouth Rock on the back. In this rendering, the nation's history begins with the seemingly peaceful appearance of European settlers and their establishment of colonies. This unquestioned presentation of a founding narrative was not accidental, but another critical opportunity to reinforce stories that shaped the nation's official historiography from a white perspective.

In 1914, the Federal Reserve's first twenty-dollar bill featured Grover Cleveland, the nation's twenty-second and twenty-fourth president. Cleveland was elected in 1884 and became the first Democrat to win the presidency since James Buchanan in 1856. He would lose his re-election in 1888 but return to the office in 1892, the only president in U.S. history to have non-consecutive terms. It is believed that he earned such an honor due to his unyielding support for the gold standard, which the United States would use to back up its currency until 1933. In terms of racial issues, Cleveland's administration demonstrated little concern for the interests of the black community and stood on the sidelines as white America visited increasing violence and segregation on African Americans.[67] Cleveland supported segregation as New York governor and was president when the pivotal 1896 *Plessy v. Ferguson* Supreme Court decision upheld the constitutionality of racial segregation under the "separate but equal" doctrine. Three of the seven justices who voted yes—Melville W. Fuller, Rufus W. Peckham, and Edward D. White— were appointed by Cleveland.

Also in 1914, Andrew Jackson made his appearance on another denomination, the new ten-dollar bill.[68] This was perhaps the biggest irony in the history of U.S. currency. No other president was as vocal an opponent of paper currency and federal banking as Jackson. Much of his presidency, when he was not dispossessing Native Americans of their land, was spent railing against the banking community. At one point, while campaigning for a second term in 1832, he said of bankers, "You are a den of vipers and thieves. I intend to rout you out, and by the eternal God, I will rout you out."[69] In his farewell address as president, in 1837, Jackson referred to paper currency as a "deep-seated evil." He elaborated:

> In reviewing the conflicts which have taken place between different interests in the United States and the policy pursued since the adoption of our present form of Government, we find nothing that has produced such deep-seated evil as the course of legislation in relation to the currency. The Constitution of the United States unquestionably intended to secure to the people a circulating medium of gold and silver. But the establishment of a national bank by Congress, with the privilege of issuing paper money receivable in the payment of the public dues, and the unfortunate course of legislation in the several States upon the same subject, drove from general circulation the constitutional currency and substituted one of paper in its place.[70]

Despite his contempt for paper money, Jackson nevertheless became the face of several denominations issued by the Federal Reserve. In 1928, Jackson's image was moved to the front and center of the U.S. twenty, but it long remained a mystery how the decision was made. In 2016, the *Washington Post* conducted an investigation to determine how it had occurred. Reporters checked with the Treasury Department and with officials at Jackson's former slave plantation, The Hermitage, now a museum and visitor's center honoring Jackson. At that point, no records of the deliberations or discussions could be found to clarify what happened. Howard Kittell, the CEO of The Hermitage, stated simply, "It's a mystery to us as well."[71] However, subsequent research by Rutgers University law professor Ruth Anne Robbins and law librarian Genevieve Tung uncovered key documents that offered a bit of an explanation.[72] On October 28, 1927, when a major redesign of all of U.S. currency was on the table, a committee studying the redesign sent a memo to Treasury Secretary Andrew Mellon listing eleven denominations and suggestions regarding who should be on them. A subcommittee had recommended that only portraits of past presidents who had striking features and were "distinguished" should be used. That list was modified by the chair of the committee to include non-presidents Benjamin Franklin and Alexander Hamilton.

The memo to Mellon read:

> In connection with reducing the size of paper currency and the revision of designs, portraits for the faces of the various denominations and pictorial embellishments for the backs of certain denomination are proposed as follows:
>
> $1 – George Washington
> $2 – Jefferson; Monticello
> $5 – Lincoln; Lincoln Memorial
> $10 – Hamilton; Treasury
> $20 – Cleveland; White House
> $50 – Grant; Capitol
> $100 – Franklin; Bureau of Engraving and Printing
> $500 – McKinley
> $1,000 – Jackson
> $5,000 – Madison
> $10,000 – Chase

While initially Grover Cleveland was recommended for the twenty and Jackson for the thousand-dollar bill, on the memo a line is drawn through Cleveland's name and another through Jackson's. Their names were apparently switched by Mellon, but no further explanation is documented.[73]

In the early twentieth century, when segregation and racial violence were at a zenith, Jackson's history of unrepentant militancy
against Native Americans and African Americans did not raise
an eyebrow with white political leaders and the majority of white
America. Race riots, public lynchings, inflammatory films such as
The Birth of a Nation, and bigoted language in public were the norm.
By 1928, Jackson had appeared on a postage stamp (1863), a bronze
equestrian statue had been erected in his honor in Lafayette Park
across from the White House, and his pro-slavery face stared out
from at least "18 pieces of U.S. currency, including a $5 bill, a $10, a
$50 and a $10,000."[74] The propagation of Andrew Jackson's image on
postage, monuments, and money enshrined the vehement enemy of
abolition and Native America as an unassailable national icon. Black
and Indigenous Americans were certainly not solicited for their
views on what Jackson may have meant to them, their ancestors, and
their communities.

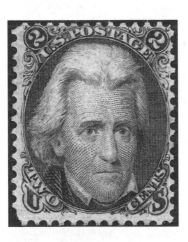

While it was at war with
the Confederacy over
slavery, the U.S. released
a two-cent stamp honoring
Andrew Jackson, who died
sixteen years before the
war started.

For most of U.S. history, representations of women and people
of color were rarely considered for inclusion in formal symbols pro-
jecting the nation's origins and ethos. As a result, the overwhelming

centrality of white men in official U.S. narratives has perpetuated distorted or false versions of the nation's political and racial history. In the process, both whiteness and maleness have long remained prerequisite conditions for access to privilege and power, while the struggles of "others" who have fought for freedom from forces far more savage and tyrannical than the British Crown have been marginalized. This process—perpetuated from the days of settler-colonialism to the present through education, media, law, monuments, and the nation's money—has indoctrinated generations to internalize the racist view that "American means white." "All others," Toni Morrison once said, "must hyphenate."

Despite the pervasiveness of U.S. history rendered from a white perspective, such renderings have never succeeded in suppressing the resistance of the millions of people left out of the official story. Such resistance inspires each new generation of people who have organized against the injustices of their time—from slavery, genocide, land displacement, and lynching to the vigilantism, police violence, anti-protest laws and voter suppression of today. One of the individuals whose acts of resistance have permanently left her mark on the nation is Harriet Tubman.

Portrait of Harriet Tubman circa 1868 or 1869. PHOTO BY
BENJAMIN F. POWELSON.COURTESY OF THE LIBRARY OF CONGRESS.

TWO

HARRIET TUBMAN REPRESENTS SOLIDARITY, STRUGGLE, AND GENUINE DEMOCRACY

"There was a glory over everything. The sun came like gold through the trees, and over the fields, and I felt like I was in heaven."
—Harriet Tubman, describing the moment
she achieved self-emancipation

"Excepting John Brown—of sacred memory—I know of no one who has willingly encountered more hardships to serve our enslaved people than you have. Much that you have done would seem improbable to those who do not know you as I know you. It is to me a great pleasure and a great privilege to bear testimony for your character and your works, and to say to those to whom you may come, that I regard you in every way truthful and trustworthy."
—Frederick Douglass, from his August 29, 1868,
letter to Harriet Tubman

BY THE TIME Harriet Tubman escaped to freedom in the late fall of 1849, resistance to slavery was intense on multiple fronts.[75] First and foremost were the black people who fought to disrupt and sabotage the daily life of their white enslavers in every possible way. The trope of the "happy slave" was a myth that belied the hellish conditions black people endured in the antebellum South. Like Tubman, thousands of enslaved black people took the perilous risk of self-emancipating by escaping to the north. In 1849, Tubman was one of at least 278 people who escaped from Maryland.[76]

Resistance to the slaveocracy of the South took many forms, including the emergence of Maroon communities—areas of liberation occupied by escaped individuals that often included Native Americans. Scores of these societies existed in the South and other parts of the country during the slavery era and after.[77] Some were large, but most were small. Some involved communities hidden deep in woods or swamps; others were more open, resembling villages. Some lasted years, while others were crushed soon after being established.

One of the most spectacular forms of collective resistance was the spate of slave rebellions that struck fear in every Southern white for the entire duration of "the peculiar institution."[78] Historian Herbert Aptheker estimated that there were at least 250 slave revolts prior to the Civil War. In every state where people of African descent were held captive, there were rebellions. While all were terrifying for white slaveowners, some uprisings became nationally renowned for their audacity and scope. In 1831, when Tubman was about nine years old, the most notorious slave revolt in U.S. history occurred less than a hundred miles from where she was enslaved. In August 1831, in Virginia, after experiencing several visions and organizing a cadre of followers, Reverend Nat Turner and his army went from plantation to plantation slaying white men, women, and children— and freeing the enslaved communities there. After two days, white militias were able to stop the revolt, capturing and killing many of those involved. Turner, however, escaped and was not found until October. He was tried and executed, but his rebellion changed the atmosphere of slavery, ensuring that few slaveholders slept easy again.[79] Certainly, Tubman was aware of, and perhaps inspired by, news of the revolt.

Another indispensable source of resistance was the community of free blacks, in the South and outside of it, who fueled the abolition movement in every possible way. Petitions, protests, and organizations that fought slavecatchers were some of the tools used by those who wanted to free their real and figurative sisters and brothers. Tubman's missions to free people from their enslavers was initially motivated by her desire to rescue her parents, her siblings, and a reluctant husband.

Vulnerable to being captured by rogue slavecatchers who presumed any available black body was prime for kidnapping, free black people were central to the clandestine operations of the Underground Railroad system.[80] Like Tubman, both escaped and free blacks ventured onto dangerous roads to go south and facilitate escapes. While Tubman has been the focus of much of the popular awareness about these liberation sojourns, she was not alone. For example, Osborne Perry Anderson was one of the few African Americans who joined John Brown's infamous and failed raid on Harpers Ferry in 1859. Remarkably, he survived and even wrote a book about his experiences, *A Voice from Harper's Ferry*.[81] Elijah Anderson, an abolitionist blacksmith in Kentucky, took advantage of his light complexion to pass as a white slaveowner in multiple operations to free enslaved people.[82]

Resistance came from both white and black leaders in the more public fronts of the abolitionist movement. The Quakers, in particular, had a long history of abolitionism in the United States. They campaigned to change laws, assisted and funded the Underground Railroad, sponsored abolitionist speakers, and more. They won the admiration of Tubman and other black leaders. Among them were Philadelphia's Anthony Benezet, an educator who in 1775 founded the Society for the Relief of Free Negroes Unlawfully Held in Bondage. Historian Maurice Jackson writes, "Unlike most of his contemporaries, even those in the antislavery movement itself, he believed that all people were born equal in God's sight."[83] After his death in 1784, Benjamin Franklin and others would rebrand the organization into the audaciously and perhaps excessively named Pennsylvania Society for Promoting the Abolition of Slavery and for the Relief of Negroes Unlawfully Held in Bondage and for Improving the Conditions of the African Race.[84] Resistance also often involved more subtle forms, such as secretly learning to read and write, and sharing this knowledge with others.[85]

Lastly, and perhaps least acknowledged, were the Northern capitalists who sought to end slavery as a means to undermine the Southern aristocrats whose power was almost wholly dependent on slave labor. Tubman's America was a nation in which two centers of economic power fought for political dominance. The anti-slavery stance of Northern capitalists, and the creation of the Republican Party in 1854, were deemed tactically necessary to overthrow the Southern aristocrats. The fact that Northern capitalists' agendas coincided with the aspirations of enslaved blacks and abolitionists was more a confluence of interests than any kind of solidarity. "The Northern capitalists sought economic control over the entire nation," writes Angela Y. Davis. "Their struggle against the Southern slaveocracy did not therefore mean that they supported the liberation of Black men or women as human beings."[86] In fact, the capitalists were not just disinterested, but opposed to the political power that the black population demanded. Once the Northern capitalists had established their hegemony, the Republican party engaged in "the systematic disenfranchisement of Black people," says Davis.[87]

As such, the convergence of interests was limited and ultimately flawed. U.S. businesspeople, wherever they were based, conducted their operations within structures of white supremacy and male dominance entrenched since the first days of settler-colonialism. Abolition of white people's right to traffic and enslave black people did not, therefore, also accomplish an end to race- and gender-based marginalization. The power shift from the Southern planters to Northern bankers and industrialists did not involve a radical democratic change that immediately expanded the basic human and political rights of America's oppressed communities. Though their interests overlapped in opposition to the South, the capitalists' goal was power and profit. Enslaved communities and their abolitionist allies were fighting for a second revolution, one based on the very same Enlightenment ideals of liberty and equality that the colonies voiced, but never realized, in their revolt against the British.

THE QUIET, UNDISPUTED DIGNITY OF BLACK WOMANHOOD

One black woman who fought for liberty and equality her entire life was Harriet Tubman. Constantly underestimated, she risked her life and freedom on countless occasions to liberate others, and until her last breath remained committed to building a political system that endowed women and people of color with the same rights as white men. She never sought fame or riches for her efforts, only the justice and fairness which she believed was a right of all.

Born enslaved in Dorchester County, Maryland, and given the name Araminta Ross, the child would later achieve national and global fame as the "Moses" of her people. There has long been a mystery surrounding the precise year and date of her birth, but recent scholarship discovered her actual birthdate to be March 15, 1822. According to Dorothy Wickenden in her book *The Agitators: Three Friends Who Fought for Abolition and Women's Rights*, scholar Kate Clifford Larson unearthed her birthday by "piecing together a notation in a slaveholder's ledger, a legal dispute about who owned her, and an October 1849 advertisement in a newspaper on Maryland's Eastern Shore for a twenty-seven-year-old runaway slave."[88] Her biography has been taught for generations to nearly every public school student in the United States as early as kindergarten, and to many around the world. Several museums and historical sites have been constructed in her honor. Among them are the Harriet Tubman Underground Railroad Monument in Dorchester County, Maryland, the seventeen-acre Harriet Tubman Underground Railroad State Park and Visitor Center in Church Creek, Maryland, and the Harriet Tubman National Historical Park in Auburn, New York.

The objective here is not to retell her entire biography but to highlight a few points relevant to debates about why she should be on the front of the twenty-dollar bill, and how her work in liberation, abolition, women's suffrage, and caring for those in need offers inspiration for all who stand up to injustice. Her refusal to accept oppression from anyone regardless of their power, status, race, or gender was as fierce as her determination to emancipate herself and others. Unlike Frederick Douglass and Sojourner Truth, two of the most important and influential black leaders of the mid to late 1880s and both friends of hers, Tubman was handicapped by a head injury and never learned to read or write. Tubman also never met with

President Lincoln. In part, this was because she was more critical of his policies. The sticking point was his initial resistance to enlisting black troops to fight the Confederacy. Sojourner Truth had invited Tubman to accompany her when she went to meet with the president, but Tubman declined. She later expressed regret that she did not get to meet "Lincoln and thank him."[89] But she was resolute that *all* black people had to be free if the country wanted to move forward.

It should be stressed that Tubman was a wanted fugitive from the time she escaped her enslavers to the end of the Civil War. As such, she was in danger wherever she went, not just when she conducted missions to liberate black people from slave states through the Underground Railroad. The Fugitive Slave Act of 1850 only increased the danger. The act required that anyone suspected of being a runaway slave be reported and captured. The act also eliminated protections for suspected runaways, and provided monetary incentives to abduct people of African descent. Slavecatchers frequently roamed the areas where free blacks lived, looking for escaped individuals hiding among them. Such threats increased the steps she took to successfully evade capture, but never deterred her. Her insurrectionary role in the public liberation of Charles Nalle, described below, demonstrates the extent of her solidarity with the oppressed and determination to overcome their oppressors, no matter the risk. The history of her escape is itself an important insight into the long struggle for black liberation.

ESCAPE TO FREEDOM

The story of Harriet Tubman's self-emancipation is a hero's tale, a daring journey into the unknown by a young woman who had never left the state of Maryland or tasted freedom. At twenty-seven, she had already faced decades of enslavement with all the brutality, torture, rape, and evil that came with it. She envisioned a wholly different future for herself, her family, and her race.

On September 17, 1849, Tubman and her two brothers, Ben and Henry, set out to escape the slave plantations of the Brodess and

Thompson families. She had become increasingly concerned that her family members would be sold to different owners upon the death of the plantation's patriarch, Edward Brodess, and the estate falling into the hands of his widow, Eliza Brodess.[90] While Tubman's father, Ben Ross, had been free since 1840, her mother, Harriet "Rit" Ross, was not. After persistent research, Tubman later discovered that a will left by Brodess's great-grandfather provided for Rit and other enslaved women to be freed upon turning forty-five years old.[91]

Heirs of slaveowners often sold enslaved people to pay estate taxes and other costs. There was no reason to expect that widow Eliza would demonstrate any hesitation in selling Tubman, her brothers, and her mother to meet her financial needs. Three of Tubman's sisters—Mariah Ritty, Linah, and Soph—had been sold off years earlier by Edward Brodess, and she carried that pain deeply.

Although the economics of slavery along the upper East Coast had changed significantly, and soil depletion made wheat more profitable than cultivation of the more labor-intensive tobacco, tens of thousands of black people were still enslaved in the region. As cotton came to dominate the Deep South's economy, the number of black people sold and shipped away from the East Coast states to Alabama, Georgia, Louisiana, and Mississippi increased. According to Walter Johnson, more than one million newly arrived Africans and older-generation African Americans were traded from the East to the South in the decades before the Civil War.[92] Like most other enslaved women, Tubman certainly had plenty of reasons to worry about the breakup of the rest of her family.

Equally worrisome, both of her parents were active agents in the Underground Railroad that assisted black people to escape their enslavers, a dangerous endeavor that could and did have severe repercussions for those who got caught.[93] Dorothy Wickenden writes that Tubman's parents knew the many escape routes by land and water, and, like the many African Americans who were active in the Underground, they "also knew which white families provided shelter, and advised freedom seekers how to evade bounty hunters and bloodhounds."[94] Tubman absorbed this information and the stealth art and skills of disappearing runaways from the intense searches of slave-catchers and vengeful slave masters. Her father gave her lessons that would later prove indispensable during the many trips she made back and forth to the South, Angela Y. Davis writes. "He taught her how to walk soundlessly through the woods and how to find food and medicine among the plants, roots and herbs. The fact that she never once suffered defeat is no doubt attributable to her father."[95] In preparation for her self-emancipation, Araminta changed her name to Harriet, after her mother, and assumed her husband's last name, Tubman.[96]

It was Harriet who convinced Ben and Henry to leave with her that day in mid-September. Although she was leaving behind her beloved parents and her husband of five years, John Tubman, it is reasonable to assume that even then she was thinking that she would come back for them someday. John was actually "free" and could have left on his own if he so desired. As such, he had misgivings about his wife's desire to free herself by escaping to the North. In 1840 he had become a legally free man, joining the community of thousands of other free blacks in Maryland. In 1851, Harriet sought to reunite with John and convince him to leave with her, but she discovered that he had remarried. He refused to go, thus ending that relationship for good.

As unique as Tubman would turn out to be, her high-risk decision to escape was not. As noted earlier, according to Kate Clifford Larson, in 1849, the year of her absconding, hundreds of enslaved black folks fled Maryland.[97] Larson notes that this was surely an undercount, given that plantation owners did not always want to make it known that they could not control their black population. Slavery in the eastern shore area of Maryland where Harriet lived dated back to the arrival of Africans in chains in 1619. And from that barbaric act going forward, black people would flee the savagery of enslavement whenever they could.

When Tubman and her brothers escaped, they violated the state and federal laws of their time. Under Article 4, Section 3 of the U.S. Constitution, "No Person held to Service or Labour in one State, under the Laws thereof, escaping into another, shall, in Consequence of any Law or Regulation therein, be discharged from such Service or Labour, but shall be delivered up on Claim of the Party to whom such Service or Labour may be due." This "fugitive slave" clause in the U.S. Constitution was reinforced in 1793 with the passage of the first of two Fugitive Slave Acts.

Refusing to be complicit in the institution of slavery, most Northern states intentionally neglected to enforce the law. Several even passed "Personal Liberty Laws" that gave accused runaways the right to a jury trial and also protected free blacks, many of whom had been abducted by bounty hunters and sold into slavery.

Despite the profusion of states' ideologies, black folks fleeing slavery were not to be protected from extradition regardless of the anti-slavery proclivities of receiving states. However, the law was so brazenly ignored that in 1850—the year after Tubman's escape— Congress passed a second Fugitive Slave Act. The purpose of this white supremacist law was to strengthen the ability of slavers to recapture the black folks who had self-emancipated. The law incentivized police officers and judges with bonuses for arresting and convicting people who had escaped, while adding severe penalties for officers not arresting suspected escapees or individuals who helped them.[98]

Tubman was unwavering about her right to freedom. "I started with this idea in my head, there are two things I've got a right to, and these are, Death or Liberty—one or t'other I mean to have. No one will take me back alive; I shall fight for my liberty, and when the time has come for me to go, the Lord will let them kill me."[99]

A few days after their escape, Harriet's former enslaver, Eliza, placed an advertisement in the *Cambridge Democrat*, the local paper, for the three runaway siblings, reading (verbatim):

> three negroes, named as follows: HARRY, aged about 19 years, has on one side of his neck a wren, just under the ear, he is of a dark chestnut color, about 5 feet 8 or 9 inches high, BEN, aged about 25 years, is very quick to speak when spoken to, he is of a chestnut color, about six feet high; MINTY, aged about 27 years, is of a chestnut color, fine looking and about 5 feet high.

The advertisement uses Tubman's nickname, Minty. It is notable that Eliza referred to her as "fine looking," a compliment she probably never gave to Tubman in person. Eliza offered one hundred dollars for each person if they were captured out of state, and fifty dollars if caught in Maryland. Three hundred dollars total reward in 1849 would be the equivalent of approximately ten thousand dollars today, signaling how valuable Tubman and her brothers were to Eliza.[100]

Shortly after taking off, and learning about the bounty on their heads, Ben and Henry got cold feet and wanted to return. Unable to convince them to continue, but also fearful they could not get back safely on their own, Tubman returned with them. Shortly after coming back, she heard rumors that she was to be sold as soon as possible due to her insubordination. Upon learning that, and not giving up on her dream, she again made plans to leave, this time alone and with no possibility of stopping until she had reached "free" soil.

Not long after, she sang her way to freedom. In recalling her departure, she stated that she was singing as she walked away from the plantation to which she had been rented. As she did, the plantation owner, Anthony Thompson, happened to ride up on horseback. Tubman gave him a bow as she crooned:

> I'm sorry I'm gwine to lebe you,
> Farewell, oh farewell;
> But I'll meet you in the mornin',
> Farewell, oh farewell.

According to her account of it to Sarah H. Bradford, once he passed, she continued singing:

> I'll meet you in the mornin',
> I'm boun' for de promised land,
> On the oder side of Jordan,
> Boun' for de promised land.[101]

Traveling alone, Tubman followed the North Star and advanced with support from the Underground Railroad. By the 1840s, the network of abolitionists helping people escape their enslavers was vast, interracial, and efficient. At the beginning of her journey, a white woman that Tubman never identified by name provided her with contacts and directions. She went to different safe houses, hid in wagons, slept in the woods, and walked and walked and walked.

When she crossed the Maryland-Pennsylvania line, as indicated by a stone marker on the road, Tubman stated, "I looked at my hands to see if I was the same person. There was a glory over everything. The sun came like gold through the trees, and over the fields, and I felt like I was in heaven."[102] However, she felt almost immediately that she would need to go back and rescue those she had left behind.

Her first attempt to do so occurred only one year later. In December 1850, after being informed that her beloved niece, Kessiah, and her two children, James Alfred and Araminta, were going to be sold, she returned to Maryland and plotted their way to freedom with other relatives and friends. They were audaciously spirited away in the midst of physically being sold on the auction block, and were delivered to Tubman in Baltimore. After hiding them for a few days, she got them safely to Philadelphia's growing black community.[103]

Over the years, Tubman made thirteen return trips to Maryland to help people self-emancipate. As a result of these efforts, between seventy and eighty individuals found freedom, including her parents, other relatives, and complete strangers.[104] Incredibly, she did not lose a single person either to capture by slavecatchers, an untimely accidental death, illness, or injury. For years, Maryland slaveowners were mystified about the black person who was successfully helping enslaved individuals escape. Some even believed that there was a white man masquerading as a black woman. Some abolitionists knew her or called her "Moses," while she also used the name "Harriet Garrison."

To evade them she traveled through farmland, bush, forests, rivers, wetlands, thickets, and virtually every terrain that existed between Maryland and areas due north. Many of her trips, almost always at night, were in the frost of winter. This significantly increased the perils of the journey with the threat of hypothermia, frostbite, flu, and other winter-related challenges. The fact that many fugitives could not swim made crossing streams and rivers exceptionally challenging. Hiding in covered wagons, baskets, holds of ships, and other claustrophobic places of concealment was terrifying to many.

Tubman became a master of disguise and often dressed as an old, feeble woman or a young man. A network of enablers including hundreds of free blacks were her army. Strategically, she would leave with her flock on Saturday evenings. This would give her a head start before any notice could be printed in the newspaper or on flyers on Mondays. In fact, she also hired those she trusted to "follow white masters and slavecatchers as they posted reward notices . . . and tear the notices down."[105] She continued to make freedom runs right up until the outbreak of the Civil War. Her last trip was in December 1860, when she helped seven individuals cross into "Jordan."

It should be remembered that Tubman carried extraordinary personal health burdens during this period. Her seizures and blackouts would have crushed someone of lesser determination, resilience, and fortitude. She viewed them as blessings that offered moments of spiritual guidance for the work she was doing. While she received financial help here and there, she worked mostly menial jobs between her rescues to raise money to live on, help family members, and to pay for her extraction trips in and out of Maryland.

"AFRICAN FURY" AND THE LIBERATION OF CHARLES NALLE

We will never know the details of many of the missions Tubman undertook, nor the stories of most of the people she helped find their way to freedom. However, in the spring of 1860, one of her most audacious liberation actions was witnessed by crowds, reported in the press, and later recounted by Tubman herself. While traveling to Boston to give a talk at an abolitionist rally, she stopped in Troy, New York, to visit a cousin, John Hooper, and some comrades active in the Underground Railroad. During her stay, news reached her that Charles Nalle, a married father of six who had fled from slavery eighteen months earlier, had been captured and was being held at the local U.S. Commissioner's office. Born around 1821, Nalle was the son of a white slaver and a black slave. Called an "octoroon" in his time, he grew up on his father's farm in Culpeper County, Virginia, before being inherited by his white half-brother, Blucher Hansbrough.[106]

When news of the capture reached Tubman, she immediately went to Nalle's location and joined an angry crowd outside the building where he was being detained.[107] Rumor spread that Nalle was going to be returned to the South without a trial or a hearing. This meant the abolitionist community had to act fast.

The crowd outside the building was comprised of free blacks, escapees, and whites, men and women. Tubman disguised herself as an old woman and somehow managed to enter the building and witness what was happening on the upper floor where Nalle's fate was being determined. After a while, some in the crowd feared that the authorities had somehow gotten Nalle out through an unseen exit, but as long as they saw Tubman's bonnet through a window, they were reassured that Nalle could still be rescued. Hoping to amass more people in the streets, Tubman sent some children to yell "fire." As a result, the size of the crowd outside the building increased to "nearly a thousand persons."[108]

Harriet Tubman's biographer, Sarah H. Bradford, relayed Tubman's account as follows:

> Offers were made to buy Charles from his master, who at first agreed to take twelve hundred dollars for him; but when this was subscribed, he immediately raised the price to fifteen hundred. The crowd grew more excited. A gentleman raised a window and called out, "Two hundred dollars for his rescue, but not one cent to his master!" This was responded to by a roar of satisfaction from the crowd below. At length the officers appeared, and announced to the crowd, that if they would open a lane to the wagon, they would promise to bring the man down the front way.
>
> The lane was opened, and the man was brought out—a tall, handsome, intelligent *white* man, with his wrists manacled together, walking between the U. S. Marshal and another officer, and

behind him his brother and his master, so like him that one could hardly be told from the other. The moment they appeared, Harriet roused from her stooping posture, threw up a window, and cried to her friends: "Here he comes—take him!" and then darted down the stairs like a wild-cat. She seized one officer and pulled him down, then another, and tore him away from the man; and keeping her arms about the slave, she cried to her friends: "Drag us out! Drag him to the river!" They were knocked down together, and while down, she tore off her sun-bonnet and tied it on the head of the fugitive. When he rose, only his head could be seen, and amid the surging mass of people the slave was no longer recognized, while the master appeared like the slave. Again and again they were knocked down, the poor slave utterly helpless, with his manacled wrists, streaming with blood. Harriet's outer clothes were torn from her, and even her stout shoes were pulled from her feet, yet she never relinquished her hold of the man, till she had dragged him to the river, where he was tumbled into a boat, Harriet following in a ferry-boat to the other side. But the telegraph was ahead of them, and as soon as they landed he was seized and hurried from her sight.[109]

Tubman and hundreds of others took a ferry to West Troy in pursuit. When they got to Nalle's location, a battle was already raging between armed officers and abolitionists. Shots were fired and at least two men lay wounded on the ground. During that melee, Tubman and "other colored women," as reported in the press, rushed in over the downed men, grabbed Nalle and spirited him away a second time. At one point, Nalle was knocked unconscious. According to Tubman, "I throw him across my shoulder like a bag of meal and tote him away out of there."[110] They put him in a wagon and brought him to a place of hiding in Schenectady. Falsely reported to be in Canada, Nalle remained in hiding nearby while the local abolitionist network raised enough money to buy his freedom.[111] The efforts of Tubman and the other black rescuers were captured in press reports on the incident that stated, while "lawyers, editors, public men, and private individuals" participated, "African fury is entitled to claim the greatest share in the rescue."[112] Tubman's role in Nalle's miraculous emancipation occurred in public and was witnessed by many and reported in the press. This elevated her status as a living Moses figure and the guerrilla general John Brown knew her to be.[113] But Tubman could never have freed Nalle alone. This episode demonstrates her leadership and the level of unwavering solidarity present in the black freedom struggle.

Physical efforts to stop bounty hunters and armed authorities from returning self-emancipated black folks took place on numerous occasions in the North, frustrating Southern attempts to consolidate their regime of slavery. In many ways, these were countervailing interpretations of the Constitution and the principles the nation claimed to uphold. The question of democracy for some or democracy for all has been a dividing line that has plagued the nation from the time of its founding, through Tubman's era, to the present day.

COMBAHEE RIVER RAID

At the age of forty-one, in the middle of the bloodiest days of the Civil War, Tubman led a raid from Beaufort, South Carolina, against Confederate forces along the Combahee River, becoming "the first woman to plan and execute an armed expedition during the Civil War."[114] On the night of June 1, 1863, Tubman and Colonel James Montgomery set sail with an estimated three hundred black soldiers on three gunboats, *John Adams, Harriet A. Weed*, and *Sentinel*, two of which were converted steamboats. Montgomery was a committed abolitionist and had been close to Tubman's friend John Brown, who in October 1859 had led an unsuccessful, but highly impactful raid on the U.S. federal arsenal in Harpers Ferry, Virginia. Brown had hoped the assault would inspire slave rebellions across the region. Reportedly, Montgomery intended to rescue Brown from jail after his capture, but a severe snowstorm scuttled his plans.[115]

Aware of her scouting skills and knowledge of the area, General David Hunter asked Tubman to lead the daring raid into Confederate territory. Hunter was an advocate for immediate abolition and for building an all-black regiment, both positions that President

Lincoln rejected at the time. Tubman agreed to the mission, but only if Colonel James Montgomery was in command. Her role was critical due to her network of scouts who collected crucial information about Confederate positions and activity.[116] That allowed her to report back the locations where Confederates had placed torpedoes in the river—essential intelligence so that the Union armada could navigate safely. As Paul Donnelly recounted in the *New York Times* in 2013, "The Combahee raid was planned and executed primarily as a liberation raid, to find and free those who were unable or unwilling to take the enormous risks to reach Union lines on their own. That's how Tubman conceived of it."[117] Donnelly describes what happened next as "arguably the most beautiful scene ever recorded in war."

Illustration of the Combahee River Raid published in *Harper's Weekly*, July 4, 1863. COURTESY OF THE LIBRARY OF CONGRESS.

Using intelligence gathered by Tubman, black troops landed and advanced into Confederate territory. They sabotaged bridges and rails, burned plantations and barns, destroyed crops and rice fields, and took important food and farm animals. While their enslavers' homes burned, hundreds of black families defied attempts to keep them from bolting. Sarah H. Bradford described Tubman's account of how black families ran for the gunboats:

> They came down every road, across every field, just as they had left their work and their cabins; women with children clinging around their necks, hanging to their dresses, running behind, all making at full speed for 'Lincoln's gun-boats.'
>
> "I nebber see such a sight," said Harriet; Here you'd see a woman wid a pail on her head, rice a smokin' in it jus' as she'd taken it from de fire, young one hangin' on behind, one han' roun' her forehead to hold on, 'tother han' diggin' into de rice-pot, eatin' wid all its might; hold of her dress two or three more; down her back a bag wid a pig in it. One woman brought two pigs, a white one an' a black one; we took 'em all on board; named de white pig Beauregard, and de black pig Jeff Davis. Sometimes de women would come wid twins hangin' roun' der necks; 'pears like I nebber see so many twins in my life; bags on der shoulders, baskets on der heads, and young ones taggin' behin', all loaded; pigs squealin', chickens screamin', young ones squallin.'"
>
> And so they came pouring down to the gun-boats. When they stood on the shore, and the small boats put out to take them off, they all wanted to get in at once. After the boats were crowded, they would hold on to them so that they could not leave the shore. The oarsmen would beat them on their hands, but they would not let go; they were afraid the gun-boats would go off and leave them, and all wanted to make sure of one of these arks of refuge. At length Colonel Montgomery shouted from the upper deck, above the clamor of appealing tones, "Moses, you'll have to give 'em a song."

Tubman then lifted up her voice and sang lyrics she made up on the spot:

Come from the East;
Come from the West;
'Mong all the glorious nations
This glorious one's the best.
Come along, come along; don't be alarmed,
For Uncle Sam is rich enough
To give you all a farm.[118]

Because of Tubman's efforts, more than seven hundred black people escaped in the mission, and not one Union soldier died in the process.

Back in Beaufort, Tubman, Montgomery, the troops, and the newly freed were greeted with cheers from people in the streets. Tubman and Montgomery later spoke to those gathered at a packed church event celebrating the mission. Her speech was referred to as one of "sound sense and real native eloquence."[119] Nearly all men who had been freed by the raid soon enlisted in South Carolina's Third Regiment.[120]

In her own words, Tubman said, "We weakened the rebels somewhat on the Combahee River, by taking and bringing away seven hundred and fifty-six of their most valuable live stock, known up in your region as 'contrabands,' and this, too without the loss of a single life on our part. . . . Nearly or quite all the able-bodied men have joined the colored regiment here."[121]

On July 10, 1863, a public account of the operation was published in a Boston-based abolitionist journal, *The Commonwealth*:

Col. Montgomery and his gallant band of 300 black soldiers, *under the guidance of a black woman*, dashed into the enemy's country, struck a bold and effective blow, destroying millions of dollars worth of commissary stores, cotton and lordly dwellings, and striking terror into the heart of rebeldom, brought off near 800 slaves and thousands of dollars worth of property, without losing a man or receiving a scratch. It was a glorious consummation.

After they were all fairly well disposed of in the Beaufort charge, they were addressed in strains of thrilling eloquence by their gallant deliverer, to which they responded in a song. *"There is a white robe for thee,"* a song so appropriate and so heartfelt and cordial as to bring unbidden tears.

The Colonel was followed by a speech from the black woman, *who led the raid and under whose inspiration it was originated and conducted.*

Those exact words were used more than once. Reporting on the operation to Secretary of War Edwin Stanton, Brigadier General Rufus Saxton, the military governor of Beaufort, said, "This is the only military command in American history wherein a woman black or white led the raid and under whose inspiration it was originated and conducted."[122]

On July 17, 1863, a lengthy front-page report by Franklin Sanborn about Tubman was published in *The Commonwealth.* Sanborn was one of the "Secret Six" who had funded John Brown's raid on Harpers Ferry and a member of the Concord literati, which included Henry David Thoreau, Ralph Waldo Emerson, and Nathaniel Hawthorne. Sanborn's feature was the first time Harriet Tubman was publicly identified, linked with her clandestine reputation as Moses, and heralded by name for her leadership role in the spectacular success of the Combahee River operation.[123] News of the raid and her liberation missions made Tubman internationally famous in her time, and have been inspiring movement groups and people of conscience ever since.

In 2021, Tubman was inducted into the U.S. Military Intelligence Corps Hall of Fame and honored by the U.S. Army as a black woman, leader, warrior, and intelligence operative of the highest caliber:[124]

She was given recognition by Queen Victoria for her service, but until now, U.S. recognition has been less than she earned through her dangerous work as a Soldier, a spy, and an operative for the Union government. In 2020, the Military Intelligence Corps made her an honorary member.

There can be no doubt that women have had active roles in the nation's history. Even long before the United States claimed its independence, women worldwide had been known to lead armies, fight wars, and take great personal risk to fight for the causes they believed in. Because they were women, their roles often went unbelieved or highly criticized because their actions were thought to be inappropriate or impossible for women. These traditional gender roles are now known to be false. . . . Harriet Tubman Davis is a testament to the capabilities of African Americans, women, and the disabled alike. A leader, a warrior, and a Military Intelligence operative of the highest caliber . . . the U.S. Army Intelligence Center of Excellence and the Military Intelligence Corps honor her service.[125]

TUBMAN'S ACTIVISM IN THE POST-SLAVERY PERIOD

During the Obama era, a movement emerged to place women on U.S. currency, and Harriet Tubman's image was overwhelmingly favored as the lead choice. This took place even though Tubman's relationship with the women's rights movement—and its perception of her role in it—have both been complex and at times even contentious. For many, the way Tubman has been perceived by the broader women's rights movement has revealed the single-issue focus that the intersectionality approach seeks to address and overcome. Historically and symbolically, Tubman's treatment has been emblematic of the often turbulent political relationship experienced by black women within a feminist movement that has been dominated by white women. For black women, liberation has involved confronting multiple forces of oppression, not just those that target their gender, a matter the larger feminist movement has been slow to address. Women of color, whether they identify as feminist or not, have long understood how the oppressive power dynamics of race, class, gender, and sexual orientation collectively define their lived experiences and socio-economic status. How the women's movement during Tubman's lifetime understood these overlapping identities zigzagged politically and set the context for her engagement with it.[126]

Following the historic 1848 Seneca Falls Convention that many consider the birth of the U.S. women's movement, an alliance of sorts was forged between the abolitionists and women demanding equal rights and suffrage. Frederick Douglass attended the Seneca

Falls Convention, reportedly the only African American present, and drew the link between abolition and rights for women. Douglass publicly advocated not just for women's rights, but for the view that women and men are equally entitled. In an essay published in his *North Star* newspaper immediately following the Convention, he wrote: "In respect to political rights, we hold woman to be justly entitled to all we claim for man. We go further, and express our conviction that all political rights which it is expedient for men to exercise, it is equally so for women."[127] Susan B. Anthony, who would become the nation's most prominent women's rights activist, shared stages with Douglass as they both advocated for abolition and women's suffrage. The two soon became friends. Douglass and his family moved to Rochester, New York, where Anthony lived, and they visited each other often.

Douglass and Anthony had a falling-out after the Civil War, however, when the 14th Amendment granted free African Americans full citizenship rights, and the 15th Amendment granted the franchise to black men. Anthony and some of the other well-known suffragist leaders were incensed that women were not included in either amendment, especially when Douglass and other black leaders supported both. As white attacks on black people intensified following the Civil War, Douglass spoke bluntly about the critical importance of black America winning the right to vote:

I must say I do not see how any can pretend that there is the same urgency in giving the ballot to woman as to the negro [*sic*]. With us, the matter is a question of life and death, at least, in fifteen States of the Union. When women, because they are women, are hunted down through the cities of New York and New Orleans; when they are dragged from their houses and hung upon lamp-posts; when their children are torn from their arms, and their brains dashed out upon the pavement; when they are objects of insult and outrage at every turn; when they are in danger of having their homes burnt down over their heads, when their children are not allowed to enter schools; then they will have an urgency to obtain the ballot equal to our own.[128]

Douglass was responding to a bitter diatribe from Elizabeth Cady Stanton, another prominent suffrage leader, at a political meeting at New York's Steinway Hall in 1869. Voicing raw white supremacist opposition to the 15th Amendment, she rhetorically asked, "Shall American statesmen, claiming to be liberal, so amend their constitutions as to make their wives and mothers the political inferiors of unlettered and unwashed ditch-diggers, bootblacks, butchers and barbers, fresh from the slave plantations of the South and the effete civilizations of the old world?"[129] Her "indisputably racist ideas," writes Angela Y. Davis in *Women, Race & Class*, "indicate that Stanton's understanding of the relationship between the battle for Black Liberation and the struggle for women's rights was, at best, superficial."[130]

The issue would also fracture the women's movement from within. In 1866, the American Equal Rights Association (AERA) was formed by a coalition of abolitionists and feminists. However, in the battle over the 15th Amendment, which was ratified in 1870, the organization split and fell apart when some women supported it and others did not, including Anthony and Stanton. Both quit the AERA and formed the National Woman Suffrage Association. Their former colleagues created a rival organization with a similar name, the American Woman Suffrage Association. It would be two decades before the hatchet was buried and the two organizations would merge in 1890 to form the National American Woman Suffrage Association.[131]

It was during this period and into the 1890s that Harriet Tubman became more visible at meetings of women's rights groups up and down the East Coast. Usually speaking from the floor as a visitor, she talked about her experiences freeing the enslaved, her wartime work, and about rights for African Americans. Tubman also used these opportunities to raise funds for her charity work assisting aged and indigent black people. Most white women she encountered in this context often seemed more patronizing to her concerns than genuinely engaged with them. Few were active in fighting for the rights of African American women, and few spoke out forcefully against the increasing institutionalization of segregation or the rise of white violence against black people. There were exceptions, however, such as Frances Seward, as noted earlier, and Quaker activist and writer Martha Coffin Wright, who helped organize the Seneca Falls Convention and was a close confidant of Frederick Douglass. Journalist and writer Dorothy Wickenden beautifully documents the close friendship between Seward, Wright, and Tubman in her book *The Agitators: Three Friends Who Fought for Abolition and Women's Rights.*[132]

Tubman's most celebrated appearance at a women's movement gathering was on November 18, 1896, at the New York State Woman Suffrage Association conference in Rochester. Tubman was led to the stage by none other than Susan B. Anthony. Both were in their late seventies and in the twilight of their careers. Tubman spoke about her experiences helping people escape slavery, telling one gathering of activist women, "Yes, ladies, I was the conductor on the Underground Railroad for eight years and I can say what most conductors can't say—I never ran my train off the track and I never lost a passenger."[133]

In 1900, Carrie Chapman Catt was voted in as president to fill the seat vacated by the elderly Susan B. Anthony. Astonishingly, Catt later stated to researcher Earl Conrad, "I never heard of Harriet Tubman."[134] Conrad was trying to establish the nature of Tubman's relationship to the women's rights movement and asked her to reflect on Tubman. "[Tubman] did not assist the suffragists or the woman suffrage movement at any time," Catt later wrote to Conrad in 1939. "It was they who were attempting to assist her. . . . There was no leadership on the part of the colored people at that time and there is very little even now."[135] Many other white feminists had similar prejudicial views. Susan B. Anthony's niece, Lucy E. Anthony, told Conrad, "Harriet Tubman is just a name to me which I just remember Aunt Susan mentioning from time to time."[136] There is little evidence that the women's suffrage movement, as opposed to some individual feminists, actually helped Tubman, as Catt claims. "Catt's utter disregard for Tubman's life history is striking, and her careless assessment of contributions of African American women to the suffrage movement presaged the reception Tubman's biography would continue to receive for several more decades," writes Kate Clifford Larson.[137] Catt is also incorrect in her erasure of black women from women's rights movements. Black women scholars and activists, such as Angela Y. Davis, Patricia Hill Collins, Nikki Giovanni, Beverly Guy-Sheftall, bell hooks, Barbara Smith, and many others have thoroughly documented black women's activism as well as the racism in the women's suffrage movement.[138]

Catt and Lucy E. Anthony's dismissive view of African Americans —and African American women in particular—characterized the white supremacist views that increasingly dominated women's organizations at the end of the nineteenth century. Black women's rights and suffrage organizations, black women activists within white-dominated women's groups, black women's scholarship, and black women's struggles within civil rights organizations were simply not acknowledged by the middle-class white women whose leadership guided the women's movement into the twentieth century, and in some instances, continues to this day. For example, Harriet Tubman's entry in the National Women's Hall of Fame still lacks mention of her activities in the suffrage movement.[139]

Despite the accounts of white suffragist leaders, black women were involved at every stage of the movement's development, from the antebellum era up through the passage of the 19th Amendment and beyond. Among the many organizations from that time period were the National Association of Colored Women's Clubs, National League for the Protection of Colored Women, National Council of Negro Women, and Southeastern Federation of Colored Women's Clubs. To a significant degree, these organizations were also long written out of mainstream black history texts, but rescued in the literature of black women scholars in the latter third of the twentieth century. In real time, these institutions were vital to the black community. Thousands of black women were involved, and their organizing was often intergenerational. In some instances, mothers and daughters were active together for decades.

For example, women in the Philadelphia-based Forten family worked together to secure the vote for women and end slavery. Activist and poet Charlotte Vandine Forten, her daughters Harriet and Margaretta, and Charlotte's niece Harriet Purvis were central to the effort within the Philadelphia Suffrage Association and the Philadelphia Female Anti-Slavery Society. The Grimké family, who were related to the Fortens, produced similar leaders. Angelina Weld Grimké, who was mixed race, and her aunt Charlotte Forten Grimké, who was also a poet, were both active in the movement in Washington, D.C. as writers, teachers, and organizers.

In 1878, black journalist, editor, and lawyer Mary Ann Shadd Cary attended and gave remarks at the National Woman Suffrage Association Convention. She was the first and only woman to join the Howard University Law School's very first class of forty-six students in September 1869.[140] She became one of the first black women to obtain a law degree in the United States, which she earned at the age of sixty after a long struggle with the university.[141]

Mary Ann Shadd Cary was born October 9, 1823, in Washington, D.C., and was active in both the United States and Canada, where her family moved in the 1850s. Although her family was free, the passage of the 1850 Fugitive Slave Act increased the efforts of slave-catchers, motivating many black people to seek safety in Canada. In 1853, the thirty-year-old founded *The Provincial Freeman*, an anti-slavery newspaper and the first created by an African American woman, albeit in Canada. She traveled back and forth between the two nations promoting her newspaper, delivering anti-slavery speeches, and, along with family members, playing an active role in the Underground Railroad. After the Civil War she moved to Washington, D.C., where she founded a school for the children of the newly freed.

Mary Ann Shadd Cary became deeply involved in the women's movement through her work with the National Woman Suffrage Association. In fact, she gave testimony before the House of Representatives Judiciary Committee on the issue of women's suffrage alongside Susan B. Anthony and Elizabeth Cady Stanton in

January 1874, noting that as a "colored woman" and "taxpayer" she was unjustly denied the rights that men enjoyed. Cary is believed to be the first black woman to create a suffrage organization. In 1880 she founded the short-lived Colored Women's Progressive Franchise Association, a forerunner of the Black all-women's clubs that were to come in the 1890s.[142]

Not only were black women an active part of the nineteenth-century women's movement, they were also vocal regarding the racial inequality within it. Frances Ellen Watkins Harper, for example, called out white women and their white-skin privilege in her fiery speech at the eleventh National Women's Rights Convention held in New York City in May 1866:

> You white women speak here of rights. I speak of wrongs. I, as a colored woman, have had in this country an education which has made me feel as if I were in the situation of Ishmael, my hand against every man, and every man's hand against me. . . . While there exists this brutal element in society which tramples upon the feeble and treads down the weak, I tell you that if there is any class of people who need to be lifted out of their airy nothings and selfishness, it is the white women of America.[143]

She went on to become a founding member of the American Woman Suffrage Association, the group that broke away from Susan B. Anthony, and even gave the closing speech at its convention in New York in 1873.[144] She later became one of the initiating members of the 1894 National Association of Colored Women.

Scholar Anna J. Cooper, who lived to be 106, wrote one of the first books on black feminism in 1892, *A Voice from the South*, advocating education and suffrage for African American women.[145] In that work she famously wrote, "Only the Black woman can say, 'when and where I enter, in the quiet, undisputed dignity of my womanhood, without violence and without suing or special patronage, then and there the whole *Negro race enters with me*.'"[146] Cooper received a PhD in history from Sorbonne University in France in 1925 when she was sixty-six years old.[147] She was born in the last years of slavery in 1858 and passed away during the era of civil rights and black power in 1964.

These women and many, many others were determined and unrelenting in fighting for justice and equity for black women and the black community as a whole. The brief sketches above are only the tiniest rendering of the known and unknown activists and warriors who married the struggle against racism and slavery with that of women's rights, suffrage, and social justice.[148]

While Tubman never led a women's rights organization or seemed to be an ongoing active member of any one group, the last decades of her life were largely spent working with and speaking for suffrage and women's rights. For the most part, her remarks were not documented.

On July 21, 1896, Tubman attended the inaugural meeting of the National Association of Colored Women Clubs (NACWC) as an honored guest. One of the women celebrating Tubman at that meeting was Rosetta Douglass, the daughter of Frederick Douglass.[149] The NACWC advocated for voting rights for women, but unlike the white-dominated suffragist organizations, the organization fought for a broader agenda that included advocacy against segregation. The organization was a merger of three black women's organizations: National Federation of African-American Women, Woman's Era Club of Boston, and National League of Colored Women of Washington, D.C., known by its motto, "Lifting as we climb."[150]

COMBAHEE RIVER COLLECTIVE & THE TUBMAN LEGACY

Tubman's importance to the agency of black women has been continuous. In the 1970s, frustrated with feminist groups controlled by white women and finding themselves in ideological disagreement with a major national black feminist organization, a small network of radical black lesbian feminists developed their own collective. Among the founders, active members, and supporters were Barbara Smith, Beverly Smith, Audre Lorde, Sharon Page Ritchie, Cheryl Clarke, Margo Okizawa Rey, Gloria Akasha Hull, and Demita Frazier. In 1974, Barbara Smith broke with the National Black

Feminist Organization and began to meet with other black women in Boston who adhered to a vision of change that included "the destruction of the political-economic systems of capitalism and imperialism as well as patriarchy."

Barbara Smith states that "we decided that we wanted to be a collective and not be in a hierarchy organization because it was antithetical to our beliefs about democracy."[151] In 1977 the group issued a widely influential statement that many consider a precursor to contemporary intersectionalist theory. They wrote, "We are actively committed to struggling against racial, sexual, heterosexual, and class oppression and see as our particular task the development of integrated analysis and practice based upon the fact that major systems of oppression are interlocking. The synthesis of these oppressions creates the condition of our lives. As Black women we see Black feminism as the logical political movement to combat the manifold and simultaneous oppressions that all women of color face."[152]

In many ways, the collective pioneered centering on identity—multiple, overlapping, intersecting identities—as essential to the struggle for social justice. They wrote, "We believe that the most profound and potentially most radical politics come directly out of our own identity, as opposed to working to end somebody else's oppression."[153]

Members of the group were active around a range of issues in the Boston area. Boston had long been seen as hostile to African Americans, and its notorious reputation took an even darker turn in the spring and summer of 1979, when thirteen women—twelve black and one white—were brutally murdered in the city. Many of the women had been raped, dismembered, strangled, and stabbed. Their bodies were found, with one exception, in the city's black neighborhoods. Smith and others protested and organized to expose the epidemic of violence toward women of color.[154]

Smith wanted to name the collective after a political action.[155] After studying Earl Conrad's *Harriet Tubman: Conductor on the Underground Railroad*, she discovered not only a political action for liberation, but one led by an abolitionist black woman. The event was the June 1–2, 1863, raid down the Combahee River led by Harriet Tubman. Inspired by the legacy of those events, Smith and the group decided to call themselves the Combahee River Collective. Smith would recall, "For us to call ourselves the Combahee River Collective, that was an educational [tool] both for ourselves and for anybody who asked, 'So what does that mean, I never heard of that?' It was a way of talking about ourselves being on a continuum of Black struggle, of Black women's struggle."[156]

A NATION IN TRANSITION

Harriet Tubman was surrounded by family and friends when she passed away on March 10, 1913, five days before what may have been her ninety-first birthday. The world was in transition. Woodrow Wilson was inaugurated four days before she died, and World War I would begin the next year. Anti-lynching activism was rising, workers' organizations were growing, and African Americans would soon be leaving the South in massive numbers. Tubman lived through twenty-two presidential administrations, and almost two hundred years after her birth she would be linked to Obama, whose administration sought to honor her by placing her image on the twenty-dollar bill.

That decision would also tie her to another former president. In 1828, around the time Tubman turned six, Andrew Jackson was elected the nation's seventh president. Impetuous and violent, Jackson had previously served as a U.S. general and senator, and was a hero among a large segment of the white population for being an enemy of Native Americans and abolitionists. At sixty-one, he had spent decades fighting to maintain white people's right to breed, traffic, and enslave black people. He was the militant embodiment of white supremacy and Manifest Destiny. Tubman and Jackson never met, and she is not known to have expressed any opinions about him nor him of her. However, it is very likely that his enslaved knew of her and, if given the opportunity, would have joined her on one of her rescue journeys North.

Born in the kitchen of The Hermitage, Alfred was one of the many people Andrew Jackson enslaved. One day in 1848, two of Andrew Jackson's grandchildren and their tutor, Roeliff Brinkerhoff, strolled past Alfred. In a gloomy mood, Alfred commented, "You white folks have easy times, don't you?" Brinkerhoff responded by saying, "Freedom has its burdens, as well as slavery." Alfred looked at the man and asked, "How would you like to be a slave?"[157] PHOTO COURTESY OF ANDREW JACKSON'S HERMITAGE.

THREE

ANDREW JACKSON'S FACE IS A MEME FOR WHITE SUPREMACY

"A man nicknamed 'Indian killer' and 'Sharp Knife' surely deserves the top spot on a list of worst U.S. Presidents."
—Bertram Wyatt-Brown

"Before turning to conquest and colonization west of the Mississippi, the slavery-based rule of the Southeast would be ethnically cleansed of Indigenous peoples. The man for the job was Andrew Jackson."
—Roxanne Dunbar-Ortiz, *An Indigenous Peoples'*
History of the United States

NEGRO FORT was a garrison that was abandoned by the British during the War of 1812 and subsequently became a refuge for people who escaped slavery, Native Americans, and free blacks. Located near what is now Sumatra, Florida, at the time it was an area that was outside the United States and became one of many autonomous maroon territories.[158] Negro Fort—originally called Fort Magazine by the British—was left fully armed when the British fled in 1815.[159] People on the run from their white enslavers came from as far away as Virginia, Tennessee, and Mississippi. Andrew Jackson's role in the brutal seizure of the fort in July 1816 would be one of the signature campaigns that built his military fame and ultimately propelled him to the White House.

Slavers in the region were fearful of Negro Fort and the message it sent about black autonomy. Many complained to state and federal authorities that residents of the fort were raiding their plantations for food and supplies. President James Madison looked to

General Andrew Jackson to end this affront to white society. When Jackson's request to the Spanish governor of Florida to destroy the fort was rebuffed, he sent instructions to Major General Edmund P. Gaines, commander of U.S. military forces "in the Creek nation," to "restore the stolen negroes and property to their rightful owners."[160] Skirmishes began on July 15, 1816, when black and Indigenous fighters from Negro Fort killed several U.S. soldiers who had come ashore at Apalachicola Bay. Over the next two weeks, clashes took place in the thick woods surrounding the fort, at times descending into hand-to-hand combat. After a pause in the ground fighting, Jackson's vessels attacked with cannon fire. The fort's defenders held their own until the morning of July 27, 1816, when a hot cannonball struck Negro Fort's stockpile of gunpowder. The impact set off a massive explosion that killed almost everyone inside the fort. The very few who survived were either executed or enslaved by Jackson's men.

There is some controversy regarding how many people died that day. The official historical marker at the site reads: "It is hard to imagine the horrible scene that greeted the first Americans to stand here on the morning of July 27, 1816. The remains of the 270 persons killed in the magazine explosion lay scattered about." However, a study by scholar Claudio Saunt argues that many had left before the decisive battle, and "probably no more than forty" had been killed by the blast and inferno.[161]

In any case, Jackson's willingness to wage war against blacks and Native Americans had no bounds. His obsession with expanding slavery westward at the expense of Native lands and lives would define the rest of his military and political career. "Andrew Jackson was the implementer of the final solution for the Indigenous peoples east of the Mississippi," writes Roxanne Dunbar-Ortiz in her book *An Indigenous People's History of the United States*.[162] The Negro Fort episode was a harbinger of things to come.

Jackson was an anti-abolitionist and a slaver with a clear and brutal record of massacring Native American people. Old Hickory, however, is more often than not portrayed as a populist and national "father figure" of sorts. He is credited with being one of the founders of the Democratic Party in the 1820s and a successful advocate for the expansion of voting rights and political participation for working-class white men. His savagery and white supremacy have been played down or ignored for too long. As Ronald Takaki points out, in biographies like Arthur Schlesinger Jr.'s *The Age of Jackson*, African Americans and Native Americans are mostly erased, and Nat Turner's 1830 rebellion and Jackson's successful push for the Indian Removal Act simply go unmentioned.[163] Some authors, like historian Robert V. Remini, have tried to have it both ways, but the result is to portray him as a badass hero:

> He was one of the greatest of generals, and wholly ignorant of the art of war. A writer brilliant, elegant, eloquent, without being able to compose a correct sentence, or spell words of four syllables. The first of statesmen, he never devised, he never framed a measure. He was the most candid of men, and was capable of the profoundest dissimulation. A most law-defying, law-obeying citizen. A stickler for discipline, he never hesitated to disobey his superior. A democratic autocrat. An urbane savage. An atrocious saint.[164]

This type of bromance with Andrew Jackson has certainly factored into his placement on U.S. currency and glorification in books, monuments, and official U.S. narratives. However, a more honest acknowledgement of the mass suffering and death inflicted by his racism and greed should dispel any notion that he continues to deserve to be uncritically honored on national platforms such as currency, or anywhere else.

FROM ORPHAN TO PRESIDENT

As previously mentioned, Andrew Jackson was born on March 15, 1767, ironically sharing a birth date with Harriet Tubman. He was orphaned at the relatively young age of fourteen, and grew up poor, deprived, and rough. He joined the colonial army during the American Revolution, at age thirteen or fourteen. Stories of his bravado, perhaps exaggerated, describe personality traits of stubbornness, tenacity, and a dogged resilience that would shape his path going forward. He left the military after the Revolutionary War but would later return and ultimately rise to the rank of general and commander. In this role, the carnage at Negro Fort would be one of many massacres he would lead.

Jackson's career zigzagged as he dipped into the legal field, business ventures, and political interests, as well as the military. Over the course of his life he became an enslaver, human trafficker, attorney, solicitor, U.S. representative, U.S. senator, land speculator, Tennessee Supreme Court justice, store owner, military commander, Tennessee governor, and president of the United States. He achieved all these positions with little education.

Like Donald Trump, Andrew Jackson was also involved in a disputed presidential election result. Jackson ran for president in 1824 against John Quincy Adams, the son of the nation's second president. The two other candidates in the race were Henry Clay and William H. Crawford. Although Jackson won the popular vote, he did not win enough votes in the electoral college. As a result, the decision on the election went to the U.S. House of Representatives. After much debate and backroom deal-making, the presidency was awarded to John Quincy Adams and the vice presidency to John C. Calhoun, enraging Jackson.

RESULTS OF 1824 AMERICAN PRESIDENTIAL ELECTION

Candidate	Popular Vote	Electoral Vote
John Quincy Adams	108,740	84
Henry Clay	47,531	37
William H. Crawford	40,856	41
Andrew Jackson	153,544	99

Sources: Electoral and popular vote totals based on data from the United States Office of the Federal Register and Congressional Quarterly's Guide to U.S. Elections, 4th ed. (2001).

Jackson abandoned the National Republican Party, helped to start the Democratic Party, and benefited from expanding voting rights to working-class white men. As a result, from 1824 to 1828, the voting population went from around 365,000 to over one million, launching what many historians have dubbed the era of Jacksonian Democracy. The rise of political parties and the end of property requirements drove the surge in voting among white men.[165] Jackson's anti-elite rhetoric openly excluded women, African Americans, and Native Americans without apology or regret. For First Americans, Jackson was the "Sharp Knife" that stabbed their hearts while slashing them apart from their ancestral land. For black families, he was another white slaver determined to keep them in chains.

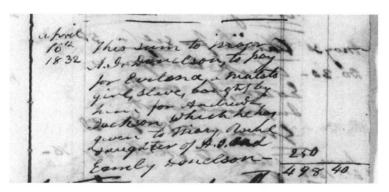

Excerpt from Andrew Jackson's bank book for April 16, 1832, showing a check to his adopted nephew, Major A. J. Donelson, for "a mulato girl, slave, bought by him for Andrew Jackson, which he has given to Mary Rachel, daughter of A. J. and Emily Donelson." PHOTO COURTESY OF THE WHITE HOUSE HISTORICAL ASSOCIATION.

JACKSON AND SLAVERY

One of Andrew Jackson's slave plantations was known as "The Hermitage" and was located in Davidson County, Tennessee. Today, The Hermitage is a tourist destination that lures visitors with the call to "Experience the historic mansion and tranquil beauty" of the 1,000-acre plantation.[166] In fact, Jackson's livelihood was almost wholly dependent on the cotton produced by the people he enslaved and the income he earned by breeding and selling them. Jackson purchased his first human being when he was around twenty-four years old, a six-year-old boy named Aaron, and continued to purchase black people and engage in the slave trade itself. He brought people he enslaved to the White House from Tennessee and bought more during his presidency to serve his family.[167]

At the time of his death in 1845, Jackson owned approximately 150 people, a significant increase from the nine he owned when he purchased the Tennessee land for The Hermitage in 1804. According to the White House Historical Association:

> In January 1829, less than two months before he became president, Andrew Jackson ordered an inventory of his slaves. The inventory recorded the names, ages, and familial relationships of ninety-five enslaved individuals who lived and worked at The Hermitage, his Tennessee plantation. When President-elect Jackson left for the White House, he brought some of these enslaved people with him. The 1830 census listed fourteen enslaved individuals in Jackson's household—eight women and six men—and many scholars suggest that his household grew during the course of his presidency.[168]

Among the individuals he enslaved were "Seamstress" Gracy; "Cooks" Old Hannah, Betty, Maria, Mary, and Old Dick; "Body Servant" George; "Carpenters" Ned and Henry; and "Weavers" Eliza, Gincy, and Big Sally. People without specific jobs were listed as either "House Slaves" or "Field Slaves," the latter constituting the largest number of those owned by Jackson. Many of the individuals were in families that were, of course, torn asunder when Jackson so desired.[169]

By all accounts, he did not hesitate to work the people he enslaved as hard as possible. An example of Jackson's cruelty could be found in how he attempted to capture a person who had escaped from his plantation. In 1804, Jackson posted an advertisement describing the person who had escaped to freedom as a "Mulatto Man Slave, about thirty years old, six feet and an inch high, stout made and active, talks sensible, stoops in his walk, and has a remarkable large foot, broad across the root of the toes." Jackson speculated, "He will make for Detroit, through the states of Kentucky or Ohio, or the upper part of Louisiana." He offered what was likely a normal reward of fifty dollars—about $1,202.19 in 2022 dollars.[170] However, he included an additional incentive in his post. He pledged to pay an extra ten dollars, for a total of about $1,442.62 in 2022 dollars, "for every hundred lashes any person will give to the amount of three hundred," encouraging others to do his dirty work for him.[171] His maximum offer of a possible $300.00 was equivalent to $7,213.12 in 2022 dollars. Historian Robert P. Hay points out that many of Jackson's biographers either did not know of this particular advertisement or ignored it in in an effort to try to dishonestly make that case that "he was the most indulgent, patient and generous of masters" and that he oversaw his enslaved with a "patriarch's care," or that he was "an ideal slave-owner."[172]

On Jackson's plantation, violence was used to maintain the racial hierarchy. In 1815, one of Jackson's nephews informed him, "Your wenches as usual commenced open war" against the overseer. The black women were "brought to order by Hickory oil," wrote the nephew, a reference to being whipped. Understanding use of the term in this manner strongly suggests that Jackson may have been nicknamed "Old Hickory" as a reference to the hickory switches used on plantations to beat black people into submission. In the classic slave narrative *Slavery in the United States: A Narrative of the Life and Adventures of Charles Ball, a Black Man*, Ball writes, "If a slave gives offence, he is generally chastised on the spot, in the field where he is at work, as the overseer always carries a whip—sometimes a twisted cow-hide, sometimes a kind of horsewhip, and very often a simple hickory switch or gad, cut in the adjoining woods."[173] Being named after the simple weapon used by white enslavers to impulsively whip black people would have been fitting for Jackson, who was notorious for flying into violent rages.

Andrew Jackson enslaved many people at his plantations, including Betty and the children shown here. PHOTO COURTESY OF ANDREW JACKSON'S HERMITAGE.

But Old Hickory was also known for calmly ordering violence against the black people who resisted his and his wife's dictates. For example, in 1821, the Jacksons were living in Florida while Andrew served as territorial governor. During one of his absences, his wife Rachel wrote to him that her slave, Betty, "has been putting on some airs, and been guilty of a great deal of impudence." Her sin was washing clothes for individuals in the neighborhood without

Rachel's "express permission." Jackson instructed his staff to punish Betty with fifty lashes at "the public whipping post" if she refused to obey his wife. Betty was "capable of being a good & valluable servant," he wrote one of the men, "but to have her so, she must be ruled with the cowhide."[174]

Jackson despised abolitionists and worked to perpetuate and expand slavery in the United States. In his multiple positions as an attorney, military officer, Congressmember, governor, and certainly as the nation's seventh president, he did all he could to ensure lands seized or purchased westward would be welcome spaces for white people to profit from trafficking and enslaving people of color.

Jackson also supported efforts of other white supremacists to target the free speech of Americans active in anti-slavery networks. During his second presidential term (1833–37), the abolition movement organized a mail campaign to flood Southern states with anti-slavery literature. The campaign prompted widespread public protest and attention throughout the white South.[175] In July 1835, a local postmaster in Charleston, South Carolina, Alfred Huger, discovered a cache of abolitionist literature mail en route from Philadelphia's American Anti-Slavery Society. While not wanting to assist abolitionists, but hesitant about violating his responsibility to deliver the mail, Huger stopped the literature from going forward and wrote U.S. Postmaster General Amos Kendall, an enslaver himself, for some guidance. When white people in the community found out about the stalled mail, they took matters into their own hands. A mob formed, took the materials, and publicly burned them. At the same time, a committee of prominent Tennessee citizens formed and issued a statement that they would support banning anti-slavery mail and advocate that any similar materials be set on fire.

Postmaster Kendall sent Southern postmasters instructions to withhold abolitionist mailings unless recipients requested the literature. When he consulted with President Jackson about the situation, Jackson approved of the intervention even though it clearly violated

Americans' rights and the U.S. Constitution. In a private letter sent August 9, 1835, "Jackson himself denounced the 'monsters' who were using the items 'to stir up amongst the South the horrors of a servile war' and called for them 'to atone for this wicked attempt, with their lives,'" writes Mark R. Cheathem in a 2020 article for the *Washington Post.*

> He also recommended that Southern postmasters make a list of the people in their communities who wanted the material so that they could be "exposed" in the media "as subscribers to this wicked plan of exciting the negroes to insurrection and to massacre." Jackson hoped that his fellow White Southerners would force those sympathetic to the abolitionist cause to "desist" in their support of freedom for enslaved people "or move from the country." Instead of trying to be a leader for all Americans, Jackson used the language of an enslaver who saw the threat that holding out hope of freedom to enslaved people posed not just to his livelihood but also to his entire way of life.[176]

About five months later, Jackson spoke publicly about the issue in an address to Congress. Jackson proposed legislation that would "prohibit, under severe penalties, the circulation in the Southern States, through the mail, of incendiary publications intended to instigate the slaves to insurrection."[177] No bill was ever passed by Congress, so Jackson simply allowed Southerners to continue to illegally seize and destroy black freedom literature.

INDIAN REMOVAL

Howard Zinn described Andrew Jackson as "the most aggressive enemy of the Indians in early American history."[178] His most infamous move as president was to push through the 1830 Indian Removal Act. When elected president in 1828, Jackson vowed that he would complete the work of President Thomas Jefferson, who in 1802 signed the "Georgia Compact" and in 1803 completed the

Louisiana Purchase. Those two actions set the stage for the forced removal of the Creeks and Cherokees living in Georgia, Alabama, and Mississippi. The Georgia Compact was an agreement between the U.S. government and Georgia in which the latter agreed to cede claim on Alabama and Mississippi—states cut out of territory controlled by Georgia—in exchange for a commitment on the part of the federal government to purge Native Americans, specifically the Cherokees, from those areas, despite their titles to the lands. The understanding was that at some point the First Americans would be resettled elsewhere. The "elsewhere" was some of the vast territory acquired with the Louisiana Purchase. This agreement was accomplished without input or consent from the Cherokees, and naturally, they resisted. Jefferson would later state that he did not have the power to force them to relocate or surrender their titles to the land.

Jackson felt no such qualms or constitutional constraints. The situation had reached something of a stalemate until his election. He came into office determined to implement a removal plan. Southern congressmembers supported Jackson, as they wanted Native American land to expand their slave-based economy. On December 8, 1829, the top priority in Jackson's first State of the Union address was pitching legislation for Native removal. Six months later, the bill came up for a vote in Congress. The vote was close—28 to 19 in the Senate and 102 to 97 in the House—but Jackson prevailed and signed the bill into law on May 28, 1830.[179] With the bill's passage, Jackson had the authority to "exchange" Indian lands in the South for some western territories, whether the Indigenous nations wanted to or not.

While the Indian Removal Act called for negotiations, it was clear to all that force would be used if necessary. Legendary frontiersman and U.S. Representative Davy Crockett voiced strong opposition to the bill. On May 26, 1830, he stated on the floor of Congress that he viewed "the native Indian tribes of this country as a sovereign people" and that "removing them in the manner proposed" would not protect them as the United States was bound to do.[180] He said he did not trust the Jackson administration to efficiently spend the $500,000 that had been allocated, nor that appropriate land would be available. He contended that he personally knew of some Cherokees who vowed never to leave their ancestral land, and he thought they should not be forced.

Crockett's passions notwithstanding, Jackson's long record of bloody battles against Native peoples had already set the path he would follow. By the time of his 1828 presidential victory, Jackson's attitude toward Native Americans was well documented. He referred to Indigenous people as "savage bloodhounds" and "blood thirsty barbarians," a view perpetrated by white people in the Americas since the days of the conquistadors. As a military leader, Jackson personally initiated and led numerous atrocities, including massacres. One bloody conflict took place on March 27, 1814, at the Battle of Horseshoe Bend on the Tallapoosa River in what is now Alabama. Referring to the upcoming fight, he wrote to one of his generals, "I must destroy those deluded victims doomed to distruction [*sic*] by their own restless and savage conduct."[181] Historian Ronald Takaki wrote that Jackson's stance was that "'foreign' governments could not be tolerated, and the Indians would have to submit to state authority."[182]

With a bloodlust that is difficult to fathom, Jackson and his men, which included some Cherokees and even a few Creeks, attacked and killed eight hundred Creek children and adults in a community of one thousand. After the slaughter, Jackson's men skinned many of the corpses and removed the noses. The skins were then used to make bridle reins. Jackson took clothes off the bodies of women and, as he noted in a letter to his wife, took a "warrior's bow and quiver" for their son Andrew.[183]

Proud of the devastation that he caused, Jackson wrote, "What good man would prefer a country covered with forests and ranged by a few thousand savages to our extensive Republic, studded with cities, towns, and prosperous farms . . . filled with all the blessings of liberty, civilization, and religion?"[184] Following the massacre, the Creeks signed the Treaty of Fort Jackson, which forced them to cede 22 million acres, including a huge tract in southern Georgia. Jackson, some of his relatives, and some of his associates then began buying the seized land.[185]

In 1832, the Supreme Court, adhering to the 1802 Indian Trade and Intercourse Act, upheld the law that "states could not legally extend their jurisdiction into Indian territory."[186] They ruled that the federal government, not the states, had the authority to negotiate land issues. Jackson blatantly ignored that decision and through nonenforcement essentially gave states the green light to begin the process of dispossessing Indian Nations of their ancestral lands.[187]

JACKSON AND THE TRAIL OF TEARS

"During the Jacksonian period," writes Roxanne Dunbar-Ortiz, "the United States made eighty-six treaties with twenty-six Indigenous nations between New York and the Mississippi, all of them forcing land cessions, including removals."[188] The federal government often refused to honor its treaties guaranteeing that lands would not be violated or taken, as was the case with the Cherokee people. Jackson, as he had done on other occasions, forced negotiations that led to a treaty signing for Cherokee removal in 1835. Anti-removal tribal leaders and the vast majority of tribal members were marginalized and ignored. When the majority refused to budge, Jackson sent the military to drive the Cherokees off their land.

Before being forced to walk 1,200 miles in the dead of winter to current-day Oklahoma, Indigenous families were first rounded up and placed in detention camps—a legacy that echoed in the internment of Japanese Americans in the 1940s and migrant families in 2019. More than half of the sixteen thousand Cherokee children, women, and men forced to march on Jackson's Trail of Tears died on the way.[189] Some black families, who were enslaved to the Cherokees, were also forced to march.[190] By 1835, as many as 1,600 black people were enslaved to the Cherokee nation.[191]

Dunbar-Ortiz relates that, after the Civil War, journalist James Mooney interviewed people who had been involved in the forced removal. Based on firsthand accounts, Mooney described the scene:

> Under [General Winfield] Scott's orders the troops were disposed at various points throughout the Cherokee country, where stockade forts were erected for gathering in and holding the Indians preparatory to removal. From these, squads of troops were sent to search out with rifle and bayonet every small cabin hidden away in the coves or by the sides of mountain streams, to seize and bring in as prisoners all the occupants, however or wherever they might be found. Families at dinner were startled by the sudden gleam of bayonets in the doorway and rose up to be driven with blows and oaths along the weary miles of trail that led to the stockade. Men were seized in their fields or going along the road, women were taken from their wheels and children from their play. In many cases, on turning for one last look as they crossed the ridge, they saw their homes in flames. fired by the lawless rabble that followed on the heels of the soldiers to loot and pillage. So keen were these outlaws on the scent that in some instances they were driving off the cattle and other stock of the Indians almost before the soldiers had fairly started their owners in the other direction. Systematic hunts were made by the same men for Indian graves, to rob them of the silver pendants and other valuables deposited with the dead. A Georgia volunteer, afterward a colonel in the Confederate service, said: "I fought through the civil war and have seen men shot to pieces and slaughtered by thousands, but the Cherokee removal was the cruelest work I ever knew."[192]

Some historians have tried to overlook Jackson's atrocities against First Americans by pointing to his "adoption" of a young Creek infant orphan. They tend to underplay or not mention that Jackson was the reason the boy became an orphan in the first place.

On November 3, 1813, Jackson and his soldiers attacked a small Creek Indian village, Tallushatchee. The assault was meant as vengeance for violence by the Red Sticks, a faction of Creeks, against whites in the area. The village became a killing field that has been called "beyond bloody," a "massacre," and a "revolting scene."[193] Babies, children, and adults were shot, burned, and beaten to death. Not one of the 186 men in the village was left alive. At some point after the slaughter ended, one of Jackson's interpreters brought him a small child who had somehow miraculously survived. Jackson decided that he would take the child, whom he called a "savage," and send him to his five-year-old son as a "pett" to "amuse him."[194] The Indigenous child was named Lyncoya. As Jackson wrote to his wife Rachel, Lyncoya was to be given to Andrew Jr. to replace Andrew's previous pet, also a Creek child, Theodore. Jackson wrote, "He is about the size of Theodore and much like him."[195] According to the U.S. National Park Service, Theodore was likely captured when U.S. forces overran the Creek village of Littafuchee on October 27, 1813, and died soon after arriving at The Hermitage. A third Creek child, renamed Charley, was presented to Jackson as a gift by Jim Fife, a member of the Creek National Council.[196]

As *Slate* researcher Rebecca Onion noted, "Defenders of Jackson have long used Lyncoya to finesse Jackson's historical reputation in relationship to Native Americans."[197] Notably, there is scant record of Lyncoya's views on the massacre of his family and village, adoption by Jackson, and life at The Hermitage. It is known that he ran away on several occasions in an effort to return to the Creek nation.[198] When he was about ten years old, he wrote Jackson a letter in which he asked to be able to call him "Father" and wanted him to be proud one day to be able to say, "This is the Indian boy I [once] raised."[199] But that's not how things went for Lyncoya. When he died of tuberculosis at age sixteen or seventeen, Jackson had him buried, like a pet, in an unmarked grave.[200]

But Jackson's pet was useful to him beyond the amusement of his son, Andrew Junior. As his political ambitions grew, Jackson presented himself as a strong fighter but with a soft edge, a counter to his well-known history as an "Indian killer." Jackson worked the Lyncoya story to propagate a "benevolent father figure" narrative about himself. According to historian Dawn Peterson, in 1816 he went as far as to ask Tennessee senator George Washington Campbell to use his adoption of Lyncoya as an example to his congressional colleagues that stories of Jackson's raging temperament toward Native peoples were overblown.[201]

In his farewell address to Congress, Jackson spoke derisively and paternalistically about how Native Americans had fared under his presidential tenure. He stated:

> The States which had so long been retarded in their improvement by the Indian tribes residing in the midst of them are at length relieved from the evil, and this unhappy race—the original dwellers in our land—are now placed in a situation where we may well hope that they share in the blessings of civilization and be saved from that degradation and destruction to which they were rapidly hastening while they remained in the States; and while the safety and comfort of our own citizens have been greatly promoted by their removal, the philanthropist will rejoice that the remnant of the ill-fated race has been at length placed beyond the reach of injury or oppression, and that the paternal care of the General Government will hereafter watch over them and protect them.[202]

References to Native peoples as "evil" and "ill-fated" captured the genuine attitude of Jackson toward First Americans and his policies while in office. References to so-called "paternal" care were just treacle to mask racial conquest. Jackson's near-pathological goal to seize Native lands was meant to enrich himself and the sprawling white enslaver class of which he was a part.

Charles C. Mann's research indicates that that there were probably more people living in the Americas in 1491 then there were in Europe. The real history of the United States is not one of a "nation of immigrants," Dunbar-Ortiz writes, but one of erasure and exclusion shaped by greed and white supremacy. For the millions of American people committed to justice and equality—not just those whose ancestors were butchered, enslaved, robbed, and left in unmarked graves like Lyncoya—the face that sneers out at them every day from their twenty-dollars bills is the vulgar embodiment of unfreedom, injustice, racial disunity, censorship, and death.

A preliminary design of the Tubman twenty was produced in 2016 by the
Bureau of Engraving and Printing.[203]

FOUR

THE MOVEMENT TO TRANSFORM THE FACES ON U.S. CURRENCY

"It's not about supplication, it's about power. It's not about asking, it's about demanding. It's not about convincing those who are currently in power, it's about changing the very face of power itself."
—Kimberlé Williams Crenshaw

IN JULY 2014, a nine-year-old girl from Massachusetts named Sofia noticed during a classroom assignment that all the images on U.S. currency portrayed men. She went home and wrote a letter to the president of the United States, then Barack Obama, suggesting that he put a woman on U.S. money. She wanted to know "why there aren't many women on the dollars/coins for the United States."[204] Sofia even included a list of women to be considered: Michelle Obama, Rosa Parks, Abigail Adams, Helen Keller, Eleanor Roosevelt, and, with some prescient flavor, Harriet Tubman, among others. As Sofia explained, "if there [were] no women, there wouldn't be men." The next year, on February 11, 2015, Obama responded to Sofia on official White House stationery, thanking her for "such a good idea."[205]

Sofia was not the first person to recognize the absence of women on the currency. As far back as 1947, the U.S. Treasury Department received a letter from a high school business class inquiring why more women were not honored by having their images appear on U.S. money. Evidently unaware that First American Pocahontas had briefly appeared on a bill, they asked why Martha Washington had been the only woman to be represented on U.S. currency.[206] To that query and similar ones, the response has been bureaucratic evasions.

Although Obama did not promise Sofia that he would specifically seek to make the change, other developments were under way to transform U.S. currency. As far back as 2012, the notion of getting a woman on U.S. paper money began getting traction. Barbara Ortiz Howard, an independent businesswoman in New York, had an epiphany. When she noticed while getting coffee one day that there were no women on the money in her possession, she "realized the lack of women representation in the cultural landscape was a fundamental reason why women had yet to achieve equal status in everyday life and hoped she could interest others to include getting women on currency on their agenda to celebrate the centennial of the 19th Amendment in 2020."[207] When she could find no takers, she resolved to do something about it.

Soon thereafter she founded Women On 20s, an organization committed to replacing Andrew Jackson with the image of a woman. From the beginning, Ortiz Howard and her team felt that Jackson's abysmal record of Indian displacement and genocide alongside his slave trading required his removal from the twenty. They also believed that his replacement should be chosen by a campaign that involved input from as many people as possible. In 2015, after a group of one hundred advisors arrived at a list of fifteen possible candidates based on a weighted scale of perceived contribution to society and level of difficulty in achieving that contribution, Women On 20s used social media and the internet to solicit votes and comments on the list.

In the first round of feedback, 250,000 people cast votes over five weeks. Based on those results the list was pared down to four women: Native American activist Wilma Mankiller, civil rights activist Rosa Parks, former first lady Eleanor Roosevelt, and anti-slavery insurgent Harriet Tubman. The second round drew even more participants, around 360,000 votes, and Tubman won.

Meanwhile, the Advanced Counterfeit Deterrence Steering Committee (ACD) had determined that it needed to redesign the ten-dollar bill for security reasons, and decided to use the opportunity to propose having a woman replace Alexander Hamilton on the front of the redesigned bill. The ACD is comprised of representatives from the Department of Treasury, Federal Reserve, Secret Service, Currency Technology Office, and the Bureau of Engraving and Printing. Established in 1982, the ACD's responsibility is to bring together the tasks of currency design and protection against counterfeiting.[208] On June 17, 2015, Treasury Secretary Jacob J. Lew announced that a woman would be chosen based on public input conducted through town hall gatherings and online responses. His goal was to release the new bill in time to celebrate the hundredth anniversary of the 19th Amendment, which gave U.S. women the right to vote.

At a speech at the National Archive on June 18, 2015 Lew stated:

> America's currency is a statement of who we are as a country. Our bills—and the images of great leaders, landmarks, and symbols— have long been a way to honor our past and express our values. And despite those who might think that with the growth in plastic and electronic payments, physical currency is outdated, it is important to point out that the use of paper money keeps going up. In fact, we continue to break circulation records. And just recently, we hit an all-time high of more than 1.3 trillion American dollars in circulation around the world. This means that more people handle more currency than ever before, and paper money remains a powerful tool for commerce and a canvas to reflect our values.
>
> To the Americans who use it, our new 10 dollar bill will convey something powerful. It will deliver the message that our nation is an inclusive democracy, where opportunity, justice, and equality are not limited to a few, but available to all—no matter where you grew up, what god you worship, what your last name is, what you look like, or who you love. And this message will ripple beyond our borders. The U.S. dollar remains the most trusted currency in the world. Every day, millions around the globe hold one of our bills in their hands. This is a chance to speak to the world about what we cherish and what we stand for. . . . I would like to say something to everyone involved in the Women on 20s campaign—we thank you for your passion and your citizenship. Your campaign is exactly what democracy is about—making your voice heard.[209]

While Women On 20s was encouraged by Lew's initiatives, the organization strongly preferred that the twenty-dollar bill be redesigned first and inquired why the two bills could not be produced at the same time. Just prior to Lew's announcement, Susan Ades Stone and Ortiz Howard met with U.S. treasurer Rosa Gumataotao Rios and other officials to register their objections to the focus on the ten. According to Ortiz Howard, they were told that the ten-dollar bill was more frequently counterfeited. "We countered that the counterfeiting of the twenty causes more than double the damage in absolute dollars. We also pointed out that the twenty was last redesigned in 2003, while the ten was redesigned in 2006. The twenty should be next in line to redesigned, not the ten-dollar bill."[210]

Despite Lew's announcement about the new ten, which gave many a reason to cheer, Women On 20s continued to vigorously organize and advocate for a redesign of the twenty. Lew hedged on getting rid of Hamilton. It is unclear if he was aware of longstanding criticisms of Hamilton by scholars and others regarding slavery. Hamilton had been placed on the ten-dollar bill, as had all the other portraits on contemporary currency, in 1928 by Treasury Secretary Andrew Mellon, the third-richest person in the United States. It is believed that Mellon deeply admired Hamilton's banking-friendly policies during his tenure as the nation's first Treasury chief. Hamilton was far from an uncontroversial choice. Then, as now, many historians and economists questioned Hamilton's policies and even argued that he leaned toward undemocratic methods and ideas. Researcher Matt Stoller states bluntly, Hamilton "was an authoritarian, and proud of it."[211]

Hamilton presented himself as an abolitionist and is on the record speaking out against slavery. Many scholars contend, however, that there is more to the story than just Hamilton's declarations. Ankeet Ball, who was involved in a project looking at the relationship between Columbia University and slavery, wrote, "Hamilton detested the institution of slavery with fervor, but whenever the issue of slavery came into conflict with Hamilton's central political tenet of property rights, his belief in the promotion of American interests, or his own personal ambition, Hamilton allowed these motivations to override his aversion to slavery."[212]

In Ball's works and others', Hamilton's abolitionist credentials are also shown to be in contrast with the fact that he actually enslaved people.[213] Scholar Michelle DuRoss dryly notes, "Hamilton's involvement in the selling of slaves suggests that his position against slavery was not absolute." She further observes, "Hamilton conducted transactions for the purchase and transfer of slaves on behalf of his in-laws and as part of his assignment in the Continental Army." Hamilton, unlike some of his contemporaries, did support a plan to grant manumission to enslaved black men who joined the fight against the British. However, this was for selfish reasons as well. DuRoss contends Hamilton supported freeing people from their white enslavers if they joined the Continental Army because Hamilton "believed it was in the best interest of America, not because he wanted to free slaves."[214]

Despite this, there were plenty of people who were unhappy with the announcement to remove Hamilton. Former Federal Reserve chairman Ben Bernanke wrote on his blog, five days after Lew's statement, that he considered Hamilton "Jack Lew's most illustrious predecessor" and Jackson to be a "man of many unattractive qualities and a poor president."[215] He advocated that Hamilton not be replaced. The conflicting views were destined to grow more intense.

However, what Women On 20s, Bernanke, and others were unable to accomplish by argument was done by Broadway. Historian Ron Chernow's 2004 glowing biography, *Alexander Hamilton*, became the inspiration for what became a smash hit, sold-out Broadway musical in 2015.[216] The play became so popular, playgoers had to purchase tickets months in advance. In 2016, Lin-Manuel Miranda's *Hamilton* won endless awards including eleven Tony Awards (including for best musical), the Grammy Award for Best Musical Theater Album, and the Pulitzer Prize for drama. Given the accolades, massive fan base, and agitation by Hamilton fans, Lew had permission to rethink his position to protect Hamilton, and Women On 20s saw more opportunity to replace Jackson.

Writer Ishmael Reed was so incensed at the rehabilitation of Hamilton and other Revolutionary-era figures in *Hamilton* that he wrote his own play, *The Haunting of Lin-Manuel Miranda*, a slap at the producer and star of the Broadway hit. In Reed's drama, Miranda is visited by ghosts of many characters in U.S. history—including Harriet Tubman—who seek to correct the historical record.[217] After a viewing of the play, Reed wrote, "My headline would be that 'Hamilton' is bad jingoistic history salvaged by the brilliant performance of a multicultural cast."[218] At least one other notable African American literary figure was also unhappy with *Hamilton*. Legendary author Toni Morrison agreed with Reed's assessment and provided him with financial assistance. According to Reed, Morrison "was the second largest patron" of *The Haunting of Lin Manuel Miranda*, which ran at the Nuyorican Poets Cafe in 2019.[219]

Keeping the promise he made at the National Archives, Lew engaged in a far-reaching campaign seeking the public's suggestions for which woman should be on the redesigned ten. He held town hall discussions and roundtable conversations, and received "more than a million responses via mail and email, and through handwritten notes, tweets, and social media posts."[220] Despite Toni Morrison and Ishmael Reed's interventions, the Broadway-driven popularity for Hamilton influenced Lew's decision to back off a redesign of the front of the ten. In April 2016, a year after his presentation at the National Archives, Lew said:

> Over the course of the last 10 months, you put forth hundreds of names of people who have played a pivotal role in our nation's history. Many of you proposed that our new currency highlight democracy in action and reflect the diversity of our great nation. Some of you suggested we skip the redesign of the $10 note, which is the next in line for a security upgrade, and move immediately to redesigning the $20 note. And others proposed unconventional ideas, such as creating a $25 bill.

I have been inspired by this conversation and today I am excited to announce that for the first time in more than a century, the front of our currency will feature the portrait of a woman—Harriet Tubman on the $20 note.

Since we began this process, we have heard overwhelming encouragement from Americans to look at notes beyond the $10. Based on this input, I have directed the Bureau of Engraving and Printing to accelerate plans for the redesign of the $20, $10, and $5 notes. We already have begun work on initial concepts for each note, which will continue this year. We anticipate that final concept designs for the new $20, $10, and $5 notes will all be unveiled in 2020 in conjunction with the 100th anniversary of the 19th Amendment, which granted women the right to vote.

The decision to put Harriet Tubman on the new $20 was driven by thousands of responses we received from Americans young and old. I have been particularly struck by the many comments and reactions from children for whom Harriet Tubman is not just a historical figure, but a role model for leadership and participation in our democracy. You shared your thoughts about her life and her works and how they changed our nation and represented our most cherished values.

Looking back on her life, Tubman once said, "I would fight for liberty so long as my strength lasted." And she did fight, for the freedom of slaves and for the right of women to vote. Her incredible story of courage and commitment to equality embodies the ideals of democracy that our nation celebrates, and we will continue to value her legacy by honoring her on our currency. The reverse of the new $20 will continue to feature the White House as well as an image of President Andrew Jackson.[221]

According to Barbara Howard, at a meeting with Lew after his 2016 announcement, a group of women, including journalist Cokie Roberts, complained loudly that Lew did not keep his promise to have a woman on the ten-dollar bill. Women On 20s insisted—and continues to insist—that Andrew Jackson must be completely removed and that Native American recognition is imperative.

Ultimately, Obama's Treasury decided to make sweeping changes to most of the paper currency: Hamilton would remain on the front of the ten, but the back would include images of women suffragists Susan B. Anthony, Lucretia Mott, Elizabeth Cady Stanton, Alice Paul, and Sojourner Truth. Changes to the five were unexpectedly announced with Abraham Lincoln staying on the front and Martin Luther King Jr., Marian Anderson, and Eleanor Roosevelt at the Lincoln Memorial dignifying the back.

Women On 20s met with Lew after his announcement about Tubman. Perhaps anticipating that Hillary Clinton, then the presumptive presidential nominee for the Democratic Party, could lose and derail his plan, Lew informed the group and public that the Treasury Department would expedite the changes to the currency. His anxiety would prove to be well founded.

In November, Clinton lost the electoral vote, and Donald Trump, at Steven Bannon's bidding, began a bromance with Andrew Jackson.[222] Within weeks of his inauguration, a portrait of Andrew Jackson went up in the Oval Office, and Trump visited Jackson's infamous slave plantation, The Hermitage, and laid a wreath on his hero's tomb. "Inspirational visit, I have to tell you. I'm a fan," said Trump. It is also important, of course, to acknowledge what Trump did not say. He called The Hermitage a "great landmark," but never revealed that it was a slave plantation where brutal and unspeakable acts against enslaved people occurred. According to The Hermitage's website, the "great landmark" was a "self-sustaining plantation" that "relied completely on the labor of enslaved African American men, women and children." [223]

Under Trump, the Treasury Department quickly purged its website of any trace of the Tubman twenty and the millions of Americans who participated in the process of identifying her as their number-one choice for the front of the redesigned bill. It was obvious that the new Jackson-idolizing president wanted to nix the Tubman twenty, and his Treasury Department announced that its release would be, at best, delayed. The news was met with outrage. House Speaker Nancy Pelosi (D-CA) said it was an "insult to the hopes of millions," while Senator Jeanne Shaheen (D-NH) said the delay sends an "unmistakable message to women and girls, and communities of color."[224] "It says everything you need to know about President Trump's values that he can't even do the lightest of lifts to honor Harriet Tubman," said Senator Chuck Schumer (D-NY) in a statement. "He's refusing to put her portrait on the $20 bill, but he's continuing to honor Confederate generals who fought to preserve slavery."[225] Governor Larry Hogan of Maryland—Tubman's birthplace—wrote a letter to Treasury Secretary Steve Mnuchin urging him to find a way to speed up the process. "I hope that you'll reconsider your decision and instead join our efforts to promptly memorialize Tubman's life and many achievements," wrote Hogan, a Republican.[226] "The Trump administration's indefinite postponement of this redesign is offensive to women and girls, and communities of color, who have been excitedly waiting to see this woman and civil rights icon honored in this special way," said New Hampshire senator Jeanne Shaheen, a Democrat.[227]

A July 2019 report by Jeff Stein in the *Washington Post* complicated matters even more. According to Stein, a former government official appointed by Obama said the Tubman twenty had always been scheduled for release toward the end of the 2020s. Stein reported: "A confidential 2013 report by the Advanced Counterfeit Deterrence committee, an interagency group that oversees the redesign of U.S. currency, said the $20 would not enter circulation until 2030, similar to the timeline announced by the Trump administration, according to Larry R. Felix, director of the Bureau of Engraving and Printing from 2006 to 2015."[228]

In fact, the fate of redesigned money is tethered to a court injunction that long precedes Sofia's letter to President Obama. Evoking section 504 of the Rehabilitation Act, a 2002 lawsuit by the American Council of the Blind against the U.S. Treasury Department sought new features on money to enable the visually impaired to determine denominations by touch. At the time of the lawsuit, it was estimated that eight million to twelve million Americans were visually impaired, including approximately 300,000 to 1.3 million who were blind. Accordingly, on October 3, 2008, the district court issued an injunction ordering the Treasury Department to "take such steps as may be required to provide meaningful access to [each denomination of] United States currency for blind and other visually impaired persons not later than the date when a redesign of that denomination is next approved" by the Treasury.[229]

As a result of this injunction, the rollout of a Tubman twenty is tethered to the Treasury's mandate to produce currency legible to the visually impaired and blind, and to address "significant developments in counterfeiting technology" that were announced in 2016 court filings.[230]

In June 2020, as sustained anti-racism protests prompted the removal of symbols of white supremacy, a justice-seeking public demanded that Trump confirm that the Tubman twenty would be released without delay. Trump's obedient Treasury chief, Steven Mnuchin, demurred and stated that a new twenty would not be released until at least 2030, with no commitment that the image of Tubman would be on it. "This is something that is in the distant future," he stated.[231]

On June 14, 2019, the *New York Times* published an article by Alan Rappeport titled "See a Design of the Harriet Tubman $20 Bill That Mnuchin Delayed." In a challenge to the Trump administration, the *Times* report suggested that Mnuchin's claim that work on implementing new security features were responsible for the delay was highly suspect. "In fact, work on the new $20 note began before Mr. Trump took office, and the basic design already on paper most likely could have satisfied the goal of unveiling a note bearing Tubman's likeness on next year's centennial of the 19th Amendment, which granted women the right to vote," Rappeport reported.[232] Kate Clifford Larson notes that she witnessed a full-color design that was well on its way as early as 2017.

Not only had the Obama administration moved the design along, but "a metal engraving plate and a digital image of a Tubman $20 bill" existed, a copy of which was published by the *Times*.[233] However, as noted, the Treasury Department had made a determination prior to Trump that it would take until at least the late 2020s before the bill could be rolled out. New security elements, for example, would impact the recalibration of ATM machines not only in the United States, but around the world. This does not excuse the Trump's administration ideological opposition and lack of efforts to speed up the process where possible.

Some in Congress fought back against the Trump administration's lack of interest. In their view, the image of Harriet Tubman did not have to wait a decade for security concerns to be fleshed out. In February 2019, Congressmen John Katko (R-NY)[234] and Elijah Cummings (D-MD) introduced the Harriet Tubman Tribute Act, which directed the Treasury Department to place Tubman's image on twenties printed after December 31, 2020. The Tubman Act had bipartisan support.[235] On the Senate side, Senator Jeanne Shaheen (D-NH), introduced the measure a month later in March. Neither bill, however, got past the committee level. Though well-intended, the Tubman Act ignored the fact that the slowed process for developing the Tubman twenty, perceived as a delay, began while Obama was in office, Trump's hesitancy notwithstanding.

Senator James Lankford (R-OK) proposed a Senate resolution to remove Jackson and replace him with the image of a woman. His proposal states, in part, "the forced removal of American Indians by Andrew Jackson and the subsequent inhumane settlement of Indian lands represent a major blight on the proud history of the United States."[236] According to the data from the 2020 census, Oklahoma has the second-largest Native American population (523,360) in the United States, behind California (757,628), and the second-highest percentage (13.36 percent), behind Alaska (19.74 percent). [237]

A rubber stamp of Tubman produced by Dano Wall allows individuals to create their own "Tubman twenty."

One enthusiastic supporter of the change, designer Dano Wall, did not wait for the Treasury to print the Tubman twenty. He designed a stamp that allows anyone to simply brand their twenties—or any other denomination for that matter—with Tubman's image. "Putting Harriet Tubman on the front of the $20 bill would have constituted a monumental symbolic change, disrupting the pattern of white men who appear on our bills," he said, "and, by putting her on the most popular note currently in circulation, indicates exactly what kind of a life we choose to celebrate; what values we, as a country, most hope to emulate. Harriet Tubman's unparalleled grit, intelligence, and bravery over the course of her long life certainly make her worthy of such an honor."[238] Many others, including Women On 20s, also had Tubman stamps and encouraged adding her image to bills.

A poll taken soon after the Treasury Department's announcement about the coming Tubman twenty found that 56 percent of Americans supported removing Jackson and replacing him with Tubman.[239] Support, however, broke down along racial and political lines: 80 percent of African Americans, 61 percent of Latinx people, and only about 51 percent of white folks polled favored the change. Even more Democrats—81 percent—supported the redesign. On the other side, about 70 percent of Trump supporters thought adding Tubman to the currency was a bad idea.[240]

Within days of being sworn in to office, the Biden administration pledged to restart and aggressively push for the production of the Tubman twenty. On January 25, 2021, White House press secretary Jen Psaki stated, "It's important that our notes—our money, if people don't know what a note is—reflect the history and diversity of our country, and Harriet Tubman's image gracing the new 20-dollar note would certainly reflect that."[241] The NAACP's chief executive and president, Derrick Johnson, said in a statement: "Harriet Tubman lived at a time when Congress, the Supreme Court and our nation [were] abhorrently paralyzed over whether it was legal to allow one person to own another. In a true act of liberty and independence,

Tubman freed herself from slavery, only to return south 19 more times, risking her own life and freedom, to save her family and hundreds of others from a life spent in slavery. The legacy of Harriet Tubman and other Black Americans who built the nation we know today must be recognized and celebrated in our schools, culture and currency. The NAACP applauds the Biden administration's announcement to change the design of the $20 bill to commemorate the full story of the significant figures in our history."[242]

Meanwhile, Women On 20s has continued to organize and advocate for the Tubman twenty, including submitting a new petition with more than 1,300 names in response to a Treasury Department survey about what it could do to advance racial equity. Despite multiple inquiries, as of April 2022, the Treasury Department had yet to respond. A coalition of Tubman family members, Native American leaders, the American Council of the Blind, Women On 20s, and this author seeks an audience with the Treasury to identify a path to truly expedite the production and circulation of the Tubman twenty without further delay.

Support and opposition have gone beyond surveys, polls, and politicians. The issue has opened a public debate that reflects a range of contemporary race, gender, and ideological differences. The next two chapters take a deeper dive into the support for and opposition to the Tubman twenty.

Mural of Harriet Tubman painted by Michael Rosato on the side of the
Harriet Tubman Museum & Educational Center in Cambridge, Maryland.

FIVE

HONORED OR EXPLOITED? THE TUBMAN TWENTY—BLACK SUPPORT AND OPPOSITION

"I think of the $20 as a way to keep her moving in the world. It keeps her in motion. And I mean subconsciously, eventually that will seep into the national consciousness just like the rest of the figures on our coins."[243]

—Judith G. Bryant, descendant of Tubman's brother
William Henry Stewart Sr.—one of the brothers she rescued
from Eastern Shore Maryland on Christmas Day in 1854

"[T]he image of Tubman on our currency as some sort of corrective action for centuries of oppression and subjugation, or as a symbol of how far we've come in ending racism, is more symbolic of our fundamental misunderstanding of race in America."

—Ijeoma Oluo

"Regarding the detractors, we can yawn and agree with them that Tubman opposed our monetary system, but it is also true that she deserves to be honored, and what better way than on a widely circulated symbol of that which held her in oppression? Portraits on American currency represent the best and brightest lights produced by this country, and in that regard, Harriet Tubman certainly qualifies. Until some better honor is brought forth, this one will more than suffice. *A luta continua.*"

—*Chicago Crusader*, a weekly African American newspaper

IT WOULD SEEM AT FIRST a safe bet to assume that most African Americans, virtually all of whom grew up hearing stories about Tubman's heroism, would eagerly support any effort to honor her, including her image being placed on a twenty-dollar bill. If all goes as planned, she will become the first African American to appear on U.S. paper currency, and the third woman. She has been the subject of several biographies and two Hollywood films, and is referenced frequently in both academia and popular culture. Following the announcement of the Tubman twenty, much of black America lit up with excitement. Given all the buzz and the deep love held for Tubman, one could be excused for thinking that black women in particular would universally welcome the Tubman twenty. But this has not been not the case. Blogger Chanelle Adams wrote that African Americans were "feeling all types of ways" about the decision. She noted accurately that the responses ranged from "debates about capitalism and representation to celebrations and cynicism."[244] While noting the complexity of the issue, she opined, "Black people literally have been, and still are, the currency that the United States was founded upon."[245] One theme that stood out in the examples that Adams provided was the outrage that Jackson might remain on the back of the bill.

BLACK SUPPORT

Enthusiasm for the Tubman twenty emanated from various sections of the black community. Members of the Congressional Black Caucus (CBC) issued gushing statements of support and elation almost immediately after Treasury Secretary Lew's press conference. Congressman G. K. Butterfield (D-NC), the caucus chairman, stated, "It brings me great joy to learn that the United States will honor abolitionist Harriet Tubman by placing her image on the $20 bill. An African American woman, former slave, freedom fighter, and leader for women's rights, Ms. Tubman was a true visionary who is most deserving of this recognition." He went on to add, "Furthermore, the $5 and $10 bills will also feature new historic images that remind us of the activists that have made America a more perfect union. These designs will represent a more inclusive America by finally representing women, many of whom have been absent in important historical accounts of American history."[246]

Another Black Caucus member, Congresswoman Maxine Waters (D-CA), stated, "These depictions on our nation's currency are long overdue and will show the world the remarkable progress our country has made on the road to equality. The Secretary's decision recognizes the important contributions of women and people of color to our society. I look forward to the circulation of these bills so that we can all feel the weight of history in our hands."[247]

Statements from other members of the Congressional Black Caucus at the time included:

- Congressman John Lewis (D-GA): "It is so fitting and appropriate that this woman, this fighter, this warrior for freedom be on the $20 bill."
- Congressman Cedric Richmond (D-LA): "I'm going to start carrying more twenties now."
- Congresswoman Gwen Moore (D-WI): "I'm straight out of Racine, Wisconsin, the place where the runaway slaves went, so I think she is a dynamic heroine for all Americans."
- Congresswoman Barbara Lee (D-CA): "Long overdue, long overdue. I am so proud."
- Congressman Bennie Thompson (D-MS): "The fact that this will be the first person of color is tremendous and that it will be a female is even more noteworthy."
- Congressman Elijah E. Cummings (D-MD): "Too often, our nation does not do enough to honor the contributions of women in American history, especially women of color. Placing Harriet Tubman on our U.S. currency would be a fitting tribute to a woman who fought to make the values enshrined in our Constitution a reality for all Americans."[248]

A. Shuanise Washington, at that time president and CEO of the Congressional Black Caucus Foundation, a separate entity from the

CBC, commented: "The ground-breaking decision by the Treasury Department—to add Harriet Tubman, a well-known abolitionist and former slave, to the $20 bill and Sojourner Truth, a leader in the women's suffrage movement, to the $10 bill—reflects the changing tide across America. . . . The legacies of Tubman and Truth resonate with millions and transcend ethnicity, gender, and creed."[249] "People other than white men built this country," said Representative Ayanna Pressley, a Democrat and the first African American woman to represent Massachusetts in Congress. She said that Tubman is an "iconic American," and it's past time that our money reflects that.[250]

Today, however, a very different metric is held by many in the black community, particularly young people of color, who are not willing to accept compromise when it comes to symbolism without substance. Black debate on the matter has ranged from strong backing to absolute rejection of Harriet Tubman's image on American money.

Beyond the elected officials, other voices in the black community signaled their support. Lonnie G. Bunch III, the founding and first director of the Smithsonian Institution's National Museum of African American History and Culture, asserted at the time, "For me, having Harriet Tubman on the $20 bill really says, first of all, that America realizes that it's not the same country that it once was—that it's a place where diversity matters. And it allows us to make a hero out of someone like Harriet Tubman, who deserves to be a hero."[251]

Mary C. Curtis, an award-winning journalist, penned an extensive defense of the twenty even while recognizing the conflicting opinions and perceived tokenism it generated. She wrote:

> This one honor won't solve all American society's ills, and it may even be seen as crass—using money to reward a woman who fought against being treated as the spoils of a transaction. But that's a lot of weight to put on this one honor, way too much for it to bear. Are there positives? There is the satisfaction of knowing there will be an instant, though momentary reminder of Tubman's place in

American history each time an ATM spews a $20. That is a rather cool, even subversive notion, since those who object to the choice will have to bear it or boycott the bill. And to young women, especially young African American women, who are still striving against the odds, Tubman is an example of grace, grit, and spirit in one body. The woman born a slave survived so much, overcame crushing odds, and achieved far beyond what America expected or deserved.[252]

BLACK OPPOSITION

Challenges to changes on the currency came shortly after speculation began in 2015 that a woman—perhaps a black woman—would replace one of the white men appearing on all U.S. paper currency. Journalist Kirsten West Savali, writing on the popular black news website *The Root*, argued that no black woman should appear on U.S. currency. She wrote:

> Specifically, there is something both distasteful and ironic about putting a black woman's face on the most frequently counterfeited and most commonly traded dollar bill in this country. Haven't we been commodified and trafficked enough? Slapping a black female face, one of our radical icons, on a $20 bill as if it's some attainment of the American dream would be adding insult to injury.
>
> When nearly half of all single African-American women have zero or negative wealth, and their median wealth is $100—compared with just over $41,000 for single white American women—it is an insult. When black women are the fuel for the prison-industrial complex, with incarceration rates increasing 800 percent since 1986 and black girls being the fastest-growing population of a corrupt juvenile-criminal system, it is an insult. When African-American women earn on average 64 cents for every dollar paid to white, non-Hispanic men, compared with the 78 cents that white women earn for every dollar paid to white, non-Hispanic men, it is an insult. . . .
>
> I don't want Harriet Tubman's face on a $20 bill; I want our people to be free from the chains of institutionalized racism and economic slavery. That's how we honor her.[253]

Savali's indignation with institutionalized racial and economic injustice makes focusing merely on symbols seem like a cosmetic diversion from the ongoing oppressive realities Tubman fought to abolish. According to the U.S. Bureau of Labor Statistics, in December 2021, the unemployment rate for black women was 6.2 percent, higher than the rate for white women (4.51 percent) or Latino women (4.9 percent).[254] The unemployment numbers were linked to what Brookings researchers called an "alarming increase in Black women exiting the labor force."[255] Their participation rate dropped to 60.3 percent between October 2021 and November 2021, wiping out employment gains that had occurred over the previous summer.[256]

According to the Department of Labor, long-standing earnings inequality continued as, "Black women earn 63 cents for every dollar earned by white, non-Hispanic men."[257] The data demonstrated that the differences had little to do with other factors. African American women earned less than white men "even when there was equal educational attainment."[258]

The criminal justice system has also been a source of disproportionate suffering by African American women. According to the Sentencing Project, while the rate of incarceration has been dropping, "In 2019, the imprisonment rate for African American women (83 per 100,000) was over 1.7 times the rate of imprisonment for white women (48 per 100,000)."[259] This inequality also existed for young black girls. The incarceration or placement rate for young white girls was 29 per 100,000, but for their black counterparts it was 94 per 100,000.[260] These are disturbing facts. For these reasons and more, Savali calls the government's plan to put black women on U.S. currency "hush money."[261]

Feminist activist and writer Feminista Jones was another early critic. She argues that all women should be kept off U.S. currency. Responding to the Women On 20s effort, she writes:

> As a feminist, I think this campaign is well-intentioned. Women are rarely acknowledged as important contributors to the creation and development of the United States, and Tubman especially is

regularly overlooked. I even named her on my own list of candidates, initially. But I was hesitant to support Women On 20s's goals from the beginning, and now that Tubman has been selected, I'm certain: There's no place for women—especially women of color—on America's currency today.[262]

Jones contends, essentially, that Tubman was an anti-capitalist of sorts, writing, "Her legacy is rooted in resisting the foundation of American capitalism. Tubman didn't respect America's economic system, so making her a symbol of it would be insulting."[263] While there is no record of Tubman specifically speaking out against capitalism, the political economy of her time was certainly a racist and capitalist one that enslaved her and millions of others for centuries. "She repeatedly put herself in the line of fire to free people who were treated as currency themselves," says Jones.[264] Tubman did try her hand as a small businesswoman, but with little success.

Jones makes the point that U.S. currency is "viewed as a place to honor people of historic political influence" and "to suggest that black women are part of that club by putting Tubman's face on the $20 simply would cover up our nation's reality of historic and lingering disenfranchisement."[265] Jones says she would be for the change if having Harriet Tubman's face on the $20 bill would actually help women or improve their lives, but the consequence is more likely to "distort Tubman's legacy and distract from the economic issues that American women continue to face."[266]

Black Agenda Report writer Margaret Kimberley makes a similar argument. She states, "It is an insult, an offense, to be told that putting Tubman's image on the symbol of her oppression is in any way praise worthy."[267] Kimberley argues that Lew's proposal is a double insult: it's exploitative of Tubman's heroic work and it insults Tubman by keeping Jackson on the back of the bill, making it "an even greater mockery of her legacy."[268] She points out the hypocrisy of ostensibly celebrating the progressive and heroic politics of Tubman and declaring that to be the justification for replacing the deplorable Jackson—and then having him remain on the back of the currency.

Kimberley goes on to say, "There is a larger question about how black freedom fighters should be honored and by whom. Black people should need no stamp of approval on their heroic figures. It is enough that we remember Harriet Tubman and tell her story and ours."[269]

Writing in the *Guardian*, Ijeoma Oluo expresses similar sentiments, arguing that putting Tubman on the twenty-dollar bill "papers over racism."[270] She links slavery not as much to racism as to the economics of capitalism and the need for a moral justification. Whether it was in the era of slavery, Jim Crow, or contemporary post-industrial America, it was an oppressive economic system that gave rise to racism and the resistance to it. In Oluo's words, "It's always been money."[271] She makes the salient and ironic point that "Tubman's life was offered up for five of the $20 that will now bear her image," referring to the hundred-dollar bounty that was placed on her capture after she escaped.[272]

Brittney Cooper, author of *Eloquent Rage: A Black Feminist Discovers Her Superpower*, suggests that a better way of furthering Tubman's legacy would be to tackle the racial and economic injustices that continue to this day:

> Putting Tubman on legal tender, when slaves in the U.S. were treated as fungible commodities is a supreme form of disrespect. The imagery of her face changing hands as people exchange cash for goods and services evokes for me discomfiting scenes of enslaved persons being handed over as payment for white debt or for anything white slaveholders wanted. America certainly owes a debt to Black people, but this is not the way to repay it. . . .
>
> If Tubman is going to be linked to conversations on capital, that conversation must be about a redistribution and funneling of resources and money into Black communities, to deal with wealth and wage disparities, access to education and safe housing, and a comprehensive plan of action to redress the social determinants of poor Black health. Anything else is downright disrespectful. Perhaps we need the Harriet Tubman Reparations Act or the Harriet Tubman Abolition of Prisons Act. What we don't need is Harriet Tubman on twenties.[273]

Despite the principled opposition, most African Americans want the Tubman twenty *and* change. The debates, for the most part, have been healthy and reinforce the view that symbolic change is just one of many essential and interconnected struggles. The fight for justice has multiple fronts, and requires a long view that keeps an eye on the prize. All-white narratives that purport to explain the nation's history and nature, in whatever form, are simply no longer acceptable. Formally replacing the image of a white male enslaver with one of an insurgent, self-emancipated black woman will further a needed shift in national consciousness and the fight against organized forgetting. "She is a ray of hope," says Mary C. Curtis, "and her face on the $20 would fill in one more space missing in all those history books of the contributions of Americans of every color and gender whose blood, sweat, hard work, and sacrifice are part of this all-American soil."[274]

But there's another reason a Tubman twenty is a good idea: deleting Jackson's face and replacing it with Tubman's will lower a pro-slavery, anti-Indigenous flag from a national stage and raise in its place one that truly symbolizes solidarity and liberation. The next chapter examines the sector of white America that finds that idea frightening.

SIX

CONSERVATIVE HOSTILITY TO THE TUBMAN TWENTY

"You want to put that face on the twenty-dollar bill?"
—Donald Trump

IT WAS CLEAR from their initial responses that many on the right had never given much thought to the possibility that a woman, black or otherwise, would be considered for a major place on U.S. currency. However, once they realized it was not only a possibility but an unfolding reality, many reacted as if the move posed an existential threat.

During a September 2015 presidential debate, Republican contenders were asked what woman they would prefer to be on the ten-dollar bill. The debate took place after Treasury Secretary Jacob Lew had announced the previous April that the Treasury Department was seeking suggestions for a woman to replace Alexander Hamilton on the ten, but before the announcement that Jackson would be removed from the front of the twenty instead. Lew's plan was already becoming controversial. The answers of those who replied, without elaboration, were:

Jeb Bush: "Margaret Thatcher"
Ben Carson: "My mother"
Chris Christie: "Abigail Adams"
Ted Cruz: "Keep Hamilton. Put Rosa Parks on the $20."
Carly Fiorina: "Don't change it."
Mike Huckabee: "My wife"
John Kasich: "Mother Theresa"

Rand Paul: "Susan B. Anthony"
Marco Rubio: "Rosa Parks"
Donald Trump: "My daughter, Ivanka," or "Rosa Parks"
Scott Walker: "Clara Barton"

Not a single candidate named Harriet Tubman. Three of the candidates—Cruz, Rubio, and belatedly, Trump—named Rosa Parks. Cruz tried to have it both ways by recommending that Hamilton remain on the ten while placing Parks somewhere on the twenty. Trump initially suggested his daughter, Ivanka, and when he could not think of another American woman, named Parks. Bush and Kasich named women who were not U.S. citizens: former British prime minister Margaret Thatcher and India-based religious activist Mother Theresa. The only black candidate on stage, surgeon Ben Carson, suggested his mother. The only woman candidate in the GOP race, businesswoman Carly Fiorina, stated she did not think any change should happen at all. It is likely that she had actually given it some thought and made the political calculation that Republican voters did not want to sniff any signs of feminism coming from the only woman in the race.[275]

At the time, the candidates initially seemed to take the question as a throw-away with little relevance to their political aims, but for other conservatives, the eventual plan for Tubman to replace Hamilton or Jackson embodied the evil of "political correctness." Moving forward, Republican leaders and the entire spectrum of right-wing media denounced the plan as liberal extremism.

In 2020, conservatives found a new term with which to badger progressives: cancel culture. Similar to right-wing tropes about political correctness, attacks against so-called cancel culture were further attempts to defend white political behavior and avoid responsibility for structural racism, sexism, homophobia, and other bigotries. Trump, however, sought to cancel everyone and everything from Colin Kaepernick, Arnold Schwarzenegger, and Black Lives Matter to MSNBC host Joy Reid, the *New York Times*, and the NBA. At the 2020 Republican National Convention, Trump bellowed: "The goal of cancel culture is to make decent Americans live in fear of being fired, expelled, shamed, humiliated, and driven from society as we know it."[276] By "decent Americans" Trump meant his base of followers. They felt particularly put-upon in 2020 as a powerful national movement emerged following the killing of George Floyd.

THE REPUBLICAN TROPE OF POLITICAL CORRECTNESS AND THE ATTACK ON DEMOCRACY

> "I think the big problem this country has is being politically correct. I've been challenged by so many people and I don't, frankly, have time for total political correctness."
>
> —Donald Trump

In many ways, using the label of political correctness pejoratively is an attempt to thwart the democratic transformations that have been won since the 1960s. Rather than accept that the nation has actually become more democratic, conservatives have sought to delegitimize these victories and justify right-wing assaults on rights that are necessary for a fair society. In particular, conservative officials have weaponized the replacement fears of their white base against people of color, Muslims, immigrants, the LGBTQ community, and the left. All of these sectors are portrayed as a threat to "making America great again" for working-class white Republicans. Lowering Jackson's flag to raise Tubman's strikes at the very heart of their racial replacement anxiety.

Thwarting "political correctness" became Trump's go-to justification for rejecting any policy he did not like. When challenged on his racism, sexism, climate-change denial, anti-immigrant bigotry, Islamophobia, anti-LGBTQ policies, and overall assaults against democracy, he lashed back with loud and dismissive accusations of over-the-top "political correctness." While he almost universally leveled these charges against Democrats and progressives, he has thrown it at the Republican establishment as well. In 2015, during his presidential run, he told a crowd in Florida that he believed the other nominees were ganging up on him and he was "so tired of this politically correct crap."[277] In attempting to lure evangelicals and signal his disdain for other religions, he stated, "We're going to protect Christianity. We don't have to be politically correct about it."[278] A study in the *Journal of Social and Political Psychology* argued that, in 2016, those voters who most perceived restrictions on their communication—i.e., felt they were forced to accept "political correctness" regarding social policies and cultural behavior—flocked to Trump rather than Hillary Clinton.[279] While the researcher does not link these perceptions to views on race and changing demographics, they underscore the effectiveness of Trump's attracting white voters by denouncing anything that decenters the cultural dominance of white people and white men.

WHITELASH

White backlash to the Tubman twenty and other planned changes to U.S. currency was unsurprisingly swift. Tennessee lawmakers were the first to defend their homeboy, Jackson. Senator Lamar Alexander (R-TN), following Trump's post-Charlottesville "good people on both sides" playbook, said "United States history is not Andrew Jackson versus Harriet Tubman. It is Andrew Jackson and Harriet Tubman, both heroes of a nation's work in progress toward great goals. . . . It is unnecessary to diminish Jackson in order to honor Tubman."[280] Alexander's false equivalence of Jackson's record of atrocities with Tubman's record of liberation reveals the ongoing ways white supremacy evades ethical responsibility for historical facts by ignoring them.

The most zealous resistance to the Tubman twenty has come from well-known white supremacist and pro-Trump former congressmember Steve King (R-IA). Within weeks of Lew's announcement, King introduced an amendment that, as the *Huffington Post* put it, "would bar the Treasury Department from spending any funds to redesign paper money or coin currency," despite the fact that the Treasury Department was already under court order to redesign the currency.[281] The amendment went nowhere, but that did not stop King's attempts to scuttle the proposal and misinform the public. King called the plan to put Tubman on the bill "sexist" and "racist."[282] He attempted to disparage Tubman by making the ignorant claim, "As much as she did, she didn't change the course of history."[283]

Steve King had plenty of company opposing the Tubman twenty. He was joined by other notable conservatives, including presidential candidates and those in the far-right media. Ben Carson, toeing the Republican line, said that Jackson should stay on the twenty and that "we can find another way to honor her. Maybe a $2 bill."[284] Carson made his suggestion only days after Trump said the same thing, perhaps already preparing for the sycophant role he would play in his administration. Overlooking Jackson's heinous acts as a slaver and human trafficker, Carson said he was "a tremendous president . . . the last president who actually balanced the federal budget where we had no national debt."[285]

FOX NEWS AND RIGHT-WING MEDIA ON TUBMAN

It was no surprise that Fox News pundits went after Obama for the Tubman twenty. Some went as far as believing the decision was the equivalent of starting a new Civil War. Then–Fox News host Greta Van Susteren slammed Lew's plan for the Tubman twenty as "awful," "dumb," and "stupid." She said: "Rather than dividing the country between those who happen to like the tradition of our currency and happen to want Andrew Jackson to stay put and those who want to put a woman on the bill, . . . give Tubman her own bill, like a $25 bill."[286] The notion of creating a twenty-five-dollar bill that itself would not also be viewed as divisive seems, at best, naïve, given that the opposition was not based on the denomination.

Within days of Lew's announcement, black conservative Crystal Wright went on Fox and blamed liberals, Democrats, Black Lives Matter (whom she referred to as "mobs"), and, of course, political correctness as the culprits that forced the purge of Jackson from the front of the bill. She accused Democrats of "using our currency as a political weapon to pander to their constituents."[287] She disingenuously argued that Lew was being coerced to put a woman on the currency. Ms. Wright also ignored the fact that the Treasury Department had to make changes for security reasons, and that a court order had already compelled it to make the U.S. bills more secure from counterfeiting and more functional for the disabled.[288]

Other conservatives lobbed in some snark as well. The alt-right website InfoWars saw the decision as part of an ongoing "war on cash" and said that somehow removing Jackson would lead to the "enslavement" of "the masses."[289] Right-wing media icon Matt Drudge took to Twitter and wrote sarcastically, "Obama Moves to Change $5, $10 and $20 Bills . . . Beyoncé on the $100?"[290]

CONSERVATIVE DEMOCRAT DEFENSE

It wasn't just right-wingers who shaded the decision to roll out a Tubman twenty. Jim Webb, Virginia's Democratic senator from 2007 to 2013, wrote one of the worst and most self-serving apologies for Jackson imaginable. In an April 2016 piece in the *Washington Post* titled "We Can Celebrate Harriet Tubman Without Disparaging Andrew Jackson," Webb defends not only Jackson, but the entirety of white Americans with Southern roots—completing ignoring white people outside of the South who engaged in and benefited from slavery. Responding to articles in the *Huffington Post, Washington Post*, and elsewhere that were critical of Jackson based on historical facts, Webb blusters that "summarizing his legendary tenure as being 'known primarily for a brutal genocidal campaign against native Americans,' offers an indication of how far political correctness has invaded our educational system and skewed our national consciousness."[291]

In a defensive posture, he declares that "any white person whose ancestral relations trace to the American South now risks being characterized as having roots based on bigotry and undeserved privilege."[292] Webb accuses unnamed sources of spreading "libels" against Jackson but offers no proof. He does not quote a single example of the slander he rails against.

Webb celebrates Jackson as "self-made" and notes that "he found wealth in the wilds of Tennessee and, like other plantation owners such as George Washington, Thomas Jefferson and James Madison, owned slaves."[293] By tying Jackson to other presumably more accepted white enslavers, Webb's piece serves to normalize white supremacy and insulate its history from criticism. Webb does not discuss the fact that Jackson's wealth was extracted from the labor of the black families he bred, trafficked, and enslaved. He ignores Jackson's animosity for abolitionists, his brutality toward the people he enslaved, and the racial violence he waged to dispossess Native Americans of their land. Webb, like other leaders who refuse to acknowledge and critique the legacies of white supremacy, perpetuates them.

Webb's defense of Jackson's war against Native Americans is appalling. First, he employs the false equivalence of "heavy casualties on both sides," suggesting that both sides were equally responsible for the violence. He acknowledges that Jackson's leadership role in the forced and murderous removal of Native populations "was a disaster." But then he asks, "Was its motivation genocide?" According to Webb (and historian Robert Remini, whom he cites), it was not. In fact, they contend Jackson's role was benevolent, and he was doing all he could to protect Native peoples. Without evidence, all Webb could do was hope his readers hadn't already heard the facts about the "pett" Jackson found among the corpses of the Indigenous community he had just slaughtered. "He brought an orphaned Native American boy from the battlefield to his home in Tennessee," writes Webb, "and raised him as his son."[294] Nowhere does Webb acknowledge that it was Jackson who slaughtered the child's entire family and village, making him an orphan. Evidently, such historical facts need not be recalled in the case of "self-made" American heroes like Jackson.

TRUMP TRASHES TUBMAN

As noted earlier, when first asked about selecting a woman to be on the new currency, Trump immediately named Ivanka Trump, the woman he has described during interviews as being "a piece of ass."[295] "If Ivanka weren't my daughter," said Trump during a television interview, "perhaps I'd be dating her."[296] When he realized the suggestion for Ivanka's image on money wasn't scoring debate points, he then mentioned Rosa Parks, an American he probably could not identify in a photo. After the debate, however, he quickly lost interest in seeing an abolitionist black woman replace a white slaver president on the front of the country's twenty-dollar bill. He hurried to defend keeping Jackson on the front, professing his admiration for the seventh president. Trump has openly acknowledged that he rarely reads, so his actual degree of knowledge about Jackson is likely feeble.[297]

Trump later stated, "Andrew Jackson had a great history and I think it's very rough when you take somebody off the bill."[298] He then suggested, as noted above, that Tubman's image could go on the least-circulated of all U.S. currency, the two-dollar bill, which currently features an image of another slaver president, Thomas Jefferson, and is sometimes rejected by retailers.[299]

According to former White House staff, Trump had an even blunter response in private. In her book, *Unhinged: An Insider's Account of the Trump White House*, Omarosa Manigault Newman writes that when she advocated Trump consider the Tubman issue after Treasury Secretary Steven Mnuchin was publicly evading the matter, his response was "You want to put that face on the twenty-dollar bill?"[300] Trump's comment is consistent with other ways he has sought to degrade women in the past. For example, in a 2015 interview with *Rolling Stone*, he insulted one of his opponents, Carly Fiorina, the only woman running in the Republican presidential race, saying, "Look at that face! . . . Would anyone vote for that? Can you imagine that, the face of our next president?!" . . . I mean, she's a woman, and I'm not s'posedta say bad things, but really, folks, come on. Are we serious?"[301]

WHOSE AMERICA?

The debate over the future of the twenty-dollar bill reveals the underlying clash between the forces of white supremacy and racial justice. On many levels, the history of the United States has been Andrew Jackson versus Harriet Tubman. At the heart of this conflict is a struggle over the meaning and future of American democracy. The message of Tubman's life—and of emancipatory politics—is that the future of democracy depends on using our privilege to help win freedom from domination and hierarchy *for everyone*. Andrew Jackson—and right-wing politics today—embody a fundamental antagonism toward such goals.

From a perspective of conscience, dignity, and justice, Andrew Jackson represents the racialized oppression, violence, and censorship of the people's "work in progress toward great goals." The nation's frantic debate over Critical Race Theory and the 1619 Project—which at its core is a conflict over national memory and narration—demonstrates the way the conflict plays out. It also reveals the willingness of conservatives to consciously perpetuate official narratives organized to erase the legacies and trauma caused by white enslavement of black people and the genocide of First Americans.

Conservatives not only run away from facts belying the vaunted values that they argue led to the founding of the United States—such as "with liberty and justice for all" and the idea that "all men are created equal"—but also seek to suppress any voice that poses a more honest counter-narrative. Life stories that serve to propagate founding myths and overlook white atrocities have long been privileged over the stories of those who actually fight for a democracy that delivers liberty and justice for all. Jackson and Tubman represent this split not just historically, but in the current unfolding political era.

The fact is, the MAGA politicians have risen to influence because they validate forms of white nationalism that still resonate with millions of Americans. Doing so requires constant disinformation and "defensive maintenance of a national memory built on lies of historical omission," as Kali Holloway notes.

Symbolic representation is an essential element of power. The urgency to defend Jackson's image and other icons of whiteness cannot be separated from the pursuit of policies that enforce racial hierarchy. Deliberately displacing the image of a prominent white enslaver with that of an insurgent black abolitionist woman will not immediately correct generations of structural injustice, historical omission, and narrative bias. But it will win a small battle, and each battle won brings us closer to the kind of liberation and solidarity that Tubman fought for us all to enjoy.

II. AND CHANGE

The debates, concerns, celebrations, and differences over the Tubman twenty are not just academic and do not occur in a vacuum. The spirit of Tubman's fierce opposition to oppression and inequality at multiple levels lives on in today's movements to dismantle white privilege, end police violence, achieve fairness in health care and medicine, and expand and protect memory, free speech, and voting for all. Tubman's legacy remains an inspiration for all who struggle for greater democracy, particularly black women, who understand how challenging it is to overcome compound injustices based in race, gender, and class. The following chapters analyze some of the most glaring of these injustices, and how today's movements, driven by individual and collective efforts, are working inside and outside of traditional politics to achieve material change.

SEVEN

FEAR OF A DIVERSE AMERICA: WHITE PANIC, RAGE, AND INSURRECTION

"Whenever the American people shall become convinced that they have gone too far in recognizing the rights of the Negro, they will find some way to abridge those rights. . . . History repeats itself."
—Frederick Douglass

"As during Reconstruction and the civil-rights era, we face once again the danger that a politics of freedom *and* equality may be eclipsed by the psychology of white resentment."
—Lawrence B. Glickman, May 2020

"A racial reckoning that ushers in racial progress is only one type of racial reckoning. Racial backlash is a kind of racial reckoning too. And the racial reckoning of this moment—one characterized by White backlash to a perceived loss of power and status—seems poised to be much more consequential."
—Hakeem Jefferson and Victor Ray

TRUMP KNEW HE COULD dismiss the Tubman twenty and pay no political price for it. In fact, he knew much of his Republican base would cheer him on. And they did. Political strategists have long understood that fear of racial replacement is a primary force driving white Americans to join the contemporary Republican Party. For some, the plan for Harriet Tubman to push Andrew Jackson off the front of a twenty-dollar bill is a visual materialization of that very fear. For many others, however, having Tubman officially replace

Jackson on a national platform is a battle won in the ongoing effort to free America from white supremacy in all its forms.

As much as Trump has been an enemy of that effort, it is the Republican Party, which spawned him and allowed itself to be restructured by him, that is truly a threat to the future of America. Despite the constant embarrassment the Trump presidency brought to the nation, Republicans still obtained seventy-four million votes in the 2020 presidential election. While the fact that Trump lost by about seven million votes gave many Americans reason to celebrate, the clear and ongoing spread of far-right culture and authoritarian politics is troubling and dangerous.

A key force driving people to embrace such politics is white replacement anxiety—the fear of losing a dominating position in America's racial caste system. At the heart of this fear is the irrational belief that as people of color advance politically and economically, white people *lose* politically and economically. This fear has been skillfully deepened by a GOP desperate to maintain relevance in a demographically changing nation. As discussed earlier, the party has fully embraced the infamous "Southern Strategy" of using racial wedge issues to build a loyal base from whites angry with the gains of Americans of color and the progressive bent of the Democratic Party.[302] Since the 1970s, the strategy has enjoyed electoral success well beyond the South, and has expanded, in part, due to the decreasing influence of ethics and truthfulness in politics and media. The facts of constant immigration, declining white birth rates, and increasing political agency of Americans of color supply Republicans with fat to throw on the fire of white replacement anxiety.

New York Times columnist and author Charles Blow has a different term for it: White Extinction Anxiety. "All manner of current policy grows out of this panic over loss of privilege and power," writes Blow: "immigration policy, voter suppression, Trump economic isolationist impulses, his contempt for people from Haiti and Africa, the Muslim ban, his rage over Black Lives Matter and social justice protests. Everything."[303]

Right-wing media—particularly Fox News—have provided Republicans with constant reinforcement. For example, conspiratorial statements like the following from Tucker Carlson in 2021 are a common part of the network's programming, and often appear intended to convert racial anger into antipathy for the Democrats: "Now, I know that the left and all the little gatekeepers on Twitter become literally hysterical if you use the term replacement—if you suggest the Democratic Party is trying to replace the current electorate, the voters now casting ballots, with new people, more obedient voters from the third world. But they become hysterical because that's what's happening, actually. Let's just say it. That's true."[304]

White supremacist groups couldn't agree more, including former KKK leader David Duke, who applauds Republicans for promoting replacement theory, which Duke has been propagating for decades.[305] "Trump really knows what his movement is based on," Duke said. "You know, [Trump] had to know that I ran my campaigns primarily on the immigration issue, on fair trade issues, on the issues of preserving American culture, on stopping the replacement of European Americans—which people are all talking about now."[306]

Carlson also repeats the white supremacist propaganda that immigrants—by which he means people of color—are "invading" the country with the goal of "replacing" Americans—meaning white people. For example, on April 2, 2018, Carlson provocatively asked, "Will anyone in power do anything to protect America this time, or will our leaders sit passively back while the invasion continues?" On August 3, 2018, he stated, "This is really destroying one culture and replacing it with the new foreign culture." On August 20, 2018, he declared, "I don't think we should sit back and get invaded by foreigners. I don't. That doesn't make me a racist, it makes me an American."[307]

Other hosts on the network, including Sean Hannity, Jeanine Pirro, and Laura Ingraham, regularly rail about the "plot to remake America, to replace American citizens with illegals."[308] Media

Matters for America, a progressive media watchdog that documents the bias and bigotry dominating the Fox News network, has compiled an extensive list of guests and hosts, including Republican officials, who have promoted the "immigrant invasion" narrative central to white nationalists.[309] The tally has included far-right proponent Patrick Buchanan, Congressman Louie Gohmert (R-TX), *Fox & Friends* host Steve Doocy, former congressman Allen West, anti-immigrant activist Mary Ann Mendoza, conservative radio host Todd Starnes, Trump's former White House press secretary Kayleigh McEnany, former Trump advisor Sebastian Gorka, far-right writer Ann Coulter, and Senator Lindsey Graham, among others.[310]

It is noteworthy that anti-immigrant replacement rhetoric has been repeated by white supremacist terrorists when perpetrating attacks. The authors of an August 2019 report in the *New York Times* titled "How the El Paso Killer Echoed the Incendiary Words of Conservative Media Stars" reveal that there is a striking similarity between the words of right-wing media personalities and the language used by the Texas man who confessed to killing twenty-two people at a Walmart in El Paso in 2019.[311] "In a 2,300-word screed posted on the website 8chan, the alleged killer, then-21-year-old Patrick Wood Crusius, wrote that he was 'simply defending my country from cultural and ethnic replacement brought on by an invasion.'"[312]

An extensive review of popular right-wing media platforms found "hundreds of examples of language, ideas and ideologies that overlapped with the mass killer's written statement—a shared vocabulary of intolerance that stokes fears centered on immigrants of color. The programs, on television and radio, reach an audience of millions."[313] For example, one poster on the website 4chan wrote, "Tucker sat down and proved white genocide was real. That white nationalists and white supremacists were 100% right and that it is being systematically implemented globally to genocide whites and make them powerless oppressed minorities within what were once their own borders. But that requires action."[314] "The 'great replacement' theory should be seen for what it is: a staple of white supremacist rhetoric," says Jonathan Greenblatt, head of the Anti-Defamation League.[315] "I think we're living in a moment where people like Tucker are writing the talking points for elected officials rather than people actually analyzing what's happening in a fact-based and responsible manner," Greenblatt observes.[316] "We know where this ends," he said to *Rolling Stone*. "The shooter in Pittsburgh invoked the great replacement theory. The shooter in Christchurch invoked the great replacement theory. The shooter in El Paso invoked the great replacement theory. That's where this goes."[317]

What the far right has deemed existential "replacement" is, in fact, a nation diversifying as a result of decades-old declining white birth rate, immigration from the developing world, an increase in interracial relationships, and larger black and brown families. A study by Maureen A. Craig and Jennifer A. Richeson, "On the Precipice of a 'Majority-Minority' America," examined how "perceived status threat from the racial demographic shift affects white Americans' political ideology" and impacts the widening partisan divide.[318] Writer Ezra Klein summed up the study and similar ones: "Even gentle, unconscious exposure to reminders that America is diversifying—and particularly to the idea that America is becoming a majority-minority nation—pushes whites toward more conservative policy opinions and more support of the Republican Party."[319] Strategists on the right thus have a good reason to propagate rhetoric about white replacement, as doing so "pushes whites" away from the Democrats.

While this approach has had some success at state and local levels, the same cannot be said for presidential contests. Republicans have lost the popular vote in all but one presidential election since 1988, when George H. W. Bush soundly defeated Michael Dukakis. Republican presidential candidates lost the popular vote in 1992, 1996, 2000, 2008, 2012, 2016, and 2020. George W. Bush fell short of about 500,000 votes to Al Gore, yet took control of the Oval Office in 2000. In 2016, Trump lost by three million votes to Hilary Clinton, but the electoral college system, founded to prop up enslaver states centuries ago, came through for Republicans.[320] The events of January 6, 2021, demonstrate that Republicans are now willing to engage in sedition—including mobilizing violent militias and mobs—when they can't legally tweak the system fast enough to obtain power.

Prior to Trump, a twice-elected black president led some to conclude that white supremacy was no longer relevant, and that the nation had fully entered a "post-racial" phase.[321] Such conclusions were fatally inaccurate. Persistent police killings in black communities, voter-suppression campaigns targeting populations of color, anti-protest laws passed as backlash to the rise of black influence following Black Lives Matter, and armed vigilantism along the U.S. border are constant reminders of the deeper racist moorings that persist across America. Rather than attempt to mitigate these issues, the GOP and right-wing media have deliberately exacerbated them.

In their June 13, 2021, *Atlantic* article, "The Myth of a Majority-Minority America," Alba Morris Levy and Dowell Myers write:

> The majority-minority narrative contributes to our national polarization. Its depiction of a society fractured in two, with one side rising while the other subsides, is inherently divisive because it implies winners and losers. It has bolstered white anxiety and resentment of supposedly ascendant minority groups, and has turned people against democratic institutions that many conservative white Americans and politicians consider complicit in illegitimate minority empowerment. At the extreme, it nurtures conspiratorial beliefs in a racist "replacement" theory, which holds that elites are working to replace white people with minority immigrants in a "stolen America."

Given these challenges, an essential part of securing the peaceful collapse of America's racial caste system involves successfully educating the nation about diversity as a strength of American democracy and community. Part of that process includes understanding white supremacy as the structural through line connecting Anglo settler colonialism to slavery, Indian Removal, Manifest Destiny, the

Civil War, Jim Crow, voter suppression, and current-day Republican politics. The Civil Rights and Black Power movements of the 1950s, 1960s, and 1970s had many achievements, but consolidating a popular definition of structural racism that was grounded in an understanding of that historical through line was not one of them. Since then, the influence of the Black Lives Matter movement has made substantive advances in popularizing a critique rooted in acknowledgment of structural racism.

However, for every advance toward greater racial justice, there has been white pushback. Republican-controlled Florida's recently proposed "Stop W.O.K.E. Act"—and the 104 education gag orders pending in states across the country as of March 28, 2022—clearly expose the anti-black racism at play in America today.[322] For example, a December 15, 2021, press release from Florida Governor Ron DeSantis announcing the Stop W.O.K.E. Act describes it as "a legislative proposal that will give businesses, employees, children and families tools to fight back against woke indoctrination. The Stop W.O.K.E. Act will be the strongest legislation of its kind in the nation and will take on both corporate wokeness and Critical Race Theory."[323] Among the outrages that the bill hopes to prevent in the future are middle school classes "simulating a Black Power rally to 'free Angela Davis' from prison" and corporate trainings "that encourages white employees to confront their 'privilege,' reject the principle of 'equality,' and 'defund the police.'"[324]

Kimberlé Crenshaw, a central figure in the development of intersectional and critical race theories, said in a May 2021 interview that critical race theory "just says, let's pay attention to what has happened in this country, and how what has happened in this country is continuing to create differential outcomes. . . . Critical race theory . . . is more patriotic than those who are opposed to it because . . . we believe in the promises of equality. And we know we can't get there if we can't confront and talk honestly about inequality."[325]

Animating white backlash to critical race theory is an existential denial that the United States was founded, structured, and historically narrated as a white state. In his November 2021 essay for PEN America, Rutgers University professor Gregory Pardlo writes,

> The popular (among some) objection is that CRT teaches children and young people that America is racist at its core. This is true. That is, America is indeed racist at its core. And it is a dishonest—not to mention illogical—rhetorical move to make that assertion mean "all white Americans are racist," which is what CRT-baiters would have us believe is the hidden agenda. Equally dishonest is the effort to have the words "racist" and "racism" describe only the willful and overt racial hatred expressed by a conscious actor. Defining racism like this prevents us from examining the ways that laws, policies, practices and institutional cultures might bear the imprint of earlier generations' racial attitudes and beliefs. Defining racism in this limited way precludes the possibility that an institution can act on its own, independently from its individual constituents, which, of course, is the very thing institutions are designed to do.[326]

Today, many Republicans continue to insist that U.S. history—like Trump and the GOP—is not racist, and the wave of educational gag orders, some of which are openly designed to prevent white people from getting "uncomfortable," is intended to enforce that view.[327] In response to one such bill in Florida (SB148), in January 2002 Democratic state senator Shevrin Jones said, "This isn't even a ban on Critical Race Theory, this is a ban on Black history. They are talking about not wanting White people to feel uncomfortable? Let's talk about being uncomfortable. My ancestors were uncomfortable when they were stripped away from their children."[328] The NAACP of Florida, the Florida PTA, Equality Florida, and the American Civil Liberties Union all testified against SB 148.[329]

Such laws expose how white supremacy is struggling to maintain a footing in a nation increasingly shaped by its rapidly diversifying population. Despite the obvious racism in such measures, for many, though not all, only the placing of a burning cross or calling someone the "N-word" constitutes a bona fide act of white supremacy. It is undeniable that people's individual actions can be bigoted and racist.

Yet it is the quotidian violence of America's racial caste system—which structures institutions, government, policing, education, and social norms and gives rise to white supremacist groups and militias—that poses the most critical threat to communities of color and democracy itself. Ultimately, it is that system, and the narratives that validate it, that must be overthrown.

DOES WHITE SUPREMACY REALLY EXIST?

Not according to some Republicans.

During the summer of 2019, Trump escalated his attacks on four progressive congresswomen of color who had called him out for his racist, misogynist, and xenophobic policies and statements. Dubbed "The Squad," Congresswomen Alexandria Ocasio-Cortez (D-NY), Ayanna Pressley (D-MA), Ilhan Omar (D-MN), and Rashida Tlaib (D-MI) became a favorite target of Trump's venom at rallies and online. On July 14, 2019, he posted the following tweet:

> So interesting to see "Progressive" Democrat Congresswomen, who originally came from countries whose governments are a complete and total catastrophe, the worst, most corrupt and inept anywhere in the world (if they even have a functioning government at all), now loudly . . . and viciously telling the people of the United States, the greatest and most powerful Nation on earth, how our government is to be run. Why don't they go back and help fix the totally broken and crime infested places from which they came.[330]

Trump, a self-proclaimed "extremely stable genius," knew that all four congresswomen were U.S. citizens and only one, Omar, had been naturalized.[331] However, he was also aware that "othering" his opponents would prove to be enormously popular with potential Republican voters, as had been the case when he expanded his supporter base by questioning the birthplace of Barack Obama. Three days after the tweet, on July 17, 2019, those gathered at the Republican leader's rally chanted "Send her back!" while a smug and preening Trump stood back and basked in his handiwork.[332]

Virtually all Republican officials claimed that the statement was not racist, as did much of their base. One former Republican New Hampshire state representative, Dan Hynes, defended Trump on Facebook, where he posted the following: "If Trump is the most racist president in American history, what does that say about all of the other presidents who owned slaves?"[333] Hynes's effort to pivot attention away from the Republican figurehead is a common evasive tactic. In response to that question from Hynes, Republican New Hampshire state representative Werner Horn replied, "Wait, owning slaves doesn't make you racist."[334] He later claimed, after severe criticism, that his intent was sarcasm and that he thought "slavery's not okay." However, Horn's white supremacist views could not be hidden and became repulsively clear in a series of subsequent interviews. In one he stated, "The U.S. had abolitionists since the start, people who felt slavery wasn't moral. But [slaveowners] weren't enslaving black people because they were black. They were bringing in these folks because they were available. What they were looking at was whether they were fit enough to do the demanding work that needed to be done. It was an economic reality."[335] In another interview, he stated, "My comment specifically was aimed at a period of time when that was how you survived, that's how you fed your family. It wasn't 'I want to own a black person today.' It was, 'I need to feed my family; I need five guys who can work stupidly long hours in the sun without killing themselves.'"[336] Horn's comments expose the reasoning inherent in America's racial caste system: Those at the top of the hierarchy get to feed their families by exploiting those below them to the edge of death. How those forced to toil "stupidly long hours in the sun" feed their families is not a concern.

As is common among white supremacists today, Horn ignores the entire system and ideology of racial capitalism that was inherent in white people acquiring land through "Indian Removal" and breeding, trafficking, and enslaving black people for profit. The organized forgetting of black and Indigenous misery, unfreedom, and death for the sake of white people's economic enrichment is part of the ongoing legacy of settler-colonialism and white supremacy today. Such historical erasure is inherent in the educational gag orders and the absence of black, Indigenous, Asian, and Latinx women and men in official U.S. narratives, including those enshrined on money and monuments.

Despite this, most Republicans continue to believe that African Americans face little discrimination. Based on poll data culled from the National Opinion Research Center since the 1940s, researcher Mike Tesler reports that Republicans' denial of Trump's racist tweets "fits a long American history of denying racism."[337] In 1944, when Jim Crow was the law across the South and in practice in many other parts of the country, black and white Americans were asked the question, "Do you think negroes in the United States are being treated fairly or unfairly?" A sizable majority of white people, about 60 percent, said, "fairly," a number that has held steady for decades. This was compared to about 11 percent of African Americans who said the same. In the 1940s and 1950s, white terrorism against people of color still occurred regularly throughout the United States, and African Americans and other people of color were politically disempowered. As recently as 2018, a Cooperative Congressional Election Study found that 53 percent of whites believed "blacks didn't face a lot of discrimination."[338]

Right-wing media continue to provide reinforcement for these views on a twenty-four-hour basis. For example, in 2019 Tucker Carlson said on his widely viewed Fox News show that white supremacy is "actually not a real problem in America. This is a hoax, just like the Russia hoax. It's a conspiracy theory used to divide the country and keep a hold on power."[339] After a firestorm of criticism, he evaded the specific issue of white supremacy by saying, "racism is one of America's problems," which can mean many things, including that people of color are guilty of it.[340]

WHITE SUPREMACIST THREATS TO NATIONAL SECURITY

Despite right-wing propaganda to the contrary, evidence of white supremacy is overwhelming and irrefutable. FBI director Christopher

A. Wray, in his July 2019 testimony before the Senate Intelligence Committee, stated that of the ninety or so domestic terrorist cases in which the FBI had made arrests, a "majority . . . are motivated by some version of what you might call white supremacist violence."[341] He later modified his statement to clarify that he meant a majority of the domestic terrorism cases involving race were linked to white supremacy.[342] Wray added, "We also found ideologically motivated murders by white supremacists increased in 2018 to 17, from 13 in 2017," while violent jihad-related killings "dropped to only one."[343] Wray's testimony echoed the May 2018 testimony of the FBI's assistant director of the Counterterrorism Division, Michael McGarrity, before the House Committee on Homeland Security. McGarrity stated that the FBI was investigating about 850 cases of domestic terrorism, about 40 percent of which were related to white supremacists.[344]

A 2018 Department of Homeland Security report was more explicit about the dangers of white supremacy. The report stated that white supremacist extremists "will remain the most persistent and lethal threat in the Homeland."[345] On September 29, only a week before the report was issued, Trump had declined to condemn white supremacists at the second presidential debate. When challenged to publicly denounce the violent far-right group the Proud Boys, Trump refused and said, "Proud Boys, stand back and stand by." Gleeful with the shout-out from the commander in chief, many Proud Boys responded on social media with the words "standing by," which they did until they began complying with the president's instructions to go to D.C. on January 6 and "stop the steal."[346] In October 2020, the Department of Homeland Security (DHS) annual threat assessment went even further, reporting that violent white supremacy was the "most persistent and lethal threat in the homeland."[347] In its November 2021 *National Terrorism Advisory System Bulletin*, in a clear reference to white supremacists, DHS wrote, "Through the remainder of 2021 and into 2022, racially or ethnically motivated violent extremists and anti-government/anti-authority violent extremists will continue to pose a threat to the United States."[348]

BLACK IDENTITY EXTREMISM VS. "HARD WORK, LOVE AND UNITY"

The Department of Homeland Security's Countering Violent Extremism (CVE) program was developed under the Obama administration. It is run by a joint task force of representatives from DHS, FBI, Department of Justice (DOJ), and other agencies to engage in "proactive actions to counter efforts by extremists to recruit, radicalize, and mobilize followers to violence."[349] As noted by DHS, "Fundamentally, CVE actions intend to address the conditions and reduce the factors that most likely contribute to recruitment and radicalization by violent extremists."[350] Notably, it has a broad mandate and has been used to address domestic terrorism, including white supremacist violence. In 2017, the incoming Trump administration considered its mandate too widely focused. Two weeks after taking office, Trump sought to change the name and mission of the program to either "Countering Islamic Extremism" or "Countering Radical Islamic Extremism." As Reuters noted, if the administration had its way, CVE would "no longer target groups such as white supremacists who have also carried out bombings and shootings in the United States."[351] After significant resistance, the administration backed off the name change.

Although the name stayed, the work of the CVE program realigned with Trump's bigoted priorities. As the Brennan Center documents, "Despite the prevalence of high-profile mass killings by white perpetrators, Muslims and other minority groups are explicitly targeted in 85 percent of Homeland Security Department grants devoted to Countering Violent Extremism in the U.S."[352] Furthermore, despite the fact that significant funding was supposed to go to community organizations, under Trump those funds were cut while the amount of CVE funding going to law enforcement tripled, from $764,000 to $2,340,000.

Meanwhile, on May 10, 2017, the FBI and DHS issued a report titled "White Supremacist Extremism Poses Persistent Threat of Lethal Violence," which detailed attacks by white supremacist extremists (WSE) from 2000 to 2016 and sought to provide new insight into the state of white supremacist extremism violence in the United States.[353] After reviewing attacks since 2000, the report found that "racial minorities have been the primary victims of WSE lethal violence."[354] The Department of Homeland Security and the FBI defined white supremacist extremists as "individuals who seek, wholly or in part, through unlawful acts of force or violence, to support their belief in the intellectual and moral superiority of the white race over other races."[355]

It is important to note that the report was in preparation before the Trump administration came to power and before Jeff Sessions became the country's attorney general. The report did not reflect the new administration's views or values. While the Obama administration felt the urgency of investigating white supremacy, the Trump administration absolutely did not. Under the Republicans' Justice Department, addressing "extremism" meant locking on a new target: "Black Identity Extremists."

On August 3, 2017, three months after the report on white extremists, Trump's Justice Department issued another report, titled "Black Identity Extremists Likely Motivated to Target Law Enforcement Officers."[356] The report assessed that the genesis of this contemporary "movement" was the black community's reaction to "alleged" incidents of police abuse, violence, and murder of African Americans. The opening lines of the report state:

> The FBI assesses it is very likely "Black Identity Extremist" (BIE) perceptions of police brutality against African Americans spurred an increase in premeditated, retaliatory lethal violence against law enforcement and will very likely serve as justification for such violence. The FBI assess it is very likely this increase began following the 9 August 2014 shooting of Michael Brown in Ferguson, Missouri, and the subsequent Grand Jury November 2014 declination to indict the police officers involved. The FBI assesses it is very likely incidents of alleged police abuse against African Americans since then have continued to feed the resurgence in ideologically motivated, violent criminal activity within the BIE movement.[357]

While the term "Black Identity Extremists" was new, the report notes that an earlier FBI report issued on March 23, 2016, while Obama was president, raised concerns about what it termed "Black Separatist Extremists."[358] But what was seen by the previous administration as individual acts of violence was elevated to a movement by the Trump administration. Although only five incidents are cited in the report, the danger was hyped. Further, Trump's FBI fancifully argued that "black extremist" actions dated back to at least the 1960s and 1970s, citing the Black Liberation Army as an example.[359]

The FBI refused to accept that perhaps the incidents of violence were committed by individuals acting without a base in the black community. It responded that this "alternative" explanation was "very unlikely in the cases analyzed in this assessment because strictly criminal subjects typically commit spontaneous, 'defensive' acts of violence against police rather than proactive targeting, and use idiosyncratic reasons unrelated to ideology, such as financial gain and personal disputes, to justify their actions."[360]

The designation of Black Identity Extremist was not just theoretical. The FBI actually tracked and arrested individuals who it argued fit the profile. In December 2017, in Dallas, one such target was Christopher Daniels, aka Rakem Balogun, who "was arrested during a raid on his home and charged with the unlawful possession of a firearm, the result of more than two years of FBI surveillance," according to the *Atlantic Black Star*.[361] Even though the FBI admitted it "had no evidence of Balogun making any specific threats about harming police," he was held without bail for five months and lost his home during his incarceration.[362] "It's tyranny at its finest," said Balogun, a father of three. "In a letter Balogun wrote to the *Guardian* from jail, he said he felt he had been 'abducted' by the FBI, a 'prisoner of war on free speech and the right to bear arms.' Authorities were targeting him for promoting black-led community groups and fighting 'government abuse,' he wrote, adding he was never a threat to anyone: 'Violence is the method of our oppressor, our method is hard work, love and unity.'"[363] The charges against Balogun were eventually dropped in May 2018.

During hearings in the U.S. House of Representatives, Congresswoman Karen Bass (D-CA) vigorously asked Attorney General Sessions and other DOJ officials about the Black Identity Extremist designation and the racial biases underlying it. She attempted to get to the bottom of who in the Justice Department ordered the report in the first place. While Deputy Attorney General Rod Rosenstein denied ordering the report, Sessions and FBI Director Christopher Wray demurred and promised to get back to Representative Bass, which they never did. She pointed out that the FBI was targeting black activists who were protesting police abuse, even though there was often no evidence of "extremism."[364]

On March 20, 2018, the Congressional Black Caucus (CBC) Task Force on Foreign Affairs and National Security held a hearing to discuss the Black Identity Extremist issue. In her report following the meeting, Bass, who chaired the Task Force, stated that evidence and testimony at the hearing raised further questions about the origins of the report. "The need for a total retraction of this report is absolutely imperative so that the follow-up message sent to the 16,000 local offices that received the initial report is one of lawful protection and service, not one of bigoted investigation and surveillance. I'm thankful for my colleagues in the CBC who continue to shine light on this important issue."[365]

Under severe pressure from Congresswoman Bass and others, FBI Director Wray testified in 2019 that the designation was no longer being used. Social justice leaders and activists welcomed this change. Kristen Clarke, president and executive director of the Lawyers' Committee for Civil Rights Under Law, stated:

> The abandonment of the FBI's "Black Identity Extremism" category is a win for civil rights lawyers and advocates who have fought to expose the agency's manufactured, false threat category. The "Black Identity Extremism" [category] harkened back to the darkest days of the Civil Rights Movement, when the agency abused its power and resources to silence the work of African American activists. Despite this, we must remain vigilant as the Bureau carries out its

intelligence activities in this era. It is critical that the Bureau continue to track the very real threat of white supremacist violence, and call it out by its name.[366]

Clarke's warning to remain vigilant was on the mark. According to the ACLU, Wray's abandonment of the term Black Identity Extremist appears to have been an effort to bamboozle critics. The ACLU reported that the FBI started a new program, titled "IRON FIST," which was essentially a rebranding. Documents were leaked that exposed the sham change. On August 9, 2019, the ACLU's deputy director of racial justice, Nusrat Choudhury, stated:

> The FBI wasted resources to target Black people because of protected First Amendment activities. . . . The Black Identity Extremist label is baseless, and earlier this year, bureau director Wray testified that the label is no longer in use. But, based on these documents, it appears that the FBI simply renamed the label. Even more, the documents show the bureau implemented a program, titled "IRON FIST," to target department resources on spying, surveilling, and investigating Black activists, including through undercover agents.[367]

Choudhury's sentiments were echoed by Steven Renderos of MediaJustice, who stated, "There is no indication that IRON FIST or any other programs used to target Black people for surveillance have been dismantled. Instead, these documents suggest that the FBI under Trump continues to prioritize criminalizing Black dissent while minimizing the threat of white supremacy."[368] White criminalization of black agency and dissent is as old as the "hickory oil" approach used by Jackson on his plantation. Further efforts to silence black political dissent escalated following the uprisings of 2020, discussed in more detail in Chapter 9.

"WHITE ALONE" IN DIVERSE AMERICA

White fear that the racial caste system is facing demographic challenges is based in fact. For years, the Census Bureau has projected that white people will become a minority population in the United States by 2044.[369] For younger Americans, that time has already arrived. By 2018, according to the Census, there were more children of color than white children in the group nine years old and younger.[370] By 2019, the age group had risen to sixteen and younger.[371] In the decade between 2010 and 2020, Census reports indicated that the Asian population had grown by almost 30 percent, the Latinx population by 20 percent, and the black population by 12 percent. The white population, meanwhile, declined by about 9 percent.[372]

It is critical to note that there are scholars who strongly believe the Census Bureau made a mistake in declaring that whites would lose their majority status without addressing the complex subtleties of white racial identity in the United States. Among the nuances that need to be understood is the changing structure of how the Census gathers data. Chief among these are the separate race and ethnic questions that are confusing to some, and the policy that allows one to select "white" and any other racial or ethnic category.[373] In other words, the number of "white" people in the nation depends on whether being white is defined by the "white alone" box, or the "white alone" *and* "white in combination" boxes together. In comparing 2010 to 2020, the "white alone" box saw an 8.6 percent drop. However, in comparing the "white alone" plus the "white in combination," the number grew by about 2 percent.[374]

Furthermore, as mandated by the White House Office of Management and Budget, the Census Bureau officially defines "white" as anyone with "origins in any of the original peoples of Europe, the Middle East or North Africa." This definition is clearly out of date, and out of touch with the lived reality of many light-skinned individuals with roots from parts of the world not included in the official definition.[375] What matters here is that relative to the population increase of Americans of color, the fact of white population decline is fueling a resurgence of white nationalism. The anxiety triggered by this trend is fed, tapped, and manipulated by the Republican Party at national, state, and local levels.

For example, in a January 2018 White House meeting, Trump sneered, "Why are we having all these people from shithole countries come here? We should have more people from Norway."[376] Though Trump refused to acknowledge making the comment, the extremely stable genius and his staff clearly understood that a large sector of the country wants to keep the United States politically white for as long as possible. CNN White House reporter Kaitlan Collins reported that Trump staffers seemed to relish the fact that the president's insults "actually resonate with his base."[377]

One of the real predictors of support for candidate Trump was where voters stood on the issue of immigration, specifically immigration from the global South. The more anti-immigrant an individual voter, whether they identified as either an independent, Democrat, or Republican, the more likely they were to strongly support Trump. Political scientists Marc Hooghe and Ruth Dassonneville studied the 2016 election and found that "despite ongoing discussion about the empirical validity of racist resentment and anti-immigrant sentiments, both concepts proved to be roughly equally powerful in explaining a Trump vote."[378] They concluded that "negative attitudes toward ethnic minorities and immigrants swayed independents and some Democrats to opt for candidate Trump, thereby considerably strengthening his electoral-support base."[379] Understanding this offers clear incentive to propagate "negative attitudes toward ethnic minorities and immigrants" to those interested in luring white voters to the right.

PERCEPTION OF ANTI-WHITE RACISM, ETHNIC ANTAGONISM, AND AUTHORITARIANISM

"A Trump administration is a return to the America that won the West, landed on the moon, and built an economy and military that stunned the world. Non-whites can participate in this, but only if they accept the traditional (which is to say, white) norms of American culture."

—A Trump supporter, writing in the white supremacist journal *American Renaissance*

145

Not only do demographic changes frighten many white Americans, a significant number also feel that they are victims of "reverse racism"— i.e., that acts of bigotry are perpetrated against them because they are white. A pioneering study by scholars Michael I. Norton and Samuel R. Sommers in 2011 found that African Americans and white Americans both believed that anti-black racism had decreased since the 1950s.[380] The nation had elected its first African American president, and black celebrities, sports figures, news anchors, and political voices seemed omnipresent. What was truly new in Norton and Sommers's study was the finding that a significant number of whites felt anti-white racism had increased, and by the early 2000s was a greater concern than anti-black bias. On a ten-point scale that measured perceptions of anti-black and anti-white bias, 11 percent of white people gave the maximum ten points to anti-white bias while only 2 percent did so for anti-black bias.[381]

This trend continued and deepened in the Trump era. Poll after poll confirmed that a majority of white Americans believed that racial discrimination was more prevalent against white people than against people of color. A November 2017 poll by National Public Radio, the Robert Wood Johnson Foundation, and the Harvard T. H. Chan School of Public Health asked white respondents, "Generally speaking, do you believe there is or is not discrimination against white people in America today?" A majority—55 percent—answered in the affirmative, while 43 percent said no.[382]

The areas in which white discrimination was being claimed included applying for jobs (19 percent), being paid or promoted equally (13 percent), applying or attending college (11 percent), interacting with police (10 percent), trying to rent or buy housing (5 percent), going to a doctor or health clinic (5 percent), and trying to vote or participate in politics (4 percent).[383] Notably, those who claimed personal discrimination held a higher belief in a general atmosphere of anti-white discrimination than those who did not.

Robert Blendon, a co-director of the survey, concluded, "What's striking about these findings is the significant gap between many white Americans' general belief that white people are discriminated against in America, and their relatively limited reporting of being personally discriminated against in their own lives."[384] In other words, there are far more white people who appear to fear discrimination than there are who actually experience such discrimination.

A September 2016 Quinnipiac University poll also found great anxiety from pro-Trump voters about "reverse racism" and the "United States becoming a majority non-white country."[385] About two-thirds (64 percent) of Trump voters who were "very concerned" or "somewhat concerned" about "reverse racism" described it as "discrimination against white people." Only about 20 percent of Democrat voters felt the same way. In the same poll, 40 percent of Trump voters felt "very concerned" or "somewhat concerned" about "the United States becoming a majority non-white country." Only 9 percent of Democrat voters shared those concerns.[386]

After losing the 2020 election, Trump became more explicit in advancing the view that white Americans were being discriminated against, including in terms of access to COVID-19 treatments. At an Arizona rally on January 15, 2022, he falsely claimed, "The left is now rationing life-saving therapeutics based on race, discriminating against and denigrating, just denigrating white people to determine who lives and who dies."[387] To the cheers of the nearly all-white crowd, including cheers from the Blacks for Trump cult whose members are often seated behind Trump at rallies, he stated, "In New York state, if you're white, you have to go to the back of the line to get medical health."[388] His statements contradicted the facts and CDC data that African Americans and Latinos were less vaccinated and more likely to die from COVID-19, and that many in the medical community say that race is a "risk factor" that should be considered when distributing limited supplies of certain treatments.[389]

On the other hand, Trump voters felt a lot less concern about discrimination against African Americans. A June 2019 poll conducted by *The Economist*/YouGov found that 90 percent of black people surveyed believed that they faced "a great deal" or "a fair amount" of discrimination in the United States. While 44 percent of Republicans overall felt that was true about anti-black discrimination, only 33 percent of Trump voters did.[390] In other words, about two-thirds of Trump voters do not view racism against African Americans as a problem, despite vast evidence to the contrary.

An Ipsos poll conducted in August 2020, in the midst of widespread protests for racial justice across the nation, found that a whopping 72 percent of whites believed "reverse racism" to be a problem, compared to blacks (49 percent), Hispanics (54 percent), and Asians (49 percent).[391] Overall, the poll found wide differences between white Americans and African Americans who answered yes on issues such as whether institutional racism exists (blacks 83 percent vs. whites 50 percent), whether reparations should be paid (blacks 80 percent vs. whites 21 percent), and whether the country needs to continue to create policies designed to achieve equal rights (blacks 89 percent vs. whites 51 percent).[392]

Today's Republican Party also demonstrates a disturbing affinity for authoritarian policies and anti-democratic views toward other Americans. A study in the *Proceedings of the National Academy of Sciences of the United States* by Larry Bartels found that a near majority or majority of self-identified Republicans and Republican-leaning independents agreed:

- "The traditional American way of life is disappearing so fast that we may have to use force to save it." (50.7 percent)
- "A time will come when patriotic Americans have to take the law into their own hands." (41.3 percent)
- "Strong leaders sometimes have to bend the rules in order to get things done." (47.3 percent)
- "It is hard to trust the results of elections when so many people will vote for anyone who offers a handout." (73.9 percent)[393]

Bartels, a political scientist at Vanderbilt University, found, "The strongest predictor by far of these antidemocratic attitudes is ethnic antagonism—especially concerns about the political power and claims on government resources of immigrants, African Americans, and Latinos. The strong tendency of ethnocentric Republicans to countenance violence and lawlessness, even prospectively and hypothetically, underlines the significance of ethnic conflict in contemporary US politics."[394]

In another study, researchers Bob Altemeyer and John Dean used a research tool called the "right-wing authoritarian scale" to measure authoritarian tendencies in a population. They polled 990 voters in autumn 2019 and concluded that "the stronger a person supported Trump, the higher he or she scored" on the scale of authoritarian tendencies.[395] Their conclusion on about half of Trump voters was brutal and frightening, declaring that they "are submissive, fearful, and longing for a mighty leader who will protect them from life's threats. They divide the world into friend and foe, with the latter greatly outnumbering the former."[396] Their research was published in their book, *Authoritarian Nightmare*. Ominously, they conclude that "even if Donald Trump disappeared tomorrow, the millions of people who made him president would be ready to make someone else similar president instead."[397] This insight is shared by Dr. Mary L. Trump, a psychologist, author, and niece of the former television game show host.[398] Dr. Trump calls for not overfocusing on Donald, but for recognizing the broader population and interests that he represents and attracts. As she pointedly writes, "Donald was incompetent, but others in Donald's administration were anything but. What they built was a lean and ruthless machine for advancing fascism. With the help of some luck, complicit institutions, an unprepared media, and a party of willing converts, that machine largely succeeded."[399]

When Altemeyer and Dean employed a racial resentment test, they concluded that "economic anxiety isn't driving racial resentment; rather, racial resentment is driving economic anxiety."[400] In other words, the perception of losing dominance in America's racial caste system engenders other white fears and motivations. Moreover, the greater the degree of racial resentment, the greater the support for the Republican Party. It can be inferred, therefore, that Republicans politically benefit from increasing racial antagonism in the United States.

According to a study by Samuel Sommers and Michael Norton, white fear of losing racial dominance in America is driven by the belief that any improvements for black Americans "are likely to come at a direct cost to whites. Black respondents in our surveys, meanwhile, report believing that outcomes for blacks can improve without affecting outcomes for white Americans."[401]

> Indeed, research points to people's pervasive fear that they will end up on the bottom of the status pile—a fear called "last place aversion." That may further increase opposition to the gains of other groups: If "they" are moving up in the world, "we" must be moving down. Such fears might be particularly pronounced for a group, like white Americans, that has always been at the top of the racial hierarchy and therefore has the furthest to fall.[402]

While the presidential runs of Republican racial populists George Wallace (1964 and 1968) and Pat Buchanan (1992, 1996, and 2000) failed, in 2016 Republicans succeeded in clinching a surprising victory in the electoral college for their racist presidential candidate. This included winning votes from whites who had previously voted for Obama. Republicans, however, failed to pull it off twice. Thanks, in part, to the power of the racial justice movement that swept the nation after the police killing of George Floyd, a diverse tapestry of Americans overwhelmingly voted Republicans out of the White House in 2020. Following their humiliating loss, however, much of the Republican Party, led by their lame duck leader, launched a multipronged effort to overthrow the national elections and illegally seize power. One prong involved inciting mob violence.

INSURRECTION

> "Statistically impossible to have lost the 2020 Election. Big protest in D.C. on January 6th. Be there, will be wild!"
> —President Donald Trump tweet, December 19, 2020, 1:42 p.m.

After months of relentlessly disinforming the public that the Democrats were guilty of rigging the 2020 election, Trump directed the American people to go to Washington, D.C., to "stop the steal." On January 6, 2021, tens of thousands of deceived Americans heeded the president's call. Angry throngs—including members of white nationalist militias—attacked police and smashed their way into the building looking for their enemies: Mike Pence, Nancy Pelosi, Alexandria Ocasio-Cortez, Maxine Waters, Jim Clyburn, and other lawmakers who were poised to certify that Joe Biden was, in fact, the nation's new, fairly elected president and commander in chief.[403] In some instances, marauders came close to actually finding the government officials they were hunting. As the mob that chanted "Hang Mike Pence" came within one minute of reaching them, Vice President Pence, his wife, daughter, and members of his staff hid in a parking garage in the building's basement.[404] While Vice President Pence hid, at 2:24 p.m. Trump incited the mob's ire by tweeting: "Mike Pence didn't have the courage to do what should have been done to protect our Country and our Constitution, giving States a chance to certify a corrected set of facts, not the fraudulent or inaccurate ones which they were asked to previously certify. USA demands the truth!"[405]

Some of the attackers were armed with zip-tie flex cuffs for the purpose of taking prisoners. Others, like Garret Miller, who has since been arrested for threatening to assassinate Ocasio-Cortez, carried rope.[406] Guy Wesley Reffitt, who was convicted on March 8, 2022, of multiple crimes relating to January 6, was armed with an illegal pistol during the attack.[407] Outside the Capitol building, a gallows with a noose was erected.

During the assault, at least 150 police officers were seriously injured, and five police officers subsequently died, one from a stroke and four from suicide. At least seven other individuals who were present died, either on January 6 or soon thereafter, and hundreds of workers were traumatized by the mob.[408] Three of the deaths were a result of medical emergencies. Ashli Babbitt, a QAnon follower, was shot by Capitol police while climbing through a smashed window inside the building as she tried to reach the dozens of House members and staffers who were trapped within.[409]

More than a dozen white supremacist organizations and far-right militias were involved in mobilizing for the day, including the Oath Keepers, Proud Boys, Three Percenters, Boogaloos, 1st Amendment Praetorian, and NSC-131 (the Nationalist Socialist Club).[410] Preparing for violence was part of the groups' planning. In December 2021, Washington, D.C., attorney general Karl Racine filed a federal lawsuit against both the Proud Boys and the Oath Keepers over their role in the attacks. The eighty-four-page civil complaint describes how dozens of members of the groups violated local and federal laws, including a statute stemming from the 1871 Ku Klux Klan Act, which targets violent conspiracies.

In early January 2022, Stewart Rhodes, the leader of the Oath Keepers, was arrested. He and ten other members of the group were charged with seditious conspiracy.[411] The indictment against them describes how they recruited participants, organized trainings in paramilitary combat, coordinated travel teams and logistics, and brought weapons to Washington, D.C., on January 6 in an attempt to keep Trump in office.[412] The indictment asserts that members of the Oath Keepers under Rhodes's command breached the Capitol in military-style formation and went in search of Speaker Nancy Pelosi.[413] Other Oath Keepers were stationed in nearby hotels as an armed "quick reaction force," ready to rush into action if so instructed.[414]

Racist symbols were seen everywhere throughout the siege.[415] A large Confederate battle flag was paraded throughout the breached Capitol Rotunda—something that has never happened previously in the nation's history. Many involved in the assault were seen carrying smaller versions of the flag or wore Confederate patches. Anti-Semitism was also on open display. One person was photographed wearing a sweatshirt printed with the slogans "Camp Auschwitz" and "Work Brings Freedom," a reference to the German words *arbeit macht frei* appearing over the entrance to the infamous Nazi death camp. *Washington Post* staff observed that the nooses seen on January 6 echoed a fictional insurrection described in the 1978 novel *The Turner Diaries*, written by William Luther Pierce, a white supremacist. In it, white terrorists lynch individuals they consider "race traitors"—politicians, journalists, and people in interracial relationships—on a day of executions known as the "day of the rope."[416] Flags associated with the white nationalist website VDARE, which gets its name from Virginia Dare, supposedly the first white child born in the New World, were also on display on January 6.

While the vice president's entourage and other government officials hid, their protectors came under attack. In their testimony before Congress and to the media, black police officers reported being called racial slurs by the angry mob. Capitol police officer Harry Dunn recalled that when he calmly told some in the crowd, "Well, I voted for Joe Biden. Does my vote not count? Am I nobody?," one woman wearing a MAGA shirt responded, "You hear that guys? This nigger voted for Joe Biden." Others in the crowd began to chant, "Boo! Fucking nigger."[417] Dunn stated that he talked to other officers who had similar experiences that day, one noting he had been told, "Put your gun down, and we'll show you what kind of nigger you really are." Another veteran black officer told *Buzzfeed* that "I got called a nigger 15 times today."[418]

HOLDING REPUBLICANS RESPONSIBLE

While it is easy—and justified—to blame Trump for attacking the 2020 election results, he was far from alone. According to reporting by Alan Feuer in the *New York Times*, as of early 2022, the government estimated that "as many as 2,500 people who took part in the events of Jan. 6 could be charged with federal crimes."[419] Among the first scheduled to stand trial was Robert Gieswein of Colorado, "a self-proclaimed militiaman charged with assaulting officers with a chemical spray. In court papers, the government has indicated that it intends to show the jury videos of Mr. Gieswein's assaults and to offer evidence that he told a reporter he was at the Capitol on Jan. 6 'to execute these fascists.'"[420]

There were "thousands of posts—with tens of thousands of comments—detailing plans to travel to Washington and engage in violence against the U.S. Capitol," said Daniel Jones, a former FBI analyst and longtime Senate investigator.[421] According to Insurrection Index, a searchable database of records on individuals and organizations in positions of public trust, as of March 2022, there were 1,098 such people and 398 organizations identified as accomplices in the attempt to overturn the 2020 election result, either by participating in 6 January or by helping to spread disinformation about voter fraud.[422] The index is a project of Public Wise, a voting rights group. Among those identified by the index were "213 incumbents in elected office and 29 who are running as candidates for positions of power in upcoming elections. There are also 59 military veterans, 31 current or former law enforcement officials, and seven who sit on local school boards."[423]

Not all the perpetrators fit stereotypes of those one might expect to find in a violent white lynch mob. For example, a study led by Robert Pape, the director of the Chicago Project on Security and Threats at the University of Chicago, examined the demographics of 716 people charged or arrested for crimes related to the January 6 assault. Of the 501 arrested or charged for which there is employment data, "more than half are business owners, including CEOs, or from white-collar occupations, including doctors, lawyers, architects, and accountants." Moreover, "only 7 percent were unemployed at the time, almost the national average, compared with the usual 25 percent or more of violent right-wing perpetrators arrested by the FBI and other U.S. law enforcement from 2015 to mid-2020."[424] Furthermore, when researchers examined the counties where the 716 live, the key characteristic uniting them is that they come from counties where the white share of the population is declining fastest relative to people of color. This further confirms that replacement anxiety is not only driving white Americans to the right, but also driving some of them to commit acts of violence and sedition.

JUSTICE AND DEMOCRACY IN THE POST–JAN. 6 ERA

One year after the attacks of January 6, 2021, none of the high-level organizers—including Trump, plotters in his inner circle, funders, and likely even some Republican members of Congress who may have facilitated the insurrection—had been arrested, charged, or held accountable in any way. This glaring fact has not been lost on judges hearing cases of foot soldiers who acted on the Republicans' disinformation about rigged elections and followed their instructions to "be there" to "stop the steal." "Judge Amit P. Mehta told John Lolos, a defendant clearly disoriented by election fraud conspiracies, that not only had he been lied to, but those who had done the lying were not 'paying the consequences.' . . . 'Those who orchestrated Jan. 6 have in no meaningful sense been held accountable.'" The judge continued, "In a sense, Mr. Lolos, I think you are a pawn."[425]

While a mob of pawns attacked police outside the Capitol, a political assault was occurring within Congress as MAGA senators and representatives objected to the Arizona election results in an unprecedented effort to stop the legally required certification of state votes. This forced the joint session to end and the two chambers to meet separately to debate the issue. Given the majority held by the Democrats in the House, and with most Senate Republicans on the record to follow precedent and vote to accept the results, there was no legitimate reason to raise objections other than to show fealty to Trump. It was during this interregnum, shortly after 2:00 p.m., that the mob stormed into the Capitol. Order was restored after five hours, and the separate chambers met again to address the Arizona results. Despite having just survived a violent attack on their branch of government, dozens of Republicans continued to engage in voter nullification. On the Senate side, six Republicans voted to reject the Arizona results while 121 did so on the House side.

At the time of this writing, investigations are under way, and will likely continue for an extended period of time, perhaps years. Every day, the body of evidence grows demonstrating seditious conspiracy at the highest levels, including submitting fake electoral slate documents, plots to seize voting machines, and pressuring states where Republicans lost to overturn results.[426] With the exception of a few outliers such as Congressmembers Liz Cheney (R-AZ) and Adam Kinzinger (R-IL), the current Republican political machine appears willing to do everything in its power to prevent those responsible for the failed coup from being held accountable—and also determined to make white Americans "comfortable" again through educational gag orders, anti-protest laws, voter suppression tactics, and MAGA politics that reinforce an apartheid system that is racist to its core.

In the same way that Harriet Tubman fought to free as many people as possible *and* abolish the system of slavery, we must bring all responsible for January 6 to justice *and* dismantle the structures of white supremacy and political impunity upon which such assaults depend. To do otherwise would be to allow the racial hierarchy, authoritarianism, and political violence of a Jacksonian past to keep a white knee on our future.

EIGHT

FROM 1619 TO COVID-19, RACISM IS A PRE-EXISTING CONDITION

"The old African-American aphorism 'When white America catches a cold, black America gets pneumonia' has a new, morbid twist: when white America catches the novel coronavirus, black Americans die."

—Keeanga-Yamahtta Taylor

"[I]t took a plague to make some of the people realize that things could change."

—Octavia Butler

"Of all the forms of inequality, injustice in health is the most shocking and the most inhuman because it often results in physical death."

—Martin Luther King Jr.

"As far as I'm concerned, this period has been the most interesting era. . . . the coming together of the pandemic and recognition regarding structural racism, especially with respect to Black and indigenous people. And the lynching of George Floyd, precisely because of that conjunction, compelled people to recognize the structural and systemic character of racism in the police department, in prisons, in the university, in health institutions."

—Angela Y. Davis, interview with *The Student Life* newspaper, October 2021

HARRIET TUBMAN suffered from debilitating headaches all her life. She would sometimes fall into a daze in mid-sentence. She would wake after a while and continue what she was doing or saying. Physicians suspect she had temporal lobe epilepsy, an illness that generates spontaneous sleeping spells, seizures, and hallucinations.[427] Whatever the specific condition may have been, the source of it was not a mystery. When Tubman was a teenager, she was hired out by her owner, Edward Brodess, to work on someone else's plantation in town. While she was at a store with the plantation cook, an overseer from another farm confronted a black man suspected of having escaped his enslaver. The overseer demanded that Tubman help capture the young man, and being who she was, she refused. As the young man attempted to run away, the overseer grabbed a weight of some sort and threw it at the fleeing man. Instead of hitting him, the heavy object struck Tubman, splitting her skull and knocking her unconscious.

Tubman would later say, "That was the last thing I knew."[428] She was in and out of consciousness for three days, and lost a profuse amount of blood. Though injured, she was sent back to work in the field "with blood and sweat rolling down my face till I couldn't see."[429] Since she was now "damaged," she was sent back to Brodess. After seeing how seriously she was hurt, rather than having her rest or seeking treatment for her, he attempted to sell her to his neighbors, but found no buyers. Tubman stated, "They said they wouldn't give sixpence for me."[430] The health aftereffects of the incident challenged Tubman the rest of her life, underscoring how remarkable her daring missions to free enslaved people truly were.

The medical condition of enslaved people only mattered to plantation owners to the degree that it threatened their bottom line. White slavers treated the black folk they owned much the way they did their livestock. For generations, slaveholders not only denied black people access to proper health care and medical remedies, but subjected them to inhumane medical experiments. This little-known history is documented in Harriet Washington's award-winning *Medical*

Apartheid: The Dark History of Medical Experimentation on Black Americans from Colonial Times to the Present. "Physicians had every motive to skew narratives against their black subjects," Washington argues, "not because they were especially racist or unfair (although many were) but because the culture of American medicine has mirrored the larger culture that encompassed enslavement, segregation, and less dramatic forms of inequity."[431]

Among the most notorious cases of such medical apartheid involved syphilis experiments conducted on black men—without their knowledge or consent—right up to the 1970s.[432] In 1932, for example, a barbaric forty-year experiment began when the U.S. Public Health Service (PHS) started its "Study of Syphilis in Untreated Negro Male," more popularly known as the "Tuskegee Experiment" because it took place in and near Tuskegee, Alabama. (Neither the city of Tuskegee nor Tuskegee College had a role in the project.) In an area where the median income was a dollar a day, impoverished African American men were promised free medical care to treat syphilis. Instead, for four decades, the white doctors who ran the study held back treatment, even after penicillin was developed in 1947, in order to study the progress of the disease in more than six hundred black men. The enterprise was exposed and shut down in 1972 after twenty-seven-year-old Peter Buxtun, an ethical PHS employee, became aware of what was happening and leaked the story to the press. News of the experiment spread in the black community, though often with the misunderstanding that the white doctors injected their black patients with syphilis. A successful lawsuit in 1974 won more than $10 million for survivors, a pittance in the face of the destructive nature of the crimes perpetrated against the black men, their families, and their communities. Descendants of many of the victims formed the nonprofit Voices of Our Fathers Legacy Foundation, and in 2021 became involved in the effort to persuade hesitant African Americans to take the COVID vaccine.[433]

Systemic racism in the U.S. medical field today can be traced back to the antebellum era. Oliver T. Brooks, president of the

National Medical Association representing more than 50,000 black physicians, calls the generations of "discrimination, unequal treatment, and injustices in healthcare, criminal justice, and employment" the "Slave Health Deficit."[434] The ongoing legacy of this deficit continues to menace America in the COVID-19 era. While people in the United States continue to be denied equal access to the high-quality health care granted in other developed countries, it is America's communities of color that bear the most deleterious impacts of the current system.

Tubman recognized the need to intervene and be proactive in helping elderly and ill African Americans. In 1903, she transferred title from a twenty-five-acre property that she owned in Auburn, New York, to the AME Zion Church with the stipulation that it would be turned into a place for older and infirm African Americans. It would take five more years of fundraising, planning, and hard work, but on June 23, 1908, her long-sought goal was realized: the Harriet Tubman Home for Aged and Infirm Negroes was christened, with her as the guest of honor. In addition, a parade, presentations, a dinner reception, and a dance were held. One of the main buildings was named after John Brown, Tubman's friend who had attempted to spark a regional slave revolt to end slavery in 1859. When her own health deteriorated due to old age and the persistent effects of a brutal life under slavery, she ended her days in the senior home that she created, passing away there surrounded by family and friends on March 10, 1913.[435]

Five years later, the deadly 1918–1919 flu pandemic swept the United States and the world. More than 50 million people died globally, including over 675,000 in the United States.[436] Musicians responded to the crisis. At least four jazz or blues songs were written about the virus: "The Influenza Blues" by Happy Klark and Arthur C. Brown (1919); "The Influenza Blues" by Walter A. Mooney (1919); "Influenza Blues" by Malvin M. Franklin and Robert B. Smith (1919); and "1919 Influenza Blues" (undated).[437] The "1919 Influenza Blues," of unknown origin, circulated in the 1930s and captured the horrific nature of the virus. In a version recorded by Essie Jenkins, she sings about the cross-class impact:

> It was nineteen hundred and nineteen;
> Men and women were dying,
> With the stuff that the doctor called the flu.
> People were dying everywhere,
> Death was creepin' all through the air,
> And the groans of the rich sure was sad.[438]

Similar to COVID-19, in its worst version, the 1918–19 flu was a painful and cruel way to die:

> Influenza is the kind of disease,
> Makes you weak down to your knees,
> Carries a fever everybody surely dreads,
> Packs a pain in every bone,
> In a few days, you are gone.
> To that hole in the ground called your grave.[439]

The pandemic was incorrectly labeled the "Spanish flu,"—much like Republicans' xenophobic reference to the COVID-19 virus as the "China flu"—smearing and stigmatizing a whole nation and its people.[440] Notably, the flu pandemic occurred in the segregation era, and that, along with black Northern migration, qualitatively shaped the way African Americans were impacted by the virus. Even prior to the outbreak, racist tropes regarding the health of African Americans dominated reporting on the black community, especially regarding recent migrants from the South. A March 5, 1917, *Chicago Daily Tribune* headline read, "Rush of Negroes to City Starts Health Inquiry." The wording clearly implies that the mere presence of African Americans generated a health crisis. A few months later, the paper ran another inflammatory headline: "Half a Million Darkies from Dixie Swarm to the North to Better Themselves," employing both a white supremacist slur and a narrative that black people arriving from the South represented a "swarm," i.e., a dangerous invasion.[441] At the same time, segregated hospitals and bigoted white physicians often denied service to black families, and refused to employ black medical professionals. Other regions echoed these sentiments about African Americans. In Pennsylvania, during the worst of the pandemic, the Philadelphia Hospital for the Insane advertised for four assistant physicians. The first qualification was that applicants "must be white."[442]

The medical racism of the era did not go unchallenged. W. E. B. Du Bois took it on in his study, *The Health and Physique of the Negro American*, which he presented to the Eleventh Conference of the Study of the Negro Problem at Atlanta University on May 29, 1906. In it, Du Bois documents every element of health affecting African Americans, including physical measurements, psychological issues, the "black" brain, skin type and color, black mortality, and even disparities in health insurance. On the positive side, he detailed the important existence of black medical schools, including McHarry Medical School, Howard University Medical School, Shaw University's Leonard Medical School, New Orleans University's Flint Medical College, and Louisville National Medical College.[443] These institutions were critical in generating medical professionals and a system of health care that was an alternative to the Jim Crow health structure. Du Bois also documented the number of black physicians, dentists, and pharmacists in the nation.

It should be noted that some of the data employed by Du Bois, who was not a medical doctor, repeated the racist stereotypes of the white medical community. These included musings on the skull size, facial angles, and body length of people of color. This was somewhat ironic because part of what Du Bois was trying to do was refute the white supremacist theories of Frederick L. Hoffman and his book, *Race Traits and Tendencies of the American Negro*. Hoffman, a statistician at the Prudential Life Insurance Company, wrote, "It is not in the conditions of life, but in race and heredity that we find the explanation of the fact to be observed in all parts of the globe, in all times and among all peoples, namely, the superiority of one race over another, and of the Aryan race over all."[444] This was raw white supremacy passing itself off as objective science.

During the 1918–1919 flu pandemic, African Americans were forced to use segregated hospitals that became overwhelmed as cases grew. In addition, they were forced into unhealthy quarantine situations in crowded, often unsanitary areas. Little attention was paid by government agencies to the real needs of the black community. One hundred years later, similar trends emerged during the COVID-19 pandemic.

RACIAL INJUSTICE AND THE COVID PANDEMIC

In the face of the most dangerous global public health crisis in a century, the U.S. for-profit health system all but guaranteed that the official response would be uneven, its defects visited disproportionately on working-class people and communities of color. According to the U.S. Centers for Disease Control and Prevention (CDC), when the pandemic hit, 31.2 million Americans under the age of sixty-five were uninsured.[445] Tens of millions more were underinsured.[446] As a result, many relied on emergency rooms and commercial urgent care centers for critical medical treatment after hesitating to seek help earlier due to the expense of medical bills.

The first official case of COVID-19 in the U.S. occurred in January 2020 in Snohomish County, Washington.[447] President Trump was dismissive and repeatedly stated that the virus would just vanish. On January 22, 2020, he stated, "We have it under control. It's going to be just fine."[448] A month later, on February 26, Trump said that cases were "going to be down to close to zero."[449] The extremely stable genius was wrong. According to the CDC, on February 1, 2020, there was one case in the United States and zero deaths.[450] On March 1, those numbers grew to 88 and two. On March 12, Trump said, "It's going to go away."[451] Then the sledgehammer began to come down: by April 1, there had been 241,007 cases and 6,080 deaths. By May 1, the number mushroomed to 1,122,851cases and 67,264 lives lost, with new variants on the way. Trump was bringing untold suffering and death for countless American families who allowed themselves to be guided by his comments. Instead of going away, the crisis intensified. Six months into the pandemic, by August 1, there were more than 4.6 million cases and well over 160,000 deaths. Trump continued to downplay the lethal seriousness of COVID until he lost the election and was forced to leave the White House in January 2021. On Trump's watch, one in three Americans contracted COVID, and approximately 385,000 died.[452]

As reported by the CDC, 2022 began with the highest infection rate to date, but with a lower fatality rate than was seen at the pandemic's onset. On January 1, 2022, there were 267 deaths and 273,940 new cases. Two days later, the number of new cases mushroomed to 954,009. By May 25, 2022, the CDC's online data tracker reported that there had been a total of 83,408,645 cases and more than one million lives lost in the United States since the pandemic began.[453]

The CDC didn't need a crystal ball to see COVID coming. The agency had also anticipated the pandemic's impact on communities of color before it hit. In early December 2020, a CDC report marked for "agency use only" dated December 4, 2020 was leaked to the press. Titled "COVID-19 Science Update," the report states:

> Unfortunately, discrimination, which includes racism, exists in systems meant to protect well-being or health. Discrimination can lead to chronic and toxic stress and shapes social and economic factors that put some people from racial and ethnic minority groups at increased risk of COVID-19. There is increasing recognition that addressing the underlying inequities in social determinants of health is key to improving health and reducing health disparities.[454]

At every level—from health effects and employment to treatment of the incarcerated and policing—racial disparities defined not only the path of the virus, but the response by federal, state, and local officials. While African Americans constituted about 13 percent of the U.S. population in 2020, they were an estimated 23 percent of those who died from the virus according to the COVID Racial

Data Tracker.[455] By August 1, 2020, this meant that close to 800,000 African Americans had contracted the virus, with more than 35,000 black lives lost. Black Americans were dying at a rate 2.5 times that of white Americans.[456]

In state after state, the rate of death for black people—especially compared to other racial groups—was exceedingly high. According to the APM Research Lab Staff, at the end of November 2020, the rate was 111 per 100,000 for African Americans compared to 80 for American Indians, 60 for Pacific Islanders, and 75 for Latinx people.[457] The rate for white Americans was 53 deaths per 100,000. However, the toll was much greater in individual cities and states. In Chicago, where African Americans were 32 percent of the population, they comprised 67 percent of the deaths. In Louisiana, blacks comprised 32 percent of the population and 70 percent of the deaths, while in Michigan, blacks were 14 percent of the population and 41 percent of those who died. These disparate numbers would appear across the nation as one black community after the other was devastated by COVID-19. From large majority-black cities such as Detroit, New Orleans, and St. Louis to small black towns and communities nationwide, the lethal virus raged. The death rate was so high among African Americans that 31 percent of black adults knew someone who had died of the virus, compared to 9 percent for white adults and 17 percent for Latinx adults, according to a June 9–14, 2020, survey by the *Washington Post*.[458]

A report in *Health Affairs* found that pandemic mortality rates were higher for black people than they were for any other group.[459] In their July 2021 article, researchers Sarah Miller, Laura R. Wherry, and Bhashkar Mazumder found that while mortality for uninsured whites and uninsured Hispanics increased by roughly 20 percent, the figure shot to 65 percent for African Americans. It did not get much better for those who were insured. In that group, white mortality grew by about 5 percent, Hispanic by less than 20 percent, but for African Americans it was about 50 percent. In other words, in 2020, during the COVID pandemic it was better to be white and uninsured than African American and insured.

Even greater disparities were discovered when focusing on family income. Impoverished African Americans saw their mortality rate leap by almost 80 percent compared to Hispanics (20 percent), and whites (10 percent). For middle-class African Americans, the figure was about 40 percent, which was still significantly higher than for Hispanic and white groups (20 percent and 10 percent, respectively). Ditto for upper-income families, where the black mortality increase was about 45 percent—for some reason higher than that for the black middle-class category—compared to Latinx (less than 20 percent) and whites (less than 10 percent). Again, it was better to be impoverished and white than to be upper-income and black.

While COVID-19 disproportionately impacted African Americans early in the pandemic, other people of color would soon face daunting outbreaks of cases and deaths as the virus spread. Native American communities have been severely harmed by the virus. By early March 2020, in Arizona, they were 15 percent of those infected and 20 percent of those who died, yet were only 4 percent of the state's population. The rate of death was 234 per 100,000, while the rate for whites was 23 per 100,000, a tenfold difference.[460] In Mississippi, the death rate of Native Americans was 983 per 100,000 compared to whites' rate of 28 per 100,000. In New Mexico, it was 280 per 100,000 compared to 11 per 100,000.[461] A year later, in March 2021, the numbers remained disproportionate in the same three states: in Arizona the death rate was 483 per 100,000 for Native Americans while it rose to 201 per 100,000 for white Americans; in Mississippi the death rate decreased for Native Americans to 832 per 100,000 compared to 216 per 100,000 for white folks; and in New Mexico, the Native American death rate ballooned to 581 per 100,000 and to 142 per 100,000 for white people.[462]

The Navajo Nation was hit especially hard. With a population of less than 174,000, and more than 4,000 cases, at one point in mid-May 2020, the Navajo Nation had the highest infection rate in the United States, surpassing New York and New Jersey.[463] While New York had a staggering rate of 1,806 per 100,000, the Navajo

Nation superseded it at 2,304 cases per 100,000. The Navajo Nation government was forced to declare a state of emergency, issue a daily curfew from 8:00 p.m. to 5:00 a.m., and shut down all nonessential operations.[464] The pre-pandemic conditions facing Navajo people made it difficult to fight the spread of the virus. As recently as 2016, about one-third of tribal residents lacked clean water and 38 percent did not have water pumped into their homes.[465]

It was a similar tragedy for Latinx communities. In workplaces such as meatpacking plants and farms, Latinx workers were quickly overwhelmed with infections. Spikes in the South and West, with significant Latinx populations, increased through the summer of 2020. In California, Latinx communities were "39 percent of the state population, but 46 percent of all virus deaths and 57 percent of virus deaths reported in the last week of June."[466] In the South and the Midwest, disparate outbreaks occurred. In this early period of the virus, in North Carolina, Latinx communities were 9.3 percent of the population but 44 percent of the cases, while in Wisconsin, they were 9 percent and 37 percent respectively.[467]

Contrary to the general trend of COVID-19 deaths disproportionately affecting older people, young people of color comprised a significant number of those under sixty-five killed by the virus. In the first six months of 2020, the median age of young people of color who died was 31 compared to a median age of 44 for young whites. People in black, Latinx, Native American, and Asian American communities "accounted for 40.2% of deaths under 65, though they make up just 23 percent of those under 65 nationally," and black people alone accounted for 30 percent of that number.[468]

The disparities in infections, unfortunately, did not spare children of color. While there was very little peer-reviewed research on children with COVID-19, one fairly comprehensive August 2020 study on about 1,000 children in the Washington, D.C., area found that about 20 percent of children tested positive at one drive-through site. However, when disaggregated by race, about 30 percent of black children and 45 percent of Latinx children were positive, compared to 7 percent of white children. The median age of these children was 11, with children from lower-income families (40 percent) testing positive more often than those at the top end of the income scale (10 percent).[469] The emergence of the Omicron variant in late 2021 spelled even more danger for children. By the end of 2021, according to the CDC, hospital admissions for children reached a record high of 378 per day by the third week of December, reflecting a streak of tens of thousands of children being hospitalized that fall.[470] According to the American Academy of Pediatrics (AAP), as of January 6, 2022, a total of 8,471,003 cases of children with COVID-19 had been reported, and children represented 17.4 percent of all cases (8,471,003 out of 48,641,190). However, AAP reported that cases among children spiked dramatically in 2022 during the Omicron surge, with more than 4.8 million additional pediatric cases reported from the beginning of January 2022 to the beginning of March. For the week ending March 3, 2022, almost 69,000 additional child COVID-19 cases were reported. Throughout the pandemic, the majority of the children who tested positive were unvaccinated, although many were eligible.

In 2021, another racialized front in the COVID war opened with the release of vaccines that have greatly reduced the risk of death, hospitalization, and severe symptoms. However, what most would see as a miracle invention that would or could help the entire world recover from the deadly pandemic became another ideological battleground in which race would play a role. COVID accounted for 14 percent of all deaths in the United States from March 2020 until all adults became eligible for the vaccine in April 2021, compared with 11 percent of deaths from then to the end of December 2021.[471] Paradoxically, in the initial rollout of the vaccine, poor planning led to disproportionate access by affluent whites, at the same time that resistance emerged from disproportionately white anti-vaxxers. Although the vaccine was free, its early distribution required making online appointments or using other methods that were obstacles to many working-class and low-income people. In New York, Washington, D.C., and elsewhere, wealthy and middle-class whites traveled to black and brown areas of the city to receive vaccine shots while those who lived in the very same neighborhood were unable to get any.

On March 4, 2021, the *New York Times* reported that people in underserved neighborhoods were "tripped up by a confluence of obstacles, including registration phone lines and websites that can take hours to navigate, and lack of transportation or time off from jobs to get to appointments. But also, skepticism about the shots continues to be pronounced in Black and Latino communities, depressing sign-up rates."[472] Among other factors, reports indicate that black and Latinx people are less likely than whites to have internet access reliable enough to make online appointments; to have work schedules flexible enough to take any available opening; and to have access to transportation to vaccine sites.[473]

The kinks were largely smoothed out, and African American vaccination rates began to rise. This was primarily due to intentional mobilizing by health activists in the black community pushing back against the normalization of access disparity. By the beginning of November 2021, 48 percent of the eligible black population had been partly or fully vaccinated, compared to 55 percent of whites, 53 percent of Hispanics, and 71 percent of Asians.[474]

The dynamics of African Americans opposed to or reluctant about getting the vaccine was rooted in the racialized history of medical care in the United States, noted above, and rampant conspiracy theories that also have an extensive history. A dividing line of sorts emerged where many black Americans were "vaccine hesitant," as opposed to the "vaccine-never" position held by many MAGA Republicans. A full-court press was launched by black opinion leaders, activists, athletes, and entertainers who discussed the life-saving benefits of the vaccine, and reminded the community that the Tuskegee Experiment was about African American men *not* receiving medicine that would have helped to ease or eliminate their suffering. Given that history, it was understandable that there would be reluctance among African Americans to accept health care.

Although vaccines had been given for decades, opportunists on the right saw political benefits to fanning the embers of the anti-vax proponents. Virtually all the GOP and conservative media voices who promoted vaccine resistance, including the entire roster of Fox News personalities, had themselves received the shots, as had the president and the first lady. Nevertheless, they aggressively spread rumors and disingenuously tied the vaccination effort to narratives about violations of personal freedom. As *Vanity Fair* noted, 90 percent of Fox News employees were vaccinated by September 2021, but Fox News host Laura Ingraham claimed that promoting the vaccine was "anti-freedom."[475] A Media Matters for America study of Fox News found that "in the 254 days since Biden took office (from January 20 through September 30), Fox undermined the vaccination efforts at least once on 238 of the days (94%). The network's efforts to undermine inoculations increased as we got further into Biden's presidency; from January 20 through March 31, Fox undermined the vaccine effort at least once on 80% of the days (57 out of 71), but from April 1 through September 30, the network undermined the vaccine efforts at least once on 99% of the days (181 out of 183)."[476]

While few in the black community bought into those arguments, some high-profile black celebrities, such as rapper Nicki Minaj and NBA player Kyrie Irving, spread unfounded stories or refused to get the vaccine on spurious grounds. Minaj tweeted, "My cousin in Trinidad won't get the vaccine cuz his friend got it & became impotent. His testicles became swollen. His friend was weeks away from getting married, now the girl called off the wedding."[477] Beyond the general fact that there was no evidence the vaccine had the side effects that Minaj cited, an investigation by Trinidad and Tobago's health minister Terrence Dyalsingh found no truth in any of her assertions, nor could it find the "cousin's friend." In fact, Dyalsingh was incensed that his office "wasted so much time" dealing with the "false claim."[478]

Meanwhile, Kyrie Irving stated cryptically that his decision not to get vaccinated was "bigger than the game." This was likely a reference to his team, the New York Nets—and New York City policies—that would not let him play or practice without being vaccinated.[479] His "personal choice" decision received almost immediate support from multiple right-wing conservatives, including Donald Trump Jr., Fox News host Laura Ingraham, and one of the most politically extreme and misinformed members of Congress, Representative Marjorie Taylor Green (R-GA), who referred to the NBA as "fascist."[480] Twitter permanently suspended the Congresswoman's personal account for repeatedly violating its policy on COVID misinformation after she falsely tweeted about "extremely high amounts of COVID vaccine deaths."[481] According to January 2022 reporting in the *New York Times*, Twitter considered Green's statement a "fifth strike," which meant that her account will not be restored. "The company had issued her a fourth strike in August after she falsely posted that the vaccines were 'failing.' Ms. Greene was given a third strike less than a month before that when she had tweeted that COVID-19 was not dangerous and that vaccines should not be mandated."[482]

Although these and other conservatives had long records of racist attacks on professional athletes for their political views and support for Black Lives Matter—Ingraham infamously told community-engaged NBA star Lebron James to "shut up and dribble" when in an interview he called out Trump's profound ignorance as president—Kyrie Irving never refuted the right-wing support.[483] In late March 2022, New York City lifted the ban that had prohibited Irving and other athletes and performers from working.

Basketball legend Kareem Abdul Jabbar was not having any of it. He called out Irving for rejecting "the expertise of prominent immunologists without reason," and "contributing to vaccine hesitancy" in the black community."[484] In a deeply insightful article in *Jacobin*, Abdul Jabbar wrote, "His lack of regard for Black lives doesn't deserve acceptance, nor does his lack of regard for the health and welfare of the NBA community."[485]

Another high-profile NBA player, Bradley Beal, had also initially hesitated to get the shot, stating publicly he had questions about the efficacy of the vaccine since some who had been vaccinated had died. Yet when Senator Ted Cruz (R-TX) attempted to link him to right-wing anti-vaxxism, Beal didn't hesitate to furiously reject his support, stating, "I don't support you or anything you do. . . . Ted, you know damn well I ain't rockin' with you. You're not going to get no cool points if that's what you're in it for."[486]

At the same time, numerous black cultural figures spoke out during the crisis. For example, Canadian rapper Dax released "Coronavirus (State of Emergency)." Dax raps about how COVID harms your lungs, and speaks out against anti-Asian racism. "Forgetting that the problem stems from something we can't grasp / Before you yell 'conspiracy,' before you tweet at Donald like it's really gonna fix the situation / But you have no validity, before the stocks plummet, before every industry realizes that its workers who slave actually run it," he says. Dax ends his song emphasizing solidarity: "Before you go crazy, just know—we're all part of the remedy, we're on the same team, and corona is the enemy."[487] Video of Dax rapping the song has been viewed millions of times on YouTube.[488]

While the forty-fifth president of the United States was telling the country COVID was going to disappear, in March 2020, rap artist Cardi B uploaded a short video to Instagram. She pushed back against messaging from the White House: "Government! Let me tell y'all motherfuckers something. I know what the fuck this coronavirus is about. . . . I'm telling you, shit is real. Shit is getting real!"[489] Claire Stern wrote in *Elle*, "The rant was subsequently reposted and even remixed, reaching full viral status, but the words rang hauntingly true," adding "Cardi was right, and we should've listened."[490]

ECONOMIC IMPACT

In mid-March 2020, virtually overnight, the U.S. economy shut down. Although there was never a national lockdown, "non-essential" businesses, schools, parks, government offices, closed in nearly every state. Only essential businesses—liquor stores were classified essential, bookstores were not—remained open, and even then in a limited way. Many of those who were forced to stay home lost their jobs as businesses lacked income to pay their workers, and some businesses shuttered permanently. At the same time, essential workers became highly vulnerable to the virus as they faced more challenges in being able to physically distance or gain access to personal protective equipment. These workers were more exposed in their travel to and from work, and at their high-risk places of work, including hospitals, nursing homes, grocery stores, public transportation, and meatpacking factories, among many other sites that could not or did not close down. An analysis by the Hamilton Project found that African Americans (16 percent) and Latinx people (21 percent) accounted for more than a third of all essential workers, while white people comprised about 55 percent.[491]

A racial divide quickly emerged between those who were able to work safely at home, and those who had to choose between going to work and risking getting the virus, or losing their job. Using data from 2017–2018, the Economic Policy Institute estimated that while 29.9 percent of white people were able to telework, only 19.7 percent of black workers and 16.2 percent of Latinx workers could do so.[492] In addition, the lower the income, the less likely a person was able to work from home.

During the onset of the pandemic, unemployment skyrocketed for black and Latinx workers, reaching levels not seen since the Great Recession of 2008. African Americans' labor participation, for those sixteen or older, fell below 50 percent in spring 2020.[493] Latinx workers also saw significant declines over the period. Even when there was a slight drop in overall unemployment in May 2020, there was an actual increase for black and Asian workers.

Women of color suffered job loss more severely than did men. According to the Pew Research Center, while all men saw job declines (white, 9 percent; black, 13 percent; Asian, 17 percent; Hispanic, 15 percent), the drop for women across the board was higher (white, 13 percent; black, 17 percent; Asian, 19 percent; Hispanic, 21 percent).[494]

There was a significant decline in the number of small businesses as a result of the pandemic. The decline in white small businesses between February and April 2020 was 17 percent. For black businesses the number was 41 percent, the worst impact suffered by any racial group.[495] This was significantly higher than that of Latinx businesses (32 percent), Asian businesses (26 percent), and white businesses (17 percent).[496] According to *CBS News*, this meant that by mid-April 2020 approximately 400,000 black small businesses had permanently closed.[497] "Part of the struggle for Black businesses stems from their difficulty securing bank loans during the first wave of the pandemic," reported *CBS News* in February 2021, "while many report being left out of the Paycheck Protection Program (PPP), a federal lending initiative geared to smaller employers."[498]

In an effort to mitigate the economic crisis, Congress passed several laws to provide urgent assistance. On May 15, 2020, the U.S. House of Representatives, controlled by the Democrats, passed the $3 trillion Health and Economic Recovery Omnibus Emergency Solutions Act, or the HEROES Act. It included rental and mortgage assistance; aid to local, state, tribal, and territorial governments; funding for job training; $800 million for minority-owned lenders to help minority-owned businesses; and $1.7 billion for historically black colleges and universities and other institutions of higher education that serve communities of color.[499] The U.S. Senate, however, refused to pass the bill, as Republicans in charge of the chamber killed it. Earlier, on March 27, 2020, Congress had passed and the president signed the $2 trillion Coronavirus Aid, Relief, and Economic Security (CARES) Act to provide economic help to struggling businesses. This package gave assistance in four areas: to workers, with a one-time $1,200.00 maximum payment; to certain industries to maintain employees; to state, local, and tribal governments; and to small businesses through the CARES-created Paycheck Protection Program.

Although the need was greater, businesses owned by black and Latinx people received proportionately less aid under the PPP than did businesses owned by white people. The program granted millions in loans, including ones that did not need to be repaid if they were used to keep employees on the payroll. A study by Accountable. US found that the "10 congressional districts with the lowest black populations got over 64,000 more PPP loans than the 10 districts with the most black residents."[500] As reported in the *New York Times*, only 12 percent of black and Latinx applicants were able to get loans from the PPP, according to a survey by the Global Strategy Group on behalf of Color of Change and UnidosUS.[501] Another 26 percent "received only a fraction of what they requested." In response, "Rashad Robinson, the president of Color of Change, said the new survey showed that 'if we don't get policies to protect these communities, we will lose a generation of black and brown businesses, which will have deep impacts on our entire country's economy.'"[502]

The Center for Responsible Lending wrote that the PPP "has failed to fairly serve businesses owned by people of color, causing spill-over harms throughout communities of color, states, and regions." It went on to elaborate:

> The scarcity of funding relative to the demand strongly favored relatively well-connected, well-resourced businesses with existing commercial lending relationships with a bank or credit union. These entities were able to get their application accepted and processed quickly to claim their share while the funding lasted. This strongly disfavored business owners of color, who generally do not have these relationships and access. Moreover, the program incentivizes lenders to favor larger loans, which yield larger fees, and these require payrolls larger than those of the vast majority of businesses of color.[503]

While small black businesses struggled to receive PPP funding, a large list of very wealthy, very connected, very famous celebrities were raking it in. Among the multimillionaires and billionaires was MAGA-man Kanye West, who received $2 million to $5 million for his Yeezy clothing and sneaker company. Unlike other struggling black companies, Kanye didn't need the welfare, but took it anyway. At the time, Kanye claimed his company was worth $3 billion.[504] As what appears to be a big favor to Trump, Kanye launched his own presidential campaign in an effort to lure black votes away from Joe Biden. Roger Sollenberger, William Bredderman, and other journalists documented that GOP operatives with ties to Trump played a critical role in administrating, managing, and financing West's campaign.[505] Tallies from the Associated Press estimated that Kanye spent $9 million—approximately $150 per vote—to render 60,000 Americans' votes irrelevant in twelve states.[506] Jay-Z's Malibu Entertainment and Reese Witherspoon's Draper James clothing brand also received government assistance.[507] Country clubs and private jet companies were among the beneficiaries as well.

To add insult to the race-and-class bias of the program, at least ten organizations listed as hate groups by the Southern Poverty Law Center received funding. Those groups included the Center for Immigration Studies and the Federation for American Immigration Reform, both anti-immigrant organizations. Groups dedicated to thwarting LGBQT rights also received funding, including the Pacific Justice Institute, American Family Association, Liberty Counsel, and Concerned Women for America. The vehemently anti-Muslim Center for Security Policy also obtained PPP funds.[508]

IMPACT ON THE INCARCERATED

Virus outbreaks among the incarcerated and staff who work in those enclosed and often under-ventilated facilities have been severe. According to the U.S. Bureau of Prisons (BOP), in mid-August 2020, eight months after COVID was discovered in the United States, approximately 1,300 federal inmates and 571 staff members at 113 BOP facilities had tested positive for COVID-19. According to the Marshall Project, which was set up specifically to track the spread of COVID-19 among the incarcerated and those who work there, by mid-August 2020, in local and state jails and prisons, more than 95,000 inmates tested positive and hundreds of deaths were reported.[509] Social justice activists and progressive policy makers called for humane decarceration to save lives and relieve suffering. Specifically, they called for early or complete release for low-level, nonviolent offenders, pregnant women, seniors, and inmates with compromised immune systems. By July 2020, twenty-one states had released inmates at the state level, and twelve states had released inmates on the local level in an effort to mitigate the spread of COVID-19.[510]

Prior to the Omicron outbreak in late 2021, the data showed that the death rate from COVID-19 in prisons was more than double that of the general U.S. population, a staggering 200 deaths per 100,000 incarcerated people.[511] By October 2021, more than 2,800 people had died of COVID-19 in state and federal prisons across the country. Nearly 438,000 people had been infected, and thousands of additional cases were linked to individual county jails.[512] By late December 2021, the Marshall Project reported that Omicron had arrived and that many prisons and jails were not ready. "In the Philadelphia jail the number of COVID-19 cases has tripled in the last two months. In Chicago's lockup infections have increased 11-fold in the same period. And in New York city jails are struggling with a mushrooming 13-fold increase in less than a month. From local lockups in California to prisons in Wisconsin to jails in Pennsylvania, COVID-19 is once again surging behind bars, posing a renewed threat to a high-risk population with spotty access to health care and little ability to distance."[513]

By January 10, 2022, overall, there had been more than 460,911 cases among the incarcerated in prisons, resulting in at least 2,739 deaths of prisoners and more than 140,000 cases among prison staff, with at least 256 deaths, according to the COVID Prison Project.[514] After the development of the vaccine, by January 2022, more than 518,000 prisoners and 142,000 staff had received at least one dose.[515] One caveat is that the COVID Prison Project reported collecting complete data from only twenty-eight prison systems.

While neither the U.S. Bureau of Prisons nor the Marshall Project nor the COVID Prison Project stated how the data broke down by race, it seemed fairly logical that a large percentage of those impacted were black, brown, and Indigenous prisoners. In 2020, people of color constituted about 37 percent of the 2.2 million people in U.S. prisons and jails.[516] A significant number of prison staff are also people of color.

WHY COVID-19 HAD SUCH A DEVASTATING IMPACT ON AFRICAN AMERICANS

When it became clear that African Americans were contracting COVID and dying at much higher rates than others, a range of arguments emerged to explain why. The "comorbidities" analysis came to dominate. According to this approach to the data, African Americans became sicker and died at higher rates due to "pre-existing" health conditions or comorbidities such as high blood pressure, diabetes, asthma, and obesity. Health stats demonstrated that wide racial disparities do exist relative to these conditions. According to the *Journal of the American Heart Association*, African Americans are two times more likely than white people to develop hypertension by the time they turn fifty-five.[517] More than 40 percent of non-Hispanic African American men and women manage high blood pressure. For African Americans, high blood pressure also develops earlier in life and is usually more severe.[518] Similarly, diabetes, diagnosed and undiagnosed, is more prevalent among black Americans than among white Americans and most other racial and ethnic groups. The prevalence of diabetes for African Americans is 16.4 percent, compared to 14.7 percent for Latinx Americans, 14.9 percent for Asian Americans, and 11.9 percent for white folks.[519] The group with the most elevated level was Native Americans, with a rate of 33 percent.[520] These pre-existing conditions have fed racialized notions that African Americans themselves are at fault for their susceptibility to the worse effects of COVID-19. As Ibram X. Kendi writes, "Americans are blaming black people" for their medical conditions "but, crucially, they're not explaining why. Or they blame the choices made by black people, or poverty, or obesity—but not racism."[521]

In other words, what were the conditions in the first place that led to these disparities in health situations? Why have they been permitted to persist? What is being done to eliminate them? Not only were these questions not being asked regarding the roots of the pre-existing conditions in the black community, but queries as to why African Americans are so vulnerable to becoming infected were being ignored. Black voices in the medical and social justice community began to push back against racist explanations for black suffering.

Writing in the *New York Times*, Professor Sabrina Strings sees the ongoing legacies of white supremacy as the root of contemporary health disparities between people of color and white people. She writes, "The era of slavery was when white Americans determined that black Americans needed only the bare necessities, not enough to keep them optimally safe and healthy. It set in motion black people's diminished access to healthy foods, safe working conditions, medical treatment and a host of other social inequities that negatively impact health."[522] The legacies of white supremacy have not only caused health discrepancies, but continue to perpetuate narratives that blame African Americans themselves for poorer health. Professor Strings and other researchers, in fact, believe that the standard medical metric known as BMI, or Body Mass Index, was created based on white male body types. Despite this, the index is still used to determine whether nonwhite folks are in a healthy weight category. Professor Strings argues, "It is racist, and also sexist, to use mostly white men within your study population and then try to extrapolate that and create norms and expectations for women and people of color."[523] According to the Body Mass Index standards, African Americans adults have the highest proportion of "obesity," i.e., a BMI reading over 30. While that reading alone cannot determine the overall health of an individual, it feeds racialized and gendered narratives not only about individuals, but about whole groups of people.

RACISM AND TREATMENT OF AFRICAN AMERICANS IN THE U.S. HEALTHCARE SYSTEM

Despite generations of progress, structural racism in the medical system persists today. A study by the biotech data company Rubix Life Sciences, for example, found that African Americans with COVID-like symptoms, such as a persistent cough or fever, were not treated the same way as white patients with similar symptoms.[524] The company reviewed medical billing data across a number of states and concluded that in the early days of the pandemic "an African American with symptoms like cough and fever was less likely to be given one of the scarce coronavirus tests."[525]

This unjust treatment correlates with other studies showing that a disturbing number of white people, including those with medical training, continue to believe there are biological differences between African Americans and white Americans. In one study, published in the *Proceedings of the National Academy of Sciences of the United States of America* (PNAS), participants were asked to reply to a series of medical and health-related statements regarding the two groups. Among the statements posed, all false, the percent of white respondents saying yes were:

- Blacks' nerve endings are less sensitive than whites' (20 percent).
- Black people's blood coagulates more quickly than whites' (39 percent).
- Whites have larger brains than blacks (12 percent).
- Blacks' skin is thicker than whites' (58 percent).
- Blacks have stronger immune systems than whites (14 percent).[526]

A second study, also published in *PNAS*, focused on medical students and residents. It concluded that "many white medical students and residents hold beliefs about biological differences between blacks and whites, many of which are false and fantastical in nature, and that these false beliefs are related to racial bias in pain perception."[527] More stunning, the study found that the white medical students who held these erroneous racial assumptions "endorsed views such as that black patients felt less pain than whites" and that the white medical students "were less accurate with black patients with their treatment recommendations."[528]

Other research revealed similar bias. According to the website blackdoctor.org, African Americans "were 40% less likely to receive medication to ease acute pain" and "34% less likely to receive opioids for acute pain" compared to white Americans.[529] Latinx were 25 percent and 13 percent less likely, respectively, compared to whites.[530] These racist practices have clearly led to higher levels of preventable suffering among African Americans and Latinx people.

Republicans—Trump included—relentlessly sought to destroy the Affordable Care Act (ACA) for years. The ACA has been instrumental in providing healthcare insurance to tens of millions of people in the United States who were previously uninsured, including numerous African Americans.[531] All plans offered by the Affordable Care Act have covered a two-dose vaccination, a booster shot, and diagnostic testing, "even if you don't have symptoms, or don't know if you've been exposed to COVID-19. For example, if you want to make sure you're COVID-19 negative before visiting a family member, you pay nothing to get tested."[532]

This signature legislation of the Obama-Biden administration helped decrease the number of African Americans without health insurance from 18.9 percent to 11.8 percent from 2010 to June 2021.[533] Yet black people still have a significantly higher uninsured rate than do white people (7.5 percent) or Asian Americans (6.3 percent).[534] As of the first half of 2021, almost a quarter of the Latinx population did not have health insurance, up from a historical low of 19.3 percent in 2016.[535] Until states and cities began to provide free COVID-19 tests, few could afford to pay the steep cost of determining whether or not they had the virus. Due to lack of insurance and potentially overwhelming medical bills, many black families hesitated to go to the doctor when experiencing COVID-like symptoms. As a result, many waited until symptoms became severe, and then went to the emergency room. Treating the infection earlier would have likely saved lives.

In one challenge to racist medical practices, Michigan governor Gretchen Whitmer issued an executive order declaring "racism a public health crisis," echoing the views of most black medical professionals. On August 5, 2020, under Executive Order 2020-163, she created the Black Leadership Advisory Council, whose objectives were to "elevate Black voices" and "make health equity a major goal."[536] A few months earlier, in April 2020, she had established the Michigan Coronavirus Task Force on Racial Disparities, which was chaired by Michigan's lieutenant governor, Garlin Gilchrist. The sixteen-member council was tasked with reviewing state laws for their impact on racial inequality and making recommendations "to remedy structural inequities." More important, the task force was to be a vehicle for the state's black communities to have a seat at the table relative to policies that are of concern to them. African American communities in Michigan have been among the hardest hit by COVID-19 in the United States. As of December 2021, they comprised about 15 percent of confirmed cases and 20 percent of deaths where race was identified. African Americans made up about 14 percent of the state's population.[537] By early 2022, they had experienced more than 195,000 cases and over 5,300 deaths.[538]

Racial disparities would also ensue once the vaccines became available to prevent serious illness—and death—from the virus. Complaints were almost immediate that distribution of the vaccines was racially uneven. Black and Latinx communities struggled to get the same level of access as white communities. It is unclear how many hospitalizations and deaths could have been prevented. According to a *New York Times* analysis of state-reported race and ethnicity information published in early March 2021, two months after the first vaccine became available, "Communities of color, which have borne the brunt of the COVID-19 pandemic in the United States, have also received a smaller share of available vaccines. The vaccination rate for Black people in the United States is half that of white people, and the gap for Hispanic people is even larger."[539] "People of color are getting vaccinated at rates below their representation of the general population," said Dr. Marcella Nunez-Smith, the chair of President Biden's coronavirus equity task force. "This narrative can be changed. It must be changed," she said.[540] Until it changes, black, Latinx, and Indigenous families will continue to suffer and lose loved ones as a result of structural racism.

DISINFORMATION

A 2020 study by Brandi Collins-Dexter, a visiting fellow at Harvard Kennedy School's Shorenstein Center on Media, Politics and Public Policy, states, "The health misinformation surrounding COVID-19 poses an immediate threat to the health of Black people, and is a symptom of an information ecosystem poisoned by racial inequality." Collins-Dexter's research identified four initial falsehoods targeting the Black community:

- Black people could not die from COVID-19.
- The virus was man-made for the purposes of population control.
- The virus could be contained by taking herbal remedies.
- 5G radiation was the root cause of COVID-19.[541]

Such disinformation about the crisis, coupled with historical awareness of the Tuskegee horrors, initially impacted black views about getting free injections developed under a president who was seen as antagonistic to their interests. To a degree, distrust about getting vaccinated was overcome when trusted sources—family members, friends, black scientists, black doctors, and faith leaders—vouched for the safety of the vaccine.

RACIALIZATION OF THE PANDEMIC

Republicans racialized the pandemic in numerous ways. First, Trump blamed China for the crisis and referred to the virus as the "Chinese flu" or, even more derogatory, the "Kung flu." Before the virus spread around the world, Trump initially praised China's handling of the virus on at least fifteen occasions, according to *Politico*. On January 24, 2020, Trump sent a tweet that said, "China has been working very hard to contain the Coronavirus. The United States greatly appreciates their efforts and transparency. It will all work out well. In particular, on behalf of the American People, I want to thank President Xi!"[542] On February 10, during a *Fox Business* interview, Trump said, "I think China is very, you know, professionally run in the sense that they have everything under control. I really believe they are going to have it under control fairly soon. You know in April, supposedly, it dies with the hotter weather. And that's a beautiful date to look forward to. But China, I can tell you, is working very hard."[543] Speaking at a February 29, 2020, press conference held by the newly created Coronavirus Task Force, Trump stated, "China seems to be making tremendous progress. Their numbers are way down. . . . I think our relationship with China is very good. We just did a big trade deal. We're starting on another trade deal with China—a very big one. And we've been working very closely. They've been talking to our people, we've been talking to their people, having to do with the virus."[544]

However, as the pandemic took hold in the U.S. and criticism of his mishandling of it grew, Trump shifted all blame to China. "The world is now suffering as a result of the malfeasance of the Chinese government," he said, and "countless lives have been taken, and profound economic hardship has been inflicted all around the globe."[545] In one infamous incident, *Washington Post* photographer Jabin Botsford captured a picture of Trump's notes for a March 19 Coronavirus Task Force press conference. The printed phrase "corona virus" had been changed. "Corona" had been crossed out and replaced in Trump's unmistakable black-marker writing with the word "Chinese."[546] Bashing China quickly became a repetitive feature of Trump's public messaging about the pandemic.

At the same time that Trump was verbally attacking China for COVID-19, there was a surge in physical attacks against Asians in the United States. These attacks harked back to the 1882 Chinese Exclusion Act that banned Chinese labor immigration for ten years and ruled that all Chinese immigrants were ineligible for naturalization. In that era, fears about job competition and narratives of drug-induced crime and depravity dominated U.S. views of Chinese people. Public campaigns against heroin and marijuana at the turn of the 20th century and in the 1930s, respectively, also fed fear and excoriation of Asians.

During World War II, the U.S. government notoriously rounded up and interned thousands of individuals of Japanese ancestry, including U.S. citizens. Racist war fervor by white Americans supported the measures. Similar to the original U.S. Constitution that did not explicitly use the words "slave" or "slavery," President Franklin D. Roosevelt's infamous February 19, 1942, Executive Order 9066 authorizing the process did not include the word "Japanese," but it was clearly understood who was being targeted. They would remain detained until mid-December 1944, when two Supreme Court decisions, *Korematsu v. United States* and *Ex parte Mitsuye Endo*, determined that their internment was illegal.[547]

In the 1970s, Japan was blamed for the downturn in the auto industry. In addition to an increase in vandalism of Japanese-produced cars such as Toyotas and Hondas, Asian individuals were physically and verbally assaulted. Among the most notorious cases was the murder of Vincent Chin in the Detroit area by two white men, Ronald Ebens, a supervisor at a Chrysler plant, and Michael Nitz, a laid-off Chrysler autoworker. On June 19, 1982, twenty-eight-year-old Chin had been at a strip club with some friends celebrating his upcoming wedding when a verbal altercation with Ebens and Nitz led to a brawl. Blows were exchanged with minor injuries. The situation escalated after racial slurs and charges of taking American jobs were hurled at Chin. At the time, increasing sales of Japanese cars, a downturn in the U.S. auto industry, and a 17 percent Detroit unemployment rate fed anti-Japanese sentiments.[548]

Chin was of Chinese heritage, although knowing that fact would likely not have mattered to Ebens and Nitz. Activist and writer Helen Zia, who was an unemployed autoworker in Detroit during that time, stated, "Anyone who looked Japanese in the early 1980s or any Asian American, we all felt like moving targets. . . . People who drove cars of Japanese models were shot at on the freeway."[549]

After the brawl in the strip club ended and the two groups went their separate ways, Ebens and Nitz spent up to a half hour in a vengeful search for Chin, and eventually found him at a McDonald's. While Nitz held him down, Ebens beat him savagely with a baseball bat. Chin died in a local hospital after spending four days in a coma.

Despite the brutal, egregious, and premeditated nature of the killing, Ebens and Nitz were allowed to negotiate the initial charges of second-degree murder, which carried substantial prison time, down to manslaughter, for which they were wrist-slapped with a $3,000 fine, $780 in court costs, and three years of probation. They did not spend a single day incarcerated for the brutal murder they committed.[550]

This history echoed loudly as COVID-19 spread and Republicans and right-wing media relentlessly disparaged China. By February 2020, human rights groups and civil rights organizations began to receive reports from around the United States of abuse and insults visited on Asian American and Pacific Island individuals. According to one report by Stop AAPI Hate, more than 1,700 racist incidents were reported against Asians in forty-five states over the period from March to May 2020, about 70 percent of them related to COVID-19.[551] In fact, there were so many instances that the database created ten distinct ways to categorize how the racist attacks were waged. These included "Verbal harassment," "Shunning," "Physical assault," "Coughed/spat on," "Workplace discrimination," "Online," "Barred from establishment," "Barred from transportation," "Vandalism," and "other." While about 40 percent of the victims were Chinese American or of Chinese descent, most were East Asian or descendants from other parts of Asia. There were also numerous racist attacks of online webinars, classes, and meetings of Asian Americans where hateful slogans and images were posted to the chat rooms.

On April 1, 2020, in Pittsburgh, an Asian woman was told by another shopper in a grocery store she "should be rounded up with the virus and shipped back to China." In San Leandro, California, on May 22, a woman posted fliers in her neighborhood that read, "In this place, no Asians allowed." Before his arrest in the Bronx, a man shouted, "Asians caused the virus!" and spat on an Asian woman on the subway on July 31. Video recorded on July 18, 2020, in Sacramento shows an assailant telling an Asian restaurant owner to "Go back to China, you COVID ass."[552]

Even Asian medical professionals were subject to racism and abuse. A patient in a Connecticut emergency room was comfortable with the on-duty doctor while his face was covered with protective gear. Once the patient heard the doctor's Asian name, however, he said, "Don't touch me" and requested another doctor.[553] The anti-Asian climate manufactured by the MAGA right helped fuel such incidents.

While Republicans were in charge of the U.S. Senate there was no possibility of strong congressional action to combat racism. On September 17, 2020, House Democrats passed Resolution 908, which was strong on language but lacked legislative authority to do anything. The Resolution condemned "all manifestations of expressions of racism, xenophobia, discrimination, anti-Asian sentiment, scapegoating, and ethnic or religious intolerance," and called for "all public officials to condemn and denounce any and all anti-Asian sentiment in any form" and "to hold the perpetrators of those crimes, incidents, or threats accountable and bring such perpetrators to justice."[554]

On January 26, 2021, during his first week in office, President Biden signed a memorandum that denounced racism targeting

Asian Americans and Pacific Islanders. The memorandum provides stronger guidance toward the Department of Justice to oversee and investigate cases of anti-AAPI violence and harassment, a posture that did not exist under Trump. In a sharp, unapologetic swipe at Republicans, the memo states, "The Federal Government must recognize that it has played a role in furthering these xenophobic sentiments through the actions of political leaders, including references to the COVID-19 pandemic by the geographic location of its origin."[555] Three months later, Congress passed the "COVID-19 Hate Crimes Act" which seeks to strengthen the ability of the Justice Department to address hate crimes related specifically to the pandemic. Asian American members of Congress, in particular Congresswoman Grace Meng (D-NY) and Senator Mazie Hirono (D-HI), drove the legislation.

The health consequences and economic impact of the constantly mutating coronavirus have been severe in the United States. With multiple variants of COVID still spreading at the time of this writing in April 2022, the United States continues to have the most cases overall, the most deaths, and the highest death rate. The nations that did best during the initial onset of the pandemic all had national healthcare systems. China, Japan, New Zealand, Cuba, and other nations that flattened the curve were able to do so because they had national health systems that were not driven by profit maximization. The Obama administration provided its successor with a plan for dealing with a pandemic, the sixty-nine-page "Playbook for Early Response to High-Consequence Emerging Infectious Disease Threats and Biological Incidents." Obama also conducted pandemic planning briefings with the transition team, but Trump threw it all out the window.[556] He never implemented a national strategy; his failed approach led to the preventable suffering of millions and the death of hundreds of thousands.

White supremacy and racial injustice have skewed medical practices just as they have skewed everything else. Despite decades of advocacy, disparities based on race, gender, and income persist.

While the Affordable Care Act has made a profound difference for many, people of color continue to suffer under a racialized system that refuses to operate in a fair and efficient manner. Epidemics and pandemics will continue, and without substantial change to the U.S. healthcare system, each future outbreak will only aggravate social cleavages. A single, national, tax-funded healthcare system that covers all U.S. citizens and residents with zero-to-minimum individual costs—sometimes referred to as "Medicare for all" or "single-payer"—is urgently needed.[557] But that is not enough.

The adverse pre-existing health conditions that exacerbate the potential harm of COVID-19 are by-products of a social system biased to favor white people and the wealthy. Establishing a genuinely just national healthcare regime means abolishing these biases. As the CDC itself says, "addressing the underlying inequities in social determinants of health is key to improving health and reducing health disparities." Doing so is also a necessary prerequisite for freeing ourselves from the injustices that continue to be imposed on us today. Achieving health justice won't happen by itself any more than the Combahee River Raid happened on its own. First, we need to imagine it can be done. Then we need to organize and make it happen together.

Images of George Floyd, Harriet Tubman, Frederick Douglass, and others were projected by Dustin Klein and Alex Criqui on the statue of Robert E. Lee in Richmond, Virginia, in solidarity with the Black Lives Matter protests of 2020. PHOTO BY ZACH FICHTER, "RECLAIMING THE MONUMENT," 2020.

NINE

WHEN PROTEST BECOMES A MOVEMENT: THE GEORGE FLOYD CATALYST

"You're going to kill me, man."
—George Floyd to former police officer Derek Chauvin

"What did you expect? I don't know why we're so surprised. When you put your foot on a man's neck and hold him down for three hundred years, and then you let him up, what's he going to do? He's going to knock your block off."
—Lyndon Johnson, on the uprisings that followed the killing of Martin Luther King Jr.

CENTRAL TO THE POWER of any nation state is the capacity to impose violence on a population. In the United States, where forces of white supremacy have sought to subjugate people of color since the nation's inception, such violence has assumed many forms. Being at the bottom of America's racial caste system has meant enduring repressive laws, exploitative conditions, an unjust carceral system, terrorism, and murder. For example, in the groundbreaking report "Lynching in America: Confronting the Legacy of Racial Terror," the nonprofit Equal Justice Initiative documents that there were more than four thousand terror lynchings—horrific acts of violence whose perpetrators were never held accountable—in the United States between 1877 and 1950.[558] The racial terrorism documented in the report includes hangings, burnings, shootings, and beatings. Simply breaking white-determined norms was often enough to trigger anti-black violence. For example, accusing a black male of insulting a white woman was a quick way to send him to a noose without slowing things down with a trial, as was the case for Emmett Till, a boy of fourteen. White terrorists also often struck black families if they moved too close to a white part of town. As Angela Y. Davis notes, for example, during her childhood, black folks called Birmingham "Bombingham" due to the frequency with which black families were firebombed by white terrorists. The neighborhood where Angela's family lived was called "Dynamite Hill" for exactly this reason.[559]

In the United States, black, brown, Indigenous, Latinx, and Asian communities have endured such violence for centuries. Yet from settler-colonial times through Harriet Tubman's era to the rise of Black Lives Matter (BLM), there have always been networks of organizing, solidarity, and resistance. They have always been there, and are there today. Those who look, find them. At key turns in U.S. history, these networks swell into national movements capable of making changes that previously seemed impossible. We have been living through such a turn.

A MODERN SOUTHERN LYNCHING: THE MURDER OF AHMAUD ARBERY

As Keeanga-Yamahtta Taylor notes, "Every movement needs a catalyst, an event that captures people's experiences and draws them out from their isolation into a collective force with the power to transform social conditions."[560] Mass resistance to the traumatizing murders of a black teenager and two black men—Trayvon Martin in Florida on February 26, 2012, Eric Garner in New York on July 17, 2014, and Michael Brown in Ferguson, Missouri, on August 9, 2014—catalyzed protests, uprisings, and organizing that gave rise to the Black Lives Matter movement that would sweep the nation after George Floyd was lynched.

While Floyd's killing drove millions into the streets on a daily basis for months, several other recent police murders had already brought America close to the boiling point. On Sunday, February 23,

2020, shortly after 1:00 p.m., Ahmaud Arbery, twenty-five, was jogging a short distance from his home in the mostly white suburb of Satilla Shores outside of Brunswick, Georgia. He often jogged with no problem. On that day, two white men, Gregory McMichael and his son Travis McMichael, begin to chase Arbery in their truck, falsely accusing him of burglarizing a property being built in the neighborhood. They would be joined by their neighbor William Bryan, also white, in his truck and with a phone camera, after he made a 911 call to report seeing a "Black guy running down the road."[561]

Although none of the three white men had witnessed Arbery break any laws, they were determined, they later claimed, to make a "citizen's arrest," legal at the time in Georgia, but repealed in early 2021. Georgia's "citizen's arrest" law was passed in 1863 in the middle of the Civil War, and was in play during the 589 known lynchings that occurred in Georgia in the decades between the Civil War and the 1960s.[562] The law was promoted and essentially written by Georgia attorney Thomas R. R. Cobb, a staunch pro-slavery advocate and Confederate States Army officer who also wrote several white supremacist treatises. In one he stated that an enslaved man's health is improved by his enslavement, and that he "has arrived at his greatest development while in slavery."[563] Cobb's citizen's arrest law was still in place in Georgia in February 2020, and Arbery's killers sought to use it to justify their murder and claim self-defense.

The men who hunted down Arbery were armed with a .357 Magnum and a shotgun. They tried to box him in and then hit him with their vehicle, and when that failed, they got out of their truck and attacked him physically. Arbery fought back, the only person on the scene who legitimately had the right to assert self-defense. During the struggle, Travis McMichael shot him to death with blasts to the chest and wrist. Bryan, the McMichaels' friend, filmed the entire atrocity. The video became another in a long series of filmed murders of unarmed black people.[564] Bryan later turned the film over to the police hoping that it would acquit him and the McMichaels. It did not, and, justly, would be the trio's undoing.

The three assailants' white supremacist views became clear as the investigation unfolded. According to a prosecutor, Travis McMichael called Arbery a "fucking nigger" as he lay dying on the ground.[565] Prosecutors also stated in court documents that they found texts on Bryan's cell phone that were "replete with racist remarks."[566]

Arbery's family and the black community were outraged that local authorities did not immediately arrest the McMichaels. Although the McMichaels killed Arbery in late February, they were not arrested until May 7. Bryan was arrested two weeks later on May 21. It turned out that George McMichael was a retired Glen County police officer with friends in high places. He had served as an officer from 1982 to 1989, and then as an investigator in the prosecutor's office. When the Glen County police first interviewed the McMichaels, they accepted their story of "self-defense" at face value and released them. When the police contacted Arbery's mother, Wanda Cooper-Jones, to tell her that her son had been killed, they told her that he had been involved in a house burglary and was killed by the home-owner, all of which was false. Ms. Cooper-Jones fought relentlessly to get justice for her son, and others as well. Her energy and commitment played a role in the passing of Georgia's first hate crime law, signed by Governor Brian Kemp on June 26, 2020.[567]

The local prosecutors' involvement was even more egregious. The Brunswick district attorney at the time, Jackie L. Johnson, was forced to recuse herself, given the fact that Gregory McMichael had previously worked in her office.[568] That did not stop her from first telling police officers not to arrest the McMichaels. No arrests were made in the case until about seventy days after the incident, when the video was leaked online by Alan Tucker, an attorney who had consulted with the suspects. After losing her re-election bid in September 2021, Johnson was indicted on multiple charges for her misconduct in the case, including violating her oath of office and obstructing the police investigation, as well as not treating the Arbery family "fairly and with dignity."[569]

Johnson referred the case to the Waycross district attorney, George E. Barnhill, who wrote a letter to the Glen County Police

Department on April 2, 2020, exonerating the killers. The letter contends that the three had "solid firsthand probable cause" to suspect Arbery was a burglar and that he initiated the fight, giving Travis McMichael the right to "use deadly force to protect himself" under Georgia's citizen's arrest law.

They were eventually charged with felony murder, malice murder, aggravated assault, false imprisonment, and criminal attempt to commit false imprisonment, among other charges. In April 2021, a federal grand jury also indicted the three men for violating a federal hate-crime law, bringing charges of "Interference with Rights," "Attempted Kidnapping," and "Use of a Firearm During a Crime of Violence."[570] Due to a carefully argued case by prosecutor Linda Dunikoski, all three were found guilty of murder on Thanksgiving Eve, November 24, 2021, after a three-week televised trial in Georgia.[571] Travis McMichael was found guilty of both felony murder and malice murder, as well as seven other charges. Both Gregory McMichael and Bryan were convicted on felony murder and other charges. Travis and Gregory McMichael were both sentenced to "life in prison without the possibility of parole," while Bryan received life with the possibility of parole after serving at least thirty years.[572]

HER NAME WAS SAID: BREONNA TAYLOR

On March 13, 2020—less than a month after Arbery's murder—a seven-member squad of Louisville police officers killed Breonna Taylor, a twenty-six-year-old emergency medical technician, in her apartment. Within three minutes of the police arriving at her apartment, Taylor, who could not possibly have known what was happening or who was at her door, was on her hallway floor dying of multiple bullet wounds. The police were pursuing drug-related charges against her ex-boyfriend, who was nowhere near the scene. Many of the painful details described below come from an investigation conducted by Richard A. Oppel Jr., Derrick Bryson Taylor, and Nicholas Bogel-Burroughs for the *New York Times*.[573]

Taylor and Kenneth Walker, her partner, both African American, were in bed around 12:40 a.m. when they heard what sounded like someone breaking into their apartment. The police were supposed to be using a "knock and announce" warrant. That turned into a "no knock" warrant used for suspects who are considered dangerous, which Taylor was not.

When Walker heard the noise at the door and saw the door being hit by an object, he grabbed his gun, which he owned legally. Forty-five long seconds had passed. As he and Taylor stood at the end of the hallway facing the front door, they repeatedly asked who was there, but received no verbal response from the police on the other side. Instead, they witnessed their apartment door being smashed from its hinges. In defense, Walker fired a shot at the unannounced intruders. A bullet struck Sergeant Jonathan Mattingly in the leg. In violation of police protocol and training, Officer Mattingly was at the scene in plainclothes.

In response, three of the white officers on the scene—Sergeant Mattingly, Detective Myles Cosgrove, and Detective Brett Hankison—began to fire blindly into Taylor's apartment and an adjacent apartment. Although their shots miraculously missed Walker, six police bullets struck Taylor in her abdomen, chest, arm, leg, and foot.

In total, the officers fired thirty-two bullets into eight different rooms in Taylor's apartment and two others. The officers, who were not in uniform and had arrived in unmarked cars, fired indiscriminately through closed doors, seemingly not caring whom they might hit. In Taylor's apartment, bullet holes were found in the living room, dining room, her bedroom, and her sister's bedroom. Bullets were found in her shower, cereal boxes, a wall clock, cell phones, shoes, and cleaning equipment. Two shots went through the ceiling and into the apartment above Taylor's, which was occupied by a man named Aaron Sarpee, his two-year-old daughter, and her babysitter. The twenty-two bullets that rained into Taylor's apartment and the one above, fired from the front door, came from Mattingly and Cosgrove. Cosgrove fired sixteen shots, emptying his gun.

After the shooting began, Hankison went around to the front patio and fired ten shots through drawn curtains. Five went into Taylor's sister's bedroom, two of which went through the wall into the apartment to the left of Taylor's. In that unit were a pregnant woman and a small child, who both survived without injuries. Hankison fired five more bullets into Taylor's bedroom. Walker and Taylor were both on the floor and were not struck by any of his shots.

The police operation violated the couple's rights in every possible way. None of the officers had their body cameras on, a violation of Louisville police policies. Rather than assist Ms. Taylor or check to see if anyone had been injured in the apartments, the police team called in SWAT. Eventually more than forty police vehicles arrived on the scene.

Taylor did not receive any medical attention for more than twenty minutes, although an ambulance was outside the apartment building working on Mattingly. At one point, the ambulance was sent away. After the shooting had stopped and the police were gathering outside, Walker called 911 and stated in distress, "Somebody kicked in the door and shot my girlfriend," indicating that he really did not know who was trying to get into the apartment. As Taylor lay dying, the traumatized Walker was arrested and jailed for two weeks. After charges against him were dropped, Mr. Walker filed a federal lawsuit against the Louisville Metro Police.[574]

Officer Hankison had previously served on the Lexington, Kentucky police force. His former supervising sergeant, Patrick McBride, penned a brutal note regarding Hankison after he resigned. He wrote, "Based on my observations and supervision of this officer for the past calendar year, I would not recommend him for reemployment at any time in the future. Due to his actions in violation of standing orders, refusal to accept supervision, and general poor attitude toward the Division of Police and its commanding staff, I would in fact be strongly against the same."[575] Yet Hankison was hired by the Louisville Police Department, issued a gun, and placed back on the streets.

The officers lied to the media, and on the official police report falsely stated that Taylor's injuries were "none" and that they had not broken into the apartment. Taylor's mother and other family members found out that police had killed Breonna from media reports. Months went by before the local authorities did anything around the case. Tens of thousands rallied to call for justice for Taylor after her family began to organize and speak out.[576] For more than six months, demonstrations demanding justice were held every day. Eventually, a grand jury was empaneled.

On September 23, 2020, Kentucky attorney general Daniel Cameron stated that the killing "was justified" and that the grand jury would bring no charges against any of the officers involved in Taylor's death. He stated that Hankison was being charged with "wanton endangerment," a felony, for shooting indiscriminately into the adjacent apartment and thus endangering those who lived there.[577]

Hankison's random shots into Taylor's apartment were also "justified" by a grand jury. Some members of the grand jury would later state that Cameron clearly presented a case that rationalized the shooting on behalf of the police. At the press conference, Cameron also did not address the fact that in 2018, five of the officers involved in the incident and on the scene, including Hankison and Cosgrove, had been involved in a similar attack on another innocent family.[578]

There was a discrepancy about whether the police announced who they were. Cameron accepted the police assertion that they did. He did not note that while one person the police spoke to claimed to have heard the police announce themselves, there were a dozen or so other neighbors on site who did not, as discovered by the *New York Times* and at least one other investigative report. In addition, the one witness cited by the police, Sarpee, in the apartment above Taylor's, did not state that he heard the supposed announcement until his third interview, months later.[579]

Attorney General Cameron also failed to mention that the police and prosecutors had sought to pressure Taylor's ex-boyfriend, Jamarcus Glover, to implicate Taylor in some kind of drug crime, and that he refused to do so. Glover was actually the subject of the search warrants the night the police killed Taylor. He had been arrested and was in custody before the police got to Taylor's apartment. Louisville prosecutors, as reported by the *Washington Post*, offered Glover a devil's bargain where he "could turn a possible 10-year prison sentence into a probation" if he stated that Taylor was part of his "crime syndicate," disregarding the fact there was no evidence to support that theory.[580] He turned them down. It must be noted that no illegal substances were found in Taylor's apartment.

Cameron—the first African American to serve as attorney general in Kentucky—continued to endorse Trump's re-election as "the best for this country" during the summer of 2020, and gave a full-throated endorsement of Trump at the Republican National Convention. Trump had supported Cameron's run for attorney general in 2017, and had even listed him as a potential Supreme Court nominee. Cameron was also a protégé of Senator Mitch McConnell (R-KY) and at one point had served as his counsel. Given that he had argued "self-defense" before a grand jury, Cameron's bias towards the police was expected.[581]

Despite Cameron's manipulations, the Taylor family was awarded $12 million in a wrongful death settlement for Breonna's murder, and the city committed to making some reforms within the Louisville Police Department.[582] The payment conflicts with the idea that the officers acted properly. No officer was charged in Taylor's killing. Hankison and Cosgrove were fired by the department, and Mattingly wrote a disingenuous book, *12 Seconds in the Dark: A Police Officer's Firsthand Account of the Breonna Taylor Raid*, in which he blames everyone but himself for Taylor's murder.[583] As discussed below, in June 2020, Louisville passed "Breonna's Law," which finally bans no-knock warrants.[584]

TWENTY DOLLARS AND MURDER

Watching that man die slow left a hole
He cried for his mama as the murder unfold
If it wasn't for those phones, Chauvin would be at home
Feeling justified because of George's skin tone
I'm telling those with melanin, you're not alone.

—L. L. Cool J, untitled

George Floyd was a double victim of the COVID-19 pandemic, like millions of other workers around the nation. When Minnesota governor Tim Walz (D–Farmer-Labor Party) issued a stay-at-home order and shut down the state on March 25, 2020, Floyd lost his job as a bouncer at the nightclub El Nuevo Rodeo.[585] Floyd, a forty-six-year-old black man, had already survived a case of COVID-19. He had every reason to feel good about that. A twenty-dollar bill would change everything.

Shortly before 8:00 p.m. on May 25, 2020, Floyd left the Cup Foods grocery store in Minneapolis after purchasing cigarettes. A recently hired clerk in the store, nineteen-year-old Christopher Martin, notified his manager that he suspected Floyd had passed a counterfeit twenty-dollar bill. Martin testified that he had a friendly discussion with Floyd about his height—he was six feet six inches—and whether he played baseball. Martin said he "felt like George didn't really know it was a fake bill." Martin testified later that he offered to pay out of his pocket after Floyd left the store.[586] However, the store manager told Martin that it was store policy to report to the police about counterfeit money. He sent Martin out to find Floyd and have him return to the store. But Floyd was already in a car with some friends, and he refused twice to go back into the store. At that point another clerk from the store called the police. Floyd was a regular at the store and friendly with the owner, Mahmoud Abumayyaleh, who was not present. Abumayyaleh later stated, as Martin had, that even if the twenty dollars was fake, Floyd likely did not know. He referred to Floyd as a "big teddy bear" who often came to the store and was friendly. He had deep regrets about what happened and stated, "If I would have been here the authorities would not have been called. George Floyd may still be alive."[587]

Two police officers—Thomas Lane, who is white, and Alexander Kueng, who is African American—arrived at the scene around 8:08 p.m. Lane approached Floyd, who was still sitting in his car near the store, and began to question him. Floyd stated that he had done nothing wrong. Lane drew his gun, and decided to arrest him anyway. Two other officers, Derek Chauvin, who is white, and Tou Thao, who is Hmong American, arrived after Floyd had been hand-cuffed, but before anyone tried to place him in the police car.

Although videos from the scene show that Floyd was calm, he had ample cause to be apprehensive about getting in the police car. He explained that he was claustrophobic. His recent illness from COVID-19 had also likely heightened his anxieties. Perhaps experiencing a panic attack, Floyd physically resisted being placed in the car, leading to a tussle with the officers.

The four policemen responded by forcing him to the ground. Chauvin, the lead officer on the scene, placed his knee on Floyd's neck and kept it there for nine minutes and twenty-nine seconds. A crowd had gathered at that point and began pleading with the officers to address Floyd's cry that he could not breathe. Floyd stated at least twenty-eight times, "I can't breathe," or some variation.[588] This was not the first time a black man in police custody had spoken these words. On July 17, 2014, another unarmed black victim of police violence, Eric Garner, uttered the same chilling words eleven times in Staten Island, New York, as officer Daniel Pantaleo choked him to death. Although the NYPD had banned the choke hold as far back as 1993, Pantaleo and other cops used it with impunity. Daniel Pantaleo was not fired until August 2019, and was never charged with a crime in Garner's death.[589]

George Floyd was not breathing for the last three minutes or so that Officer Chauvin was on him. During the entire episode, the growing crowd of people witnessing the incident shouted at the officers to let Floyd up, to turn him over, or to get medical assistance. The officers finally called for an ambulance at 8:22 p.m., but it was a Code 2 call, deemed less of an emergency. They would eventually change it to a Code 3, signaling a more urgent circumstance.

According to a transcript of footage taken from Lane's body camera, Floyd not only stated he could not breathe numerous times, but also called for his mother and asked the officers not to kill him. The police ignored Floyd's pleas.

Floyd: I'm through, through. I'm claustrophobic. My stomach hurts. My neck hurts. Everything hurts. I need some water or something, please. Please? I can't breathe, officer.
Chauvin: Then stop talking, stop yelling.
Floyd: You're going to kill me, man.
Chauvin: Then stop talking, stop yelling, it takes a heck of a lot of oxygen to talk.
Floyd: Come on, man. Oh, oh. [crosstalk.] I cannot breathe. I cannot breathe. Ah! They'll kill me. They'll kill me. I can't breathe. I can't breathe![590]

While most attention initially focused on Chauvin after the murder, the other officers on site ignored Floyd's cries as well. At one point, the exchange went like this:

Thao: "Relax."
Floyd: "I can't breathe."
Kueng: "You're fine. You're talking fine."
Lane: "Deep breath."[591]

Floyd clearly was not fine. He seemed to feel his death was imminent. At another point in the transcript, Floyd states, "Momma, I love you. Tell my kids I love them. I'm dead."[592]

By the time an ambulance arrived on the scene, Floyd was dead or dying. In their initial official report, the police officers did not disclose that Chauvin pinned Floyd's neck with his knee, nor that they did not engage in any de-escalation tactics. They claimed that Floyd "physically resisted officers" and appeared to be "suffering medical distress."[593] Two autopsies, one by the local medical examiner and another commissioned by the family, found that he died of homicide, with the former stating he suffered "subdual, restraint, and neck compression" by arresting officers.[594]

Although multiple police cams and bystanders' videos would also show what had really occurred, a seventeen-year-old high school student would be the first to tell the nation what happened. Darnella Frazier was on her way to Cup Foods with her nine-year-old cousin to buy snacks when she saw Floyd grasping for breath under Chauvin's knee. She whipped out her cell phone and used its built in-camera to document the police.

Frazier quickly posted her video to Facebook, adding the caption: "They killed him right in front of cup foods over south on 38th and Chicago!! No type of sympathy "#POLICEBRUTALITY."[595] When the Minneapolis Police Department issued a false statement about Floyd's death called "Man Dies After Medical Incident During Police Interaction," Frazier responded at 3:10 a.m., saying "Medical incident??? Watch outtt they killed him and the proof is clearlyyyy there!!"[596]

Darnella Frazier's video of Floyd's killing immediately went viral. As it did, she received massive public support and even scholarship offers, but also death threats and abuse on social media. Public outrage over the video also had immediate impact on the Minneapolis Police Department: the false account of Floyd's death was deleted from the police website and all four officers were quickly dismissed from the force.[597] Chauvin was charged with second-degree unintentional murder, third-degree murder, and second-degree manslaughter. The other three officers were charged with aiding and abetting second-degree murder. Chauvin had a long history of complaints—at least seventeen—filed against him for abusive behavior during his nearly two decades with the department.[598] It was later discovered that both Chauvin and Floyd had worked as part-time security guards at El Nuevo Rodeo nightclub, stoking speculation the two had history with each other. As noted, the officers involved were a mix of races: Chauvin and Lane are white, Thao is Hmong American, and Kueng is African American.[599] It was the two white officers, however, whose refusal to de-escalate led to Floyd's death.

When the world witnessed Frazier's video of Chauvin slowly killing Floyd, many saw a lynching, and responded with their conscience. Protest erupted in the United States and around the world. When millions of people saw yet another white police officer casually take the life of an unarmed black man, passive or subdued rage was no longer tolerable. The dam of complacency broke, and waters of indignation flooded the streets of the world.

WHEN PROTEST BECOMES A MOVEMENT

Protests began within hours of Frazier posting her video online.[600] What was most notable about the demonstrations was not just their durability, size, and diversity, but the fact that people were willing to assemble despite official COVID-related guidelines to avoid gathering in crowds. While there have been many massive single-day protests, such as the January 21, 2017, Women's March Against Trump, not since the Occupy Movement of 2011 have there been months of sustained mass protests—and arrests—across the United States and globally.[601]

According to the Crowd Counting Consortium, more than 300,000 people marched in at least 1,164 events documented between the day of Floyd's lynching on May 25 and the last day of May 2020.[602] The following month there were at least 4,269 additional protests, with actions in every U.S. state.[603] These figures are corroborated by data from Pew, National Opinion Research Center, Civis Analytics, and Kaiser Family Foundation. On June 6, 2020, alone, "half a million people turned out in nearly 550 places across the United States."[604]

By mid-June 2020, protests demanding justice for George Floyd, defunding the police, and the dismantling of white supremacy were taking place in thousands of cities across the United States and in at least sixty nations. The theme "Black Lives Matter" was suddenly everywhere, from the floor of the 2020 NBA playoffs to the streets leading to the White House in Washington. The words appeared on T-shirts, flags, street art, face masks, lawn signs, and even in dating apps. By every indication, the anti-racism protests following the police lynching of George Floyd were the largest and most widespread, enduring, and diverse in U.S. history up to that point. By the end of June, between 15 million and 26 million people had come out to protests, including in counties where the majority of the population was white.[605] On July 3, 2020, the *New York Times* ran a report with the headline, "Black Lives Matter May Be the Largest Movement in U.S. History."[606]

Although the focus was anti-racism, and black activists—particularly black women— took the lead, there were often fewer black people in the streets than non-blacks. In small towns with minuscule populations of color, white allies organized and led the protests. The numbers ranged from small neighborhood demonstrations of fewer than twenty to marches or rallies of thousands. While nationally recognized figures would show up on occasion, the participants were overwhelmingly local. A tipping point had clearly been reached, and despite the very real risks posed by the ongoing explosion of COVID worldwide, millions of people broke from lockdown and took to the streets to demand change.

Throughout the summer of 2020, many cities, such as Washington, D.C., and Philadelphia, often had multiple demonstrations on a given day. On the Fourth of July 2020, for instance, D.C. had at least ten separate protests at different parts of the city.[607] In a count considered on the low side, the *U.S. Crisis Monitor* documented 7,750 demonstrations in the country between May 24 and August 22, 2020.[608] That was an average of eighty-six demonstrations per day. These actions were documented in "more than 2,440 locations in all fifty states and Washington, D.C."[609] Protests continued after the study's cutoff date, and the actual number of protests was likely much higher in the period monitored. As new cases of police violence continued to make headlines after Floyd's murder, calls for justice increasingly merged into the growing movement against systemic racism in America.

On the law enforcement side of things, the Major Cities Chiefs Association (MCCA)—a professional organization of police executives representing the largest cities in the United States and Canada—documented at least 8,700 protests taking place between May 25 and July 31, 2020. In the 2,440 locations where protests were studied during that period, approximately 90 percent were peaceful gatherings. However, within the 10 percent where incidents occurred, there were 2,385 instances of looting, 624 acts of arson, and 97 or more police cars burned.[610] At least 16,241 people were arrested. On one night in May 2020, eight fires erupted during protests in Philadelphia, and 109 people were arrested.[611]

As their predecessors have done for more than sixty years, Republicans and the right-wing media seized upon those incidents to attack the nationwide protests and call for "law and order." In an effort to disparage the movement, Trump called BLM protesters "terrorists" and attempted to portray them as a source of widespread disorder. The U.S. Crisis Monitor found that 93 percent of the demonstrations linked to Black Lives Matter involved no violence or property damage whatsoever, corroborating the findings of the MCCA, which concluded "the vast majority of these protests were peaceful." The same conclusion was determined by the Armed Conflict Location & Event Data Project, a nonprofit. Working in collaboration with a group of researchers at Princeton University they also found that the overwhelming majority of the more than 9,000 Black Lives Matter demonstrations that took place nationwide after the killing of George Floyd were peaceful.[612]

POLICE AND LEGAL SYSTEM VS. PROTESTERS

There is scant data about how many people were injured by police during the protests of 2020. According to data collected by the investigative website Bellingcat and the research group Forensic Architecture, at least 950 instances of police brutality against civilians and journalists took place in the five months of protests after Floyd's murder.[613] A report by Physicians for Human Rights indicated that in the two-month period from May 26 to July 27, 2020, police shot at least 115 anti-racism protesters in the head, face, and neck with various projectiles, including rubber bullets, bean bag rounds, pellets, and tear gas canisters.[614] Many of these police attacks caused serious injuries and lasting suffering. A report from *Time* describes one such case:

On July 11, Donavan La Bella was holding a stereo above his head at a Portland, Ore. protest, blasting a song by the artist Dax called "Black Lives Matter," when a line of U.S. Marshals across the street began launching smoke canisters. Cell-phone footage shows La Bella, 26, calmly kicking aside a canister that landed at his feet, then picking it up and tossing it away before lifting the stereo above his head again. Seconds later, as La Bella stands in place, not moving toward the officers, he's shot between the eyes with an "impact munition" and drops to the ground. La Bella's skull was fractured, and the bones around his left eye socket were broken. He has trouble concentrating and controlling his emotions and suffers from extreme sensitivity to light and sound and impaired vision, says his mother, Desiree La Bella. "Try to imagine having a migraine for a minimum of 12 hours a day for five, six weeks straight," his mother says. "You can't get away from that kind of pain." La Bella spent most of the past two months in the hospital, having returned there on Aug. 17 for the third time to treat a sinus and brain infection as well as a cerebrospinal fluid leak, conditions related to his injuries.[615]

The nonprofit organization Reporters Without Borders (RSF) reported that dozens of journalists were attacked, arrested, or otherwise harassed—sometimes by police and sometimes by protesters—during their coverage of the uprisings. Freelance photographer Linda Tirado was blinded in her left eye after being shot in the face with a rubber bullet by Minneapolis police on May 29, 2020.[616] While covering one of the protests on May 30, MSNBC's reporter and host Ali Velshi was struck in the knee by a rubber bullet shot by Minneapolis police. At a rally, Trump called the unprovoked police attack on Velshi "a beautiful thing."[617] RSF's secretary general, Christophe Deloire, linked the assaults on journalists to the political atmosphere generated by Trump. He stated, "President Trump's demonization of the media for years has now come to fruition, with both the police and protesters targeting clearly identified journalists with violence and arrests. It has long been obvious that this demonization would lead to physical violence."[618]

In fact, it was much more likely for activists and journalists to be attacked by the police and right-wing counterprotesters than the other way around. For example, there were more than a hundred instances where cars were used as weapons and deliberately driven into groups of demonstrators, with drivers including some individual perpetrators affiliated with the Ku Klux Klan, police, or military.[619] According to The Armed Conflict Location & Event Data Project, during the three-month period from late May 2020 to late August 2020, car-ramming attacks were also perpetrated by those affiliated with the government, "such as the military and law enforcement, including an on-duty police officer at a demonstration in Anaheim, California on 25 July (Fox11 Los Angeles, 28 July 2020); an off-duty police officer at a demonstration in Seattle, Washington on 4 July (King5, 9 July 2020); an army sergeant at a demonstration in Austin, Texas on 25 July (KTSM, 31 July 2020); and an off-duty jail correctional officer at a demonstration in Kokomo, Indiana on 30 May (Kokomo Tribune, 1 June 2020)."[620] According to researcher Ari Weil, there were 104 incidents of cars driving into protesters between May 27 and September 25, 2020, including 96 by civilians and 8 by police officers.[621]

Rather than make an effort to protect those utilizing their Constitutional right to demonstrate, Republican lawmakers and governors have sought to punish activists and shield those who attack them. On April 21, 2021, Oklahoma governor Kevin Stitt signed into law a bill that "grants immunity to drivers who unintentionally hurt or kill protesters on public streets." All such drivers need to do is claim they feared for their life or were attempting to leave a "riot" situation in order to receive civil and criminal immunity for using their vehicle as a weapon to kill. The law was passed in response to an incident in May 2020 in Tulsa, when a man rammed his pickup truck into a group of people participating in a Black Lives Matter gathering. Two days earlier, on April 19, Florida governor Ron DeSantis had signed a similar bill that "grants civil immunity to drivers who ram into protesting crowds and even injure or kill participants, *if* they claim the protests made them concerned for their own well-being in the moment."[622] (Emphasis is in the original).

Prior to the Floyd protests, the most notorious case of a driver using a vehicle to harm peaceful protesters occurred during the infamous August 2017 "Unite the Right" rally in Charlottesville, Virginia. In that tragic case, white nationalist James Alex Fields Jr. deliberately plowed into a crowd of protesters, killing anti-racist activist Heather Heyer and injuring more than thirty other people. In June 2019, Fields was sentenced to life in prison for murdering Heyer and related crimes.[623] If these laws had been in place, Fields might have walked away scot-free.

Oklahoma and Florida are not alone. Many other states, almost all Republican-dominated, are attempting to pass anti-protest legislation. According to the International Center for Non-Profit Law's U.S. Protest Law Tracker, more than a hundred anti-protest bills were introduced in multiple states during the twelve-month period following the racial justice protests of summer 2020.[624] From January 2017 to January 2022, just five years, 45 states considered 241 bills, resulting in 36 enacted laws. Forty-eighty such bills remained pending as of January 28, 2022. Conservative legislators sought to go even further in the assault on individuals exercising their free speech rights by proposing that someone convicted of a protest-related crime would lose their right to access public assistance programs such as food stamps and unemployment insurance. Federal legislation that was pending in the 117th Congress cruelly aimed to deny COVID aid to people convicted of a protest-related crime. For example, H.R. 289, introduced January 13, 2021, by Congressman Jim Banks (R-IN) was crafted with this intention:

> [to] withdraw COVID-19 unemployment benefits from and impose new costs on anyone convicted of a federal offense related to the individual's conduct at and during a protest. Such a person would be ineligible for federal unemployment aid under the CARES Act (15 U.S.C. 9023) or any other Federal supplemental unemployment compensation during the COVID-19 public health emergency. If federal agents were involved in policing the protest at issue, the person who was convicted of a related federal offense would also have to pay the cost of the agents' policing activity, as determined by the court.[625]

Considering the widespread black support for racial justice movements and the certainty of protests to come, laws like H.R. 289 plainly expose the level of white supremacy inherent in ongoing Republican efforts to suppress the political agency of people of color in America. These efforts evoke the cruel punishments white enslavers would visit upon black families for offenses such as learning to read and write or disobeying a white person's orders. Today's Republican-driven anti-protest laws are part of the Jacksonian tradition of bringing "order by Hickory oil" to those who challenge the authority of the racial caste system. The only difference between Jim Crow–era laws and these policies is that the new legislation is given a veneer of race-neutrality, but the intent is crystal clear.

THE ENDURANCE OF THE OPPRESSED

"The limits of tyrants are prescribed by the endurance of those whom they oppress. In the light of these ideas, Negroes will be hunted at the North, and held and flogged at the South so long as they submit to those devilish outrages, and make no resistance, either moral or physical."
—Frederick Douglass

What was behind the historic uprisings of 2020? First, no person of conscience could watch Darnella Frazier's video of Officer Derek Chauvin killing George Floyd without being repulsed and disturbed. Chauvin is seen for more than nine minutes looking casual and unfazed with his sunglasses on his head, his left hand in his pocket, as the black man pinned beneath his knee begs for his life. The callousness on display is infuriating to witness, and evokes centuries of black deaths at white hands. While the assassination of a well-known leader can catalyze uprisings and mass movements, so too can the killing of an ordinary person. That was the case in the savage lynching of fourteen-year-old black teenager Emmett Till in Money, Mississippi, in 1955, which helped to mobilize the Civil Rights movement. Gruesome photographs of Emmett's mutilated body in

Jet Magazine—his mother insisted on having an open coffin at his funeral in order to show America what his killers had done—galvanized black America. [626]

In 1991, video footage of the brutal beating of black motorist Rodney King by Los Angeles police officers drew condemnation and protest. A massive uprising followed the officers' acquittal. In 2012, the vigilante killing of seventeen-year-old Trayvon Martin in Florida gave rise to the Black Lives Matter movement. In 2014, the murder of black teenager Michael Brown in Ferguson, Missouri, by a white police officer sparked national outrage and a massive wave of protests, strengthening the BLM movement. The murder of black teenager Stephen Lawrence in London by a gang of white men in 1993 launched a renewed movement for racial justice across the United Kingdom. [627]

Second, years of highly publicized incidents involving police violence against people of color has led to a shift in public consciousness. Racial justice organizers, cultural workers, and public intellectuals have been able to channel the energy of that shift into movement organizing, particularly since the Ferguson uprisings in 2014. Following Ferguson, an investigation by the *Washington Post* found that the FBI had undercounted fatal police shootings "by more than half." This was "because reporting by police departments is voluntary and many departments fail to do so." [628]

It's clear from available data that police in the United States kill black Americans at a much higher rate than they kill white Americans. [629] Black Americans "account for less than 13 percent of the U.S. population, but are killed by police at more than twice the rate of White Americans. Hispanic Americans are also killed by police at a disproportionate rate." [630] According to Mapping Police Violence and Color of Change, African Americans who are fatally killed by police are 1.3 times less likely to have a weapon than white people. [631] They also reported that 99 percent of the police killings between 2013 and 2019 resulted in no officer being charged with a crime. [632] This total lack of accountability led to a breaking point.

Years prior to Floyd's lynching, three black women—Patrisse Cullors, Alicia Garza, and Opal Tometi—launched Black Lives Matter to confront violence against people of color in America. On February 26, 2012, a self-appointed neighborhood guard, George Zimmerman, shot and killed unarmed Florida teenager Trayvon Martin while he was walking home from a store. Zimmerman considered Martin suspicious for no other reason than he was a young black man. Claiming self-defense, Zimmerman was acquitted at his trial in July 2013. Indignant, Cullors, Garza, and Tometi conceived Black Lives Matter as "a call to action for Black people" after Zimmerman "was not held accountable for the crime he committed."[633] Within months of launching the #BlackLivesMatter hashtag, the group began organizing nationally "on issues of critical importance to Black people working hard for liberation, said Alicia Garza. "We've connected people across the country working to end the various forms of injustice impacting our people. We've created space for the celebration and humanization of Black lives."[634]

As Black Lives Matter grew outwardly as a movement, it also evolved internally. In her 2017 comments memorializing the work of the Combahee River Collective, described in Chapter 2, Barbara Ransby writes:

> The Black Lives Matter movement, and Movement for Black Lives, writ large, and inclusive of many organizations and coalitions, is where the contemporary Black freedom movement has landed in many ways. And this movement—not without problems or contradictions, but on the whole—has embraced a Black feminist praxis as its ideological bedrock. And that is pivotal to recognize. Because then we see, from the protests in the streets of Hamburg or London, the politics of intersectionality.[635]

Viewed in this light, the same historical tradition of black revolt and liberation struggles that emerged in 1619 and continued through Tubman's time and the Civil Rights era, persists through the racial justice uprisings, protests, and movement organizing of today.

Between its hashtag origin in response to Trayvon Martin's death and the killing of George Floyd eight years later, Black Lives Matter developed chapters across the country, setting the stage for what was to come. The shift in political awareness was deeply informed by a confluence of the black feminist praxis to which Ransby refers, including years of neo-abolitionist activism against the prison industrial complex, and many manifestations of cross-issue solidarity work. A literature of resistance and movement consciousness has also emerged, including titles like Keeanga-Yamahtta Taylor's *From #BlackLivesMatter to Black Liberation*, Mumia Abu Jamal's *Have Black Lives Ever Mattered?*, Tamika Mallory's *State of Emergency: How We Win in the Country We Built*, Patrisse Cullors and asha bandele's *When They Call You a Terrorist: A Black Lives Matter Memoir*, Barbara Ransby's *Making All Black Lives Matter: Reimagining Freedom in the Twenty-First Century*, and Alicia Garza's *The Purpose of Power*, among many others. These works were informed and preceded by the deeply influential *Are Prisons Obsolete?* by Angela Y. Davis and *The New Jim Crow* by Michelle Alexander, both of which were considered essential reading by activists during the uprisings. Michelle Alexander's book, which was first published in 2010, sold more than 400,000 copies in 2020 alone.[636] This movement literature—part of the canon of African American writing that goes back to the first slave narratives—combines historical memory, analysis, and political vision with a Tubmanesque sense of emancipatory urgency. Colin Kaepernick's publishing house was also launched during this period, as was Haymarket Press's important Abolitionist Series.

While the message of Black Lives Matter was popular with young people, who used it as a rallying cry of protest for the many unarmed black women and men who died at the hands of the police or vigilantes, it did not resonate immediately with many older African Americans or non-blacks. That changed dramatically in the wake of George Floyd's lynching. In June 2020, a Pew Research Center survey found that about 67 percent of all adults either strongly or somewhat supported the Black Lives Matter movement. Among African Americans, the number was 86 percent, followed by 77 percent for Latinx people and 75 percent for Asians. Even a majority of whites, 60 percent, felt that way. A huge partisan disparity existed, however, when parsed by party affiliation. While 91 percent of Democrats or Democrat-leaning respondents supported the movement, only 47 percent of Republicans or Republican-leaning respondents did so, still a remarkable number.[637]

However, while black support remained steady or grew, white support dropped sharply as demonstrations continued and the Trump-led right incessantly disparaged the protesters as "thugs," "looters," "leftist extremists," "socialists," "criminals," and "antifa," a reference to anti-fascist networks. Black Lives Matter and antifa were often blamed for acts of violence that were committed by individuals not connected to the movement and, in some cases, deliberately perpetrated by far-right provocateurs. In Richmond, Virginia, for example, local police concluded that white supremacists posing as Black Lives Matter activists were responsible for instigating riots in that city during a demonstration.[638] In fact, Black Lives Matter activists were credited with trying to *stop* the impostors from acting violently. In Minneapolis, a man wearing all black, who was captured on film smashing windows and spray-painting incendiary slogans in the days after Floyd's death, was a white supremacist affiliated with the racist Aryan Cowboy Brotherhood.[639]

White supremacists also engaged in online provocations while pretending to be Black Lives Matter activists. Their efforts promoted violence. One fake Twitter account that was actually operated by a militant white nationalist group implored protesters to go to "white hoods" and "take what's ours."[640] The post was retweeted hundreds of times before being taken down. It used the handle "@ANTIFA_US" and claimed to be working with Black Lives Matter. According to the Southern Poverty Law Center, the group involved was a campus-based white nationalist formation "at the forefront of the racist 'alt-right's' effort to recruit white, college-aged men and transform them into the fashionable new face of white nationalism."[641] Founded in 2016 as Identity Evropa, the group rebranded itself American Identity Movement in 2019.[642] The organization has been a staunch supporter of MAGA politics, and its membership numbers were bolstered by Trump's election.

Despite efforts to sabotage and demonize it, Black Lives Matter became a unifying theme of rebellion, resistance, and movement building. The ubiquity of the three-word message was just a sign of the deeper organizing occurring to dismantle white supremacy and racial injustice across the country.

The third factor behind the 2020 uprisings was the forty-fifth president of the United States. Although he was not in Minneapolis when Floyd was killed, Trump's antagonism had consequences. Given his aggression against protesters, many saw Trump's knee on the neck of their communities. His relentless attacks and false accusations of criminality increased the indignation of black communities and social justice networks on the left. Evoking the threat of violent mobs of low-income black and brown people invading white areas, his rhetoric grew shriller as he fell further behind in the polls. While calling Black Lives Matter a "symbol of hate," Trump falsely claimed that people living in suburbs were increasingly threatened by having "low-income housing" built in their neighborhoods, and would see dramatic increases in crime.[643]

His racialized assault on legal protests went beyond rhetoric, and arguably condoned the use of aggressive tactics against people who joined protests. In its September 2020 report "The Law Enforcement Violence Trump Won't Talk About," the ACLU describes how Trump "called for law enforcement to 'dominate' protesters," and how authorities subsequently "used sharpshooters to maim people, swept protesters away in unmarked cars, and brutally attacked journalists, legal observers, and medics."[644] The president also passed a series of executive orders in direct response to the protests, such as increasing prison time to a maximum of ten years for damaging federal monuments, including those that honor slavers and human traffickers.[645] Yet his actions only mobilized people to protest more, generating months-long demonstrations that swelled with each new police killing.

As the demonstrations grew in Minneapolis in the days immediately after Floyd's murder, Trump inflamed the situation with an outrageous public statement. On May 29, he posted a tweet that said, "These THUGS are dishonoring the memory of George Floyd, and I won't let that happen. Just spoke to Governor Tim Walz and told him that the Military is with him all the way. Any difficulty and we will assume control but, when the looting starts, the shooting starts."[646] His use of the phrase "when the looting starts, the shooting starts" was a cut-and-paste evocation of white backlash to black revolt during the Civil Rights era. In the late 1960s, Miami's white police chief, Walter Headley, repeatedly stated, "When the looting starts, the shooting starts."[647] The message was clearly aimed at repressing the local black community. During a 1967 press conference addressing crime in the city, Headley said, "We have done everything we could, sending speakers out and meeting with Negro leaders. But it has amounted to nothing."[648] Segregationist presidential candidate George Wallace repeated the phrase in 1968 while on the campaign trail. When Trump was called out on what he said, including Twitter flagging the tweet for violating its rules against inciting violence, he attempted to backpedal, issuing the following muddled statement, "Looting leads to shooting, and that's why a man was shot and killed in Minneapolis on Wednesday night—or look at what just happened in Louisville with 7 people shot. I don't want this to happen, and that's what the expression put out last night means. It was spoken as a fact, not as a statement. It's very simple, nobody should have any problem with this other than the haters, and those looking to cause trouble on social media. Honor the memory of George Floyd!"[649]

Fourth, the failure of the capitalist economic model to meet the needs of millions of people was a factor that drove people to protest. From destruction of the environment to elimination of social safety nets, corporate interests have increasingly determined public policy to the detriment of the many. According to a January 2022 report released by the nonprofit Oxfam, "A new billionaire is created every 26 hours while inequality contributes to the death of one person every four seconds."[650] The Republicans' 2017 tax cuts further enriched the top one percent and cut the corporate tax rate from 35 percent to 21 percent, with only crumbs for working people. Wages stagnated even when the economy was doing well before the pandemic. Brutal austerity in Republican-led states and from the national budget has deepened the misery of millions. Both major political parties in the United States have failed to implement significant reforms necessary for a just economy.

The interconnected protests, uprisings, and movements of recent years have created a national opening for confronting corporate influence and linking demands for economic and racial justice with a defense of democracy itself. Black Lives Matter organizing widened the opening. The revolutionary imagination was awakened. Everything was on the table.

Despite the occasional presence of celebrities, the millions of people who took to the streets were ordinary Americans. In cities with black mayors, those officials attended demonstrations and sometimes took other symbolic actions as well. This created new opportunities for communities to directly communicate with their elected officials. Many, like Garza, pointed out that the injustices facing marginalized communities went beyond police abuse and violence. Chronic issues included high rates of poverty, dysfunctional and unequal education systems, lack of adequate housing, missing or poor healthcare plans, gentrification, and extraordinarily high unemployment or underemployment rates in certain neighborhoods. These grievances were rooted in a critique of racial capitalism and calls for the abolition of carceral systems of policing and punishment.

BATTLE IN THE CAPITOL

Washington, D.C., became the epicenter of the battle between the movement and the White House. Shortly after Floyd's murder, massive protests occurred on a daily basis directly across from the White House in Lafayette Square, as well as around the city. At one point, on Friday, May 29, 2020, Trump and family were moved to the Presidential Emergency Operations Center, a security bunker where he hid out for about an hour after protesters hopped over temporary barricades set up near the Treasury Department grounds.[651] For someone who endlessly boasted about his toughness, this was a huge humiliation and one that he would later deny happened at all. Trump was ridiculed on social media and Twitter as hashtags "#bunkerboy" and "#bunkerDon" trended widely.

Further, embarrassed by the scope of the protests and the affront to his authority, Trump ordered federal officers to flush out the protesters peacefully assembled in Lafayette Park. Around 6:30 p.m. on June 1, 2020, local and federal authorities began attacking protesters with chemical weapons. This was a half hour before the 7:00 p.m. city curfew, when most of the protesters would have dispersed anyway. Trump clearly wanted to project the image of being able to dominate protesters anytime he wished.

As the incident backfired, denials of responsibility began to fly. The U.S. Park Police, D.C. Metro Police, Secret Service, and White House all initially claimed loudly that they "did not use tear gas."[652] However, in sworn testimony at a federal court hearing, D.C. Metro Police Department lawyer Richard Sobiecki confirmed that tear gas had been deployed against the demonstrators.[653]

After the protesters were flushed out with gas, Trump and a coterie of officials paraded into the park. Among those present were Ivanka Trump, her husband and White House advisor Jared Kushner, U.S. defense secretary Mark Esper, and Joint Chiefs of Staff chairman General Mark A. Milley, among others. Trump awkwardly strolled to the parish house at St. John's Episcopal Church on the border of Lafayette Square and posed for a photo holding a bible. He did not read from the bible or say a word. After a few pictures were taken, Trump and his entourage scurried back to the White House.

Many witnesses later stated that those in Lafayette Square had been assembled peacefully when the gas attack against them took place. Major Adam D. DeMarco, the most senior D.C. National Guard officer on the scene that day, later stated that "demonstrators were behaving peacefully" and tear gas was an "excessive use of force."[654] He also contradicted Park Police claims that they gave people sufficient warning to leave. DeMarco testified that the "Long-Range Acoustic Device" that supposedly was used to make the announcement was not even on the scene. Instead, authorities used a smaller megaphone that DeMarco said even he had difficulty hearing.[655]

DeMarco revealed that the preparation for the confrontation by the White House went further than reported at the time. In sworn testimony to Congress, DeMarco stated that the Department of Defense had requested the Active Denial System—a directed-energy weapon that makes its targets feel like their skin is burning.[656] The device had never been used, due to concerns about human rights, and it was unclear whether it would even work. Reportedly, Trump's team had wanted to use the machine on people at the U.S.-Mexican border, but were dissuaded by Homeland Security secretary Kirstjen Nielsen, whom Trump later forced out, it was said, for not being cruel enough to families locked in cages at detention camps.[657]

General Milley later apologized for going to Lafayette Square with Trump, after being roundly criticized for giving the impression that the U.S. military was infringing upon U.S. citizens' expression of their First Amendment rights. Milley failed, however, to criticize the egregious behavior of Trump using the military for his partisan political interests. A Department of Interior report made the dubious claim that the decision to clear the park had nothing to do with the photo stunt, and that several police agencies had decided to do so twenty minutes before the curfew in order to install new fencing. While the *Washington Post* reported that Attorney General William Barr, who arrived in the park only minutes before the law enforcement attack, had given the order to remove protesters, the

Interior report did not interview him to determine whether that was true. In fact, as analyst Radley Balko points out, the report did not include interviews from anyone at the Secret Service, most police agencies on the scene, or any protesters.[658] Balko also notes that in a phone call to governors earlier that day, Trump sought to encourage them to "dominate" protesters and "get much tougher," telling them: "You have to dominate. If you don't dominate, you're wasting your time. They're going to run all over you, you'll look like a bunch of jerks. . . . And we're doing it in Washington, in D.C., we're going to do something that people haven't seen before. But we're going to have total domination."[659] Ominously, Trump cited the November 2011 forced removal of the Occupy movement organizers from New York's Zuccotti Park as a model of how authorities should control the Black Lives Matter demonstrations.

Republican efforts to control the movement failed. Protests continued to grow nationally and in D.C. itself. Trump and others in the administration had blamed D.C.'s mayor, Muriel Bowser, a black woman, for the local demonstrations. White House deputy press secretary Judd Deere stated, "Unfortunately, the mayor did not provide early leadership to ensure peaceful protests and prevent riots and violence."[660] Trump called Mayor Bowser "incompetent." For her part, on May 30, she slapped back with a tweet that said, "While he hides behind his fence afraid/alone, I stand w/ people peacefully exercising their First Amendment Right after the murder of #GeorgeFloyd & hundreds of years of institutional racism. . . . There is just a scared man. Afraid/alone."[661]

Four days after Trump cleared the park, he woke up to find that Mayor Bowser had ordered city workers to paint the words "Black Lives Matter" on a two-block stretch of 16th Street NW, which led directly to the White House. Furthermore, under her authority as mayor, Bowser had the area around Lafayette Square renamed "Black Lives Matter Plaza."

It should be noted that Trump was not the only one unhappy with the giant street mural on his doorstep. Some local Black Lives

Matter activists, who did not participate in painting the street, were critical of Bowser's action. They decried it as "a performative distraction from real policy changes." They tweeted, "Bowser has consistently been on the wrong side of BLMDC history. This is to appease white liberals while ignoring our demands."⁶⁶² Nevertheless, her defiance got under Trump's skin and the street became a festival of pro-BLM celebration.

Trump's conflict with D.C.'s rebellious black mayor reflected his venomous attacks on other cities headed by liberal or left-leaning African American women, including Atlanta mayor Keisha Lance Bottoms, Chicago mayor Lori Lightfoot, and San Francisco mayor London Breed. Each city had massive, ongoing demonstrations that sometimes turned violent. When they did, Trump attacked the mayors, labeling all these cities and their leadership "losers." In return, they pushed back by challenging the racism of Republican officials at every level of government, and were generally open to police reform. At the same time, there was little doubt that these cities suffered from a range of chronic economic, racial, and social injustices, including uneven access to health care, educational disparities, unemployment maladies, and housing needs driven by gentrification. Republicans and Democrats alike had made business-friendly concessions that undermined unions, constricted democratic input and transparency, and offered minimum relief for impoverished and marginalized populations.

GLOBALIZATION OF THE FLOYD PROTESTS

At the same time that demonstrations erupted in the United States, solidarity protests broke out in more than seventy nations around the globe.⁶⁶³ Some were small one-offs, but others were large and sustained for days or weeks. Many of them were self-branded as Black Lives Matter. Major international cities, including London, Paris, Berlin, Toronto, Rio, Mexico City, Berlin, and many others saw large demonstrations. In most protests, the call for racial justice for Floyd and other U.S. victims were combined with local issues of racial justice or human rights. Murals and images of Floyd, along with signs stating, "I can't breathe" appeared around the world.

In France, activists linked the Floyd murder with that of Adama Traoré, who was subdued by French police in Beaumont-sur-Oise, north of Paris, in 2016, and died in their custody. Traoré, a black man, was killed on his twenty-fourth birthday, July 19. His family has medical reports and an independent autopsy establishing that he was asphyxiated to death by the police, but the police deny responsibility. According to reporting in the *Guardian*, a firefighter who had arrived on the scene found Traoré lying face down, handcuffed, and passed out. The report noted, "One of the gendarmes said Traoré had told the police he couldn't breathe, but officers told the firefighter they thought he was faking it."[664] In 2020, the case received new attention, and Black Lives Matter activists in France supported Traoré's family as part of a broader campaign for racial justice and police reform.[665] Working-class black and Arab residents in France suffer police brutality and harassment issues similar to those faced by their U.S. counterparts. Assa Traoré, Adama's sister, became the chief advocate for justice. Police arrested her when she released a letter in which she named the officers she believed to have committed the killing, an act that is illegal under French law. In May 2020, the officers involved were cleared of any wrongdoing.[666] Earlier in 2020, forty-two-year-old Cédric Chouviat, a delivery driver, was held down by three French police officers and put in a choke hold. He repeated at least seven times the French equivalent of "I can't breathe," and later died. In Chouviat's case, multiple videos of the killing were made by bystanders.[667]

U.S. embassies were the target of protests in many countries, including Denmark, Ireland, New Zealand, Mexico, and Poland. On June 5, 2020, a haka dance was done in front of the embassy in Auckland, New Zealand. The haka is a high-energy traditional dance performed by Indigenous Maori people. According to the activists, the dance was meant both to express solidarity with the U.S. movement, and to protest a new policy of arming police in New Zealand.

Also on June 5, the U.S. embassy in Mexico City was forced to shut down due to the intensity of protests. Demonstrations in Mexico were inflamed by the recent police killing of construction worker Giovanni López a month earlier in Jalisco. In Warsaw, crowds gathered peacefully with flowers and chanted slogans, including "Black Lives Matter!" and "No Justice, No Peace!"[668]

Even in small nations that rarely receive global attention, Floyd's lynching had an impact. In June 2020, the hashtag, #Papuanlivesmatter was trending in Indonesia. It reflected a new awareness of not only the struggle of the Papuan people of Papua New Guinea for self-determination after centuries of colonialization and oppression, but also their sense of solidarity with the black freedom struggle in the United States. Long ignored domestically and internationally except by human rights groups, Indonesian attacks on activists fighting for peaceful change and against racism gained new attention as the Black Lives Matter uprisings forced many nations to look inward at their own issues of injustice. The former Dutch colony came under Indonesian control in May 1963 with the latter promising—but never allowing—full independence for the Papuan people. Periodic rebellions and ongoing resistance have resulted in an estimated 100,000 people being killed by police and military forces since the 1960s, with little to no accountability.[669]

Beyond suffering brutal policing, according to the *Los Angeles Times*, Papuans endure persistent racism, with the result that "few good jobs and threadbare health and education systems have contributed to the highest poverty rates, lowest literacy rates and highest mortality rates for children and expectant mothers in Indonesia."[670] They face quotidian bigotry that includes Papuans being denied service in stores and restaurants, or denied rental opportunities by landlords.

Nevertheless, activists believed that change was becoming acceptable in 2020 due to the uprisings breaking out everywhere at that time. Local advocates stated, "Black Lives Matter has triggered support for oppressed Papuans" and "Many Indonesians wouldn't be reflecting on the injustice toward Papuans if it wasn't for George Floyd."[671] In at least one instance, a group arrested for demonstrating had their time reduced. Facing seventeen-year prison terms, in July 2020 a group known as the "Balikpapan 7" had their sentences reduced to only months as a consequence of widespread public demands for racial justice, and by August 2020, all were free after getting credit for the months they had spent in jail awaiting trial.[672]

It is worth repeating that these rallies and demonstrations took place despite a global pandemic in which millions died and countless numbers became ill. While the United States had the most cases and deaths during the summer of 2020, other nations that suffered devastating losses, including Brazil, India, and South Africa, also had demonstrations during the pandemic.

REIMAGINING POLICING AND DECARCERATION IN THE TWENTY-FIRST CENTURY

"We want the laws enforced against rich as well as poor; against Capitalist as well as Laborer; against white as well as black. We are not more lawless than the white race, we are more often arrested, convicted, and mobbed. We want justice even for criminals and outlaws."

—W. E. B. Du Bois

"We can never be satisfied as long as the Negro is the victim of the unspeakable horrors of police brutality."

—Martin Luther King Jr.

Ongoing demands for justice are anchored in rejection of institutional and systemic racism in policing. It would be an understatement to simply say that black communities have been targeted to a degree of violence and intimidation never visited upon white communities. From the slave patrols of the settler-colonial era and the white supremacist organizations that arose after the Civil War, to the predation of majority-white police departments on black communities in places like Ferguson, the U.S. justice system has been weaponized against African Americans.[673] While the election of black mayors and appointment of black police chiefs has brought a degree of relief, it has not eliminated systemic racism in policing in the United States. At every point in the criminal justice system, racial disparities persist. Today, African Americans continue to be disproportionately stopped on the streets, pulled over in their cars, and underrepresented as judges and attorneys. Blacks are also disproportionately arrested, convicted of a crime, incarcerated, and then disenfranchised.

This chain of despairing engagement with America's criminal justice system begins with the police. A range of excellent empirical and historically grounded studies make it abundantly clear that the "one bad cop" theory that attributes black victimization to lone rogue officers is fiction. The institutional racism inherent in policing and the carceral state is detailed and elucidated in Paul Butler's *Chokehold: Policing Black Men*; Angela J. Davis's *Policing the Black Man: Arrest, Prosecution and Imprisonment*; Angela J. Hattery's *Policing Black Bodies: How Black Lives Are Surveilled and How to Work for Change*; Jamie Thompson's *Standoff: Race, Policing, and a Deadly Assault That Gripped a Nation*; and Alex S. Vitale's *The End of Policing*; among other important books, including aforementioned works by Angela Y. Davis and Michelle Alexander.[674] The revolutionary work of Ruth Wilson Gilmore and contemporary feminist abolitionists calls on us to "change everything," beginning with abolishing prisons. The through line is a persistence for the emancipatory organizing required to reconstruct society to be fair, equitable, restorative, and humane.

In addition to this scholarship, much work is being done on the ground. The efforts of Kimberlé W. Crenshaw, Luke Harris, and the rest of the team at the African American Policy Forum; Phillip Atiba Goff at the Center for Policing Equity; Color of Change's Rashad Robinson; Bryan Stevenson and the Equal Justice Initiative; and the legal activists at the Innocence Project have been indispensable for their approaches to securing justice for black people and others unfairly treated by biased policing and courts. Their efforts have also advanced narratives for what a genuine people-centered justice system can look like. These activists and visionaries pressure the structural biases and inequities in a criminal justice system that has steadfastly resisted change.

Demands to "Defund the Police" have drawn much-needed attention to a criminal justice system that does not meet the needs of black communities, and never has. Such demands insist that funding shift from a focus on increasingly militarized policing to a model that centers on community well-being, restorative justice, and social solidarity. The right, moderates, and even some on the left have made erroneous claims that defunding the police would leave communities completely exposed to criminal predation. Contemporary abolitionism, as human rights lawyer Derecka Purnell notes, is "a bigger idea than firing cops and closing prisons; it include[s] eliminating the reasons people think they need cops and prisons in the first place."[675] In thinking innovatively, as Purnell points out, abolitionists "have developed alternatives to 911, created support systems for victims of domestic violence, prevented new jail construction, reduced police budgets, and shielded undocumented immigrants from deportation," among other transformative approaches to justice and security.[676]

Activist Mariame Kaba, author of *We Do This 'Til We Free Us: Abolitionist Organizing and Transforming Justice*, contends that the goal is to make the police obsolete. "We are not abandoning our communities to violence," she states. "We don't want to just close police departments. We want to make them obsolete." This is accomplished, she says, by redirecting "billions that now go to police departments toward providing health care, housing, education and good jobs. If we did this, there would be less need for the police in the first place."[677]

Abolitionist activists and scholars argue that modern policing perpetuates settler-colonial legacies of white supremacy originally forged to dominate black and Indigenous populations. Today, communities of color continue to be surveilled, policed, and criminalized at higher rates than white communities. Such oppressive disparities include being subjected to lethal overuse of force. Even so-called "wellness" checks, or responses to individuals who are having a mental health or medical crisis, have led to serious injuries and deaths of black people by police. In Rochester, New York, on March 30, 2020, forty-one-year-old David Prude was killed by police. David's brother, Joe Prude, called the police for help after David went out into the street naked and in severe stress as a result of mental health issues and perhaps drug intoxication. The police subdued him and placed a plastic bag over his head. According to the subsequent investigation, Prude died of asphyxiation while in police custody. Although the local police attempted to label his death a drug overdose, Dr. Nadia Granger, the Monroe County Medical Examiner, ruled it a homicide.[678] This is but one of literally countless examples.

In addition to removing non-security functions from policing, it is critical to have community oversight and review of policing functions in order to regularly assess the impact of department policies and outcomes from a racial justice perspective. These include street stops, car stops, arrests, use-of-violence or physical altercations, searches, and use of warrants, among others. Such oversight should involve community-level committees in the process of creating changes.

NEW LAWS

The movement to save black lives and build diverse communities exists because the harassment, injury, and murder of unarmed people of color by police and vigilantes persists. Nevertheless, there have been victories, small and large, because of the protests. Cities and states have seen some unprecedented changes.

In the wake of Breonna Taylor's killing, for example, Louisville passed "Breonna's Law"—legislation addressing aspects of the long-standing systemic racism of the city police. These reforms, which could have prevented Taylor from being killed by police, include a measure that bans no-knock warrants. It also mandates officers to comply with the following when executing a warrant:

- Physically knock on an entry door to the premises in a manner and duration that can be heard by the occupants.
- Clearly and verbally announce as law enforcement having a search warrant in a manner that can be heard by the occupants.
- Absent exigent circumstances, wait a minimum of fifteen seconds or for a reasonable amount of time, whichever is greater, for occupants to answer the door, before entering the premises.[679]

Had these policies been in place and enforced, there is a chance that officers would not have shown up at Breonna Taylor's home after midnight. The new law also requires use of body cameras in the execution of search warrants. It specifically states, "No later than five minutes prior to all warrant executions, each officer on the premises must activate their body camera recording equipment and may not deactivate the equipment any sooner than five minutes following the completion of the execution [of] the warrant."[680] Had this policy existed and been enforced, the officers would not have felt that they could so easily lie on the official incident report and get away with it.

Across the nation, BLM protests won victories in gaining re- forms that had long been resisted by the police, police unions, and pro-police elected officials. In Minneapolis, where Floyd died under the knee of police, new rules require police "to intervene and make a report if they witness excessive use of force" by other officers and ban them from using choke holds.[681] In June 2020, the *New York Times* reported that nine members of the Minneapolis city council— a veto-proof majority—pledged "to dismantle the Police Department, promising to create a new system of public safety in a city where law enforcement has long been accused of racism."[682] That pledge made it to the ballot during the November 2021 elections there, but was not voted into law. In Dallas, the police adopted a "duty to intervene" policy requiring police officers to stop other officers thought to be using an excessive amount of force handling a suspect. The "blue wall" of police silence and complicity undermines any argument that there are only a few bad police officers, as the so-called good officers witness and fail to act to stop killings and injuries by their colleagues.

According to a survey by the *Washington Post*, within months of Floyd's killing, over 60 percent of the nation's largest police departments explicitly prohibited both carotid holds and choke holds in their use-of-force policies.[683] Chemical weapons such as tear gas were outlawed or put on moratorium in Philadelphia, Seattle, Berkeley, San Francisco, and Washington, D.C. Similar to Louisville, many cities and states passed or strengthened laws requiring police officers to turn on their body cameras. In June 2020, mayors and governors in Seattle, Denver, Houston, and Connecticut, among others, issued executive orders related to body cameras. Almost all these changes occurred in jurisdictions with Democratic governors, mayors, and city councils.

Local actions were necessary, in part, because of years of inaction at the federal level. For decades, in matters of criminal justice legislation, Congress passed putative legislation that was more police-friendly than justice-driven. However, 2020 saw a change of direction by some members of Congress. While Republicans attacked racial justice protesters, the Democrat-controlled House of Representatives passed H.R. 1280, the "George Floyd Justice in Policing Act," on June 17, 2020, by a vote of 236 to 181. Congresswoman Karen Bass (D-CA), the former Congressional Black Caucus chair, led the fight to write and build support for the legislation. However, the bill had little chance of passing in the U.S. Senate under the leadership of then–Senate leader Mitch McConnell (R-KY). In the 117th Congress, with the Democrats still in control of the House, the bill passed again on March 3, 2021, with a vote of 220 to 212. Although the Democrats had won control of the U.S. Senate in January 2021, the threat of a Republican filibuster and reluctance by some Democrats to get rid of or modify the filibuster rule caused the legislation to die in committee. Senator Tim Scott (R-SC) was tasked with representing the GOP side in negotiations, but despite the willingness of the Democrats to make compromises, there were not ten Republicans who would break the filibuster.[684]

If the George Floyd Justice in Policing Act ever passes, the new law will:

- Prohibit federal, state, and local law enforcement from racial, religious, and discriminatory profiling, and mandate training on racial, religious, and discriminatory profiling for all law enforcement.
- Ban choke holds, carotid holds, and no-knock warrants at the federal level and limit the transfer of military-grade equipment to state and local law enforcement.
- Mandate the use of dashboard cameras and body cameras for federal officers and require state and local law enforcement to use existing federal funds to ensure the use of police body cameras.
- Establish a National Police Misconduct Registry to prevent problematic officers who are fired or leave an agency from moving to another jurisdiction without any accountability.
- Amend the federal criminal statute from a "willfulness" to a "recklessness" standard, to successfully identify and prosecute police misconduct.
- Reform qualified immunity so that individuals are not barred from recovering damages when police violate their constitutional rights.
- Establish public safety innovation grants for community-based organizations to create local commissions and task forces to help communities re-imagine and develop concrete, just, and equitable public safety approaches.

- Create law enforcement development and training programs to develop best practices, and require the creation of law enforcement accreditation standard recommendations based on President Obama's Taskforce on 21st Century Policing.
- Require state and local law enforcement agencies to report use of force data, disaggregated by race, sex, disability, religion, and age.
- Improve the use of pattern and practice investigations at the federal level by granting the Department of Justice Civil Rights Division subpoena power, and create a grant program for state attorneys general to develop authority to conduct independent investigations into problematic police departments.
- Establish a Department of Justice task force to coordinate the investigation, prosecution, and enforcement efforts of federal, state, and local governments in cases related to law enforcement misconduct.[685]

Without using the phrase "defund the police," the legislation includes a section titled "Empower Our Communities to Reimagine Public Safety in an Equitable and Just Way." Finally, the bill addresses another long-overlooked issue. Police rapes and sexual assaults—especially against women of color—have rarely been acknowledged, let alone prosecuted. The bill proposes that it become "a crime for federal enforcement officer to engage in a sexual act with an individual who is under arrest, in detention, or in custody." The declaration of consent, often used by officers disingenuously, would no longer be an admissible defense.[686]

While these initiatives are steps in the right direction, they underestimate the degree to which bias in the criminal justice system requires a more fundamental transformation. In the current neoliberal era—a time ripe for authoritarianism and proto-fascism—movement demands for racial justice and equality are seen as threats to a system hardened against redistributive programs that benefit the many. Biases in bail, selection of judges, and felony disenfranchisement remain mostly untouched, although their impacts are severe and wide-ranging.

Recognizing the limits of the bill, the Movement for Black Lives, an activist coalition of 150 racial justice organizations, also opposed the legislation. Instead, they promote the visionary BREATHE Act, a 128-page bill written by their Electoral Justice Project. "History is clear that we cannot achieve genuine safety and liberation until we abandon police, prisons, and all punishment paradigms," says the organization.[687] Championed by congresswomen Ayanna Pressley (D-MA) and Rashida Tlaib (D-MI), the comprehensive bill is divided into four sections: "Divesting federal resources from policing and incarceration & ending criminal legal system harms"; "investing in new approaches to community safety and utilizing funding incentives"; "allocating new money to build healthy, sustainable & equitable communities for all people"; and "holding officials accountable & enhancing self-determination of black communities."[688] It specifically calls for funding related to employment, high-quality and affordable housing, and a universal minimum livable income.

In a letter to Congresswoman Bass, Congresswoman Sheila Jackson Lee (D-TX), Senator Cory Booker (D-NJ), and Congressman Jerry Nadler (D-NY) write, "Justice in Policing, by its very name, centers investments in policing rather than what should be front and center—upfront investments in communities and people." They argue that any new legislation needs to address the fundamental causes of police brutality and killings of unarmed individuals. They write, "There's this thought that Black people are dying at the hands of police officers because individual officers are bad actors, but it is actually a systemic issue, and if you understand it to be systemic, then the solutions must also be systemic." The BREATHE Act, if passed, would transform the nation's criminal justice system through sweeping changes such as eliminating the Drug Enforcement Administration, halting the use of surveillance technology, abolishing mandatory minimums, and ending life sentences."[689]

A VERDICT BUT NOT VINDICATION FOR FLOYD

On April 19, 2021, people around the world held their breath in anticipation of the verdict against George Floyd's killer, Derek Chauvin. Despite overwhelming evidence in the form of video footage, spellbinding eyewitness statements, forensic evidence, and police testimony against Chauvin—including that of black police chief Medaria Arradondo of Minneapolis—many braced for a possible acquittal. Most police officers involved in killings are not even charged with a crime, and those who are, overwhelmingly end up being acquitted. The doctrine of "qualified immunity" is a legal principle that employs the highly subjective "reasonableness" standard, which gives police officers the benefit of the doubt in cases involving potential criminal behavior. Prosecutors and judges also tend to lean toward the police as a knee-jerk first instance. The data support this behavior. A study of the period from 2005 to 2021 by the Henry A. Wallace Police Crime Database found that out of thousands of police killings, only about 140 police officers were arrested on murder or manslaughter charges. Of that number, about a third were convicted of any charges at all, and only seven were convicted of murder, a rate of five percent.[690] Based on these statistics alone, it would have been reasonable to expect Chauvin to walk free.

However, after a three-week trial packed with emotional intensity, the jury reached a unanimous decision finding Officer Chauvin guilty on all three charges of second-degree murder, three-degree murder, and second-degree manslaughter. A collective sigh of momentary relief could be heard around the nation. On April 20, 2021, he was sentenced to twenty-two and a half years in prison. In February 2022 the other three officers were found guilty for failing to intervene.[691] They and Chauvin also faced federal civil charges.

Darnella Frazier's testimony at Chauvin's trial was riveting and reflected the excruciating trauma that she and other witnesses of police killings endure. She testified that when Chauvin had his knee on Floyd's neck, Floyd "was terrified. He was suffering." As she stood there she knew what was happening "wasn't right." She also spoke of how the incident had impacted her conscience. She described many sleepless nights where she found herself "apologizing to George Floyd for not doing more and not physically interacting and not saving his life."[692]

She and her family would face more tragedy. In a prescient moment during her testimony, she stated, "When I look at George Floyd, I look at my dad. I look at my brothers. I look at my cousins, my uncles, because they are all Black. I have a Black father. I have a Black brother. I have Black friends. And I look at that, and I look at how that could have been one of them." In early July 2021, only a couple of months after the trial, one of Frazier's uncles was inadvertently killed by Minneapolis police when they crashed into Leneal Frazier's car. The police were pursuing a robbery suspect at the time of the crash. The suspect escaped. Darnella Frazier mourned on Facebook, "Another black man lost his life [at] the hands of the police! Minneapolis police [have] cost my whole family a big loss."[693] Brian Cummings, the officer who recklessly drove the police car that led to Leneal's death, was later charged with second-degree manslaughter and criminal vehicular homicide.[694]

On May 25, 2021—the one-year anniversary of Floyd's death— Darnella Frazier posted the following statement on social media:

A year ago, today I witnessed a murder. The victim's name was George Floyd. Although this wasn't the first time, I've seen a black man get killed at the hands of the police, this is the first time I witnessed it happen in front of me. Right in front of my eyes, a few feet away. I didn't know this man from a can of paint, but I knew his life mattered. I knew that he was in pain. I knew that he was another black man in danger with no power. I was only 17 at the time, just a normal day for me walking my 9-year-old cousin to the corner store, not even prepared for what I was about to see, not even knowing my life was going to change on this exact day in those exact moments . . . it did. It changed me. It changed how I viewed life. It made me realize how dangerous it is to be Black in America. We shouldn't have to walk on eggshells around police officers, the same people that are supposed to protect and serve. We are looked at as thugs, animals, and criminals, all because of the color of our skin. Why are Black people the only ones viewed this way when every race has some type of wrongdoing? None of us are to judge. We are all human. I am 18 now and I still hold the weight and trauma of what I witnessed a year ago. It's a little easier now, but I'm not who I used to be. A part of my childhood was taken from me. My 9-year-old cousin who witnessed the same thing I did got a part of her childhood taken from her. Having to up and leave because my home was no longer safe, waking up to reporters at my door, closing my eyes at night only to see a man who is brown like me, lifeless on the ground. I couldn't sleep properly for weeks. I used to shake so bad at night my mom had to rock me to sleep. Hopping from hotel to hotel because we didn't have a home and looking over our back every day in the process. Having panic and anxiety attacks every time I seen a police car, not knowing who to trust because a lot of people are evil with bad intentions. I hold that weight. A lot of people call me a hero even though I don't see myself as one. I was just in the right place at the right time. Behind this smile, behind these awards, behind the publicity, I'm a girl trying to heal from something I am reminded of every day. Everyone talks about the girl who recorded George Floyd's death, but to actually be her is a different story. Not only did this affect me, my family too. We all experienced change. My mom the most. I strive every day to be strong for her because she was strong for me when I couldn't be strong for myself. Even though this was a traumatic life-changing experience for me, I'm proud of myself. If it weren't for my video, the world wouldn't have known the truth. I own that. My video didn't save George Floyd, but it put his murderer away and off the streets. You can view George Floyd anyway you choose to view him, despite his past, because don't we all have one? He was a loved one, someone's son, someone's father, someone's brother, and someone's friend. We the people won't take the blame, you won't keep pointing fingers at us as if it's our fault, as if we are criminals. I don't think people understand how serious death is . . . that person is never coming back. These officers shouldn't get to decide if someone gets to live or not. It's time these officers start getting held accountable. Murdering people and abusing your power while doing it is not doing your job. It shouldn't have to take people to actually go through something to understand it's not ok. It's called having a heart and understanding right from wrong. George Floyd, I can't express enough how I wish things could have went different, but I want you to know you will always be in my heart. I'll always remember this day because of you. May your soul rest in peace. "May you rest in the most beautiful roses."—Darnella Frazier[695]

Frazier's bravery was recognized far and wide. She won the Benenson Courage Award from PEN America, a leading free-speech advocacy organization, with the award presented to her by Spike Lee. PEN America CEO Suzanne Nossel stated, "With nothing more than a cell phone and sheer guts, Darnella changed the course of history in this country."[696] On June 11, 2021, she won a special award and citation from the Pulitzer Prize board for "courageously reporting the murder of George Floyd, a video that spurred protests against police brutality around the world, highlighting the crucial role of citizens in journalists' quest for truth and justice."[697] Previous winners in the category of Special Citations and Awards include anti-lynching journalist Ida B. Wells (2020) and singer and humanitarian Aretha Franklin (2019).

BLACK MOVEMENTS MATTER

How many mothers have to cry?
How many brothers gotta die?
How many more times?
How many more times?
How many more marches?
How many more signs?
How many more lives?
How many more times?
—Trey Songz, "2020 Riots: How Many Times"

Within twenty-four hours of Chauvin's trial, there were six more killings by police. These included Ma'Khia Bryant in Columbus, Ohio; Brian Deleon in San Antonio, Texas; Terry Wayne Bishop, also in

San Antonio; Steven John Olson in Escondido, California; Andrew Brown in Elizabeth City, North Carolina; and Phet Gouvonvong in Worchester, Massachusetts.[698] Bryant, whose killing was recorded by a police body camera, was a sixteen-year-old African American shot by Columbus police in an incident that involved a conflict between her and an adult woman. The shooting occurred just fifteen minutes before the Chauvin verdict was announced. Bryant held a knife and passions were inflamed, but there was no effort to de-escalate the situation before Officer Nicholas Reardon fired four shots into the teenager. The Columbus Police Department and many others defended Reardon's action as justified. Yet the department's overall record on shootings and excessive use of force reveals a disturbing anti-black bias. Although African Americans constitute less than 30 percent of the local population, they are on the receiving end of 55 percent of the violence perpetrated by the police. Bryant's killing was not just a failure of the local police, but also a failure of a foster care system that cycled her and her younger sister, Ja'Niah, through multiple unstable placements.[699] A headline in the May 8, 2021, *New York Times* summed up the tragedy: "Ma'Khia Bryant's Journey Through Foster Care Ended With an Officer's Bullet." In March 2022, a grand jury decided Officer Reardon was innocent of wrongdoing and brought no charges against him.

Perhaps more to the point, and to push back against the argument that Chauvin's conviction demonstrated that the system works, two years after the Floyd uprisings there was no sign of decline in the rate of police killings. Despite the high degree of scrutiny generated by the Floyd protests and local, state, and federal action, police killed 999 people in the United States in 2019, 1,021 people in 2020, and 1,055 people nationwide in 2021, "the highest total since *The Washington Post* began tracking fatal shootings by officers in 2015—underscoring the difficulty of reducing such incidents despite sustained public attention to the issue."[700]

While a pandemic raged and a swooning president kept Andrew Jackson's racist legacy alive, a movement of networks embodied

Harriet Tubman's mission of connecting people with aspirations for restorative justice, freedom, and liberation. The Floyd catalyst became an inflection point that has directly challenged the narratives of the nation. The movement decried the devaluation of black life and took to the streets, the media, the courtroom, the classroom, and the halls of Congress.

Many see parallels with the 1960s. As Elizabeth Hinton documents in her important 2021 book, *America on Fire: The Untold History of Police Violence and Black Rebellion Since the 1960s*, the hundreds of urban uprisings that took place in that period were almost universally prompted by police violence and harassment of black communities. Hinton's book carefully documents the following: in 1964 and 1965 there were 4 rebellions each year, in 1966 there were 17, in 1967 there were 75, in 1968 there were 504, in 1969 there were 613, in 1970 there were 632, in 1971 there were 319, and in 1972 there were 71 rebellions.[701] The National Advisory Commission on Civil Disorders, known as the Kerner Commission, did a post-rebellion assessment on the cause and potential ways to prevent more violence. Related to policing, it reported, "The Commission condemns moves to equip police departments with mass destruction weapons, such as automatic rifles, machine guns, and tanks. Weapons which are designed to destroy, not to control, have no place in densely populated urban communities."[702] As with other recommendations by the Commission, this admonition was ignored. Weaponized *control* of populated urban communities, however, is not acceptable either.

While there are parallels to the rebellions of the past, the current era unfolds in a time of state retreat on social responsibility and commitment, increasing corporate power, and a genuine drift toward authoritarianism. Federal, state, and local policies form a perfect network of debilitating economic and political disempowerment of local communities that especially impacts people of color, even though in many jurisdictions black elected officials are in charge. The Floyd uprisings and movements they catalyzed remind us that police brutality, vigilantism, and racial capitalism—not property damage—are the real domestic threats to national security. Persistent racial disparities in health, education, employment, environmental safety, criminal justice, and other areas of U.S. life and society demand a broad agenda of transformation that has yet to be realized.

In the same spirit that Harriet Tubman's vision of freedom extended beyond ending slavery, today's movement for social and racial justice extends beyond demanding individual perpetrators be held accountable, and toward structural change and collective possibilities for an emancipatory future. In the area of police accountability, reforms have occurred at the local level, where activists fought tremendous odds, but also at the national level, where they were able to change the discourses about race and criminalization and push for changes that were previously not on the table.

Imagining such changes is the first step toward enacting them, and the volcanic resistance that emerged in 2020 has energized both. As Keeanga-Yamahtta Taylor writes: "Democracy, where we see all our aspirations, our failures, and our endeavors as connected, means trying to bring in as many as possible and figuring out how to make it work. Black lives *can* matter. But it will demand a struggle to not only change the police but to change the world that relies on the police to manage its unequal distribution of the necessities of life."[703] That struggle will continue in many forms, and will be carried on the shoulders of generations to come. Our work is to lighten their load.

Bree Newsome Bass ascends flagpole on June 27, 2015, to liberate the community from the white supremacist battle flag. VIDEO STILL COURTESY OF BREE NEWSOME BASS.

TEN

MONUMENTAL CHANGE: ABOLISHING SYMBOLS OF WHITE SUPREMACY

"Monuments aren't history lessons—they're pledges of allegiance."
—Erin L. Thompson

"My body and blood are a tangible truth of the South and its past. The black people I come from were owned by the white people I come from. The white people I come from fought and died for their Lost Cause. And I ask you now, who dares to tell me to celebrate them? Who dares to ask me to accept their mounted pedestals?"
—Caroline Randall Williams

IN THE TRADITION OF HARRIET TUBMAN, Ida B. Wells, Rosa Parks, Fannie Lou Hamer, and so many others, one determined black woman decided to place her life on the line to strike out against injustice. On June 27, 2015, Brittany Ann Byuarim "Bree" Newsome Bass, thirty, climbed into history when she scaled a flagpole in Columbia, South Carolina, and removed the Confederate flag that had been flying at full mast.

Bree's career as a musician, songwriter, and performer took a sharp turn during her university years. She attended New York University's Tisch School of the Arts to study filmmaking and worked at Saatchi & Saatchi as an artist in residence during the Occupy movement. Two years later, she relocated to North Carolina, where she participated in the massive "Moral Mondays" protests at the North Carolina state capitol led by Reverend William Barber. The broad-based multiracial, multi-issue campaign fought to reject the hyper-conservative agenda North Carolina's Republican legislators were trying to impose on the state. In response to the tragic Florida murder of black teenager Trayvon Martin in 2012, she joined others working on the front lines against ongoing killings of unarmed African Americans by police and white vigilantes.

Bree's commitment to racial justice, voting rights, and civil rights flowed, in part, from a family background deeply rooted in black politics. Her mother, Lynne Platt Newsome, had long worked on issues related to educational equity. Her father, Reverend Dr. Clarence G. Newsome, had worked as dean of Howard University's Divinity School and as president of Shaw University—both historically black institutions—and had been president of the National Underground Railroad Freedom Center. Perhaps Bree also got her athleticism from her father. He was one of the first two black football players on athletic scholarship at Duke University. Although his college football career ended early due to injuries, he went on to earn his bachelor's, master's, and doctoral degrees at Duke University.[704]

In the statement they prepared for the flag removal action, Bree and her colleagues wrote, "We removed the flag today because we can't wait any longer. We can't continue like this another day. It's time for a new chapter where we are sincere about dismantling white supremacy and building toward true racial justice and equality."[705]

In 1961, almost a quarter century before Bree Newsome was born, the Confederate flag was raised over the state capitol dome in Charleston as South Carolina and other Southern states commemorated the hundred-year anniversary of the start of the Civil War. These events were not staged to critique and accurately document what happened, but to celebrate and validate Southern defiance against the Union and, more contemporaneously, push back against the struggle for racial equality and justice. Other Southern states also flew some version of the Confederate flag, including Mississippi, Georgia, and Alabama.

Segregation was still legal and enforced in 1961 despite the 1954 *Brown v. Board of Education* Supreme Court decision that declared "separate but equal" Jim Crow segregation unconstitutional. The year 1961 was also a high tide of civil rights activism that included the Freedom Rides challenge to segregation in the South's interstate bus system. The raising of the flag in South Carolina was linked to Southern opposition to the Civil Rights movement and was a states' rights rebuff to desegregation.[706] In fact, legal segregation impacted the event itself. President John Kennedy, who attended the commemoration, was forced to move some events to an integrated naval base because African American attendees were denied entrance at segregated hotels.[707]

African Americans in South Carolina continually protested the flying of the Confederate flag and, in 2000, won a minor victory when it was moved from the dome of the Capitol building to a flagpole adjacent to the Confederate soldier monument on the statehouse grounds. There it would fly until Bree decided it would not.

As she waited in a café for the signal from her colleagues that the coast was clear for her to begin her ascent up the flagpole, her thoughts surely went back to the unspeakable act of racist terrorism that had catalyzed her ten days earlier.

On June 17, 2015, South Carolina state senator Reverend Clementa C. Pinckney and twelve worshipers gathered for a prayer meeting at the legendary "Mother" Emanuel African Methodist Episcopal (AME) church in Charleston, South Carolina. Mother Emanuel is the oldest AME church in the South and has a storied history in struggles for social justice. One of AME's founders was Denmark Vesey, a free black man who, in 1822, heroically organized thousands of slaves to revolt in what would have been the nation's largest uprising had the plan not been betrayed.[708] When it was, 313 alleged participants were arrested. Thirty-five—including Vesey—were executed.[709]

The church was destroyed in the aftermath, but members of the congregation continued to meet in secret. A new church was designed by Vesey's son Robert after the Civil War. It stood from 1865 to 1886, when it was leveled by an earthquake. The church was rebuilt in 1891 and continues to stand today with the original altar, communion rail, pews, and light fixtures.[710] The church has continuously served as a center for activism from the Jim Crow and Civil Rights eras to the present day.

In his role as a state senator, Reverend Pinckney fought for racial justice, including police reform. In April, he had hosted rallies at the church after Walter Scott, an unarmed black man, was shot and killed by Michael Slager, a white police officer. On that fateful night in June 2015 at Mother Emanuel, among the congregants sat a hate-filled white supremacist posing as a bible worshiper. The bible study began around 8:30 p.m. and lasted for about a half hour. The group was studying Mark 4:1-20, the "Parable of the Sower," an allegory about seeds finding "good soil" in which to grow. Around 9:00 p.m., Dylann Roof stood up and stated, "I'm here to kill black people."[711] He pulled out a gun and began to methodically shoot the individuals with whom he had sat and prayed. He purposely spared one person, Polly Shepard, hoping she would spread an eyewitness account of his acts. During the shootings, as one victim asked him why he was attacking them, Roof shouted, "You rape our women and you're taking over our country."[712] He fired about seventy shots, hitting each victim multiple times.

Nine of the people at the bible study, all African Americans, died: Reverend Pinckney, Cynthia Marie Graham Hurd, Susie Jackson, Ethel Lee Lance, Depayne Middleton-Doctor, Tywanza Sanders, Daniel L. Simmons, Sharonda Coleman-Singleton, and Myra Thompson. One of the victims, Tywanza Sanders, was killed while trying to shield his eighty-seven-year-old aunt, Susie Jackson. Two of those in attendance—Sanders's mother, Felicia Sanders, and her five-year-old niece—survived by pretending to be dead. According to witnesses, Roof reloaded his gun at least five times and kept shooting until he ran out of bullets.

Roof was captured the next morning. On Roof's website and social media, investigators found photos of him surrounded by Confederate flags and symbols. One picture included the flag flying over the Confederate Monument outside the South Carolina State House. The car he was driving when captured had a "Confederate States of America" bumper sticker. Fittingly, Roof would share a cell block with former police officer Slager, who had murdered Walter Scott, as noted earlier.[713]

While in jail, Roof wrote what the *New York Times* called "a white supremacist manifesto." In it he stated, "I would like to make it crystal clear I do not regret what I did. I am not sorry. I have not shed a tear for the innocent people I killed."[714] Roof had spent six months planning the attack and researching the history of the church. He picked a date near the anniversary of Denmark Vesey's scheduled uprising to trigger what he called a "race war." When he was arrested and searched, the police found not only a list of other black churches but also the name of Denmark Vesey.[715] A federal jury found him guilty on thirty-three counts, including murder. On January 10, 2017, Roof became the first person in the U.S. sentenced to death for a federal hate crime.[716]

Three days after the murders, several thousand gathered at the South Carolina State House and demanded that the flag be taken down forever. The activist organization MoveOn.org launched an online petition and received more than 690,000 signatures of people in support of removing the flag.[717] State Republican leaders— Governor Nikki Haley, Senator Lindsey Graham, Senator Tim Scott, former governor Mark Sanford, all of whom had previously done little in response to demands to remove the flag—opportunistically got on board and called for the state legislature to vote to take the flag down, a legal requirement. Although momentum was building to remove the flag, there was no guarantee that it was going to happen, and Bree and the black community had been frustrated on too many previous occasions. An intervention was called for.

In a statement on the day of the assassinations, President Barack Obama said, "Michelle and I know several members of Emanuel AME Church. We knew their pastor, Reverend Clementa Pinckney, who, along with eight others, gathered in prayer and fellowship and was murdered last night. And to say our thoughts and prayers are with them and their families, and their community, doesn't say enough to convey the heartache and the sadness and the anger that we feel."[718]

Driving down to South Carolina on June 26, Newsome had listened to Obama deliver Pinckney's eulogy before 5,000 congregants at the College of Charleston. Obama moved the crowd not only with his words, but also with his spontaneous singing of "Amazing Grace." In his remarks, which surely had to be seen as a sign of some sort for Bree, he stated:

> Removing the flag from this state's capitol would not be an act of political correctness; it would not be an insult to the valor of Confederate soldiers. It would simply be an acknowledgment that the cause for which they fought—the cause of slavery—was wrong— [applause]—the imposition of Jim Crow after the Civil War, the resistance to civil rights for all people was wrong. [applause] It would be one step in an honest accounting of America's history, a modest but meaningful balm for so many unhealed wounds. It would be an expression of the amazing changes that have transformed this state and this country for the better, because of the work of so many people of goodwill, people of all races striving to form a more perfect union. By taking down that flag, we express God's grace. [applause][719]

The next morning, around 6:15 a.m., Bree and James Tyson got the signal that there were no police near the base of the Confederate monument. This was the green light needed to begin their operation. Tyson was a white activist who was chosen to help Bree precisely because he was white. The group of activists who planned the action wanted to show cross-racial solidarity against the flag while also recognizing the importance of having an African American woman actually remove it from its perch. With Tyson's help, and dressed in climbing gear, Bree got over the short fence around the site and, as she had trained to do a few days earlier, she scaled the pole and grabbed the flag. As she went up, the police arrived and demanded that she come down. She told them, "You come against me with hatred and oppression and violence. I come against you in the name of God. This flag comes down today."[720]

Bree and Tyson were arrested, and the flag was soon raised back to the top of the pole, but word of the action spread like wildfire. When a guard came and told them that former basketball great Dwayne Wade had offered to pay their bail, they began to realize the power of symbolism and the scope of their success.[721] Within days, the *BBC* ran an article titled, "Bree Newsome: Flag activist becomes online folk hero," reporting that "the act of civil disobedience by Newsome and spotter James Ian Tyson sparked an outpouring of support on social media sites. The hashtags #freebree, #freejames, #takeitdown and #keepitdown started trending on Twitter as soon as Newsome started descending the 30-foot pole, grasping the Confederate flag in her hand."[722]

The time had come for change, and less than two weeks later, on July 10, after decades of opposition, South Carolina passed legislation to permanently remove the flag. While not a single public policy changed as a result, some felt that progress had been made. The NAACP, for example, ended its fifteen-year boycott of the state over the flag issue.

Although forced into action, Governor Haley and others on the right did not concede on their misleading stance that the flag had "multiple meanings," including some that had nothing to do with race. In her convention speech at the Republican National Convention in July 2020, Haley contended that "America is not a racist country." Choosing to ignore the long and ongoing history of white supremacist support for keeping the flag, Haley said, "We made the hard choices needed to heal—and removed a divisive symbol, peacefully and respectfully."[723] Equally critical, she absolved Trump of any responsibility for the nation's taut racial relations and continued to support him even after the deadly January 6 coup attempt that he inspired and pushed.

In a broader statement released after her arrest, Bree spoke more fully of the link between her action and the murders of the nine church parishioners:

> The night of the Charleston Massacre, I had a crisis of faith. The people who gathered for Bible study in Emmanuel AME Church that night—Cynthia Marie Graham Hurd, Susie Jackson, Ethel Lee Lance, Depayne Middleton-Doctor, Tywanza Sanders, Daniel Simmons, Sharonda Coleman-Singleton, Myra Thompson and Rev. Clementa Pinckney (rest in peace)—were only doing what Christians are called to do when anyone knocks on the door of the church: invite them into fellowship and worship. The day after the massacre I was asked what the next step was and I said I didn't know. We've been here before and here we are again: black people slain simply for being black; an attack on the black church as a place of spiritual refuge and community organization.[724]

Bree's operation was widely covered, and served to initiate a new era of resistance to the white supremacist symbols that taunt the nation's landscape and culture.

SYMBOLS FALL AND RISE

> "Robert E. Lee led a bloody war to perpetuate slavery. . . . Either he knew what slavery meant when he helped maim and murder thousands in its defense, or he did not. If he did not, he was a fool. If he did, Robert Lee was a traitor and a rebel—not indeed to his country, but to humanity and humanity's God."
> —W. E. B. Du Bois

Public demand to replace Jackson with Tubman on the twenty is part of the larger national reckoning with the legacies of white supremacism and patriarchy. Slavery-defending Confederates, enslavers, segregationists, racial terrorists, and bigots should never have been platformed in spaces of public honor in the first place. Grassroots organizing has successfully forced the removal of such symbols despite fierce vows that they would never be retired. Protests and movement organizing by ordinary people and communities have expedited change.

The uprisings of 2020 shifted national consciousness and catalyzed countless new campaigns against racist symbols and narratives. However, it is important to underscore that people have been acting against these racist symbols for as long as they've existed. "The idea that protest against racist monuments is new—that it is an example of political correctness run amok—is completely ahistorical and untrue," says Kali Holloway, founder of the Make It Right Project, which linked people fighting to get racist monuments removed from places in the South and beyond.[725] "In fact," she says, "as soon as these statues were erected, there was pushback against them—primarily registered by black citizens, who used every means at their disposal to express their opposition to the placement of tributes to Confederates in their midst. And they did that even under the threat of reprisal in the form of racist Jim Crow terror and violence."[726]

For example, Frederick Douglass deeply opposed the statue portraying a black man kneeling beside a standing Abraham Lincoln, made by white artist Thomas Ball to celebrate President Lincoln's role in Emancipation. On April 14, 1876, a crowd of 25,000 people—including President Ulysses S. Grant—had gathered to hear Frederick Douglass speak at the unveiling of the statue, which was also the eleventh anniversary of Lincoln's assassination.[727] A plaque on the statue's pedestal explains that the sculpture was built "with funds contributed solely by emancipated citizens of the United States," beginning with "the first contribution of five dollars . . . made by Charlotte Scott a freed woman of Virginia, being her first earnings in freedom." It was her original idea, "on the day she heard of President Lincoln's death to build a monument to his memory."[728]

Douglass had known Lincoln and had advised him in several meetings.[730] "Truth compels me to admit, even here in the presence of the monument we have erected to his memory," Douglass said, "Abraham Lincoln was not, in the fullest sense of the word, either our man or our model. In his interests, in his associations, in his

Hundreds gather on June 23, 2020, to urge the removal of the
Emancipation Memorial, Lincoln Park, Washington, D.C.[729]
PHOTO BY TRACY MEEHLEIB. COURTESY OF THE LIBRARY OF CONGRESS.

habits of thought, and in his prejudices, he was a white man. He
was preeminently the white man's President, entirely devoted to
the welfare of white men. He was ready and willing at any time
during the first years of his administration to deny, postpone, and
sacrifice the rights of humanity in the colored people to promote
the welfare of the white people of this country."[731]

In a recently discovered letter by Douglass to the *National
Republican* newspaper, he extends his critique further:

ABOLISHING SYMBOLS OF WHITE SUPREMACY

To the Editor of the National Republican:

Sir: Admirable as is the monument by Mr. Ball in Lincoln Park, it does not, as it seems to me, tell the whole truth, and perhaps no one monument could be made to tell the whole truth of any subject which it might be designed to illustrate. The mere act of breaking the negro's chains was the act of Abraham Lincoln, and is beautifully expressed in this monument. But the act by which the negro was made a citizen of the United States and invested with the elective franchise was pre-eminently the act of President U. S. Grant, and this is nowhere seen in the Lincoln monument. The negro here, though rising, is still on his knees and nude. What I want to see before I die is a monument representing the negro, not couchant on his knees like a four-footed animal, but erect on his feet like a man. There is room in Lincoln park for another monument, and I throw out this suggestion to the end that it may be taken up and acted upon.

Frederick Douglass[732]

In 1916, Freeman Henry Morris Murray, known as the "first black art historian," critiqued the monument in his book, *Emancipation and the Freed in American Sculpture*. One hundred and forty-four years after Frederick Douglass spoke at the statue's unveiling in Lincoln Park, hundreds of people gathered at the same spot to protest the artwork, vowing to tear it down. Among those gathered was twenty-year-old Glenn Foster, a student at Harvard University. According to American University Radio, Foster helped organize the protest and said he was the founder of the Freedom Neighborhood, "a youth-led revolution for our generation."[733]

"You're looking at this and you're seeing a hand over Black people, and that's always what it has been—that we've had a hand over us when it comes to our freedom, when it comes to our liberation, when it comes to being empowered, and that's not right," Foster said. "This statue represents something that is far worse for Black people. It shows that we're going to get our freedom on their timeline, and that's not right."[734]

Confederate flags and monuments, statues of enslavers, buildings and schools named after white supremacists, sport teams with racist names, bigoted historical markers and textbook accounts of history—and omission of the true extent of the suffering and resistance of people of color—have all contributed to the normalization of racial hierarchy in the United States. For many white Americans, these symbols have been mostly in the background or perhaps slightly embarrassing, but not much more. "As people of color," writes Loretta Ross, "our intersectional standpoints have compelled us to bear witness to the human tragedy of White supremacy in a way invisible to most White people."[735] For communities of color, however, racist symbols are daily reminders of a system that devalues their lives, history, and communities. Fightback has included lawsuits, protests, boycotts, art, and every other legal and political weapon available. There has been no ambiguity regarding what these symbols represent: state-approved and deliberately public narratives of white power.

In recent times, there have been three key turning points in the broad movement to rid the nation of racist symbolism: the 2015 murder of the nine black churchgoers in Charleston, South Carolina; the deadly 2017 "Unite the Right" march of white nationalists in Charlottesville, Virginia; and the 2020 police killing of George Floyd. Each moment created opportunities for exposing the real history of these symbols and the urgent need for their abolition. More than a century and a half after the Civil War and several decades after the end of legal segregation, these symbols reinforce the normalization of a white America that has historically dominated, marginalized, and lynched people of color. At every juncture, these symbols have been challenged, stoking backlash from state and non-state forces.

While the far right's response to taking down the Confederate flag in Charleston was fierce and enraged, it mostly took place online among racial extremists. Those who inhabit that fringe emerged en masse in August 2017 when they decided to turn Charlottesville, Virginia, into a battlefront. The catalyst for mustering a coalition of neo-Nazis, Ku Klux Klan members, white nationalist groups, anti-Jewish fanatics, and all sorts of far-right forces was the Charlottesville City Council decision in February 2017 to remove a statue of Confederate general Robert E. Lee from Lee Park, which would later be renamed Emancipation Park. The statue had been in the park since 1924. Protests against the decision arose almost immediately, as did public defense of the decree. An unsuccessful lawsuit and small skirmishes throughout the spring of 2017 were just the opening act.

Lee's statue and other tributes to him have stood so long partly because he was never fully repudiated for his leading role in the effort to split the nation in defense of slavery. Lee was never arrested and certainly not sent to prison for his treasonous acts.

In June 2017, Charlottesville-based white nationalist Jason Kessler began calling for a "Unite the Right" rally for the weekend of August 11–12, 2017. According to the Southern Poverty Law Center, Kessler founded a white nationalist group called Unity & Security for America. With participants emboldened by a friendly face in the White House, the goal of the rally, besides demanding that the Lee statue not be removed, was to build a united white nationalist movement.

On the night of August 11, hundreds of openly racist demonstrators descended upon the University of Virginia campus and marched with flaming torches, Nazi salutes, and chants of "Jews will not replace us" and "white lives matter."[736] At the same time, civil rights organizations and racial justice groups met in churches and peacefully assembled as a counterforce to the rally. The city was ill prepared for this combustible mix and the catastrophic violence that occurred the next day.

Both sides gathered early Saturday morning, August 12, but with very different agendas. While the social justice activists wanted to peacefully support the removal of the statute, they met gangs of armed white nationalists who attacked them with bats, batons, and other weapons. Local law enforcement officers were woefully hapless and did little to prevent individuals from getting injured. As noted in the previous chapter, the most tragic incident happened around 1:40 p.m., when a car driven by white nationalist James Alex Fields Jr. killed anti-racist activist Heather Heyer. In June 2019, Fields was sentenced to life in prison for committing federal hate crimes.

The event triggered one of the most deplorable incidents of the Trump presidency. On August 15, after several bungled and ambiguous statements, Trump said that there were "very fine people, on both sides."[737] In his view, there were some pro-Lee white supremacists marching in the streets with torches making racist chants who were fine people and some who were not. Trump did everything he could to communicate his stance for keeping the Confederate statue. To do so, he had to ignore the overt racism of the Unite the Right crowd and their violent nature. The appalling murder of Heyer and attacks on anti-racism activists demonstrated how far some would go to perpetuate symbols of white supremacy. The aftermath also demonstrated the degree to which Republican leadership was willing to cohabit with white nationalist forces.

Few of the individuals that committed violence were arrested and prosecuted, and those that were mostly received wrist-slap sentences or fines. However, rally organizers were held accountable in other ways. In November 2021, a jury found more than a dozen of the nation's most prominent white racists and hate groups guilty of conspiring to intimidate, harass, or commit acts of violence during the Unite the Right rally. The jury also decided the men and their racist organizations should pay $26 million in damages.[738]

On July 10, 2021, the city's statues of Robert Lee and Stonewall Jackson were removed from public display. Charlottesville's mayor, Nikuyah Walker, who is African American, stated as the crane was lifting the Lee statue off its base, "Taking down this statue is one small step closer to the goal of helping Charlottesville, Virginia, and America, grapple with the sin of being willing to destroy Black people for economic gain."[739] In December 2021, the Charlottesville city council decided that the 1,100-pound monument that once provoked a deadly weekend of violence in their city would be melted down and turned into a new piece of public artwork by 2024. A black-led museum, the Jefferson School African American Heritage Center, will spearhead the effort through its "Swords Into Plowshares" project. Andrea Douglas, the museum's director, said the project "will allow Charlottesville to contend with its racist past."[740]

Today, more than 150 years after the Confederacy ended, symbols that pay tribute to individuals associated with it still exist throughout America's physical and symbolic landscape. A February 2019 study by the Southern Poverty Law Center, "Whose Heritage? Public Symbols of the Confederacy," found that there were at least 1,503 Confederate symbols in public spaces, at least 109 schools named after Confederate leaders, and more than 700 monuments or statues honoring the Confederacy around the nation.[741] As Stephanie McCurry wrote in her June 21, 2020, article for the *The Atlantic*:

> The Confederate States of America was a pro-slavery nation at war against the United States. The C.S.A. was a big, centralized state, devoted to securing a society in which enslavement to white people was the permanent and inherited condition of all people of African descent. The Confederates built an explicitly white-supremacist, pro-slavery, and antidemocratic nation-state, dedicated to the principle that all men are *not* created equal. Emboldened by what they saw as the failure of emancipation in other parts of the world, buoyed by the new science of race, and convinced that the American vision of the people had been terribly betrayed, they sought the kind of future for human slavery and conservative republican government that was no longer possible within the United States. This is the cause that the statues honor.[742]

There is no way to separate Confederate symbols from the ideology of white supremacy and slavery. In February 1861, in Montgomery, Alabama, seven rebel states formed the Confederate States of America (CSA), swore in Jefferson Davis as their president, and forged a constitution. The new nation was anchored in the constitutional provision that prohibited the CSA from *ever* changing the law of slavery: "No . . . law denying or impairing the right of property in negro slaves shall be passed."[743]

Declarations made by the Confederacy's individual states further reaffirmed their racist positions. For example, Mississippi stated, "Our position is thoroughly identified with the institution of slavery," while Florida declared that it was being driven to secede by the "strength of the anti-slavery sentiment of the free States." Georgia was upset that some Northern states were promoting "negro equality." The Secessionist Commissioner of Louisiana stated, "Louisiana looks to the formation of a Southern confederacy to preserve the blessings of African slavery" and "The people of the slave-holding States are bound together by the same necessity and determination to preserve African slavery."[744]

Although the words "slave" and "slavery" do not appear in the U.S. Constitution, the document sanctioned the slave trade, obligated states to return individuals who had escaped their enslavers, and allowed the South to count "all other persons" (enslaved) as three-fifths of a person for the purpose of determining proportional representation in the U.S. House of Representatives and for taxation. The authors of the U.S. Constitution were careful about their language. The Confederate Constitution made no effort to hide its intentions. In fact, it sought to emphasize with clear language the sanctity of white people's right to own black people. The Constitution of the CSA reinforced the urgency of defending that right. In Article IV, Section II, it states:

> The citizens of each State shall be entitled to all the privileges and immunities of citizens in the several States, and shall have the right of transit and sojourn in any State of this Confederacy, with their slaves and other property; and the right of property in said slaves shall not be thereby impaired.[745]

In Article IV, Section III, it continues:

> In all such territory, the institution of negro slavery as it now exists in the Confederate States, shall be recognized and protected by Congress, and by the territorial government; and the inhabitants of the several Confederate States and Territories, shall have the right to take to such territory any slaves, lawfully held by them in any of the States and Territories of the Confederate States.[746]

Furthermore, contrary to Lost Cause arguments, Southern states were not fighting on behalf of states' rights. In fact, they were angry that Northern states were asserting their states' rights to not return individuals who had escaped from slavery and to grant, in some instances, voting rights to free African American men. More than anything, Southern states wanted the federal government, even under the leadership of what the Alabama secessionist convention resolution called the "Black Republican Party," to intervene to perpetuate slavery.[747] In fact, while Lincoln, upon getting elected, opposed the expansion of slavery to the territories, he did not plan to arbitrate and end the institution in the states where it already existed. It was never the case of states' rights vs. federalism. The rising power of financial and industrial capital in the North challenged the economic and political hegemony of the Southern aristocracy, a conflict that could only be resolved, from the Southern perspective, by secession, a move unacceptable to Northern power. Breaking Southern authority required the North to abolish slavery, but it did not require the North to institutionalize equality for African Americans. However, black people and radical Republicans linked abolition with democratic expansion and the securing of full citizenship rights. This led to the emancipatory possibilities of the Reconstruction era.

It was after Reconstruction's fall in the late 1870s that the Lost Cause narrative unfolded to reframe the Civil War as primarily a defense of Southern culture, states' rights, and opposition to federal overreach, rather than a defense of slavery. This storyline gathered strength and became popular history that eventually influenced school textbooks, Hollywood films, academic discourse, and the defense of public monuments.

The Lost Cause narrative surged again in the 1950s and 1960s as national racial justice movements made gains. Conservative white intellectuals rationalized and justified Southern retrenchment and ongoing domination of the black population. Scholar William F. Buckley Jr., perhaps the best-known conservative writer of his time, wrote in 1957,

The central question that emerges—and it is not a parliamentary question or a question that is answered by merely consulting a catalogue of the rights of American citizens, born Equal—is whether the White community in the South is entitled to take such measures as are necessary to prevail, politically and culturally, in areas in which it does not predominate numerically? The sobering answer is Yes—the White community is so entitled because, for the time being, it is the advanced race.[748]

Buckley argued that the right to vote as outlined in the Constitution was "demagogy" and that it would be only when African Americans reached "cultural equality" with white Americans—as defined by whites—that the white imposition of "superior mores" should cease.[749] Others would take a less cerebral approach. White terrorism and authoritarian rule were the defining experiences for most African Americans until the Civil Rights movement victories. Those victories have led to progress, but they have far from abolished racial injustice and the many ways life in the United States continues to enforce racial hierarchy and to privilege whiteness.

The decision by the modern Republican Party to go all in on the "Southern Strategy"—the effort to win votes from bigoted whites by signaling promises to push back against the political organizing of African Americans—also meant a defense of Confederate symbols. First Richard Nixon and then Ronald Reagan aligned with voters who opposed busing, affirmative action, minority set-asides, and expanded voting rights. They and the Republican Party quickly embraced the narrative that the Confederate symbols simply meant a defense of Southern "heritage" and "culture." The Ku Klux Klan and other violent white supremacist groups fully incorporated Confederate symbols as projections of white power. No symbol has been as ubiquitous as the Confederate flag among racist groups, or, for that matter, among ordinary whites in the South.

Under pressure from an outraged black community following the Charleston murders, some states and local areas followed South Carolina's move to distance themselves from the Confederate flag. In 2015, three Southern governors—Terry McAuliffe (D-VA), Pat

McCrory (R-NC), and Larry Hogan (R-MD)—took steps to eliminate or downplay the Confederate flag. On June 23, 2015, Governor McAuliffe announced that Virginia would gradually phase out license plates incorporating its image.[750] These plates had been produced at the request of the Sons of Confederate Veterans, a pro-Confederate group comprised of descendants of Confederate soldiers.

In North Carolina, on the same day McAuliffe made his statement, Governor McCrory also announced that it was time to end the license plate practice, stating in a press release that he would "be requesting that the General Assembly change the North Carolina statute in order to discontinue the issuance of the Confederate battle flag emblem on state-issued license plates. The time is right to change this policy due to the recent Supreme Court ruling and the tragedy in Charleston."[751]

Maryland's Governor Hogan also expressed support for ending Confederate license plates, but made it clear at the time that he did not want to remove statutes or other symbols of the Confederacy.[752] He did not address one Confederate controversy tied to the Maryland state flag. The four-square flag has two family crests on it from the family of George Calvert, who along with his sons founded the Maryland colony. The orange and black crest in the upper left and lower right represent his father's side of the family, which opposed the Confederacy. The red and white cross and backgrounds in the upper right and lower left are the crest of Calvert's mother's side, which supported the Confederacy. Maryland was one of four slave states—the others are Delaware, Kentucky, and Missouri—that did not join the Confederate States of America. There were families in Maryland, of course, that certainly did support it, and the Calvert family enslaved people. The flag was created in 1904 ostensibly to bring together the conflicting sides of the war.[753] In *Baltimore Magazine*, Ron Cassie writes,

> The bigger question may be whether Maryland should fly any flag paying homage to the Calvert family—either black and gold or red and white. The founding family's record on race is shameful. In 1639, under Cecil Calvert—the second Lord Baltimore—Maryland

became the first colony to specify baptism as a Christian did not make a slave a free person, as it did in England. In 1664, led by the third Lord Baltimore, plantation owner and Proprietary Governor Charles Calvert, Maryland became the first colony to mandate life-long servitude for all black slaves, the first to make the children of slaves their master's property for life, and the first to ban interracial marriages.[754]

The removal of the Confederate flag from the South Carolina statehouse left only one state holdout still incorporating overtly Confederate imagery in its official symbolism: Mississippi. First raised in 1894, a redesigned Mississippi state flag incorporated the canton of the Confederate "stars and bars" and three horizontal blue, white, and red stripes of equal size. As a result, an image of the Confederate battle flag hovered over the state's black community for generations as a constant reminder of the racist ethos that dominated every aspect of Mississippi's culture. While other states had abolished the flag following protests, lawsuits, and the "Unite the Right" violence in Charleston, lawmakers in Mississippi did not budge. Some cities in the state found legal means to no longer fly the state flag, including Macon, Columbus, Grenada, Magnolia, Hattiesburg, Clarksdale, Starkville, Yazoo City, and Greenwood, as did the University of Mississippi. Between 2015 and 2020, nearly two dozen pieces of legislation were proposed to change the flag, but all were rebuffed.[755]

At 38 percent, Mississippi has the largest percentage of African Americans of any state in the country. Yet the state's persistent embrace of white supremacist "heritage" has menaced its black citizens and people of conscience on a daily basis. This embrace was provocatively reinforced in 2020 when Mississippi governor Tate Reeves issued an executive order designating April as "Confederate Heritage Month."[756] This was in addition to the already existing "Confederate Memorial Day," which had been a legally designated state holiday since 1972.[757]

The state's positions were constantly challenged. Black activists have fought relentlessly to remove the flag, in efforts including those of educator Ollye Shirley, Delores Orey, Ineva May-Pittman, state senator Henry Kirksey, and NAACP leader Aaron Henry, among others. Ollye Shirley forced Jackson's board of education to remove the Confederate flag from a high school—a white majority one at that—while Orey and May-Pittman worked together to force a shopping mall to do the same.[758] According to the *Mississippi Encyclopedia*, state senator Kirksey fought for years in his capacity as a legislator to get rid of what he called the "Confederate slave flag."[759] Former Mississippi NAACP president Aaron Henry worked on a lawsuit that led to a 2001 ballot referendum on whether the flag should be removed.

The defense held, however, until the influence of the Black Lives Matter movement overpowered it. The wave of demand for change pushed some of the flag's staunchest proponents to capitulate. Even the great-great-grandson of CSA president Jefferson Davis, Bertram Hayes-Davis, supported removal, albeit for reasons that ignored the white nationalist politics it represented. He stated that "the battle flag has been hijacked" and "does not represent the entire population of Mississippi."[760] However, the flag clearly *does* represent the racist views of a significant number of white Mississippians, though no longer enough to keep it flying.

On June 28, 2020, the Mississippi House of Representatives voted 91 to 23 and the Mississippi Senate 37 to 14 to remove the Confederate-stained state flag and put it to the voters to select a new one. Two days later, after the measure was signed into law by Governor Reeves on June 30, 2020, what few would have predicted only months earlier became a reality: the flag was permanently retired.[761] In November 2020, voters in the state selected a new flag that featured a magnolia flower in the center on a dark blue background surrounded by stars and the words "IN GOD WE TRUST." After legislation passed in the Mississippi house and senate, Mississippi's Republican governor Tate Reeves signed its adoption into law on January 11, 2021.

CROSSING THE LINE: SPORTS, RACISM, AND OVERTHROWING DIXIECRAT POWER

Over the centuries, white America has perpetuated racist practices in almost every corner of the nation. The world of competitive sports has been no exception. Within that world, perhaps no sport has embodied the ethos and culture of the South's white racism more thoroughly than the National Association for Stock Car Auto Racing (NASCAR). Consequently, no sport was more invested in Confederate flag culture and symbolism than NASCAR. Founded in 1948 in Daytona, Florida, by conservative businessman Bill French Sr., NASCAR became a space for Lost Cause culture as speedways in Florida, South Carolina, and Alabama became embedded in the politics of a changing South.

At the Darlington Raceway in South Carolina, a character dubbed "Johnny Reb" dressed in a Confederate uniform, carried a large Confederate flag around the stadium, and even greeted winning cars.[762] He was not alone. The flag was omnipresent on cars, uniforms, and the clothing of white fans. *Sports Illustrated* wrote, "Confederate flags are as easy to find at NASCAR races as cutoff jeans, cowboy hats and beer."[763] Vendors sold Confederate paraphernalia, and rebel calls were frequent. Few African Americans attended races, and there were no black drivers until Wendell Scott of South Carolina entered the sport in the early 1960s. As of mid-2020, only Scott and seven other black drivers had been in the races, including Darrell "Bubba" Wallace, who has played a central role in transforming symbolism at the sport and pushing NASCAR to "evolve."[764]

Dixiecrat Senator Strom Thurmond, South Carolina's most notorious bigot, attended NASCAR regularly as a political celebrity. Thurmond and his Dixiecrats "started waving the Confederate battle flag to associate it with their pro-segregation politics," writes Joseph Goodman in the Alabama Media Group's AL.com: "Thurmond used NASCAR to advance his agenda. NASCAR was happy to help because it was a profitable partnership."[765]

When Alabama's infamous segregationist, Governor George Wallace, ran for president in 1968 and 1972, Bill French Sr.

supported him both times, stating, "George Washington founded this country, and George Wallace will save it."[766] The NASCAR founder was Wallace's campaign manager for his second presidential run in 1972. French helped him win every county in Florida in that race. As Southern whites shifted from Democrat to Republican, so did NASCAR. The Republicans' post–Southern Strategy move meant tethering the party to conservative Southern whites. As it did, the Republican Party supported the cultural norms and the historic revisionism of the Lost Cause narrative. Both Nixon and Reagan leaned into the NASCAR–Confederate flag nexus; it leaned back.

In 2016, NASCAR CEO Brian French, Bill French Sr.'s grandson, endorsed Donald Trump for president. Although French claimed that he was acting in his capacity as a private citizen, Trump's reaction to the endorsement was, "I am proud to receive the endorsement of such an iconic brand and a quality person such as Brian."[767] According to Open Secrets, of those political contributions by NASCAR-affiliated PACs and members, NASCAR employees or owners, and those individuals' immediate family members, 85.5 percent went to Republicans in 2020, and 89.16 percent went to them in 2018.[768]

Despite its strong affiliation with the conservative right, in 2015 NASCAR attempted to passively address the flag issue. In a proclamation, NASCAR said it was "asking our fans and partners to join us in a renewed effort to create an all-inclusive, even more welcoming atmosphere for all who attend our events. This will include the request to refrain from displaying the Confederate Flag at our facilities and NASCAR events."[769] Noncompliance, which was frequent, was not punished.

Earlier, in 2004, NASCAR had established a "Drive for Diversity" program to increase the number of women and people of color in the industry. Bubba Wallace graduated from the program and eventually became the first full-time racer of color in NASCAR's Cup Series since 1973.[770] Thanks to Wallace's activism and the influence of nationwide organizing to abolish racist symbolism, NASCAR was pushed to take further steps. In June 2020, as the Floyd uprisings

Bubba Wallace. PHOTO COURTESY OF WWW.BUBBAWALLACE.COM.

were taking place across the nation, Wallace called for an investigation into a noose he discovered on the garage door of the stall that had been assigned to him at the Talladega Superspeedway. The incident brought immediate scrutiny to NASCAR. Wallace received support from other drivers, professionals in other sports, and NASCAR leadership. A very public investigation discovered that the rope had been there long before Wallace was assigned the spot.

Never missing an opportunity for racial provocation, Trump wrote a tweet demanding that Wallace apologize "to all those great NASCAR drivers & officials who came to his aid, stood by his side, & were willing to sacrifice everything for him, only to find out that the whole thing was just another HOAX" that backfired.[771] Trump was factually wrong on all counts. No hoax had been perpetrated, nor had Wallace ever accused anyone in particular of placing the noose there, but had merely called for an investigation. Trump's tweet generated more vocal support for Wallace from those around NASCAR. In the aftermath, Wallace continued to raise the issue of discrimination in racing and more broadly in U.S. society. He proudly drove a car emblazoned with the words "Black Lives Matter."

Influenced by the momentum of the Black Lives Matter movement, on June 10, 2020, NASCAR issued a stronger and compulsory policy to divorce itself from its own history and ties to the Confederate flag. The statement read:

> The presence of the confederate flag at NASCAR events runs contrary to our commitment to providing a welcoming and inclusive environment for all fans, our competitors and our industry. Bringing people together around a love for racing and the community that it creates is what makes our fans and sport special. The display of the confederate flag will be prohibited from all NASCAR events and properties.[772]

THE FALL OF RACIAL SYMBOLISM

Public pressure and movement organizing have accelerated the rate that racist symbols have been challenged and replaced. According to the Southern Vision Alliance's Mapping Racist Memorials project, as of early July 2020, in the South alone, protests had led to the removal of at least seventy-seven Confederate monuments, five Columbus monuments, ten other racist monuments, the renaming of fifteen buildings and institutions, and the removal of one Confederate flag. Monuments were taken down in Alabama, Florida, Virginia, Tennessee, Georgia, North Carolina, Texas, Louisiana, Arkansas, West Virginia, Kentucky, Maryland, Washington, D.C., and Mississippi. Some of the monuments and busts were preemptively removed in response to the atmosphere of national protest, but most removals occurred as a direct result of organized efforts to correct the historical record and recognize the fact that certain public symbols represent racial subjugation.

The highest legislative body in the nation, the U.S. Congress, could not escape the reckoning. The Capitol has been a living archive of racist statues, busts, and plaques representing the Confederacy. In 2021, Democrats renewed the fight to pass legislation mandating the removal of a number of these statues in the National Statuary Hall Collection, a permanent exhibit in the U.S. Capitol. A similar bill passed in 2020, but went nowhere under Senator Mitch McConnell's Republican leadership. Among the statues targeted were ones honoring CSA president Jefferson Davis, CSA vice president Alexander Stephens, South Carolina Confederate military leader Wade Hampton, Andrew Jackson's vice president John C. Calhoun, and other white supremacists. "My ancestors built this building," said Congresswoman Karen Bass (D-CA) in passionate remarks on the House floor prior to the vote. "Imagine how they would feel, knowing that more than one hundred years after slavery was abolished in this country, we still paid homage to the very people that betrayed this country in order to keep my ancestors enslaved."[773] On June 29, 2021, the House voted 285-20 to support H.R. 3005.[774] Sixty-seven Republicans joined all the Democrats in supporting the bill. As of March 2022, the bill had not yet reached the Senate for a vote.

If it passes into law, H.R. 3005 will bring many welcome changes, including that a bust of Thurgood Marshall, the first African American judge on the Supreme Court, will replace the one of Roger B. Taney currently enjoying a place of honor in the Old Supreme Court Chamber of the Capitol.[775]

The Supreme Court's *Dred Scott v. Sandford* decision of 1857 is widely considered one of the worst in the nation's history. Dred and Harriet Scott, during their time of being enslaved in the 1840s and 1850s, were living in Missouri, Illinois, and the Wisconsin territory, all of which prohibited slavery. When their enslaver, Eliza Irene Sandford, refused to allow them to buy their freedom, they sued her. They argued that since they had lived in non-slave states, they should be free. Not only did the court rule against the Scotts by a 7-2 vote, but it went much further in defining the status of black people in the United States. In a fifty-four-page written decision, the court asserted that black people were not and could not become citizens of the United States, the federal government could make no laws governing slaveowners, and black people were property with no right to sue, adding emphatically that they "had no rights which the white man was bound to respect."

The author of that notorious and offensive ruling was Chief Justice Roger B. Taney. His ruling all but guaranteed that the issue of slavery would not be resolved short of a violent conflagration. Taney died in October 1864, before he could see the end of the war he helped to ignite. In one way, the Scotts got the last laugh. Eliza Irene's new husband, Calvin Chaffee, had abolitionist tendencies and contrived successfully to transfer ownership of the Scotts to someone who let them purchase their freedom. Eighty days after the court decision, on May 26, 1857, Dred and Harriet walked out of a St. Louis Circuit Court officially free. Replacing Taney's bust with one of Thurgood Marshall in the U.S. Capitol is a small but welcome step honoring the African American struggle to live with freedom and dignity.

STANDING UP AND TAKING DOWN: NO MORE UNREPRESENTATIVE STATUES

America's ongoing reckoning with white supremacy reaches far beyond efforts to end anti-black monuments and narratives. Symbols that honor purveyors of racism, colonialism, patriarchy, and imperialism have also been targeted for removal, particularly statues of Christopher Columbus, who never set foot in what became the United States. Native American communities have been active for generations in exposing Columbus's greed-driven violence and cruelties. As a result of their efforts, many cities and some states no longer refer to "Columbus Day" as a holiday. Instead, they celebrate "Indigenous Peoples Day" and use the occasion to teach about Native American history and the contemporary status of Native people in the United States. The replacement of Columbus Day with

Indigenous Peoples Day in many ways parallels Tubman replacing Jackson. In reference to the former, bell hooks writes in her 1994 essay, "Columbus: Gone but not forgotten":

> At the core of the new cultural values Columbus observed was a subordination of materiality to collective welfare, the good of the community. From all accounts, there was no indigenous community formed on the basis of excluding outsiders so it was possible for those who were different—in appearance, nationality, and culture—to be embraced by the communal ethos.
>
> It is the memory of this embrace that we must reinvoke as we critically interrogate the past and rethink the meaning of the Columbus legacy. Fundamentally, we are called to choose between a memory that justifies and privileges domination, oppression, and exploitation and one that exalts and affirms reciprocity, community, and mutuality. Given the crisis the planet is facing—rampant destruction of nature, famine, threats of nuclear attack, ongoing patriarchal wars—and the way these tragedies are made manifest in our daily life and the lives of folks everywhere in the world, it can only be a cause for rejoicing that we can remember and reshape paradigms of human bonding that emphasize the increased capacity of folks to care for the earth and for one another. That memory can restore our faith and renew our hope.[776]

Organized efforts to eradicate public representations of Columbus have intensified since the uprisings of 2020. Statues, monuments, and busts of Columbus were removed in Richmond, Virginia; Columbia, South Carolina; Houston and San Antonio, Texas; and other cities and towns around the nation. According to *CBS News*, at least thirty-three statues of Columbus were gone or going by September 2020.[777] In some instances, communities did not wait for officials to give formal approval. On July 4, 2020, Baltimore residents toppled a prominent marble statue of Columbus and threw it into the waters at the city's Inner Harbor. According to a report in the *Baltimore Sun*, "The Columbus statue was dragged down as people marched across the city Saturday demanding reallocation of funds from the police department to social services, a reassessment of the public education system, reparations for Black people, housing for the homeless, and the removal of all statues 'honoring white supremacists, owners of enslaved people, perpetrators of genocide, and colonizers.'"[778]

While Governor Larry Hogan, other Republican state officials, and Baltimore's Democratic mayor, Bernard C. "Jack" Young, immediately condemned the action, other local and well-known political luminaries did not. U.S. House Speaker Nancy Pelosi, who is of Italian heritage and whose family has a long history of political leadership in the city, including two members who were previous mayors, said, "People will do what they do," adding that she preferred a more public process for addressing these issues, without explaining what that process would entail. Some Italian Americans in the city retrieved the statue a few days later and brought it to a safe storage site.

The Fourth of July takedown of the Columbus monument has a parallel in early U.S. history that is worth remembering. On July 9, 1776, George Washington and some of his troops were in New York City for a public reading of a brand-new document completed only five days earlier: the Declaration of Independence. People in the crowd were so excited to hear the words calling for a revolution, they left City Hall Park, marched to nearby Broadway, and proceeded to pull down the two-ton equestrian statue of King George at the site; then, with the happy assistance of Washington's troops, the crowd smashed it into pieces. Those shards were later shipped to Connecticut and "melted down to make 42,008 bullets" that would later be flying toward British redcoats.[779]

Inspiration to remove monuments, statues, and other symbols of racism and colonialism spread beyond the United States. In the United Kingdom, a monument honoring slave trader Edward Colston was pulled down during a gathering of about 10,000 Black Lives Matter protesters in June 2020.[780] The statue was dragged through the streets of Bristol and then tossed into the harbor. It was estimated that the Royal African Company, of which Colston was a member, trafficked "about 80,000 men, women, and children from Africa to the Americas."[781]

Colston's statue was replaced by a black resin sculpture of local

Black Lives Matter organizer Jen Reid. The statue depicts her with her fist raised in a Black Power salute. Just as the activists did not seek permission to take down Colston's statue, neither did they ask to erect the one of Reid. While some officials, including Prime Minister Boris Johnson, called the action criminal, Bristol mayor Marvin Rees, who is black, had no problem with the statue coming down. He stated, "People in Bristol who don't want that statue in the middle of the city came together and it is my job to unite, hear those voices and hold those truths together for people for who that statue is a personal affront."[782] Days later, the Reid sculpture was taken down.

As in the UK, racial justice activists and policy makers in the United States sought not only to remove racist public monuments, but also to replace them with more appropriate and representative ones. In Atlanta, a statue of the late activist and congressman John Lewis was unveiled in Rodney Cook Sr. Park in July 2021. The same month in Memphis, a statue of the brilliant investigative journalist Ida B. Wells was placed in Ida B. Wells Plaza. In Philadelphia, a traveling statue of Harriet Tubman was unveiled on January 11, 2022.[783] In Newark, New Jersey, a new statue of Harriet Tubman was planned to be placed in the newly named Tubman Square (formerly Washington Park) during the summer of 2022. The Tubman statue will replace one of Christopher Columbus that was taken down in 2020.[784] "According to legend," writes Michael Hill for *PBS News Hour*, "Tubman led runaway slaves to Newark's First Presbyterian Church—which still stands in downtown Newark today."[785]

THE POLITICS OF RENAMING

In addition to accelerating the replacement of racist symbols and statues, the influence of racial justice organizing has also led to a critical review of the names of institutions and places. As a result, some states and cities, and even Congress, have taken steps to assess and potentially rename schools, buildings, streets, and public spaces that carry the name of someone whose history was out of line with the values of the users of those facilities or spaces. In some circumstances, school boards or city councils formed committees to research the history behind the names of city- or state-owned properties.

Results have been mixed. For example, in the state of Georgia, recent recommendations to change bigoted names have been rejected. According to a November 2021 report in the *Chronicle of Higher Education*, Georgia's Board of Regents for the University System entirely dismissed an advisory committee's 180-page report detailing the racist origins of names of buildings on the system's twenty-six campuses.[786] The sweeping report lists the names of white supremacists, enslavers, segregationists, vigilantes, and terrorists in whose honor buildings continue to be named. After examining 838 buildings and forty named colleges, the committee offered recommendations to change the name of seventy-five buildings and colleges bearing fifty-eight individuals' names. Among those named, for example, is Joseph Mackey Brown. The committee reports that "through his various anti-Semitic writings, Brown instigated and justified the lynch mob that killed Leo Frank in 1915. In doing so, Brown demonstrated a disregard for the humanity of Jews."[787] Georgia's Board of Regents, however, declines to rename Valdosta State University's Brown Residence Hall, which is named in honor of Brown. The report also references John Paul Illges Sr. and advocates that Columbus State University's Ilges Hall be renamed. "Illges used African American convicts as his laborers at the Muscogee Brick Company. He was obliged to house the laborers, but did so in a minimal way, forcing them to stay in cages half the size of a boxcar. In addition, Illges's company also attached spikes to the African American laborers' ankles to prevent them from escaping."[788] Georgia's Board of Regents decided that Ilges Hall, along with all the other buildings and sites, will continue to be named in honor of the racists cited in the report.

In August 2020, the District of Columbia Facilities and Commemorative Expressions Working Group, established by D.C. mayor Muriel Bowser, was tasked with evaluating "named DC

Government-owned facilities and making recommendations as to what, if any, actions need to be taken if the namesake is inconsistent with DC values and in some way encouraged the oppression of African Americans and other communities of color or contributed to our long history of systemic racism."[789] To accomplish this objective, the Working Group created a set of criteria that sought, as much as possible, to remove any subjective assessment. The five measures were as follows:

1. Participation in slavery—did research and evidence find a history of enslaving other humans, or otherwise supporting the institution of slavery?
2. Involvement in systemic racism—did research and evidence find the namesake serving as an author of policy, legislation or actions that suppressed persons of color and women?
3. Support for oppression—did research and evidence find the namesake endorsed and participated in the oppression of persons of color and/or women?
4. Involvement in supremacist agenda—did research and evidence suggest that the namesake was a member of any supremacist organization?
5. Violation of District human rights laws—did research and evidence find the namesake committed a violation of the DC Human Right Act, in whole or part, including discrimination?[790]

Based on these criteria, the Working Group concluded that there were 153 properties named for "persons of concern" out of 1,330 named properties owned by the city. This included twenty-one schools, two public libraries, twelve parks and playgrounds, ten neighborhoods, and seventy-eight streets, among other assets. The list also included federal monuments, such as the Washington Monument and Jefferson Memorial, over which the city does not have jurisdiction.[791] These were later removed from the list after the

Trump White House expressed outrage and called Bowser a "radically liberal mayor."[792] Upon further investigation, the Working Group determined there should be a "renaming," "removal," "contextualization," "clearing of the concern," or "additional research" for each of the assets.[793] The list included references to presidents who enslaved black people: Andrew Jackson, Thomas Jefferson, James Monroe, John Tyler, and Zachary Taylor. The list also referenced Woodrow Wilson, who aggressively segregated the federal workforce, U.S. National Anthem author and slaveholder Francis Scott Key, and Benjamin Franklin, a slaveholder who eventually became an abolitionist of sorts.

Washington, D.C., was not alone in confronting an uncomfortable history that would force citizens to come face-to-face with a racial justice reckoning. Across the nation, public schools, military bases, and public buildings bear the name of Confederate-era personalities, white nationalists, slavers, segregationists, and bigots. While 2020 was a banner year for raising protests against these names, the battle to change them long preceded the Floyd uprisings. In nearly every case, there was a history of resistance from people of color against these designations. Victories were rare, and most white people who weren't outright defending their permanent presence often just shrugged their shoulders. It was also common for white elected officials to equivocate and argue that both sides of the debate had some merit, then conclude that nothing could be done.

Denouncing such efforts as "cancel culture," numerous conservative politicians, including then-president Trump, absolutely refused to entertain any thought of changing the names of sites that honor white supremacists. This position led him to oppose changes that other officials in his administration wanted, including renaming ten U.S. military sites named in honor of Confederates. The list includes General Pierre Gustave Toutant "P.G.T." Beauregard (Camp Beauregard), Brigadier General Henry L. Benning (Fort Benning), General Braxton Bragg (Fort Bragg), Major General John Brown Gordon (Fort Gordon), Lieutenant General Ambrose Powell "A.P."

Hill (Fort A.P. Hill), Lieutenant General John Bell Hood (Fort Hood), General Robert E. Lee (Fort Lee), Major General George Edward Pickett (Fort Pickett), General Leonidas Polk (Fort Polk), and Colonel Edmund W. Rucker (Fort Rucker).

The issue arose with new urgency and energy in 2020 when the proposed National Defense Authorization Act included a section mandating removal of Confederate names from the military camps and bases. The legislation passed both the House (295-125) and the Senate (86-14) with veto-proof majorities.[794] There was surprising support from several congressional Republicans. Trump, however, immediately defended the Confederate labeling and vowed to never allow the name changes to happen. His veto on New Year's Day 2021 was overridden by the Democrat-controlled House (322-87) and the Republican-controlled Senate (81-13). It was Congress's only veto override of Trump during his one-term presidency. Under the new law, Congress was given three years to implement a process for renaming the military sites.[795]

Hundreds of the nation's schools, where historical accuracy is theoretically taught and cherished, still bear the names of Confederate soldiers, slaveholders, leaders of genocidal campaigns against Native Americans, and prominent segregationists. According to *Education Week* magazine, in January 2020 more than two hundred buildings were still named after Confederate figures in schools around the nation. More than fifty of them were named after Robert E. Lee. The second most popular name was Stonewall Jackson. These schools are concentrated overwhelmingly in Alabama, Georgia, Florida, Louisiana, North Carolina, Texas, and Virginia.[796] By the end of 2020, at least fifty had been renamed.

Perhaps most disturbing is that the populations of these schools are often composed of high percentages of African American and Latinx students. According to the Education Week Research Center, seventy-five of the schools have more black and Latinx students than white students, and overall, 62 percent of the students who attend Confederate-named schools are students of color.[797]

In some schools, however, African American or Latinx students are the overwhelming majority. For example, the Forrest City High School in Forrest City, Arkansas, serves a community that is 92 percent African American. The community is menaced by the fact that the town and its high school are named in honor the first Grand Wizard of the Ku Klux Klan, Nathan Forrest. Prior to terrorizing the black population through his leadership position in the Klan, Forrest fought to perpetuate slavery as a Confederate general. Under his command, Confederate troops massacred hundreds of black soldiers fighting for the Union who had already surrendered at the Battle of Fort Pillow. The racist acts he committed are honored in the name of Forrest Hill Academy in Atlanta, Georgia; 91 percent of the student body there is African American. In Pine Bluff, Arkansas, Forrest Park Prep Preschool is 97 percent African American. At the Davis Elementary School in Greenwood, Mississippi, named after CSA president Jefferson Davis, the student body is 99 percent black. Confederate General Stonewall Jackson was the namesake of the Stonewall/Flanders Elementary School in Harlandale, Texas, where the student population is 99 percent Latinx. Similarly, Robert E. Lee Elementary School in Eagle Pass, Texas, is 99 percent Latinx.[798] In a victory for activists who had been organizing to rid Memphis of all remnants of Forrest's legacy, the KKK grand wizard's remains were transferred from their burial site in Memphis to the new National Confederate Museum in Columbia in June 2021.[799]

The next month the giant bust of Forrest was removed from the Tennessee State Capitol where it has been generating controversy since it was installed in 1978. It was reinstalled in the Tennessee State Museum in a small temporary gallery adjacent to a permanent exhibition about Tennessee's role in the Civil War and Reconstruction. Forrest's role as a slave trader and Ku Klux Klan leader, among other depredations, is clearly explained in the permanent exhibition, and this historical context is very different from the place of honor the bust occupied in the Capitol. Visitors to the Tennessee State Museum learn exactly who Nathan Bedford Forrest really was and exactly which evil he fought to preserve.[800]

Beyond the Confederacy, there are schools named after notorious racists and segregationists. In March 1956, 101 members of Congress signed the Declaration of Constitutional Principles, popularly known as the Southern Manifesto. It was a fierce and defiant rejection of the 1954 *Brown v. Board of Education* Supreme Court decision that outlawed segregation in education. The statement read, in part, "This unwarranted exercise of power by the court, contrary to the Constitution, is creating chaos and confusion in the States principally affected. It is destroying the amicable relations between the white and Negro races that have been created through 90 years of patient effort by the good people of both races. It has planted hatred and suspicion where there has been heretofore friendship and understanding."[801] Assertions of "amicable relations" and "friendship and understanding" were mendacious in the extreme given the ever-present threat of racist violence on the part of white society against black people in the South.

Despite the glaring racism inherent in that history, there are at least twenty-two schools across the South that are named after signatories of the Manifesto. In Alabama, Arkansas, Florida, Georgia, Louisiana, Mississippi, North Carolina, and South Carolina, segregation-supporting members of Congress were celebrated and honored rather than condemned and criticized. Similar to schools named after slavery-defending Confederates, some of the schools had a high percentage of black students. At Wilbur D. Mills High School in Little Rock, Arkansas, named after the former congressman, black students are 63 percent of the student body. Also, in Little Rock, McClellan Magnet High School honors another Manifesto signatory, former senator John L. McClellan. The black student population there is around 89 percent.[802]

One individual whose name is emblazoned not only on educational institutions at every level, but on streets, bridges, research centers, and even a submarine is former president and segregationist Woodrow Wilson. Students and others have protested for years, if not decades, to remove Wilson's name from their facilities, given his well-known record of discrimination against African Americans during his time as president of Princeton University (1902–1910) and while in the White House (1913–1921). Although he attended the university with black students during his time there as an undergraduate in the 1870s, and was a professor when at least one black student, Irwin Roundtree, was there as a graduate student, Wilson would later deny that African Americans ever matriculated at the school. Scholar April C. Armstrong argues that he did so to provide "an inaccurate historical justification for his policy of discriminating on the basis of race."[803] Wilson responded to one potential African American student who sought admission by writing, "It is altogether inadvisable for a colored man to enter Princeton."[804]

Wilson's racist politics were on clear display on February 18, 1915, when he and his family viewed the premier screening of the film *Birth of a Nation* at the White House. A celebratory ode to the Ku Klux Klan, the film portrays African Americans as rapists, brutes, vote cheaters, intellectually backward, and power-hungry people who can only be contained by the terrorist methods of the Klan. Wilson would later claim, unconvincingly, that he did not know the politics of the film beforehand, disagreed with the film, and was just doing a favor for a friend. *Birth of a Nation* was the first motion picture ever shown in the White House. The film became a commercial success and is considered to be a leading influence behind the twentieth-century resurgence of the Klan in the mid-teens and twenties.

It was Wilson's racist policies as U.S. president, however, that generated the most lasting impact. Specifically, he aggressively segregated the federal workforce, setting back African Americans in the Washington, D.C., area for generations. As the Economic Policy Institute's Richard Rothstein writes:

> Wilson's cabinet officers demoted African Americans and denied them any further promotions, to prevent them from ever being in supervisory positions over whites. Federal departments installed curtains to separate black and white clerical workers, segregated cafeteria sections by race for the first time, and created separate

bathrooms that black workers had to use in the basements of government buildings. In 1914, the federal civil service instituted a policy of requiring photographs on all job applications, to ensure that further black workers would not be hired.[805]

For these reasons and more, the Black Justice League, a Princeton-based black student group, and Change WWS, an organization of undergraduate students at what had been the Wilson School of Public and International Affairs (SPIA), demanded not only that the name of the school be changed, but that more substantive steps be taken by the SPIA and Princeton to address issues of racial inclusion, justice, and fairness. The Black Justice League held protests in the fall of 2015 to mandate a new name and other changes. Change WWS issued a set of demands that called for modifications in the curriculum, hiring of more faculty of color, reparations, divestment from the prison industrial complex, a public renunciation of Wilson, and removal of his name.[806] The statement was signed by the Princeton Black Student Union, Princeton Association of Black Women, Princeton Black Men's Association, Princeton African Students Association, Students for Prison Education and Reform, Princeton Latin American Student Association, Black Princeton's Woodrow Wilson Accountability Task Force, Black Leadership Coalition, and Asian American Students Association.

In 2015, Princeton University trustees refused, as they had in the past, to get rid of Wilson's name. Recruiting more African American students and providing "more multi-faceted understanding and representation of Wilson" were two recommendations discussed as alternatives. For a time, the trustees were able to argue that keeping the name implied "no endorsement of views and actions that conflict with the values and aspirations of our times." [807] The overwhelming influence of the Black Lives Matter movement forced them to change their tune. On June 27, 2020, Princeton University president Christopher L. Eisgruber announced that Wilson's name would be abolished from the SPIA and the residential building.[808]

In Washington, D.C., efforts to rename "Wilson High School" also paid off. On December 7, 2021, the D.C. City Council voted to rename the school "Jackson-Reed High School."[809] The new name reflects the struggle by the African American community for equal education with namesakes Edna Jackson, the first black female teacher at the then all-white school in 1954, and Vincent Reed, the school's first black principal in 1968, who later became D.C.'s superintendent of public schools.

INDIGENOUS DIGNITY

> "We'll never change the name. It's that simple. NEVER—you can use caps."
>
> —Washington football team owner Daniel Snyder,
> May 10, 2013

One version of the origin of the word "redskin" reportedly came from a British officer who translated a letter of invitation from Chief Mosquito in 1769.[810] According to a 2005 study by the Smithsonian Institution's senior linguist, Ives Goddard, it read: "I shall be pleased to have you come to speak to me yourself if you pity our women and our children; and, if any redskins do you harm, I shall be able to look out for you even at the peril of my life."[811] Goddard notes, importantly, that the translation by the British officer—and the implication that Indigenous people referred to themselves by the term—may be inaccurate. In fact, at least one scholar, James V. Fenelon, argues that Goddard's work is shoddy and unreliable, and among its problems, he "uses deeply biased sources for his extended arguments," and only views the word as problematic in the modern era.[812]

Among Native Americans, the word is rooted in the violence of white people. The National Congress of American Indians argues, "The term originates from a time when Native people were actively hunted and killed for bounties, and their skins were used as proof of Indian kill."[813] For example, on September 25, 1863, Minnesota's *Winona Daily Republican* featured an announcement that uses the term "red-skin" as a slur: "The State reward for dead Indians has been increased to $200 for every red-skin sent to Purgatory. This sum is more than the dead bodies of all the Indians east of the Red River are worth."[814]

Whatever may actually be the etymology of the name, there is no dispute that it became attached to the football team owned by George Preston Marshall in Boston in 1933. Marshall claimed that he did not want the team's original name, "Braves," to be confused with the Boston Braves baseball team, a name that was also insulting. More dubiously, he would also state that it was chosen to honor the coach of the team, William "Lone Star" Dietz, who deceptively identified himself as Sioux when he was actually German. The team moved to Washington in 1937.

In addition to branding it with a racist name, Marshall refused to have any African Americans on the team. "We'll start signing Negroes when the Harlem Globetrotters start signing whites," he once stated.[815] The Washington team was the last in the NFL, in 1961, to roster black players. That's when the team drafted Ernie Davis, the first African American winner of the Heisman Trophy. Ten days later, however, he was traded off the team.[816]

Despite the popularity of the team with both white and black fans, opposition to the name was constant. D.C. poet Kenny Carroll referred to the team as the "Redslurs."[817] Resistance involved court cases, street protests, editorials, and other forms of public pressure through multiple changes in team ownership. The most recent owner, Daniel Snyder, vowed to never change the name and tried a number of deceptions and misleading tactics to argue that Native Americans really supported the team's name. Two polls of Native Americans, one in May 2016 by the *Washington Post* and another in 2019 by the Wolvereve polling group, reportedly demonstrated that a majority supported the team's name, an assertion Snyder and the team promoted. However, as *The New Republic* documented, "the respondents in both polls were drawn from the vast pool of Americans who 'self-identify' as Native Americans," and a large majority were not enrolled in any sovereign nations or state-recognized tribes.[818]

In other words, many white Americans who did not live in or have attachments to Native American communities were weighing in on the issue. Under the guise of being in the "fight for the preservation of Native identity," the Native American Guardians Association (NAGA) also came to the rescue of the Washington team. To the pleasure of Snyder and others with financial and cultural stakes in this exploitation, NAGA argued that Native American history and existence would be erased if these team names and Indian-themed rituals were to disappear. In 2014, NAGA wrote amicus briefs on behalf of the Washington team in a trademark lawsuit to end use of the name based on its insensitive impact. The lawsuit was eventually dismissed.[819]

Daniel Snyder had a long history of donating to Republicans and unabashedly aligned himself with Trump after he won. This included donating $1 million to Trump's inaugural events. Trump, in turn, supported Snyder's position against changing the team's name.[820] However, legal and grassroot efforts by Native American groups and their allies were relentless. Suzan Harjo (Cheyenne and Hodulgee Muscogee) and six other Indigenous activists organized to strip the team of its name by filing a legal complaint with the United States Patent and Trademark Office's (USPTO) Trademark Trial and Appeal Board in 1992. In 1994, USPTO rejected Pro Football Inc.'s motion to dismiss on the grounds of *laches*—a legal argument that a defendant has allowed too much time to elapse to make a valid claim—and other affirmative defenses because an overriding public policy issue was at stake. USPTO ordered the case to proceed to trial on the merits before the U.S. Trademark Trial and Appeal Board, whose three-judge panel ruled unanimously for the Native side in 1999.

For Harjo the fight is personal. In an article about her activism, *Washington Post* columnist Kevin B. Blackistone recounts that, when Harjo was a second-grader, she differed with a white teacher "about the facts of the Battle of the Little Bighorn, known more infamously, and oddly, by the name of its loser, Lt. Col. George Custer, rather than any of the American Indian tribes that vanquished Custer and his troops."[821] The teacher responded by spitting "dirty redskin" in her face and throwing her out the classroom window on the second story of the school.[822] A rosebush miraculously cushioned the little girl's fall. "The moment forged her to grow up to become an iconic human rights figure in this country, particularly for Native Americans, best known for being in the vanguard of the fight to erase the slur—that so stung her sensibilities over three score ago—from sports teams cheered here and around the country," writes Blackistone.

Suzan Harjo has inspired others to join the fight. Groups like Change the Mascot, Rebrand Washington Football, National Congress of American Indians, United South and Eastern Tribes, United Indian Nations in Oklahoma, Tulsa Indian Coalition Against Racism, National Indian Education Association, National Indian Youth Council, Indigenous Peoples Working Group, and many others never let up and paved the way for top-down pressure following the national protests of 2020. In early July of that year, the team's top corporate sponsors—FedEx, PepsiCo, Nike, and Bank of America—made it clear that Snyder's position would no longer be tolerated. FedEx threatened to "terminate the naming rights deal and not pay the contract's remaining $45 million if Snyder did not change the team name."[823]

On July 13, 2020, the team announced that it had surrendered. Indicative of the team's decades-long racial insensitivity, the press release was issued on letterhead that had the old name and included the name in the statement. It stated, "On July 3rd, we announced the commencement of a thorough review of the team's name. . . . Today, we are announcing we will be retiring the Redskins name and logo upon completion of this review."[824] On February 2, 2022, the team announced that its new name would be the Washington Commanders. On late night TV, Jimmy Kimmel joked, "Interestingly, the franchise now shares a name with President Biden's dog, who is also named Commander. Good thing they didn't name it after Trump's dog. 'The Washington Pences'—it doesn't have the same ring to it."[825]

Five months later, Cleveland announced that it would change the name of its baseball team. While the name "Indians" was not as ugly as that of the Washington team, it had been protested for decades. In addition, the team's mascot, a cartoon character known as Chief Wahoo, was the textbook definition of a demeaning stereotype. On July 23, 2021, the team revealed that its new name would be the Cleveland Guardians.[827] Unfortunately, as of the time of this writing, many sports teams with racist or appropriated names continue to refuse to change them, including the Atlanta Braves, Kansas City Chiefs, and the Chicago Blackhawks.[828]

It is important to underscore that while forcing the Washington team to change its name was a significant victory, and one to be celebrated, it is far from the end of the story and should not generate kudos to Snyder or any of the owners or team officials. It did not signal a recognition of either the history of exploitation of a racist brand that enriched Snyder and the owners before him, or the ongoing marginalization of Native Americans still reeling from centuries of oppression and genocide. "There is a long and ugly history here," writes Suzan Harjo. "But there is also hope. As America has matured, our country has progressed to the point where most racial and ethnic slurs are no longer tolerated in polite society. Now it is time to accord the same respect to Native Americans. Because, yes, we are still here, and we are people, not mascots."[829]

NAMING IS A CHOICE

"America's history of physical violence, malicious stereotypes, invisibility in the media and American curricula, and caricatures in both professional sports franchises and local high schools are not separate matters. They all feed the same monster of colonization."
—Nick Martin, *The New Republic*, July 10, 2020

Centuries of colonialism, racial hierarchy, and imperialism have not only caused the deaths of tens of millions, but have also resulted in the propagation of false and hegemonic narratives that have honored those practices and the individuals who carried them out. "We live with the normative ubiquity of Whiteness," says Loretta Ross, "that is the default hierarchical standard for who is human, a citizen, or an American."[830] The default hierarchical standard is reinforced, in part, by symbols, names, and images.

As Kali Holloway notes, these symbols of oppression have frequently been challenged locally, but news of such resistance has often been subjected to organized forgetting.[831] Racial justice organizing over the past decade has changed that, and since 2020 we have witnessed the largest, most enduring, and most successful resistance to racist symbols to date. No community or institution has escaped the reckoning. All have been forced to revisit and investigate histories and legacies that were, in many instances, cherished and beloved, but whitewashed to hide an ignominious and nefarious racist past.

I attended Cass Technical High School in Detroit during the late 1960s and early 1970s. The school held about five thousand students and was nationally renowned for its academic excellence. It produced numerous alumni who rose to the top in their fields. Among them were jazz greats Geri Allen, Kenny Burrell, Donald Byrd, Regina Carter, Alice Coltrane, and Ron Carter; actors Ellen Burstyn, David Alan Grier, Ella Joyce, and Lily Tomlin; singers Della Reese and Diana Ross; journalist Ed Gordon; and Congresswoman Barbara-Rose Collins.

The school was named after Lewis Cass, who served as the governor of the territory of Michigan from October 1813 to August 1831. During my time at the school, when many of us were active in the anti-war movement and black liberation struggle, none of us looked further into his background. However, in the summer of 2020, both former and current students came to realize that Lewis Cass had quite a sinister history, one that had to be addressed. It turned out that not only did Cass support slavery, but he had also served as Secretary of War (August 1831–October 1836) for Andrew Jackson and played a key role in the anti-Indian campaigns of that era. Cass helped push through the infamous 1830 Indian Removal Act that eventually led to the years of violent expulsions and the deaths of thousands of people.

As Michigan governor, Cass pressed the Anishinaabe Native communities of the Great Lakes region to give up their land for vastly undervalued sums. Almost two dozen land cession deals were conducted, according to researcher Mike Mills, ultimately sealing their displacement. Cass wrote that he was dealing with a people who were "feeble, depressed and ignorant," and, in the end, "they must remove or perish."[832] His attitude toward Native Americans, in general, was condescending and intolerant. He stated: "In the ardor of mistaken benevolence, they have elevated these little Indian communities to an equality with the civilized governments under whose protections they live."[833] In fact, it was likely Cass's ruthless dealings with Native communities in Michigan that motivated Jackson to appoint him as his Secretary of War.

Cass supported the expansion of slavery, and enslaved at least one person, a woman named Sally. In 1833, as head of the U.S. Department of War, Cass also declared martial law and sent federal troops to Detroit in an effort to suppress African Americans' efforts to free and protect a married couple who had successfully self-emancipated from their white enslavers in Louisville, Kentucky. Thanks to extraordinary solidarity from the black community, Thornton and Lucie Blackburn were able to defy the Fugitive Slave Laws. On June 16, 1833, a remarkably brave local black woman, Caroline French, managed to switch clothes with Lucie during a jail visit, allowing Lucie to walk out of jail a free black woman, while French remained jailed in her place. Hundreds of people from the black community later swarmed the jail, allowing Thornton to slip away, get on a boat, and sail across the Detroit River to Canada. When the sheriff discovered Caroline French in the jail, he threatened her with permanently taking Mrs. Blackburn's place, which meant spending the rest of her life enslaved to white people in Kentucky. In the end, however, the influence of her wealthy father and a sympathetic judge led to her release. The liberation of the Blackburns, along with further protests in Detroit, came to be known by white people as the Blackburn Riots of 1833.[834] Though he was unsuccessful in this case, Cass had intervened to suppress the black population and enforce the "law and order" of the Fugitive Slave Act.[835]

Despite this history, Cass has been lauded and honored in Michigan and beyond. There is a very prominent street named after him in central Detroit, as well as in Macomb County, Michigan. Cass River in Michigan's Thumb region and Cass Lake in Oakland County also memorialize his legacy. The city's legendary island park, Belle Isle, is named after his daughter. Outside of Michigan, a statue of Cass stands in the U.S. Capitol's Statuary Hall.

In 2018, Wayne State University law professor John Mogk argued that Cass's name needed to be "re-examined" in light of the new attention to facts regarding his role relative to slavery and attacks on Native Americans.[836] JoAnn Watson, a former City Council member, and Jamon Jordan, who operates the local tour group Black Scroll Network History & Tours, tried to get traction on changing the name but were rebuffed by the school board and the Cass Tech Alumni Association. Both the School Board and the Association argued, without much evidence, that there was no appetite for change by former and current students.[837]

In 2020, a renewed spotlight on Cass and his history resulted in his name being removed from a state-owned office building in Lansing by Governor Gretchen Whitmer. It was renamed the Elliott-Larsen Building after former state representatives Daisy Elliott, a Democrat, and Republican Mel Larsen, both of whom sponsored Michigan's 1977 Civil Rights Act.

Efforts to rename the school began again as information about Cass circulated and demands to get rid of racist names or unwarranted honors spread. Some attempted to divorce Cass from the legacy of the school and maintain loyalty to the Cass Tech label. Yet despite the popularity and pride of the "Cass Tech" brand for generations of graduates, the removal and replacement of the Cass name does not seem like a hard choice. The main argument for keeping the name has been rooted in nostalgia and the history of achievements of graduates. The name has kindled pride for generations. However, the institution's sterling reputation would not be diminished if the school renamed itself to be more representative of the values that it espouses and the working-class students of color that attend it. The school is 99 percent African American, Latinx, and Asian, which makes it even more egregious that its namesake was an enemy of those communities. There are certainly plenty of alumni and other Detroiters who are well deserving of the honor. Semaj Brown, the first poet laureate of Flint, Michigan, and a Cass Tech graduate, said it best:

> If after deep contemplation and study; if after a panoramic viewing, a complete look at this African American–driven movement happening right now with Black Lives Matter and allies; if after considering the 450-year choke hold of white supremacist systems; if after all of that, Technicians and alumni cannot shift, and remake, and by remaking, redefine, and thus rename our true legacy into something larger, and more connected and powerful, then I fear Cass Tech did not fulfill those lauded ideals of excellence.[838]

The question of who we are is asked—and answered—every day by the choices we make. The way we name our history reflects these choices. Doing so in a system skewed to advantage some and disadvantage others involves struggle, however, and equalizers come in many forms. "The power structure that enforces structural racism in every aspect of daily life is what must be dismantled for democracy to exist here," wrote Bree Newsome Bass in a Tweet on November 24, 2021.[839] Bringing down structural racism the way Bree brought down the flag will require a combination of many tools and long-term efforts. Among the most vital is protection of the right to vote.

Martin Luther King Jr. speaks at a press conference at the U.S. Capitol about the Senate debate on the Civil Rights Act of 1964. PHOTO BY MARION S. TRIKOSKO. COURTESY OF THE LIBRARY OF CONGRESS.

ELEVEN

BLACK VOTERS MATTER

"I don't want everybody to vote. Elections are not won by a majority
of the people. They never have been from the beginning of our
country and they are not now. As a matter of fact, our leverage in the
elections quite candidly goes up as the voting populace goes down."
—Paul Weyrich, founder the Heritage Foundation,
a conservative think tank

"I suffered enough to believe it."
—Harriet Tubman, on being asked if she believed
that women should vote

ON MARCH 7, 1965, now known as "Bloody Sunday," John Lewis
was infamously attacked and beaten on the Edmund Pettus Bridge.
He was marching for voting rights and in protest of the killing of
a young black man, Jimmie Lee Jackson, who had been fatally shot
by an Alabama state trooper. Edmund Pettus, whom the bridge had
been named after, was a killer of Native Americans, slavery defender,
Confederate general, and Grand Dragon of the Ku Klux Klan.[840]
Leading a march of about six hundred people walking two-by-two,
Lewis, who was chairman of the Student Nonviolent Coordinating
Committee (SNCC), and Hosea Williams of the Southern Christian
Leadership Conference (SCLC), were met by 150 Alabama state
troopers. They were given a two-minute warning to disperse, but,
as Lewis would later recall, one minute and five seconds later,
they were attacked with billy clubs, tear gas, bullwhips, and horses.
Lewis had his skull fractured, and fifty-seven others also required
hospital treatment.

On Tuesday, March 9, 1965, while Lewis was still in the hospital, Reverend Martin Luther King Jr. came to town and led a march of about two thousand people. They marched to the edge of the bridge and prayed, and then, in an agreement with the police that the marchers were not informed about, King turned the crowd around and went back to town. The day became known as "Turnaround Tuesday." Finally, on Sunday, March 21, two thousand marchers protected by U.S. Army troops and the Alabama National Guard successfully crossed the bridge on their way to Montgomery fifty-four miles away. They were led by Lewis, King, other civil rights leaders, and celebrities. This is widely viewed as the last great march of the 1960s Civil Rights movement and was instrumental in the passage of the 1965 Voting Rights Act that prohibited covered states from implementing racially discriminatory election laws or policies. This provision was enforced by the requirement that all proposals to change voting laws and policies had to first be cleared by the U.S. Justice Department or federal officials, a process known as "preclearance." President Lyndon Johnson signed the legislation into law on August 6, 1965. It would be renewed and expanded five times by Congress.

Carrie Beatrice "Mudear" Sager, my maternal grandmother, was on all three marches. Deeply religious, quick-witted, and determined, she was a longtime activist in the Bessemer-Birmingham area. Over the years, she worked with civil rights leaders such as King, Reverend Fred Shuttlesworth, and Reverend Jesse Jackson. Family stories abound of her standing up to the KKK during boycott protests in Bessemer and Birmingham. She helped organize the famous children's marches of more than a thousand children in the difficult SCLC Birmingham campaign in the spring of 1963. As reported in the *Cutoff News/Western Star Newspaper*, she was there "when the dogs and hoses were turned on the peaceful protesters."[841] Despite tremendous obstacles and restrictions, she was one of the first black people in her district in the 1950s to win the right to vote, and then became one of the county's first black elected officials in the early 1960s, winning a post as chief poll inspector in Bessemer. On February 14, 1965, Mudear was at the legendary meeting between Malcolm X, Coretta Scott King, and civil rights activists at Selma's Brown Chapel AME Church three weeks before Bloody Sunday, and seven days before Malcolm was assassinated in New York. Although she did not agree with his methods, she thought Malcolm was trying hard to bond with the crowd. Mudear passed away peacefully at the age of 101 on November 20, 2014. On January 15, 2021, Congresswoman Karen Bass introduced H.R. 323 to award a Congressional Gold Medal to Mudear "in recognition of her service to her community and nation, for peace, racial justice, and human rights."[842]

"Bloody Sunday," "Turnaround Tuesday," and the march to Montgomery may be the best-known events in a long struggle—to some, perhaps the only ones they know. Yet black Americans have more often than not been the bow on the boat of U.S. democracy. At every stage of development and crisis, it has been the struggle of African Americans and other communities of color that have sought to expand, retain, or defend the vestiges, institutions, processes, and ideas of democracy. As a result of their success advancing electoral rights, opposition to full voting access for all U.S. citizens has become the defining feature of modern conservative politics and the Republican Party. As Paul Weyrich notes, conservative leverage in the elections goes up as the size of the voting populace goes down. Obtaining that leverage has meant curtailing the vote of people of color, young people, urban-based voters, and low-income communities at every possible level. Republicans' goal is to engineer the election system so that they win power and hold it in perpetuity regardless of popular sentiment or desire. Protecting the integrity of the electoral system and advancing voting rights is key to preventing such rule.[843]

As the nation's demographic changes, consolidating permanent white minority rule has become an unspoken priority of far-right politics, particularly for MAGA Republicans. Attempts to achieve this have involved removing nonpartisan election officials and, in some cases, intimidation and threats of physical violence. Poll workers have come under so many threats that a new group was formed, the Election Officials Legal Defense Network, to protect and represent poll workers who have had to face severe bullying and pressure, particularly since Trump's 2020 defeat.[844]

In addition to those efforts, Republicans have been busy not only trying to overturn their 2020 losses, but also setting the stage for more effectively overturning future losses. Journalist Barton Gellman, in his December 2021 *Atlantic* article titled "Trump's Next Coup Has Already Begun," writes, "With tacit and explicit support from their party's national leaders, state Republican operatives have been building an apparatus of election theft." Gellman warns:

> Elected officials in Arizona, Texas, Georgia, Pennsylvania, Wisconsin, Michigan, and other states have studied Donald Trump's crusade to overturn the 2020 election. They have noted the points of failure and have taken concrete steps to avoid failure next time. Some of them have rewritten statutes to seize partisan control of decisions about which ballots to count and which to discard, which results to certify and which to reject. They are driving out or stripping power from election officials who refused to go along with the plot last November, aiming to replace them with exponents of the Big Lie. They are fine-tuning a legal argument that purports to allow state legislators to override the choice of the voters.[845]

As Gellman and others increasingly report, the right has intensified its assault on the electoral process as the GOP legislatively recodes the legal system in ways that will make it easier to reverse future lost elections. The effort is being fueled by Steven Bannon, an intellectual, con man, and propagandist who was pardoned by Trump after getting caught cheating hundreds of thousands of right-wing donors by falsely promising that their money had been set aside for new sections of border wall.[846] In a February 2021 broadcast of his *War Room* program, Bannon began instructing his followers to take up a "precinct strategy" in which they could take control of the

GOP by flooding "into the lowest rung of the party structure: the precincts."[847] "We're going to take this back village by village . . . precinct by precinct," Bannon said.

According to a *ProPublica* analysis, from February to September 2021, GOP leaders in forty-one out of sixty-five key counties have reported "an unusual increase" in precinct officer sign-ups, amounting to at least 8,500 new, low-level Republican officials. In October 2021, for example, Republican legislators in Georgia purged three black women members from the five-member Spalding County Board of Elections and replaced them with three white Republican men, while also replacing the black election supervisor.[848] In two Pennsylvania communities, MAGA candidates who propagated election fraud allegations won races in November 2021 to become local voting judges and inspectors.[849] GOP leaders in Michigan have sought to dominate election canvassing boards by appointing members who align with the MAGA disinformation campaign that the 2020 vote was rigged.[850] "In Arkansas," report Nick Corasaniti and Reid J. Epstein for the *New York Times*, "they have stripped election control from county authorities. And they are expanding their election power in many other states."[851]

There has been no parallel level of activity among Democrats. Worse, as the left fails to pass new laws for voter protection, the right is succeeding in doing the opposite. The Brennan Center for Justice reports:

> Between January 1 and December 7 [2021] at least **19 states passed 34 laws restricting access to voting.** [bold in the original] More than 440 bills with provisions that restrict voting access have been introduced in 49 states in the 2021 legislative sessions. These numbers are extraordinary: state legislatures enacted far more restrictive voting laws in 2021 than in any year since the Brennan Center began tracking voting legislation in 2011. More than a third of all restrictive voting laws enacted since then were passed this year. And in a new trend this year legislators introduced bills to allow partisan actors to interfere with election processes or even reject election results entirely.[852]

On December 22, 2021, the *Washington Post* reported that the ongoing attack on the vote "is being driven in part by well-funded Trump associates, who have gained audiences with top state officials and are pushing to inspect protected machines and urging them to conduct audits or sign on to a lawsuit seeking to overturn the 2020 results."[853] Mike Lindell, founder of MyPillow, has been among those leading the attack. According to the report, Lindell says he has spent $25 million promoting claims of election fraud. "I'm warning you that I've been going around the country," said Douglas Frank, an associate of Lindell. "We're starting lawsuits everywhere. . . . And I want you guys to be allies, not opponents. I want to be on your team, and I'm warning you." Frank, described by the *Washington Post* as "a longtime math and science teacher in Ohio who claims to have discovered secret algorithms used to rig the 2020 election," recently began calling for prison or "firing squads" for those who do not agree to hear him out.[854] In December 2021, Frank wrote that Michigan Secretary of State Jocelyn Benson, a Democrat who has refused to entertain his claims, should face a jury "capable of dispensing capital punishment."[855]

Under the guise of preventing fraud, ongoing right-wing attacks on voting rights focus on limiting mail-in voting and use of ballot drop boxes, increasing requirements on voter ID, expansion of voter-roll purges, increasing barriers for voters with disabilities, banning of providing water or snacks to voters waiting in line to vote, reducing availability of polling sites, and limiting early voting. According to Senator Dick Durbin (D-IL), it's not "voter fraud" that drives Republicans to push voter-suppression laws, because they know there is no voter fraud. "Instead," says Durbin, "it's the same animus that led to poll taxes, literacy tests, and the infamous Mississippi Plan which became the template for voter discrimination for decades."[856] The Mississippi Plan was a scheme by white Democrats in 1875, near the end of the Reconstruction era, to disenfranchise black voters in Mississippi and eventually across the entire South through poll taxes, property requirements, and felony disenfranchisement.[857] As one of the defenders of the plan noted in 1890 at a Mississippi convention to rewrite the state constitution, "We came here to exclude the Negro. Nothing short of this will answer."[858]

To illustrate his point and how contemporary assaults on voting echo the past, Durbin quotes a three-judge decision made in federal appeals court to overturn a 2013 voter restriction laws in North Carolina. The judges wrote that the law "target[ed] African Americans with almost surgical precision."[859]

African American history has been defined, in part, by struggles to neutralize that animus and dismantle the structures that target black political agency. As Tyler Stovall details in his 2021 study *White Freedom: The Racial History of an Idea*, "People of color have had to fight for inclusion into the idea of freedom, in fact not just struggling to be part of white freedom but to overthrow it as a concept and as social and political reality."[860] As a result, the fight for the right to vote has been central to the black freedom struggle and the effort to overthrow notions of America as a white concept and a white-first social and political reality.

RACE, VOTING, AND THE CONSTITUTIONAL CHALLENGE

Harriet Tubman, a strong advocate and activist for women's suffrage, died seven years before women won the right to vote through passage of the 19th Amendment in 1920. Even if she had lived to see the amendment become law, she would have been able to vote in Auburn, New York, where she lived, but it's likely she still would not have been able to vote in many places due to the prevalence of Jim Crow policies at that time. As Michelle Alexander reminds us, "Constitutional amendments guaranteeing African Americans 'equal protection of the laws' and the right to vote proved as impotent as the Emancipation Proclamation once a white backlash against Reconstruction gained steam."[861]

The power to vote is perhaps the most fundamental right of citizens in a constitutional democracy. In the United States, that right was born deformed and imperfect. It has needed to be repaired, revamped, and addressed again and again. In fact, nine of the twenty-seven amendments to the U.S. Constitution have to do with enfranchisement and the extension or curtailing of voting rights. Despite the abolition of slavery, millions of African Americans and others were denied voting rights for generations.

The 12th Amendment (1804) further empowered the undemocratic electoral college following the contested election of 1800 between Thomas Jefferson and Aaron Burr, a race that ended in an Electoral College tie. After rejecting a proposal for electing the president and vice president by a popular vote, the Amendment clarified that the president and vice president would be voted for separately by electors. After the Civil War, the 13th Amendment (1865) ended slavery and set the stage for the next two amendments. The 14th Amendment (1868) provided citizenship to the formerly enslaved, a requirement to being able to vote, while the 15th Amendment (1870), without stating so explicitly, gave black men the franchise. Despite these gains, the emergence of a racialized carceral system has ensured that black bodies disproportionately fill jails and prisons, thereby removing millions of potential black voters from electoral participation.

The 17th Amendment (1913) allowed for the popular election of senators to the U.S. Senate, an advance over their selection by governors. The amendment, however, still allows for governors, rather than voters, to fill Senate vacancies if a senator resigns or dies, until an election can be held or is scheduled. The undemocratic and unrepresentative nature of two senators per state regardless of size and demographics remains untouched. In 2021, journalist Christopher Z. Mooney noted, "57 percent of the country live in states with two Democratic senators, while only 43 percent live in states with two GOP senators," yet Republicans held fifty seats compared to the Democrats' forty-eight (plus two held by independents) in the hundred-seat Senate.[862] Racially, the smallest Republican-controlled states—Alaska, Montana, North Dakota, South Dakota, and Wyoming—average a white population of about 79 percent compared to a national average of about 60 percent.[863] These states, whose combined populations are less than half that of New York City, have ten senators. In 2021, New York City's population was listed as 8.8 million, while the combined populations of those small Republican states totaled about 4 million.

The 19th Amendment (1920), as noted above, finally gave women the right to vote, but did not address the disenfranchisement of millions of black women in the South. Professor Martha S. Jones, author of *Vanguard: How Black Women Broke Barriers, Won the Vote, and Insisted on Equality for All*, notes, "The moment looked very different to America's 5.2 million Black women—2.2 million of whom lived in the South. . . . For Black women, August 1920 wasn't the culmination of a movement. It marked the start of a new fight."[864]

With the passage of the 19th Amendment, many women's suffrage groups, most of which were primarily white, packed their bags and went home, including the National Women's Party, which shut down. Notably, in the final years leading up to the ratification of the amendment, the National Women's Party and other groups leaned in to the segregationist and racist mores of the South in their desire for support. Yet despite the obstacles of poll taxes, literacy tests, and grandfather clauses, black women in the South, to the degree possible, turned out in large numbers to register and vote, emulating their sisters in other parts of the nation.[865]

Hundreds of thousands of citizens in the District of Columbia had been deprived for decades of the right to vote in presidential elections until the passage of the 23rd Amendment (1961). The city, however, still does not have full representation in Congress as does every state. Under the current configuration of federal power over D.C., voter preferences on referendums can be overturned by Congress without recourse. Furthermore, in the event of an electoral college crisis where the decision on who becomes president is determined in the House of Representatives by the votes of states, rather than individual members, D.C. citizens do not have a voting voice in the matter.

As the Civil Rights movement grew in the late 1950s and early 1960s, the 24th Amendment (1964) addressed an issue that had been used widely in the South to deny African Americans the right to register and to vote: the imposition of poll taxes. In the beginning, grandfather clauses allowed poor whites to be exempt, but they were found to be unconstitutional in the 1915 Supreme Court case *Guinn v. United States*. The poll tax remained until the 24th Amendment prohibited poll taxes in federal elections. It did not, however, explicitly prevent the imposition of a tax at the state level. This flaw was exposed in 2020 in Florida. In 2018, approximately 65 percent of Florida voters—750,000 individuals—supported amending the state constitution to restore voting rights to most ex-felons. However, Republican state legislators reacted to this progress by passing a law in 2019 that required ex-felons to pay all court fines and fees—aka a "poll tax"—related to their crime before they could vote. U.S. District Court Judge Robert L. Hinkle ruled in May 2019 that the law was unconstitutional. The state challenged the ruling and won in an appeals court decision in which five of the six-vote majority were Trump appointees. Republican Governor Ron DeSantis signed it in June 2019. In many cases, the state could not clearly specify how much an individual owed. While some ex-felons were able to vote in the March 2020 primary, those who were listed as owing fines or fees, including those who had voted in previous elections, could not vote in the November election.[866]

The Sentencing Project documents how millions of Americans—disproportionately African American and Latinx—are disenfranchised due to felony convictions, the only circumstance that can cause a citizen to lose the right to vote. While Maine and Vermont allow individuals who are in prison to vote, more than thirty states deny the franchise in some form to those on felony probation or parole. The number of disenfranchised people has fluctuated over time. Approximately 1.17 million people were disenfranchised in 1976, 3.34 million in 1996, 5.85 million in 2010, and 6.11 million in 2016. By 2020, approximately 5.17 million Americans were prohibited from voting. The decline from 2016 to 2020—almost 15 percent—was due to states enacting new policies to end the practice. According to the Sentencing Project's 2020 report,

- One in sixteen African Americans of voting age is disenfranchised, a rate 370 percent greater than that of non-African Americans. Over 6.2 percent of the adult African American population is disenfranchised compared to 1.7 percent of the non-African American population.
- African American disenfranchisement rates vary significantly by state. In seven states—Alabama, Florida, Kentucky, Mississippi, Tennessee, Virginia, and Wyoming—more than one in seven African Americans is disenfranchised, twice the national average for African Americans.
- Although data on ethnicity in correctional populations are still unevenly reported, we can conservatively estimate that over 560,000 Latinx Americans or over 2 percent of the voting eligible population are disenfranchised.
- Approximately 1.2 million women are disenfranchised, comprising over one-fifth of the total disenfranchised population.[867]

Finally, the 26th Amendment (1971) lowered the voting age from twenty-one to eighteen. This Amendment was driven by the tragic fact that young people under twenty-one were being drafted to fight in the Vietnam War while being denied the ballot. Most felt that if young U.S. citizens can be forced to take a bullet for their country, then they should also have the right to cast a ballot.

In addition, legislation was necessary to strengthen and enforce these amendments. As noted above, the Voting Rights Act, passed ninety-five years after the 15th Amendment, was a game changer. Within a very short period, black voter registration, black voter turnout, and the number of African Americans running for and winning elected offices soared. For example, the registration gap between blacks and whites in the South dropped almost thirty percentage points to about 8 percent in the mid-1970s.[868]

According to the U.S. Census, the number of black elected officials rose from a few hundred in 1965 to 4,890 in 1980.[869] This includes the increase of black congressmembers from five in 1965 to seventeen by 1981.[870] Later, black voters were essential in the election of Douglas Wilder to become the first black governor in Virginia, the seat of the Confederacy, and Barack Obama to the White House in 2008. The preclearance provision of the Voting Rights Act constrained some of the most outrageous voter suppression schemes of the South's racist policy-makers. According to the Brennan Center, "Under preclearance, states and localities with a history of voting discrimination must get certification in advance that any election change they wanted to make would not be discriminatory. The Voting Rights Act included a formula, set out in Section 4, that identified which states and localities were subject to this review." [871] From 1998 to 2013, the preclearance provision blocked eighty-six discriminatory changes, including thirteen in the eighteen months prior to the *Shelby County v. Holder* Supreme Court case that gutted the preclearance provision in 2013.[872]

THE STATE AND CONSERVATIVES STRIKE BACK

A critical turning point in the assault against voting rights came in the *Shelby County v. Holder* Supreme Court case, which invalidated a key portion of the Voting Rights Act. On February 27, 2013, President Barack Obama, Speaker of the House John B. Boehner, Minority Leader Nancy Pelosi, Senate Majority Leader Mitch McConnell, Congressman John Lewis, and other elected officials and civil rights leaders gathered in the Capitol's Statuary Hall for the unveiling of a statue of civil rights icon and voting rights activist Rosa Parks. Her activism in the Montgomery bus boycott helped to end legal segregation and facilitate the passing of the Voting Rights Act, and she was present in the Oval Office when President Johnson signed the legislation. Ironically, while Obama's celebratory event was under way, across the street, oral arguments were being presented in the *Shelby* case.[873] Some Republicans were willing to give a nod to symbolically recognizing the accomplishments of the Civil Rights movement while supporting the eradication of the substantive gains that the movement had achieved.

In 2010, Alabama's Republican-controlled Shelby County requested that the Supreme Court declare the preclearance provision of the Voting Rights Act unconstitutional. The Republicans were seeking to reverse a ruling by the May 2012 U.S. Court of Appeals for the District of Columbia Circuit that had affirmed the provision's constitutionality. On June 25, 2013, a 5-4 Supreme Court decision declared that the formula for determining preclearance—Section 4—was outdated and unconstitutional. Writing for the conservative majority, Chief Justice John Roberts stated, "The conditions that originally justified these measures no longer characterize voting in the covered jurisdictions," arguing further that "the racial gap in voter registration and turnout" in the South had become lower than that nationwide.[874]

Roberts obfuscated the obvious point that the closure of the racial gap, to the degree that it existed, was exactly due to the measures that had been put in place, including preclearance. He chose to ignore an abundance of evidence that had been submitted in amicus briefs by a wide range of legal scholars, constitutional experts, and political scientists. For example, Professors Kareem Crayton, Matthew Barreto, Luis Fraga, Jane Junn, Terry Smith, and Janelle Wong submitted an amicus brief presenting compelling evidence that in the jurisdictions covered by the Voting Rights Act, the white population had more negative racial attitudes than elsewhere, racially polarized voting was more rampant, and voter suppression policies and laws were more likely to be passed—all indicators of the need for preclearance.[875]

Writing for the minority, Justice Ruth Bader Ginsburg argued that efforts at diluting minority votes had continued in the covered jurisdictions, including racial gerrymandering, creating at-large voting systems to limit opportunities for minority communities to win elected offices, and annexing majority white areas to increase the number of white voters.[876] At-large systems give the majority an unfair advantage. If a city that is 30 percent black has an at-large system, it is unlikely that any black candidates will win. A district-based system provides for greater chances that members of minority communities will be elected. In her dissent, Justice Ginsburg stated, "The evolution of voting discrimination into more subtle second-generation barriers is powerful evidence that a remedy as effective as preclearance remains vital to protect minority voting rights and prevent backsliding."[877]

Republican legislators in Southern states immediately reacted to the *Shelby* decision by proposing new voter suppression laws. As the Brennan Center noted, "Within 24 hours of the ruling, Texas announced that it would implement a strict photo ID law. Two other states, Mississippi and Alabama, also began to enforce photo ID laws that had previously been barred because of federal preclearance."[878] Other Southern states would soon join them in proposing and implementing new laws to suppress minority voting, some of which would eventually be disallowed by the courts.

In 2021, the integrity of the electoral process suffered another serious setback in *Brnovich v. Democratic National Committee*. In two merged cases from Arizona brought by Republican state authorities, one involving whether provisional votes cast outside a voter's home precinct could be counted and another involving who could collect and return ballots from voters, the Supreme Court ruled in favor of the state. In essence, the court allows for the state to create burdens that could have a disproportionately discriminatory impact on voters of color. As Guy-Uriel E. Charles and Luis E. Fuentes-Rohwer write, "The decision is a repudiation of the core aims of [the Voting Rights Act]. Rather than engage productively in the collective enterprise of figuring out how to protect voters of color against the states, the court majority is more interested in protecting the electoral rules of the states from undue intrusion by voters of color."[879]

A BIG ENOUGH LIE

"MILLIONS OF MAIL-IN BALLOTS WILL BE PRINTED BY
FOREIGN COUNTRIES, AND OTHERS. IT WILL BE THE
SCANDAL OF OUR TIMES!"
—Trump tweet, June 22, 2020

A key part of the Republican strategy has been to wage disinformation campaigns about the results of the 2016 and 2020 elections. The purpose of the campaigns has been to manufacture public belief that Trump won the popular and electoral votes in both elections, when in fact he did not. On May 11, 2017, the Trump White House concocted the Presidential Advisory Commission on Election Integrity to give an air of legitimacy to the effort. The Commission was dominated by Republican members and stacked with individuals with long histories of advocating for voter suppression policies based on fabricated allegations of illegal behavior, especially against the black community. Members of the Commission included Vice President Mike Pence, Kansas secretary of state Kris Kobach, Ohio secretary of state J. Kenneth Blackwell, and notorious voter suppression organizer and attorney Hans von Spakovsky—"the driving force behind policies that restrict access to the ballot" for decades, according to the investigative reporting of Ari Berman and Nick Surgey in *Mother Jones*.[880]

Kobach has a despicable record of making wildly erroneous public remarks about voter fraud and pushing for policies that disproportionately target communities of color. He was a key architect of Arizona's Orwellian "show me your papers" law (SB 1070) in 2010. That law permitted the police to ask any individual that they stopped to show documents proving citizenship or legal status if police had "reasonable suspicion" the person was undocumented. The parameters of "reasonable suspicion" were not defined, leaving it to the subjective whim of individual police officers. Eventually, parts of the law were found unlawful by the Supreme Court's 2012 decision in *Arizona v. United States*.

The Brennan Center has reported that Kobach "has a long and consistent history of pursuing severe policies despite undeniable evidence that they disenfranchise eligible citizens, and of making exaggerated voter fraud allegations."[881] While campaigning for the office of Ohio secretary of state and during his tenure, Kobach repeatedly made outlandish claims about dead people and undocumented people voting, allegations that were dismissed by courts and exposed as false by numerous media investigations. Kobach also supported Trump's disinformation campaign propagating the Goebbels-level lie that he lost the 2016 popular vote due to illicit ballots cast by his estimate of "3.2 million aliens."[882]

Kobach also ran the Interstate Voter Registration Crosscheck project whose ostensible purpose was to determine whether voters were registered in more than one state. In reality, the project was used to purge hundreds of thousands of voters, disproportionately people of color.[883]

In 2017, Kobach got in trouble with the courts when he got caught lying about documents that he was photographed holding while heading into a White House meeting with Trump. The ACLU sued to get copies of the documents, which they believed were about efforts to undermine the 1993 National Voter Registration Act. The law is popularly known as the "motor voter" law, because it allows states to register individuals when they apply for a driver's license. Given Kobach's history of antagonism toward expanding voting, it was logical to assume that he was advocating such a move. Kobach not only resisted turning over the documents, but lied to the court about their content. In a June 2017 wrist slap, Kobach was fined $1,000 by U.S. Magistrate Judge James O'Hara for making "patently misleading representations" to the public and the courts.[884]

Much like Kobach, J. Kenneth Blackwell has a long and tarnished record of attacking voting rights. The former Cincinnati mayor (1979–1980) served as Ohio's treasurer from 1994 to 1999 and its secretary of state from 1999 to 2007. According to the Ohio ACLU, Blackwell "tried to reject thousands of voter registration forms because they were on the wrong weight of paper," "prohibited people who requested an absentee ballot from voting provisionally if they did not receive their absentee ballot in the mail," failed to "provide voter registration opportunities in public assistance offices as required by the National Voter Registration Act of 1993," and used his office to mobilize Republican voters to support an anti-gay-marriage ballot issue.[885] He was forced to back off the "paper weight" issue after howls of protest, and the courts ruled against him regarding the National Voter Registration Act. A federal court of appeals also found he violated the Help America Vote Act by ordering poll workers not to provide provisional ballots to voters.[886] It is no surprise that the *New York Times* concluded that under Blackwell's oversight, Ohio was an "example for every ailment in the United States' electoral process."[887]

As reprehensible as Kobach and Blackwell are, they are in the minor leagues compared to the voting suppression record of Hans von Spakovsky. Voting rights hero John Lewis once said of von Spakovsky:

> I don't know if it's something in the water he's been drinking . . . but over the years he's been hell-bent to make it more difficult—always, always—for people to vote. It's like he goes to bed dreaming about this, and gets up in the morning wondering, What can I do today to make it *more* difficult for people to vote? When you pull back the covers, peel back the onion, he's the one who's gotten the Republican legislatures, and the Republican Party, to go along with this—even though there is no voter fraud to speak of. He's trying to create a cure where there is no sickness.[888]

Von Spakovsky has held numerous positions where he could impact election policies, including special counsel at the Justice Department's Civil Rights Division and vice chair of the Fairfax County electoral board in Virginia. He was appointed to the FEC by George W. Bush during a Senate recess. However, when he came up for permanent confirmation, a half dozen of his colleagues at the U.S.

Justice Department wrote a harsh letter of opposition. They charged him of favoring a Georgia ID law that they felt harmed black voters, using a pseudonym on an article supporting voter ID laws, and generally having a "cavalier" attitude toward legal precedent. Bush was eventually forced to withdraw his nomination.[889]

Much of von Spakovsky's work has been done with voter suppression groups such as the Heritage Foundation and its sister organization Heritage Action for America, as well as Voter Integrity Project, and True the Vote. He opposed the Help America Vote Act and the National Voter Registration laws, both dedicated to expanding the franchise, and through Heritage Action he fought against new voting laws proposed by Democrats in Congress in 2021.

In April 2021 von Spakovsky and Heritage Action executive director Jessica Anderson boasted of their influence in helping to write a rush of voter suppression laws in key battleground states, including Arizona, Florida, Georgia, Iowa, Michigan, Nevada, Texas, and Wisconsin. Anderson bragged that they were planning to spend $24 million in those states in 2021 and 2022 to pass and defend the new laws.[890] Having raised more than $76 million in 2020 alone, including from corporations such Google, Amway, Citigroup, Hitachi, and GlaxoSmithKline, Anderson may have been a little too enthusiastic. Following a leak of her remarks, ethics charges were filed against her and von Spakovsky by Iowa Democrats.[891]

Trump's Presidential Advisory Commission on Election Integrity only lasted seven months. It withered and collapsed under the weight of lawsuits, resistance by states to handing over election data, and searing criticism that it was a thinly veiled effort to suppress voting. On January 3, 2018, White House press secretary Sarah Huckabee Sanders announced: "Despite substantial evidence of voter fraud, many states have refused to provide the Presidential Advisory Commission on Election Integrity with basic information relevant to its inquiry. Rather than engage in endless legal battles at taxpayer expense, today President Donald J. Trump signed an executive order to dissolve the Commission, and he has asked the

Department of Homeland Security to review its initial findings and determine next courses of action."[892] In reality, the Commission had found no credible evidence of voter fraud and issued zero reports.

Trump had other vehicles to continue his attack. Under Jeff Sessions and William Barr, Trump's Justice Department continued to file or support hundreds of lawsuits attacking voting rights. According to the Leadership Conference on Civil and Human Rights, Trump's Justice Department attempted to suppress the vote in numerous ways, including:

- Stopping challenges to voter suppression laws in Texas that sought to disenfranchise Black and Latino voters
- Arguing in a brief to the 2018 Supreme Court in *Husted v. A. Philip Randolph Institute* that it should be easier for states to purge voters from registration rolls
- Suing Kentucky to purge ineligible voters from its registration rolls following the *Husted* decision
- Supporting Alabama's restrictive absentee ballot requirements in federal court
- Issuing a memo, with no factual basis or evidence, authorizing the opening of election fraud investigations "if there are clear and apparently-credible allegations of irregularities that, if true, could potentially impact the outcome of a federal election in an individual State."[893]

It is important to reemphasize that voter fraud is virtually non-existent in the United States. Research by Professor Justin Levitt, a constitutional law expert at the Loyola Law School, only found thirty-one possible incidents of voter fraud out of roughly one billion ballots cast in the fourteen-year period from 2000 to 2014.[894] Two Arizona State University studies found ten cases of voter impersonation out of millions of votes cast nationwide between 2000 and 2012.[895] Despite Republicans' insistence to the contrary, there simply was no massive voter fraud in 2016.[896] In fact, the *Washington Post* reported that "there have been just four documented cases of voter fraud in the 2016 election."[897] Likewise, there was no meaningful voter fraud in 2020.

In addition to academic studies, federal courts and nonpartisan state governments have reached the same conclusion.[898] These fact-based decisions did not deter Republican attempts to overthrow the will of American voters. Without a doubt, the most embarrassing government-initiated effort was an "election audit" commissioned in April 2021 by GOP legislators in Arizona. In that case, the Republicans hired a Florida-based company called Cyber Ninjas, which had no experience conducting such a study. The company's CEO, Doug Logan, was a MAGA Republican who spread disinformation about the election. On December 14, 2020, he tweeted, "The parallels between the statistical analysis of Venezuela and this year's election are astonishing. I'm ashamed about how few republicans [sic] are talking about it."[899] And a week later, on December 31, he tweeted "I'm tired of hearing people say there was no fraud. It happened, it's real and people better get wise fast."

The "fraudit," as it was labeled by critics, was supposed to produce a report after a few weeks, but actually took a torturous six months. On September 24, 2021, the company issued a report indicating that no voter fraud had been found. Instead, it uncovered 261 fewer votes for Trump and 99 more for Biden, although there was no reason to trust those figures.[900] Despite the results being a humiliating blow to Trump's "Stop the Steal" campaign, Trump issued a ludicrous statement declaring that "Arizona must immediately decertify their 2020 presidential election results."[901] In January 2022, Cyber Ninjas announced it was shutting down as it faced a brutal rebuttal of its claims by the Republican-led Maricopa County Board of Supervisors and a $50,000-a-day fine for its refusal to surrender records to the *Arizona Republic*.[902] When the shutdown was confirmed by Cyber Ninja spokesman Rod Thomson, he said it was unclear whether the company would declare bankruptcy. "That did not impress the judge, John Hannah, who suggested that the shutdown might be designed 'to leave the Cyber Ninjas entity as an empty piñata for all of us to swing at,'" reported the *New York Times* on January 7, 2022. "The official Maricopa County Twitter account seized on the description, declaring that 'an empty piñata is a pretty accurate description of the 'audit' as a whole.'"[903]

Despite all the evidence, Republican disinformation escalated sharply between losing the elections and staging the January 6 coup attempt. An investigation by *ProPublica* and the *Washington Post* published in January 2022 notes:

> Facebook groups swelled with at least 650,000 posts attacking the legitimacy of Joe Biden's victory between Election Day and the Jan. 6 siege of the U.S. Capitol, with many calling for executions or other political violence. The barrage—averaging at least 10,000 posts a day, a scale not reported previously—turned the groups into incubators for the baseless claims supporters of President Donald Trump voiced as they stormed the Capitol, demanding he get a second term. Many posts portrayed Biden's election as the result of widespread fraud that required extraordinary action—including the use of force—to prevent the nation from falling into the hands of traitors.[904]

Additionally, the Brookings Institution conducted a study of 1,500 episodes from twenty of the most popular right-wing podcasts released between Election Day and January 6 and found that approximately half pushed disinformation, including that of Steven Bannon, whose show was removed from Spotify in November 2020 after he discussed beheading federal officials, but remained available on Apple and Google as of March 2022.[905] "The new research underscores the extent to which podcasts have spread misinformation using platforms operated by Apple, Google, Spotify, and others, often with little content moderation. While social media companies have been widely criticized for their role in spreading misinformation about the election and Covid-19 vaccines, they have cracked down on both in the last year. Podcasts and the companies distributing them have been spared similar scrutiny, researchers say, in large part because podcasts are harder to analyze and review."[906]

Despite the absence of any evidence and despite Republican-commissioned studies that prove otherwise, repetition of the lie about voter fraud has increased the number of people who actually believe it. On January 3, 2022, the *Washington Post* published an article by Aaron Blake titled "Birtherism Paved the Way for the 'Big Lie.' The Latter Is Proving More Pervasive and Stubborn." Blake writes that a "University of Massachusetts poll showed that 71 percent of Republicans believe Biden was not rightfully elected while another ABC News poll had an identical 71 percent saying Trump was the rightful winner of the election. You can ask the question any number of different ways, but the results are almost always the same: The theory usually finds favor with at least 70 percent of Republicans. And it has been thus for 14 months."[907]

THE COALITION OF VOTER REPRESSION GOES NUCLEAR

Democrats' clear and decisive victory in November 2020 led to an immediate increase in the right's efforts to limit voting access and restructure state operations to give Republican-controlled legislatures the authority to overthrow election results that they do not like. Trump's "big lie" became the rally call to go beyond high-profile voter suppression laws by GOP-controlled state legislatures nationwide, which were already growing fast.

Strategically, Republicans are following the so-called "Independent State Legislatures" doctrine, a theory that contends that state legislatures have supremacy over governors or state election administrators regarding the regulation of elections. As Gaby Goldstein and David Daley write, "It effectively concludes that there can be no possible checks and balances on state legislatures' authority when it comes to election law."[908] In the modern era, this doctrine was manifest in the infamous *Bush v. Gore* decision that determined the 2000 presidential election outcome.

Few noticed at the time, but in that case, Chief Justice William Rehnquist, along with Justices Antonin Scalia and Clarence Thomas, hinted at a radical reading of the Constitution's Article 1, Section 4 and Article 2, Section 1, both of which endow state legislatures with the authority to determine the "times, places, and manners of holding elections for Senators and Representatives" and allows them to appoint "a Number of Electors," respectively. In *Bush v. Gore*, the conservative majority voted 5-4 to stop the Florida recount, thus giving the state and White House to George W. Bush. According to the majority opinion, the decision was based on an interpretation of the 14th Amendment's equal protection clause. However, Rehnquist, Scalia, and Thomas also based their vote on the doctrine that the state Supreme Court cannot override the authority of a state legislature.[909]

Two decades later, that doctrine undergirded many of the court challenges, absurdly constructed in many cases, that were filed on behalf of Trump. It is difficult to find a more undemocratic argument to justify electoral disenfranchisement. The doctrine makes null and void any effort by governors (through executive action) or state courts (through judicial rulings) to positively address voting rights. The result is to surrender the final determination of election outcomes to partisan political control.

More than at any time before the Voting Rights Act, Republicans now seek to ensure that they can win by bringing election certifications and election administration under their complete control. In a number of states, the power of secretaries of state or nonpartisan state or county election boards was diminished or shifted entirely to state legislatures. "Legislation enabling partisan interference in election administration is part of a broader 'election sabotage' or 'election subversion' campaign, a national push to enable partisans to distort democratic outcomes," says the Brennan Center for Justice in a November 2021 report titled "The Election Sabotage Scheme and How Congress Can Stop It."

The effort to sabotage and subvert electoral processes in order to tip outcomes has not been a parochial and spontaneous development. An extremely well-coordinated campaign involving national organizations, billionaire funders, Republican state officials, and experienced organizers has created a machinery of voter suppression unlike any that has previously existed in the United States. The machinery that existed prior to the forty-fifth presidency grew during its term, and has accelerated and expanded its activities since Republican electoral defeats in 2020.

Among the key institutions and groups behind this effort are the Federalist Society, the American Legislative Exchange Council (ALEC), and newer entities such as the Heritage Foundation's Election Law Reform Initiative (HFELRI), Honest Elections Project, Election Integrity Project California, FreedomWorks, National Election Protection Initiative, and True the Vote. These GOP-linked formations are working nonstop at the local, state, and federal level to roll back voting rights gains made by the Civil Rights movement and other activists since the 1960s. ALEC and HFELRI have both drafted model voter-suppression legislation for Republican lawmakers to use in states around the nation, and both have been disingenuous about doing so.[910]

GERRYMANDERING

Republican efforts to redraw state and congressional districts to their own benefit—a form of gerrymandering—represent another serious affront to the integrity of the U.S. electoral system aimed at diminishing the political power of black, Latinx, and Native American people. The Republican Party has used super-majorities in state legislatures, particularly in swing states, to draw maps that give them a disproportionate number of seats. For example, in 2018, Democrats won 54 percent of the popular vote in Pennsylvania, but only held 45 percent of the state's seats in the Pennsylvania House. In Michigan, they won 60 percent of the vote, but only 53 percent of the seats. In North Carolina, the number was also 60 percent, with only 51 percent of the seats.[911]

Few states are more egregious in this matter than Ohio. In 2021, the GOP held a 64-35 supermajority in the state House and a 25-8 supermajority in the state Senate. While Republicans won an average of 54 percent of the votes in sixteen statewide elections, they sought to claim 81 percent of the seats in the state legislature by using new maps drawn up by the Ohio Redistricting Commission. The bipartisan group was composed of seven members, with the five Republicans voting yes and the two Democrats voting no.[912]

A 2019 study by the Institute for State and Global Policy identified Virginia, Wisconsin, Pennsylvania, Michigan, and North Carolina as the five worst gerrymandering states relative to state legislatures, all of them swing states that determine the outcome in presidential elections. According to the research, about "59 million Americans live under minority rule in their state legislatures."[913]

In Virginia, after 2018, Republicans won 44.5 percent of the popular vote for state House seats, yet they ended up with 51 percent of the positions. In Wisconsin, the gap was even wider in the same time period. About 45 percent of the popular vote was won by Republicans, but they sat in 65 percent of the seats.[914] Importantly, as the report noted, "in all five of these states, Democratic candidates for state house received a majority of the statewide popular vote. Because of the way that the district lines were drawn, the Republicans won more seats than the Democrats. There were no state houses where the Republican party received a majority of the vote in 2018, but where the Democratic party won a majority of the legislative seats."[915]

Redistricting, which happens every ten years, began in the summer of 2021 after the much-delayed results of the 2020 Census. The process was completed in most states in time for 2022's midterm election primaries.[916] Unfortunately, Republican momentum around gerrymandering legislation continues. "So far at least 13 bills restricting access to voting have been pre-filed for the 2022 legislative session in four states," reports the Brennan Center on Justice. "In addition, at least 88 restrictive voting bills in nine states will carry over from 2021. These early indicators—coupled with the ongoing mobilization around the Big Lie (the same false rhetoric about voter fraud that drove [2001's] unprecedented wave of vote suppression bills)—suggest that efforts to restrict and undermine the vote will continue to be a serious threat."[917] According to an analysis by the *Washington Post*, "Under new maps already finalized in more than a dozen states, Trump would have won 78 districts by more than 15 percentage points. Under 2020 lines in those states, he won 59."[918]

What might America look like if the right succeeds in sabotaging America's electoral system? According to Rick Wilson, a longtime Republican strategist who is sharply critical of the MAGA right, "We're looking at a nihilistic Mad Max hellscape. It will be all about the show of 2024 to bring Donald Trump back into power. . . . They will impeach Biden, they will impeach Harris, they will kill everything."[919]

SEIZURE OF ELECTION ADMINISTRATION

Not satisfied with voter suppression policies and extreme racial and political redistricting, the GOP has set a goal of taking partisan control of the mechanics and administration of elections at the state level. This includes a well-financed and determined strategy to win, or occupy through appointments, offices from the secretary of state and state election directors to seats on local and state election boards or local voting judgeships.[920] As Stacey Abrams noted, "Republicans are brazenly trying to seize local and state election authority in an unprecedented power grab."[921] A January 2022 analysis by the *Washington Post* found that "163 Republicans who have embraced Trump's false claims are running for statewide positions that would give them authority over the administration of elections."[922] MAGA Republicans are also seeking to replace officials across the nation, "including volunteer poll watchers, paid precinct judges, elected county clerks and state attorneys general, according to state and local officials, as well as rally speeches, social media posts and campaign appearances by those seeking the positions."[923] "The attacks right now are no longer about 2020," said Colorado secretary of state Jena Griswold, a Democrat. "It's about chipping away at confidence and chipping away at the reality of safe and secure elections. And the next time there's a close election, it will be easier to achieve their goals. That's what this is all about."[924]

In most states, secretaries of state play a central role in the certification of elections as well as setting election policies for the state. They have an outsize role in overseeing registration rules, determining how election boards are comprised, and supervising election audits, among other responsibilities. Following Trump's humiliating defeat in 2020, the GOP recognized that power, and leaned into Trump feeling burnt by Georgia's Republican secretary of state Brad Raffensperger's refusal to illegally "find" him enough votes to allow him to win the state. In response, the GOP generated a bevy of candidates for the secretary of state offices in Arizona, Georgia, Nevada, and Wisconsin, all of whom would not state that Biden won the 2020 election.[925] They had all sought Trump's endorsement, and they were all willing to sign on to the big lie.

VOTING RIGHTS LEADERS AND DEMOCRATS FIGHT BACK

In 2021, Democrats in Congress proposed two bills to address voting rights: the John Lewis Voting Rights Advancement Act and the For the People Act. The John Lewis Act proposed to reinstall and strengthen the preclearance section of the original Voting Rights Act that was undermined by the removal of Section 4(b) via the *Shelby* decision. As mentioned earlier, preclearance provides that all proposals to change voting laws and policies must first be cleared by the U.S. Justice Department or federal officials. In addition, the proposed law aims to extend voting access on tribal lands, give more power to the Justice Department to monitor and enforce voting rights, cover more states than the 1965 law did, and include changes in district boundaries under preclearance. The bill seeks to make it easier for the U.S. attorney general to assign election observers, among other changes.

On December 6, 2019, the John Lewis Voting Rights Act passed in the House of Representatives by a margin of 228-187, with Brian Fitzpatrick (R-PA) the only Republican voting for it. However, the bill went nowhere in the Republican-dominated Senate. It was re-introduced in 2021 and passed the House on August 24, 2021, with a vote of 219-212, this time without a single Republican vote. On November 3, 2021, the bill failed to pass the Senate after falling short of the sixty votes needed.

The For the People Act was a much thicker bill that sought dramatic changes in the national election system. Under the bill there would be changes in campaign finance laws, a ban on partisan gerrymandering, new ethics requirements, a historic expansion of voting rights, and even support for D.C. statehood. On March 3, 2021, the Act passed in the House, 220-210, but Republicans employed the filibuster in the Senate, obstructing its passage.

The bill was scrapped, and a diluted version—the Freedom to Vote Act—was drafted to replace it. Most voting rights activists still considered the new version a significant step forward. National voting rights leader Stacey Abrams strongly endorsed the Freedom to Vote Act, stating, "The provisions of this legislation are overwhelmingly supported by the American people across party lines, and Senators must respond to the demands of their constituents by supporting it."[926]

The passage of the legislation was dependent on not just creating a thinned-down version of the more progressive bill, but also addressing the Senate's filibuster rule, which gave Republicans veto power due to the makeup of the Senate at that point. The only option that Democrats had for eliminating or modifying the rule was to enlist all forty-eight Democrats, their two independent allies, and Vice President Kamala Harris to reach a fifty-one-vote majority for the change. However, Democratic senators Joe Manchin (D-WV) and Kyrsten Sinema (D-AZ) steadfastly refused to vote to change the filibuster, and the Democrats were unable to get new voting-rights legislation across the finish line.

The filibuster was first adopted by the Senate in 1805, and in 1917 it adopted a cloture rule (the procedure for eliminating it) that required a supermajority vote of two-thirds of the senators.[927] Prior to that, both chambers operated with simple majorities to pass legislation or to cut off discussion. Time and time again, the filibuster was used in efforts to thwart racial justice legislation: blocking a voting rights bill in 1891; the defeat of anti-lynching legislation in 1922 and 1937; and unsuccessfully attempting to stop the Civil Rights Act of 1957 and Civil Rights Act of 1964.[928] Contemporary Republicans and conservative Democrats have contributed to that history when they blocked legislation needed for voter reform.

The failure to pass Congressional legislation that would protect and extend voting rights bolstered Republican efforts to do the opposite. Voter suppression policies in key swing states, changing rules about which state officials can nullify election results, and state and federal courts packed with conservative judges—including more than two hundred appointed by Trump—have set the stage for communities with high black, Latinx, and Indigenous populations to have increasingly diminished influence in coming elections.

While Congress fiddled, the states were burning with action. Texas led the way.

In 2021, the Republican state legislators in the Lone Star State proposed one of the most severe voting suppression laws in the nation. The law bans twenty-four-hour voting and drive-through voting, creates new ID obstacles for mail-in voting, prohibits election officials from providing unsolicited mail-in ballot applications, institutes monthly checks of the voting rolls in an attempt to purge non-citizen voters, and makes assisting individuals with disabilities more arduous.

Democratic legislators in Texas fiercely opposed the bill. In order to prevent its passage, in July 2021, they fled the state in the middle of a special legislative session called by the pro-Trump governor, Greg Abbott. Fifty-six Democrats came to D.C. to help lobby Congress to pass federal legislation that would disallow the worst provisions of the Texas law. By mid-August, however, after Congress failed to pass legislation and a few members felt the urgency to return for personal reasons, the uprising waned. Eventually they all returned to Texas.

Shortly after, a quorum was declared, the Republicans pushed the bill through, and Abbott signed it with great flair and pomp.

According to the Brennan Center for Justice, by mid-January 2022, at least twenty-seven states had introduced, pre-filed, or carried over 250 bills with restrictive provisions, compared to seventy-five such bills in twenty-four states in mid-January 2021."[929] Ninety-six bills would make it harder to vote in twelve states, compared to sixty-nine such bills in twenty-three states, a thirty-nine percent increase. "In keeping with restrictive voting laws passed last year, state legislators have resumed the assault with legislation that, if enacted, would disproportionately impact voters of color."[930] Legislators in at least thirteen states have introduced forty-one bills that would "open the door to manipulating election results for partisan reasons over accuracy," according to the Brennan Center. "This legislation ranges from allowing any citizen to initiate or conduct new biased election audits; to imposing new criminal or civil penalties on election officials for making unintended errors; to allowing partisan actors to remove election officials from office. With these bills, state lawmakers are doubling down on efforts to undermine voters' trust in elections."[931]

While voting rights activists were mostly playing defense at the state level, there were some victories both in the court and legislatively, including in Indiana, Kentucky, Louisiana, and Oklahoma. As of January 2022, legislators in at least thirty-two states had also introduced, prefiled, or carried over 399 bills that expand voting access, compared to 286 such bills in thirty states on January 2021.[932] These changes were driven by activists and legislators who did not wait for Congress to act. What Congress has refused to do or block from happening has not stopped the movement on the ground, although those efforts could not quell the voter suppression storm.

Black leaders—particularly black women—have been at the forefront of these campaigns. Stacey Abrams (Fair Fight Action), LaTosha Brown (Black Voters Matter), Melanie Campbell (National Coalition on Black Civic Participation), Tamieka Atkins (ProGeorgia), Nsé

Ufot (New Georgia Project), and many other black women activists and leaders were central in the registration and turnout that put Biden and Harris in the White House. Their efforts also helped elect Georgia's Jon Ossoff and Raphael Warnock, giving the Democrats their razor-thin majority in the Senate.

Meanwhile, efforts to subvert the electoral system, suppress voters of color, and secure permanent white-minority rule continue along two general trajectories. The top-down assault is being waged from the highest levels of the Republican power structure, with the former president and those who fund him at the top. The bottom-up assault is carried out by the white supremacist foot soldiers who drink the Kool-Aid and follow leaders' dictates, standing back and standing by swarming the Capitol to "stop the steal" as instructed. Whether or not America becomes an authoritarian apartheid state—in a word, fascist—depends on stopping both trajectories. Preserving the integrity of the nation's electoral system, and the political agency of America of color, is essential to the effort. The need for action has become more urgent than ever as the forces of authoritarianism are on the march in the United States and globally.

While securing voting rights will always be a non-negotiable component of the black freedom struggle and democracy, it's not the end goal of either. The goal is to live a good life in a society organized to ensure justice, equality, freedom, and dignity for *all*. Electoral democracy is an essential part of getting there and staying there. However, the degree to which America has excluded folks from the good life and the process of securing it is the degree to which those communities have been forced to pursue change in other ways. The emancipatory imperative at the core of Tubman's legacy speaks directly to those other ways, chief among them being a willingness to engage in "good trouble."

GOOD TROUBLE AND A HARRIET TUBMAN-INSPIRED FUTURE

"Do not get lost in a sea of despair. Be hopeful, be optimistic. Our struggle is not the struggle of a day, a week, a month, or a year, it is the struggle of a lifetime. Never, ever be afraid to make some noise and get in good trouble, necessary trouble."
—John Lewis

"The truth is that as much democracy as this nation has today, it has been borne on the backs of black resistance."
—Nikole Hannah-Jones

"If you are free, you are not predictable and you are not controllable."
—June Jordan

HARRIET TUBMAN never saw a full day of democracy. She spent her whole life under various forms of racial authoritarianism, among millions of her fellow African Americans and other people of color. From her birth in 1822 until 1849, when she escaped, she was enslaved in Maryland with little hope of being free except by her own agency. From 1849 until the end of the Civil War and official end of slavery, she was a hunted fugitive despite her work as a Union spy, nurse, and military leader. From 1865 to the late 1870s, Reconstruction softened, but did not end, black marginalization and restrictions, and she struggled to survive financially, having been denied an earned pension because of her gender. And, from 1877, when Reconstruction was overturned, until her death in 1913, Jim

Crow segregation constrained what she could do as a woman, an African American, and a member of the working class. The 1896 Supreme Court apartheidization of black life would not end until forty-one years after her passing, with the 1954 *Brown v. Board of Education* Supreme Court decision. From the end of Reconstruction to the time of her passing, there were thousands of lynchings in the United States, and countless other acts of racial terrorism committed against people of color.[933]

She took on all these challenges. She spoke and organized, and risked life and limb to increase freedom and democracy so that it included everyone—even a disabled black woman like herself. Her mission was not a simple reaction to the times, but a conscious and consistent effort and vision to bend the moral arc of the nation more closely to justice.

The images on U.S. currency tell a different story and remain contested terrain. The narrative they tell—who has contributed to the nation and who has not, whose story has mattered, and whose should be ignored—is a false one. These images silently but powerfully honor men—white men—who enslaved, committed massacres, denied human rights, and served the elite at the expense of the many. Andrew Jackson reflected all of that and more. It is no wonder that some Native Americans refuse to carry twenty-dollar bills.

As Jamelle Bouie notes in his discussion of Tyler Stovall's book *White Freedom: The Racial History of an Idea*, the ongoing struggle over the future of democracy in America is "a fight, for some, to be free (or at least more free) of domination and hierarchy, and a fight, for others, to be free to dominate on the basis of those hierarchies."[934] These dueling views can be seen in the lives of Harriet Tubman and Andrew Jackson, and in those whose vision of America draws inspiration from their spirit and legacies today.

No one represents the fight to be free of domination and hierarchy—and the good trouble that it often involves—better than Tubman. She has rightfully deserved all the accolades and honor that have been bestowed upon her. In addition to the activism for which she is best known—freeing enslaved people, raising money and providing a home for the infirm, and advocating for women's rights and suffrage—it is appropriate that she also be seen not just as a steadfast warrior for freedom, but as a Founding Mother of American democracy yet to come. In this moment when the authoritarian threat is as real as it has ever been in the history of the United States, the defense and expansion of democratic rights must be linked with the fight for racial justice, an end to patriarchy, and economic restructuring. Winning the Tubman twenty represents a small but important victory over the pervasive symbolism of white male America and the marginalization of people of color, women, and those who have always been othered.

Tubman's life touched two centuries of U.S. history and the country's struggle over freedom, democracy, and racial justice. When she was born in 1822, the United States was only thirty-three years old and presidents Thomas Jefferson and John Adams were alive. Before she turned forty, she witnessed the passage of the Fugitive Slave Acts (1850), the Supreme Court's *Dred Scott* decision (1857), and her friend John Brown's 1859 rebellion at Harper's Ferry. She was thirty-nine when the Civil War began, and joined that fight to dismantle the Confederacy, end slavery, and redefine the concept of American democracy to include her as five fifths a person—100 percent black, 100 percent woman. In her late forties and early fifties, the 13th Amendment, 14th Amendment, 15th Amendment, and a Civil Rights Act were decided and enacted. She was friends with some of the greatest Americans to live, including Frederick Douglass, Sojourner Truth, and Ida B. Wells. As she grew older, she lived through the inspiring rise and cruel fall of Reconstruction (1867–1877), and the emergence of anti-black terrorist organizations. Tubman was involved in the African American racial justice movement and the struggle to win women's rights, including suffrage, all along the way.

A decade before she died, W. E. B. Du Bois penned *The Souls of Black Folk*, in which he wrote, "The problem of the 20th century is the problem of the color line," a phrase that was prescient. It is un-known whether Tubman ever read or knew that statement, but her experiences in the 19th century and beginning of the next would certainly reflect that truth. In the final years of her life, the NAACP was founded (1909), Ronald Reagan, whose racial politics would shape the modern Republican Party, was born (1911), and millions of southern African Americans—and jazz—began to spread across the nation.

From 1619 to the current era, from the famous to the unknown, black people—particularly black women—have engaged in "good trouble" to advance racial equality, social justice, and radical democ-racy. Harriet Tubman's life was an embodiment of that spirit, and honoring her legacy asks us to use what freedom and democracy we have not to benefit ourselves, but to help dismantle structures of domination and racial hierarchy that continue to make us collec-tively unfree.

Multiple and often overlapping movements have propelled both resistance and progress toward that dismantling. Political transfor-mation requires activism, mass mobilization, institutionalization, strategies aimed at winnable targets, and vision. Most of all, move-ments must be built and rebuilt. Martin Luther King Jr. wrote, "There is no tactical theory so neat that a revolutionary struggle for a share of power can be won merely by pressing a row of buttons. Human beings with all their faults and strengths constitute the mechanism of a social movement. They must make mistakes and learn from them, make more mistakes and learn anew."[935]

The racial justice movements of the past decade are on a histor-ical continuum with the slave rebellions and generations of the black freedom struggle that have followed. Today's movements are built on the shoulders of Pan Africanist, black nationalist, black leftist, civil rights, Black Power, black feminist, and anti-apartheid move-ments, all the way back to abolitionism. For every Harriet Tubman that we learn about, there have been thousands more black women who have organized, struggled, and made good trouble.

Throughout the United States today, communities of color face disparate outcomes from economic, political, and social structures that have been shaped by generations of white privilege. Diversifying U.S. institutions, from the presidency to local police departments and beyond, is part of even larger efforts to abolish inequality in America today. In the same spirit that Harriet Tubman worked relentlessly to both liberate individual black people *and* abolish the slavery system as a whole, our task is to wage small winnable struggles while organizing to achieve the larger structural transformations.

It is in this context that nationwide demand for a Tubman twenty takes place. As I have argued throughout this book, organized efforts to change monuments and money are connected to larger efforts to advance racial justice and gender equity gains in employment, economic development, criminal justice, health care, education, the environment, housing, and voting. One win makes the next easier. Democracy connects them all.

America is at a tipping point, and the challenges are immense. In 2020, the same year that millions of people took to the streets to demand racial justice, more than 73 million U.S. citizens voted for an overtly racist candidate. The fact is, an enormous percentage of the citizenry continues to rally for a political party that engages in voter suppression and is hostile toward the rights of women, people of color, the LGBTQ community, immigrants, non-Christian religions, and working people in general.

Making good trouble is an essential tactic in how we win the fights we wage, and not just for justice and freedom, but more fundamentally, for dignity and survival itself. Making good trouble is also a noble part of the black tradition and black women's leadership of which Harriet Tubman and Ida B. Wells and Rosa Parks and Toni Morrison and Angela Y. Davis and Stacey Abrams and Bree Newsome Bass and yes, my grandmother, and countless others who go unnamed are all part.

In the worst days of the civil rights struggle, after she had been jailed, beaten, and tortured, activist and leader Fannie Lou Hamer spoke about what she faced, and, more importantly, how she would face it. She stated, "I'm never sure anymore when I leave home whether I'll get back or not. Sometimes, it seems like to tell the truth today is to run the risk of being killed. But if I fall, I'll fall five feet four inches forward in the fight for freedom. I'm not backing off."[936]

It is in that spirit that the present and the future must be engaged. Whether it is taking down symbols of white supremacy, protesting police killings, passing progressive legislation, or building institutions of social justice, there can be no backing off.

ACKNOWLEDGMENTS

One does not get through writing a book, or life, successfully without copious family and friends to help guide, rescue, refine, and move that journey forward. In no particular order, other than alphabetical, I thank deeply and sincerely Karen Bass, Kenneth Carroll, Brima Conte, Cecelie Counts, Kwame Dixon, Joni Eisenberg, Michael Fauntroy, Daryl Harris, Reva Hines, Maurice Jackson, Jennifer James, Keith Jennings, Randi Gray Kristenscn, Nicole Lee, Ayo Heinegg Magwood, Darius Mans, Saje Mathieu, Gregory Moore, Nadirah Moreland, Cathy Schneider, Michael Simanga, Lester Spence, James Steele, Margaret Summers, Lisa Sweetney Swint, David Whettstone, and Ernestine "Tina" Martin Wyatt. A word here. An article there. A tea or coffee or beer break. Wisdom shared.

There were a number of individuals who took the time and energy to read drafts of the manuscript and offered important insights, corrections, and wisdom. Deep and wide appreciation to Suzan Shown Harjo, Barbara Ortiz Howard, Kate Clifford Larson, and Stacey Lewis. Your efforts and contributions certainly made this a better work. I also loved and give thanks for the perceptive and thoughtful blurbs from Keisha N. Baine, Karen Bass, Suzan Shown Harjo, Barbara Ortiz Howard, Barbara Ransby, David Roediger, and Loretta Ross.

Nothing but honor and gratitude to Kali Holloway for her powerful foreword. Her important and brilliant work at *The Nation*, *The Daily Beast*, and the Make It Right project with its effort to take down the remaining Confederate monuments that span the United States cannot be applauded enough.

The beautiful graphics and artwork in many instances were contributions, and for that I give deep thanks to Bree Newsome Bass, Dustin Klein and Alex Criqui, and Dano Wall.

ACKNOWLEDGMENTS

Thanks to Greg Ruggiero, my editor and fierce warrior who fought to see this project through from idea to print from almost a decade ago. Greg worked overtime and beyond to land this plane. He was full in on the project from the beginning and step-by-step helped transform a rough idea into the book you hold in your hand (or see on your screen). Every author would be lucky to have as dedicated, skilled, and committed an editor as I was fortunate enough to have in Greg.

As usual, the City Lights team was superb in their professional approach and tasks. Thanks to the stellar copyediting by Elizabeth Bell and guidance from the get-go by Elaine Katzenberger. City Lights continues to publish important and challenging works of literature, social thought, and texts for social change. Always proud to be one of their authors.

Finally, gratitude to family, as always. Ellington inspires me every day, and his joy, sense of justice, and spirit for life rests on every page.

ENDNOTES

1. Helen Leichner, "Combahee River Raid (June 2, 1863)," *Black Past*, December 12, 2012.

2. See www.harriet-tubman.org.

3. David Balsiger and Charles E. Sellier Jr., *Lincoln Conspiracy* (Los Angeles: Schick Sunn Classic Books, 1997).

4. Kate Larson, *Bound for the Promised Land: Harriet Tubman, Portrait of an American Hero* (New York: Ballantine, 2004), 252.

5. Larson, ibid., 252.

6. Milton C. Sernett, *Harriet Tubman: Myth, Memory and History* (Durham, NC: Duke University Press, 2007), 96.

7. Congressional Series of United States Public Documents, Volume 1627, 337–338.

8. Beverly Lowry, *Harriet Tubman: Imagining a Life* (New York: Doubleday, 2007), 330.

9. Kate Clifford Larson, correspondence with the author, April 29, 2022.

10. Ibid.

11. Lowry, ibid., 332; Larson, ibid., 252.

12. See www.harriet-tubman.org/wp-content/uploads/2014/01/Harriet -Tubman-bill-HR4982.jpg; and U.S. Senate, Committee on Pensions, Report no. 1619, 55th Congress, 3rd Session, February 7, 1899, pp. 1–2.

13. Mary Frances Berry, *My Face Is Black Is True* (New York: Alfred A. Knopf, 2005), 48–49.

14. Author interview with Ernestine Tina Martin Wyatt, November 16, 2021.

15. David Stout, "Blind Win Court Ruling on U.S. Currency," *New York Times*, May 21, 2008.

16. Breanna Edwards, "Harriet Tubman to Be New Face of $20 Bill; MLK and Marian Anderson to Be Honored on Back of New $5 Bill," *The Root*, April 20, 2016.

17. See United States Mint, "American Women Quarters™ Program 2022–2025."

18. See Arianna Eunjung Cha, "A King Statue 'Made in China,'" *Washington Post*, August 15, 2007; and Michael E. Ruane, "Amid fine weather, thousands help dedicate King Memorial on the Mall," *Washington Post*, October 16, 2011.

19. Nikki Sutton, "President Obama at the Martin Luther King Jr. Memorial

Dedication: 'We Will Overcome,'" The White House, October 16, 2011.

20. See www.si.edu/unit/african-american-museum

21. Nicholas Loffredo, "'Soul of Our Nation': African American History Museum Opens in Washington," *Newsweek*, September 24, 2016. See Obama White House on Tumblr: obamawhitehouse.tumblr.com/post/150873001186/this-national-museum-helps-tell-a-fuller-richer.

22. Katie Reilly, "Read President Obama's Speech at the Museum of African American History and Culture," *Time*, September 24, 2016.

23. Brittney Cooper, "Putting Harriet Tubman on the $20 Bill Is Not a Sign of Progress. It's a Sign of Disrespect," *Time*, January 27, 2021.

24. In a study by economists Samuel H. Williamson and Louis P. Cain, in 1860 as the Civil War loomed, the wealth in enslaved people was around $13 trillion (in 2016 dollars). Samuel H. Williamson and Louis P. Cain, "Measuring Slavery in 2016 Dollars," www.measuringworth.com/slavery.php.

25. W. E. B. Du Bois, *Black Reconstruction in America 1860–1880* (New York: Atheneum, 1979), 182.

26. See Ronald Walters, *Fighting Neoslavery in the 21st Century: The Forgotten Legacy of the NAACP* (Chicago: Third World Press, 2014); and Douglas A. Blackmon, *Slavery by Another Name: The Re-enslavement of Black Americans from the Civil War to World War II* (New York: Anchor Books, 2009).

27. Naomi Klein, *Shock Doctrine: The Rise of Disaster Capitalism* (New York: Metropolitan Books/Henry Holt, 2007).

28. Kimberlé Crenshaw, "The Structural and Political Dimensions of Intersectional Oppression," in Patrick R. Grzanka, ed., *Intersectionality: A Foundations and Frontiers Reader* (Boulder, CO: Westview Press, 2014), 17.

29. Alicia Garza, *The Purpose of Power: How We Come Together When We Fall Apart* (New York: Random House, 2020), 144–145.

30. Brendan Farrington, "Florida could shield whites from 'discomfort' of racist past," AP, January 18, 2022.

31. Jay Reeves, "John Lewis' legacy shaped in 1965 on 'Bloody Sunday,'" AP News, July 18, 2020.

32. Rebecca Bengal, "The Last Poets: the hip-hop forefathers who gave black America its voice," *Guardian*, May 18, 2018.

33. Ibid.

34. Stef W. Kight, "America's majority minority future," *Axios*, April 29, 2019.

35. William H. Frey, "The US will become 'minority white' in 2045, Census projects," March 14, 2018, Brookings Institution, March 14, 2018.

36. Ibid.

37. Tara Bahrampour and Ted Mellnik, "Census data shows the number of

White people in the U.S. fell for the first time since 1790," *Washington Post*, August 12, 2021.

38. Ibid.

39. Adam Clark Estes, "An Illustrated History of American Money Design," *Gizmodo*, April 20, 2016.

40. Ibid.

41. Ibid.

42. David Cowen and Richard Sylla, *Alexander Hamilton on Finance, Credit, and Debt* (New York: Columbia University Press, 2019); *Alexander Hamilton on the Constitutionality of a National Bank* (Ireland: Amazon Digital Services LLC-Kdp Print Us, 2016); Katy Schiel, *The Whiskey Rebellion: An Early Challenge to America's New Government* (New York: Rosen Publishing Group, 2003); Thomas Slaughter, *The Whiskey Rebellion: Frontier Epilogue to the American Revolution* (New York: Oxford University Press, 1986).

43. See James Loewen, *Lies Across America: What Our Historic Sites Get Wrong* (New York: The New Press, 2019) and James Loewen and Edward H. Sebesta, *The Confederate and Neo-Confederate Reader: The "Great Truth" About the "Lost Cause"* (Jackson: University Press of Mississippi, 2010).

44. James Loewen, *Lies Across America: What Our Historic Sites Get Wrong* (New York: The New Press, 2019), 4.

45. Pierre Fricke and Jennifer Meers, *Collecting Confederate Paper Money: Field Edition 2014* (Self-published, Pierre Fricke, 2014), 258.

46. John C. Calhoun, Speech to the U.S. Senate, February 6,1837; Kate Feldman, "Statue of former VP John C. Calhoun, who called slavery a 'positive good,' removed in South Carolina," *Baltimore Sun*, June 24, 2020.

47. Jon Meacham, *American Lion: Andrew Jackson in the White House* (New York: Random House, 2008), 158–159.

48. Jordan Baker, "Goddess Columbia: The Making of a New Goddess for a New World," *East India Blogging Co.*, November 19, 2020, Samuel Sewall quoted in Frank J. Cavaioli, "Columbus and the Name Columbia," *Italian Americana*, vol. 11, no. 1 (Fall/Winter 1992): 10.

49. Baker, ibid.

50. John Higham, "Indian Princess and Roman Goddess: The First Female Symbols of America," American Antiquarian Society, June 1, 1990, 62.

51. See Thomas J. Schlereth, "Columbia, Columbus, and Columbianism," *The Journal of American History*, v. 79, no. 3 (1992): 939; and Higham, ibid., 63.

52. Phillis Wheatley, *Complete Writings* (New York: Penguin Books, 2001), 88–90.

53. Jake Colberg, "Stabbing Westward: An Analysis of John Gast's 'American Progress,'" America Through the Ages, November 30, 2012.

ENDNOTES

54. Albinko Hasic, "The American Dollar Bill Looks the Way It Does for a Reason," *Time*, August 31, 2018.

55. See John B. Edmunds Jr., *Francis W. Pickens and the Politics of Destruction*, (Chapel Hill: University of North Carolina Press, 1986) and Lewis, Elizabeth W., *Queen of the Confederacy: The Innocent Deceits of Lucy Holcombe Pickens* (Denton: University of North Texas Press, 2002).

56. James L. Stokesbury, *A Short History of the Civil War* (New York: HarperCollins, 2011), 30.

57. See W. E. B. Du Bois, *Black Reconstruction: An Essay Toward a History of the Part Which Black Folk Played in the Attempt to Reconstruct Democracy in America, 1860–1880* (New York: Russel & Russel, 1935).

58. Estes, ibid.

59. Dr. Linwood "Little Bear" Custalow and Angela L. Daniel "Silver Star," *The True Story of Pocahontas: The Other Side of History* (Golden, CO: Fulcrum Publishing, 2007), 51

60. Ibid., 62.

61. Phoebe Farris, "Pocahontas' First Marriage: The Powhatan Side of the Story," *Huffington Post*, December 6, 2017. www.huffpost.com/entry/pocahontas-first-marriage_b_5664891

62. Matthew Restall, *When Montezuma Met Cortés: The True Story of the Meeting that Changed History* (New York: Harper Collins, 2018), 24.

63. See www.mountvernon.org/george-washington/martha-washington/martha-on-1/.

64. Aura Bogado, "The One Native Person to Ever Grace Paper Money in the U.S.: Chief Running Antelope appeared on the $5 silver note in 1899," *Colorlines*, March 5, 2015.

65. Ibid.

66. There were twenties of a sort that were issued before this one, but they were not legal tender. See Rob Wile, "The Complete Illustrated History of the $20 Bill," *Business Insider*, September 11, 2012.

67. Christopher Brian Booker, *The Black Presidential Nightmare: African-Americans and Presidents, 1789–2016* (Bloomington, IN: Xlibris, 2017), 298–307.

68. Erin Blakemore, "Andrew Jackson Wasn't Always on the $20 Bill," *Smithsonian Magazine*, June 18, 2015.

69. Thomas Greco, *The End of Money and the Future of Civilization* (White River Junction, VT: Chelsea Green Pub., 2009), 33.

70. Andrew Jackson, "Farewell Address," March 4, 1837. Collection of the Miller Center, University of Virginia.

71. Abby Ohlheiser, "Why Was Andrew Jackson Put on the $20 Bill? The Answer May Be Lost to History," *Washington Post*, April 20, 2016.

72. Annie Linskey, "When Will Harriet Tubman Adorn the $20 bill?," *Washington Post*, June 3, 2021.

73. Genevieve B. Tung and Ruth Anne Robbins, "Beyond #TheNew10—The Case for a Citizens Currency Advisory Committee," *Rutgers University Law Review*, vol. 69, no. 195: 203–206.

74. Ohlheiser, ibid.

75. Kate Clifford Larson, *Bound for the Promised Land: Harriet Tubman Portrait of an American Hero* (New York: Ballantine Books, 2004), 77–78.

76. Catherine Clinton, *Harriet Tubman: The Road to Freedom* (New York: Back Bay Books/ Little Brown and Company, 2004), 47.

77. See Timothy James Lockley, ed., *Maroon Communities in South Carolina: a Documentary Record* (Columbia: University of South Carolina Press, 2009); Sylviane A. Diouf, *Slavery's Exiles: The Story of the American Maroons* (New York University Press, 2014); and Gene Allen Smith, *The Slaves' Gamble: Choosing Sides in the War of 1812* (New York: Palgrave Macmillan, 2013).

78. The "peculiar institution" was a euphemistic term used to refer to slavery by antebellum Southerners. See Fitzhugh Brundage, "American Slavery: A Look Back at The Peculiar Institution," *The Journal of Blacks in Higher Education*, no. 15 (Spring 1997), 118–120

79. Herbert Aptheker, *American Negro Slave Revolts* (New York: Columbia University Press, 1943); Stephen B. Oates, *The Fires of Jubilee: Nat Turner's Fierce Rebellion* (New York: Harper & Row, 1975); John Henrik Clarke, ed., *William Styron's Nat Turner: Ten Black Writers Respond* (Boston: Beacon Press, 1968); Martin S. Goldman, *Nat Turner and the Southhampton Revolt of 1831* (New York: Franklin Watts, 1992).

80. See Gayle T. Tate, "Free Black Resistance in the Antebellum Era, 1830 to 1860," *Journal of Black Studies*, July 1988, 764–782; and Solomon North, *Twelve Years a Slave* (New York: Penguin Books, 2012).

81. Osborne Perry Anderson, *A Voice From Harper's Ferry*, Wikisource, 1961.

82. See Keith P. Griffler, *Front Line of Freedom: African Americans and the Forging of the Underground Railroad in the Ohio Valley* (Lexington: University Press of Kentucky, 2004); and J. Blaine Hudson, *Fugitive Slaves and the Underground Railroad in the Kentucky Borderland* (Jefferson, NC: McFarland & Company, 2002).

83. Maurice Jackson, *Let This Voice Be Heard: Anthony Benezet, Father of Atlantic Abolitionism* (Philadelphia: University of Pennsylvania Press, 2009).

84. It should be noted that Franklin became an outspoken abolitionist late in his career. When he was younger, he owned two enslaved individuals,

George and King, and his print shop published slaveowners' advertisements for escapees as well as anti-slavery documents. See Marvee S. Shah, "Benjamin Franklin and Slavery," April 29, 2013. http://www.personal.psu.edu/cjm5/blogs/benjamin_franklin_then_and_now/2013/04/benjamin-franklin-and-slavery.html.

85. Angela Y. Davis, *Women, Race & Class* (New York: Random House, 1981), 22.

86. Ibid., 74.

87. Ibid., 85.

88. Dorothy Wickenden, *The Agitators: Three Friends Who Fought for Abolition and Women's Rights* (New York: Scribner, 2021), 37–38.

89. Rosa Belle Holt, "A Heroine in Ebony," *Chautauquan*, July 1886, p. 426.

90. Jean M. Humez, *Harriet Tubman: The Life and the Life Stories* (Madison: University of Wisconsin Press, 2003), 16.

91. Wickenden, ibid., 41.

92. Walter Johnson, *Soul by Soul: Life Inside the Antebellum Slave Market* (Cambridge, MA: Harvard University Press, 1999), 5.

93. Wickenden, ibid., 41.

94. Wickenden, ibid., 42.

95. Davis, ibid., 23.

96. Harriet Tubman Historical Society, "How did Harriet Tubman escape?," www.harriet-tubman.org/escape/.

97. Larson, ibid., 1.

98. See Andrew Delbanco, *The War Before the War: Fugitive Slaves and the Struggle for America's Soul from the Revolution to the Civil War* (New York: Penguin Books, 2019).

99. Sarah H. Bradford, *Scenes in the Life of Harriet Tubman*, 1869, 18.

100. www.in2013dollars.com/us/inflation/1849?amount=300.

101. Bradford, ibid., 12.

102. Larson, ibid., 84.

103. Larson, ibid., 89–90.

104. Larson, ibid., 302.

105. Larson, ibid., 101.

106. Bradford, ibid., 100.

107. Jean M. Humez, *Harriet Tubman: The Life and Life Stories* (Madison: University of Wisconsin Press, 2003), 204.

108. Bradford, ibid., 96.

109. Bradford, ibid., 89.

110. Humez, ibid., 204.

111. Humez, ibid., 40–41.

112. Humez, ibid., 40–41; Larson, ibid., 183.

113. Clinton, ibid., 139.

114. Larson, ibid., 212.

115. William G. Cutler, *History of the State of Kansas*, A. T. Andreas, 1883, "The Era of Peace," Part 43.

116. Humez, ibid., 58.

117. Paul Donnelly, "Harriet Tubman's Great Raid," *New York Times*, June 7, 2013.

118. Bradford, ibid., 100–102.

119. Bradford, ibid.; Wickenden, ibid., 223.

120. Humez, ibid., 57.

121. Harriet Tubman, "Letter to Franklin B. Sanborn," June 30, 1863.

122. Meredith Mingledorff, "Leader, Warrior, Military Intelligence Operative: Harriet Tubman Davis Honored in Women's History," U.S. Army, March 3, 2021.

123. Clinton, ibid., 173.

124. Military Intelligence Corps Hall of Fame, "MS HARRIET TUBMAN HONORARY MEMBER," MI Hall of Fame, Intelligence Knowledge Network; DeNeen L. Brown, "Renowned as a Black liberator, Harriet Tubman was also a brilliant spy," *Washington Post*, February 12, 2021.

125. Mingledorff, ibid.

126. See Robert Allen, *Reluctant Reformers: The Impact of Racism on American Social Reform Movements* (Washington, DC: Howard University Press), 1974; Daina Ramey Berry and Kali Nicole Gross, *A Black Women's History of the United States* (Boston: Beacon Press, 2020); and Angela Y. Davis, *Women, Race, & Class* (New York: Random House, 1981).

127. Davis, ibid., 51.

128. Kathryn Cullen-DuPont, *Encyclopedia of Women's History in America* (New York: Facts on File, 2000), 12.

129. Mark Leibovich, "Rights vs. Rights: An Improbable Collision Course," *New York Times*, January 13, 2008; Susan Brownell Anthony, Matilda Joslyn Gage, and Ida Husted Harper, *History of Woman Suffrage: 1861–1876* (New York: Fowler & Wells, 1881), 354.

130. Davis, ibid., 71.

131. Sernett, ibid., 153.

132. Wickenden, ibid.

133. Lowry, ibid., 371.

134. Sernett, ibid., 153.

135. Sernett, ibid., 155.

136. Sernett, 155.

137. Larson, ibid., 292.

138. See Patricia Hill Collins, *Black Feminist Thought* (New York:

Routledge, 2009); Beverly Guy-Sheftall, ed., *Words of Fire: An Anthology of African-American Feminist Thought* (New York: New Press, 1995); bell hooks, *Feminism Is for Everybody: Passionate Politics* (Cambridge, MA: South End Press, 2000); Gloria T. Hull, Patricia Bell Scott and Barbara Smith, *All the Women Are White, All the Blacks Are Men, but Some of Us Are Brave* (New York: The Feminist Press at the City University of New York, 2015); Audre Lorde, *Sister Outsider* (New York: Penguin Books, 2020); Cherríe Moraga and Gloria Anzaldúa, eds., *This Bridge Called My Back: Writings By Radical Women of Color* (Albany: State University of New York, 2015); and Robert L. Allen, *Reluctant Reformers: Racism and Social Reform Movements in the United States* (Washington, DC: Howard University Press, 1983).

139. See www.womenofthehall.org/inductee/harriet-tubman/

140. Jane Rhodes, *Mary Ann Shadd Cary: The Black Press and Protest in the Nineteenth Century* (Bloomington: Indiana University Press, 1999), 186.

141. Rinaldo Walcott, "'Who Is She and What Is She to You?': Mary Ann Shadd Cary and the (Im)possibility of Black/Canadian Studies," *Atlantis*, Spring/Summer 2000, vol. 24 (2): 138.

142. Megan Specia, "Overlooked No More: How Mary Ann Shadd Cary Shook Up the Abolitionist Movement," *New York Times*, June 6, 2018; www .womenofthehall.org/inductee/mary-ann-shadd-cary/; Rhodes, 185, 194; and Henry Louis Gates Jr. and Evelyn Brooks Higginbotham, eds., *African American Lives* (New York: Oxford University Press, 2004), 150.

143. John M. Brown, "Editorial," *African Methodist Episcopal Church Review*, vol. 10, no. 1 (July 1893).

144. See https://suffragistmemorial.org/african-american-women-leaders-in-the-suffrage-movement/.

145. Anna J. Cooper, *A Voice from the South* (Mineola, NY: Dover Publications, 2016).

146. Cooper, ibid., 12.

147. Charles Lemert and Esme Bhan, eds., *The Voice of Anna Julia Cooper* (Lanham, MD: Rowman & Little Publishers, 1998), 6.

148. Much of the information regarding black women in the suffrage movement came from a brilliant and well-researched article by historian and curator emerita Edith Mayo, "African American Women Leaders in the Suffrage Movement (https://suffragistmemorial.org/african-american -women-leaders-in-the-suffrage-movement/). Her sources included: Rosalyn Terborg-Penn, *African American Women in the Struggle for the Vote: 1850–1920* (Bloomington and Indianapolis: Indiana University Press, 1998); Rosalyn Terborg-Penn, "African American Women and the Woman Suffrage Movement," in Marjorie Spruill Wheeler, ed., *One Woman One Vote: Rediscovering the Woman Suffrage Movement* (Tillamook, OR: NewSage Press,

ENDNOTES

1995), 135–156; Darlene Clark Hine, Wilma King, and Linda Reed, eds., *"We Specialize in the Wholly Impossible": A Reader in Black Women's History* (Brooklyn: NYU Press, 1995).

149. Lois Horton, *Harriet Tubman and the Fight for Freedom: A Brief History with Documents* (Boston: Bedford/St. Martin's, 2013).

150. See www.crusadeforthevote.org/nacw.

151. Duchess Harris, *Black Feminist Politics from Kennedy to Trump* (New York: Palgrave Macmillan, 2019), 114.

152. The Combahee River Collective Statement. www.blackpast.org/african-american-history/combahee-river-collective-statement-1977/.

153. Ibid.

154. Keeanga-Yamahtta Taylor, "Until Black Women Are Free, None of Us Will Be Free," *The New Yorker*, July 20, 2020.

155. Keeanga-Yamahtta Taylor, ed., *How We Get Free: Black Feminism and the Combahee Women's Collective* (Chicago: Haymarket Books, 2017), 31.

156. Harris, ibid.

157. Andrew Jackson's Hermitage, "History from Home—Alfred Jackson." See thehermitage.com/history-from-home-alfred-jackson/.

158. Douglas C. Lyons, "Fort Gadsden, 'Negro Fort' history buried in Apalachicola National Forest," FloridaRambler.com, December 13, 2021.

159. See Nathaniel Millett, "Britain's 1814 Occupation of Pensacola and America's Response: An Episode of the War of 1812 in the Southeastern Borderlands," *Florida Historical Quarterly*, vol. 84, no. 2 (Fall 2005), 229–255.

160. PBS, "Florida's Negro Fort 1815–1816," www.pbs.org/wgbh/aia/part3/3p1643.html.

161. Claudio Saunt, *A New Order of Things: Property, Power, and the Transformation of the Creek Indians, 1733–1816* (Cambridge, UK: Cambridge University Press, 1999), 188.

162. Roxanne Dunbar-Ortiz, *An Indigenous Peoples' History of the United States* (Boston: Beacon, 2014), 96.

163. Ronald Takaki, *Different Mirror: A History of Multicultural America* (New York: Back Bay Books/Little, Brown and Co., 2008), 6.

164. Robert V. Remini, *Andrew Jackson: The Course of American Democracy, 1833–1845* (New York: HarperCollins, 1969), 2.

165. Michael Dubin, *United States Presidential Elections, 1788–1860* (Jefferson, NC: McFarland & Company, Inc., 2002), 42–51; and US Elections results, https://uselectionatlas.org/RESULTS/. See also Donald Ratcliffe, "The Right to Vote and the Rise of Democracy, 1787-1828," *Journal of the Early Republic*, vol. 33, no. 2 (Summer 2013): 219–254.

166. See https://thehermitage.com.

167. Charlotte Zobeir Ali, "The Five Reasons Why Andrew Jackson Was a Cruel Slaveholder," *Medium*, June 25, 2020.

ENDNOTES

168. Callie Hopkins, "The Enslaved Household of President Andrew Jackson," The White House Historical Society.

169. Ibid.

170. See www.officialdata.org/us/inflation/1804?amount=300.

171. DeNeen L. Brown, "Hunting down runaway slaves: The cruel ads of Andrew Jackson and 'the master class,'" *Washington Post*, May 1, 2017.

172. Robert P. Hay, "'And Ten Dollars Extra, for Every Hundred Lashes Any Person Will Give Him, to the Amount of Three Hundred': A Note on Andrew Jackson's Runaway Slave Ad of 1804 and on the Historian's Use of Evidence," *Tennessee Historical Quarterly*, vol. 36, no. 4 (Winter 1977): 471.

173. Charles Ball, *Slavery In The United States: A Narrative Of The Life And Adventures Of Charles Ball, A Black Man* (New York: John S. Taylor, 1837), 59.

174. Mark R. Cheathem, "Hannah, Andrew Jackson's Slave," *HUMANITIES*, March/April 2014, vol. 35, no. 2.

175. Mark R. Cheathem, "Politicizing USPS is another Andrew Jackson move from Trump," *Washington Post*, August 16, 2020.

176. Ibid.

177. Remini, 258–261; and Jon Mecham, *American Lion: Andrew Jackson in the White House* (New York: Random House, 2008), 304–306.

178. Zinn, 127

179. "Cherokee Indian Removal," Sarah H. Hill, Atlanta, Georgia, www.encyclopediaofalabama.org/article/h-1433; and Francis Paul Prucha, *The Great Father: The United States Government and the American Indians* (Lincoln: University of Nebraska Press, 1984), 206.

180. *Speeches on the Passage of the Bill for the Removal of the Indians* (Boston: Perkins and Marvin, 1830), 251.

181. Takaki, ibid., 85.

182. Takaki, ibid., 87.

183. Takaki, ibid., 85; Dunbar-Ortiz, ibid., 99

184. Takaki, ibid., 88.

185. Zinn, ibid., 128.

186. Takaki, ibid., 86.

187. Takaki, ibid., 86.

188. Dunbar-Ortiz, ibid., 111.

189. Dunbar-Ortiz, ibid., 112–113.

190. Ryan P. Smith, "How Native American Slaveholders Complicate the Trail of Tears Narrative," *Smithsonian Magazine*, March 6, 2018.

191. D. Amari Jackson, "Enslaved Black People: The Part of the Trail of Tears Narrative No One Told You About," *Atlanta Black Star*, March 17, 2018.

192. Quoted in Dunbar-Ortiz, ibid., 111.

193. Rebecca Onion, "Andrew Jackson's Adopted Indian Son," *Slate*, April

ENDNOTES

29, 2016.

194. Ibid.

195. Michael Paul Rogin, *Fathers and Children: Andrew Jackson and the Subjugation of the American Indian* (New York: Knopf, 1975), 215.

196. U.S. National Park Service, "Lyncoya," www.nps.gov/people/lyncoya.htm.

197. Onion, ibid.

198. Robert V. Remini, *Andrew Jackson and the Course of American Empire, 1767–1821* (Baltimore, MD: John Hopkins University Press), 194.

199. Robert V. Remini, *Andrew Jackson and His Indian Wars* (New York: Viking, 2001), 215.

200. Michael S. Rosenwald, "Andrew Jackson slaughtered Indians. Then he adopted a baby boy he'd orphaned.," *Washington Post*, June 16, 2019.

201. Onion, ibid. See also Dawn Peterson, *Indians in the National Family: Adoption and the Politics of Antebellum Expansion* (Cambridge, MA: Harvard University Press, 2017).

202. Gleaves Whitney, *American Presidents: Farewell Messages to the Nation, 1796–2001* (Lanham, MD: Lexington Books, 2003), 71.

203. Alan Rappeport, "See a Design of the Harriet Tubman $20 Bill That Mnuchin Delayed," *New York Times*, June 14, 2019.

204. Ibid.

205. Ibid.

206. Tung and Robbins, ibid., 214–215.

207. Correspondence with the author, February 7, 2022.

208. Bureau of Engraving and Printing, U.S. Department of the Treasury, "About Advanced Counterfeit Deterrence," www.moneyfactory.gov/about/advancedcounterfeitdeterrence.html.

209. U.S. Treasury Secretary Jacob J. Lew, "Remarks of Secretary Jacob J. Lew at The National Archives," June 18, 2015; Maya Rhoday, "U.S. to Put a Woman on the Redesigned $10 Bill in 2020," *Time*, June 18, 2015.

210. Email correspondence with the author, February 2022.

211. See Matt Stoller, "The Hamilton Hustle," *The Baffler*, March 2017; and William Hogeland, "Inventing Alexander Hamilton: The Troubling Embrace of the Founder of American Finance," *Boston Review*, November 1, 2007.

212. Ankeet Ball, "Ambition & Bondage: An Inquiry on Alexander Hamilton and Slavery," seminar paper, Columbia and Slavery, Columbia University, 2015.

213. Martin Pengelly, "New Research Sheds Light on Alexander Hamilton's Ties to Slavery," *Guardian*, November 10, 2020; and Phil Magness, "Alexander Hamilton's Exaggerated Abolitionism," History News Network, June 27, 2015.

214. Michelle DuRoss, "Somewhere in Between: Alexander Hamilton and Slavery," Varsity Tutors.

215. Colby Itkowitz, "Former Fed Chair Ben Bernanke Is 'Appalled' Alexander Hamilton Is Coming Off the $10 Bill," *Washington Post*, June 22, 2015.

216. See Ron Chernow, *Alexander Hamilton* (New York: Penguin Publishing, 2005).

217. Nawal Arjini, "Ishmael Reed Tries to Undo the Damage 'Hamilton' Has Wrought," *The Nation*, June 3, 2019.

218. Ishmael Reed, "CounterPunch on Stage: The Haunting of Lin-Manuel Miranda," CounterPunch, April 12, 2019. See Ishmael Reed, "'Hamilton: the Musical': Black Actors Dress Up Like Slave Traders . . . and It's Not Halloween," CounterPunch, August 21, 2015.

219. Rishi Nath, "Exit West: An Interview with Ishmael Reed," *Asian American Writers' Workshop Magazine*, April 22, 2020.

220. U.S. Treasury Secretary Jacob J. Lew, "An Open Letter from Secretary Lew," April 20, 2016.

221. Ibid.

222. Susan B. Glasser, "The Man Who Put Andrew Jackson in Trump's Oval Office," *Politico*, January 22, 2018.

223. Jenna Johnson, "Trump pays 'inspirational' visit to his hero Andrew Jackson's Hermitage plantation," *Chicago Tribune*, March 15, 2017. According to The Hermitage web site: "In all reality, slavery was the source of Andrew Jackson's wealth." See thehermitage.com/learn/slavery/.

224. Jeff Stein, "Obama-era Officials Say Trump Administration Hasn't Delayed New $20 Bill, Despite Harriet Tubman Firestorm," *Washington Post*, July 16, 2019.

225. Alan Rappeport, "Despite Unrest, Treasury Dept. Has No Plans to Speed Tubman to the $20 Note," *New York Times*, June 11, 2020.

226. Rappeport, ibid., June 14, 2019.

227. Ibid.

228. Stein, ibid.

229. The American Council of the Blind, et al., Appellants v. Steven T. Mnuchin, Secretary of the Treasury, Appellee; No. 17-5013; decided: December 26, 2017.

230. Defendant's Supplemental Status Report, American Council of the Blind, et al., Plaintiffs, v. Jacob J. Lew, Secretary of the Treasury, Defendant; filed: May 12, 2016.

231. Rappeport, ibid., June 11, 2020.

232. Rappeport, ibid., June 14, 2019.

233. Ibid.

234. It is notable that Katko was one of only ten Republicans who voted to impeach Trump in his second impeachment case in the House of

Representatives. The other nine were Liz Cheney (R-WY), Anthony Gonzalez (R-OH), Jaime Herrera Beutler (R-WA), Adam Kinzinger (R-IL), Peter Meijer (R-MI), Dan Newhouse (R-WA), Tom Rice (R-SC), Fred Upton (R-MI), and David Valadao (R-CA).

235. "Rep. Katko and Rep. Cummings Re-Introduce Harriet Tubman Tribute Act," press release, February 7, 2019.

236. James Lankford, "Senator Lankford Introduces Resolution to Support a Woman on the $20 Bill Instead of the $10 Bill," press release, Office of United States Senator James Lankford, January 21, 2016; www.lankford.senate.gov/imo/media/doc/Woman_On_Currency_Resolution1.pdf

237. "Native American Population 2021," World Population Review.

238. DeNeen L. Brown, "Harriet Tubman Is Already Appearing on $20 Bills Whether Trump Officials Like It or Not," *Washington Post*, May 23, 2019.

239. Hanna Trudo, "Poll: 56 percent of Americans support putting Harriet Tubman on the $20," *Politico*, April 21, 2016.

240. Ibid.

241. Andrew Keshner, "Biden Revives Plans to Put Harriet Tubman on $20 Note—Why This Bill Has Special Resonance for the Civil War–era Abolitionist," *Market Watch*, January 27, 2021.

242. Jacob Bogage, "Biden administration revives effort to put Harriet Tubman on $20 bill," *Washington Post*, January 28, 2021.

243. Janell Hobson, "Family Portraits of a Legend: Conversations with the Descendants of Harriet Tubman," *Ms. Magazine*, February 9, 2022.

244. Chanelle Adams, "Black Americans Are Feeling All Types of Ways About the Harriet Tubman $20 Bill," *BGD*, April 20, 2016.

245. Ibid.

246. Congressional Black Caucus, "Congressional Black Caucus Releases Statement on the Department of the Treasury Announcement placing Harriet Tubman on the $20 Bill," Washington, DC, April 21, 2016.

247. Ibid.

248. Maya Salam, "What Might It Take to Get Harriet Tubman on the $20 Bill?," *New York Times*, May 24, 2019; Lauren Victoria Burke, "Black Caucus Members React to Tubman Replacing Jackson on the front of the $20 bill," *Washington Informer*, April 26, 2016; Christina Tkacik, "Cummings again seeks law to put Harriet Tubman on $20 bill; Mnuchin still mum," *Baltimore Sun*, March 6, 2019.

249. Congressional Black Caucus Foundation, "CBCF Statement on Harriet Tubman Replacing Andrew Jackson on the $20 Bill and New Addition, Sojourner Truth to the $10 Bill," April 20, 2016.

250. Salam, ibid.

251. Eyder Peralta and Scott Horsley, "Treasury Decides to Put Harriet Tubman on $20 Bill," NPR, April 20, 2016.

252. Mary C. Curtis, "Harriet Tubman on the $20: Token Gesture, or a Good Start?," Women's Media Center, May 22, 2015.

253. Kirsten West Savali, "Why We Should Keep Harriet Tubman and Rosa Parks Off the $20 Bill," *The Root*, April 13, 2015.

254. Kristen Broady and Anthony Barr, "December's jobs report reveals a growing racial employment gap, especially for Black women," Brookings Institution, Washington, DC, January 11, 2022.

255. Anthony Barr, Makada Henry-Nickie, and Kristen Broady, "The November jobs report shows Black women are leaving the labor force," Brookings Institution, Washington, DC, December 8, 2021.

256. Ibid.

257. Mathilde Roux, *5 Facts About Black Women in the Labor Force*, Department of Labor, Washington, DC, August 3, 2021.

258. Ibid.

259. *Incarcerated Women and Girls*, Fact Sheet, The Sentencing Project, November 24, 2020.

260. Ibid.

261. Savali, ibid.

262. Feminista Jones, "Harriet Tubman Did Not Fight for Capitalism, Free Trade, or Competitive Markets," *Washington Post*, May 14, 2015.

263. Ibid.

264. Ibid.

265. Ibid.

266. Ibid.

267. Margaret Kimberley, "Freedom Rider: Honoring Harriet Tubman," *Black Agenda Report*, April 27, 2016.

268. Ibid.

269. Ibid.

270. Ijeoma Oluo, "Harriet Tubman on the $20 bill papers over racism," *Guardian*, April 16, 2020.

271. Ibid.

272. Ibid.

273. Brittney Cooper, "Putting Harriet Tubman on the $20 Bill Is Not a Sign of Progress. It's a Sign of Disrespect," *Time*, January 27, 2021.

274. Curtis, ibid.

275. Adam Gabbatt, "Margaret Thatcher on the $10 bill? Jeb Bush floats idea at Republican debate," *Guardian*, September 16, 2015.

276. Tommy Beer, "Trump Attacks 'Cancel Culture'—But Tried Recently

to Cancel These People," *Forbes*, September 6, 2020.

277. Nick Gass, "Trump: I'm so tired of this politically correct crap," *Politico*, September 23, 2015.

278. Ruth Gledhill, "Donald Trump says he has a 'very great' relationship with God, warns Christianity is 'under siege,'" *Christian Today*, January 18, 2016.

279. Lucian Gideon Conway, Meredith A. Repke, Shannon C. Houck, "Donald Trump as a Cultural Revolt Against Perceived Communication Restriction: Priming Political Correctness Norms Causes More Trump Support," *Journal of Social and Political Psychology*, vol. 5, no. 1 (2017): 245–259.

280. Breanna Edwards, "Tenn. Senator Afraid $20 Harriet Tubman Bill Diminishes Andrew Jackson," *The Root*, April 21, 2016.

281. Zachary D. Carter, "A GOP Congressman Wants to Defund the Harriet Tubman $20 Bill Really He filed legislation to do it," *Huffington Post*, June 20, 2016.

282. Matthew Nussbaum, "House GOP Dodges Vote to Block Harriet Tubman from $20 Bill," *Politico*, June 6, 2016.

283. Gregory Krieg, "A Brief History of Steve King Criticizing Immigrants and Minority Groups," CNN, March 13, 2017.

284. Hasan Khan, "Ben Carson: Keep Jackson where he is, put Tubman on the $2 bill," CNN, April 20, 2016.

285. Bryce Covert, "Conservatives Aren't Taking the Harriet Tubman News Well," *Think Progress*, April 21, 2016.

286. Ibid.

287. Fox News, *Fox & Friends*, April 21, 2016.

288. Ibid.

289. InfoWars, April 20, 2016.

290. Matt Drudge (@drudge) April 21, 2016.

291. Jim Webb, "We Can Celebrate Harriet Tubman Without Disparaging Andrew Jackson," *Washington Post*, April 24, 2016.

292. Ibid.

293. Ibid.

294. Ibid.

295. Louis Nelson, "Trump told Howard Stern it's OK to call Ivanka a 'piece of ass,'" *Politico*, October 8, 2016.

296. Adam Withnall, "Donald Trump's unsettling record of comments about his daughter Ivanka: 'If Ivanka weren't my daughter, perhaps I'd be dating her,'" *The Independent*, October 10, 2016. See the clip here: www.you tube.com/watch?v=DP7yf8-Lk80.

297. David A. Graham, "The President Who Doesn't Read," *The Atlantic*,

ENDNOTES

January 5, 2018.

298. Covert, ibid.

299. Michael Olesker, "A tale of customer service, justice and currency as funny as a $2 bill," *Baltimore Sun*, March 8, 2005; and Ted Oberg, "Lunchroom Lunacy: ISD cops investigate $2 bill spent on school lunch," *ABC News*, April 28, 2016.

300. Ellen Cranley, "'You want me to put that face on the twenty-dollar bill?': Omarosa claims Trump slammed the idea of replacing Andrew Jackson's face with Harriet Tubman's," *Business Insider*, August 14, 2018.

301. Paul Solotaroff, "Trump Seriously: On the Trail with the GOP's Tough Guy," *Rolling Stone*, September 9, 2015.

302. See Ian Haney López, *Dog Whistle Politics: How Coded Racial Appeals Have Reinvented Racism and Wrecked the Middle Class* (New York: Oxford University Press, 2015).

303. Charles Blow, "White Extinction Anxiety," *New York Times*, June 24, 2018.

304. "What Is White Replacement Theory?," NPR, September 26, 2021.

305. Kieran Press-Reynolds, "A former leader of the KKK celebrated Tucker Carlson 'finally' sharing the white-supremacist 'great replacement' conspiracy theory," *Business Insider*, October 22, 2021.

306. Ja'han Jones, "Ex–KKK leader David Duke takes credit for Donald Trump and Tucker Carlson," MSNBC, October 20, 2021.

307. Jeremy W. Peters, Michael M. Grynbaum, Keith Collins, Rich Harris, and Rumsey Taylor, "How the El Paso Killer Echoed the Incendiary Words of Conservative Media Stars," *New York Times*, August 11, 2019.

308. Media Matters for America staff, "Fox host Jeanine Pirro pushes white supremacist 'great replacement' conspiracy theory," Media Matters for America, August 29, 2019.

309. See Matt Gertz, "Fox News is pushing white nationalism because the Murdochs want it to," Media Matters, August 8, 2019; John Whitehouse and Eric Kleefeld, "Stephen Miller emails reveal white nationalist origin of Fox News talking points," Media Matters for America, November 12, 2019.

310. Peters et al., ibid.

311. Ibid.

312. Ibid.

313. Ibid.

314. Anti-Defamation League, "White Supremacists Applaud Tucker Carlson's Promotion of Replacement Theory," April 22, 2021.

315. Ryan Boat, "Quiz: Can You Tell the Difference Between Tucker Carlson and an Admitted White Supremacist?," *Rolling Stone*, September 23, 2021.

ENDNOTES

316. Ibid.

317. Ibid.

318. Maureen A. Craig and Jennifer A. Richeson, "On the Precipice of a 'Majority-Minority' America: Perceived Status Threat from the Racial Demographic Shift Affects White Americans' Political Ideology," *Psychological Science*, vol. 25, no. 6 (2014): 1189–1197.

319. Ezra Klein, "White threat in a browning America," *Vox*, July 30, 2018.

320. Akhil Reed Amar, "Actually, the Electoral College Was a Pro-Slavery Ploy," *New York Times*, April 6, 2019.

321. A number of scholars and researchers refuted this trope, including Kalwant Bhopal, *White Privilege: The Myth of a Post-Racial Society* (Bristol, UK: Policy Press, 2018); Melanie E.L. Bush and Joe R. Feagin, *Everyday Forms of Whiteness: Understanding Race in a "Post-Racial" World* (Lanham, MD: Rowman & Littlefield Publishers, 2011), Devon W. Carbado and Mitu Gulati, *Acting White? Rethinking Race in "Post-Racial" America* (New York: Oxford University Press, 2013); Yuya Kiuchi, *Race Still Matters: The Reality of African American Lives and the Myth of Postracial Society* (Albany: State University of New York Press, 2016); Michael Tesler, *Post-Racial or Most-Racial?: Race and Politics in the Obama Era* (Chicago: University of Chicago Press, 2016); and Tim Wise, *Colorblind: The Rise of Post-Racial Politics and the Retreat from Racial Equity* (San Francisco: City Lights Books, 2010).

322. "PEN America Index of Educational Gag Orders" regularly updates these gag orders with a detailed online spreadsheet; Jeffrey Sachs, "New Stop W.O.K.E. Act Fits Disturbing Pattern in Education Culture War," PEN America, December 23, 2021.

323. Staff of Governor Ron DeSantis, "Governor DeSantis Announces Legislative Proposal to Stop W.O.K.E. Activism and Critical Race Theory in Schools and Corporations," press release, December 15, 2021.

324. Ibid.

325. David Miguel Gray, "What Critical Race Theory Is—and What It Isn't," *YES! Magazine*, July 7, 2021.

326. Gregory Pardlo, "Notes on Critical Race Theory," PEN America, November 8, 2021.

327. Amy Simonson, "Florida bill to shield people from feeling 'discomfort' over historic actions by their race, nationality or gender approved by Senate committee," CNN, January 20, 2022.

328. Ibid.

329. Jamila Bey, "Florida Lawmakers Advance Bill Intended To Protect White People From 'Discomfort' When Learning History," Black Entertainment Television, January 21, 2022.

330. Matthew Yglesias, "Trump's racist tirades against 'the Squad,'

explained," *Vox*, July 18, 2019.

331. John Fritze, Michael Collins, "Trump calls himself an 'extremely stable genius,' while responding to Pelosi criticism," *USA Today*, May 23, 2019.

332. Tom McCarthy, "Trump rally crowd chants 'send her back' after president attacks Ilhan Omar," *Guardian*, July 18, 2019.

333. Kristin Lam, "New Hampshire lawmaker Werner Horn: 'Owning slaves doesn't make you racist,'" *USA Today*, July 18, 2019.

334. Ibid.

335. Ibid.

336. Chris Folley, "New Hampshire Lawmaker Deletes Post, Clarifies After Saying 'owning slaves doesn't make you racist,'" *The Hill*, July 19, 2019.

337. Michael Tesler, "Republicans don't think Trump's tweets are racist. That fits a long American history of denying racism," *Washington Post*, July 30, 2019.

338. Ibid.

339. Tim Elfrink, "'It's not actually a real problem in America': Tucker Carlson calls white supremacy a 'hoax,'" *Washington Post*, August 7, 2019.

340. Emily S. Rueb and Derrick Bryson Taylor, "Tucker Carlson of Fox Falsely Calls White Supremacy a 'Hoax,'" *New York Times*, August 8, 2019.

341. Matt Zapotosky, "Wray says FBI has recorded about 100 domestic terrorism arrests in fiscal 2019 and many investigations involve white supremacy," *Washington Post*, July 23, 2019

342. Ibid.

343. Chris Riotta, "White supremacist violence responsible for spike in US domestic terror arrests, FBI says," *The Independent*, July 23, 2019.

344. Dan Frosch, Zusha Elinson and Sadie Gurman, "White Nationalists Pose Challenge to Investigators," *Wall Street Journal*, August 5, 2019; and Greg Myre, "FBI Is Investigating 850 Cases of Potential Domestic Terrorism," NPR, May 8, 2019.

345. Department of Homeland Security, "Homeland Threat Assessment—October 2020," 18.

346. Roger Parloff, "The Conspirators: The Proud Boys and Oath Keepers on Jan. 6," *Lawfare*, January 6, 2022; Toluse Olorunnipa and Cleve R. Wootson Jr., "Trump Refused to Condemn White Supremacists and Militia Members in Presidential Debate Marked By Disputes Over Race," *Washington Post*, September 30, 2020; and Ben Collins and Brandy Zadrozny, "Proud Boys Celebrate After Trump's Debate Callout," *NBC News*, September 29, 2020.

347. Zolan Kanno-Youngs, "Delayed Homeland Security Report Warns of 'Lethal' White Supremacy," *New York Times*, October 6, 2020.

348. "Summary of the Terrorism Threat to the U.S. Homeland," *National Terrorism Advisory System Bulletin*, Washington, DC, November 10, 2021.

349. Department of Homeland Security, "Center for Prevention Programs

and Partnerships," undated.

350. Department of Homeland Security, "Leveraging a Targeted Violence Prevention Program to Prevent Violent Extremism: A Formative Evaluation in Los Angeles," undated.

351. Julia Edwards Ainsley, Dustin Volz, Kristina Cooke, "Trump to focus counter-extremism program solely on Islam," Reuters, February 1, 2017.

352. Faiza Patel, Sophia DenUy, Andrew Lindsay, "Countering Violent Extremism in the Trump Era," Brennan Center for Justice, June 15, 2008.

353. "White Supremacist Extremism Poses Persistent Threat of Lethal Violence," *Joint Intelligence Bulletin*, Washington, DC, 1.

354. Ibid., 5.

355. Ibid., 2.

356. "Black Identity Extremists Likely Motivated to Target Law Enforcement Officers," FBI Intelligence Assessment, Washington, DC, August 3, 2017.

357. Ibid., 2.

358. Ibid., 3.

359. Ibid., 6.

360. Ibid., 7.

361. David Love, "FBI Tracks & Arrests 'Black Identity Extremist' and Hardly Anyone Is Talking About It," *Atlanta Black Star*, February 5, 2018.

362. Sam Levin, "Black activist jailed for his Facebook posts speaks out about secret FBI surveillance," *Guardian*, May 11, 2018.

363. Ibid.

364. See "Rep. Bass Grills AG Sessions On 'Black Extremism,'" Office of Rep. Karen Bass, U.S. House of Representatives, Washington, DC, November 14, 2017; "Rep. Bass Challenges FBI Director On Fictional BIE Report," Office of Rep. Karen Bass, U.S. House of Representatives, Washington, DC, December 7, 2017; and "Rep. Bass Slams Deputy AG Rosenstein on Black Identity Extremism Report," Office of Rep. Karen Bass, U.S. House of Representatives, Washington, DC, December 13, 2017.

365. "CBC Task Force on Foreign Affairs and National Security Hosts Briefing Examining FBI Black Identity Extremism Report," Congressional Black Congress Press Release, March 20, 2018.

366. Diversity MBA, "FBI Abandons Black Identity Extremism Designation," July 27, 2019.

367. "Leaked FBI Documents Raise Concerns About Targeting Black People Under 'Black Identity Extremist' and Newer Labels," ACLU, August 9, 2019; Anti-Defamation League, "Alt Right: A Primer on the New White Supremacy."

368. Ibid.

369. Census Bureau.

370. Blow, ibid.

371. Mike Schneider, "Census shows white decline, nonwhite majority among youngest," *Washington Post*, June 25, 2020.

372. William H. Frey, "The nation is diversifying even faster than predicted, according to new census data," Brookings Institution, July 1, 2020.

373. Hansi Lo Wang and Ruth Talbot, "This Is How the White Population Is Actually Changing Based on New Census Data," NPR, August 22, 2021.

374. Ibid.

375. Ibid.

376. Jen Kirby, "Trump wants fewer immigrants from 'shithole countries' and more from places like Norway," *Vox*, January 11, 2018.

377. Kaitlan Collins, tweet, January 11, 2018.

378. Marc Hooghe and Ruth Dassonneville, "Explaining the Trump Vote: The Effect of Racist Resentment and Anti-Immigrant Sentiments," *PS: Political Science & Politics*, July 2018, 528.

379. Ibid., 532.

380. See Michael I. Norton and Samuel R. Sommers, "Whites See Racism as a Zero-Sum Game That They Are Now Losing," *Perspectives on Psychological Science*, May 18, 2011, 215–218.

381. Ibid.

382. *Discrimination in America: Experiences and Views of White Americans*, National Public Radio, the Robert Wood Johnson Foundation, and Harvard T. H. Chan School of Public Health, November 2017.

383. Ibid.

384. Ibid.

385. "American Voters are Pro-Immigrant, Anti-Wall, Quinnipiac University Poll Finds, Voters Concerned About Immigrants' Values," Quinnipiac University Poll, September 16, 2016. See https://poll.qu.edu/Poll-Release-Legacy?releaseid=2380

386. Ibid.

387. Alia Shoaib, "Trump claims white people are discriminated against for COVID-19 treatment: 'If you're white you go right to the back of the line,'" *Insider*, January 16, 2022.

388. Ibid.; and Calvin Woodward and David Klepper, "Trump Seeds Race Animus With Covid Falsehood," *US News and World Report*, January 16, 2022.

389. Woodward and Klepper, ibid.; and Natalie Colarossi, "Trump Claims White People 'at the Back of the Line' for COVID Vaccines, Treatments," *Newsweek*, January 16, 2022.

390. *The Economist*/YouGov Poll, June 2–4, 2019: 1,500 US adult citizens.

ENDNOTES

See docs.cdn.yougov.com/hlzpfslijb/econTabReport.pdf.

391. "White and Black Americans Far Apart on Racial Issues," Ipsos, August 27, 2020, 4.

392. Ibid., 1.

393. Larry M. Bartels, "Ethnic Antagonism Erodes Republicans' Commitment to Democracy," *Proceedings of the National Academy of Sciences of the United States*, vol. 117, no. 37 (September 15, 2020): 22753.

394. Ibid.

395. Christopher Ingraham, "New Research Explores Authoritarian Mind-Set of Trump's Core Supporters," *Washington Post*, October 12, 2020.

396. Ibid., and Bob Altemeyer and John W. Dean, *Authoritarian Nightmare: Trump and His Followers* (New York: Melville House, 2020), 108.

397. Ibid., xiii.

398. James Poniewozik, "Donald Trump Was the Real Winner of 'The Apprentice,'" *New York Times*, September 28, 2020.

399. Altemeyer and Dean, ibid., 139.

400. Ibid.

401. Samuel Sommers and Michael Norton, "White people think racism is getting worse. Against white people," *Washington Post*, July 21, 2016.

402. Ibid.

403. Meredith Deliso, "Capitol rioter who allegedly tweeted he wanted to 'assassinate' Alexandria Ocasio-Cortez faces 5 charges," *ABC News*, January 23, 2021.

404. Jacob Pramuk, "Capitol rioters came within a minute of reaching Pence, report says," CNBC, January 15, 2021; Josh Dawsey and Ashley Parker, "Inside the remarkable rift between Donald Trump and Mike Pence," *Washington Post*, January 11, 2021; Ashley Parker, Carol D. Leonnig, Paul Kane and Emma Brown, "How the rioters who stormed the Capitol came dangerously close to Pence," *Washington Post*, January 15, 2021; Tom Porter, "An ABC reporter said there are pictures of Pence 'holed up in a basement' hiding from the Capitol rioters but he can't show them," *Business Insider*, November 9, 2021; Heather Cox Richardson, "Details Emerge How Trump Incited Mob to Lynch Vice President Mike Pence for Not Overturning Election," *Milwaukee Independent*, January 9, 2021.

405. Pramuk, ibid.

406. Deliso, ibid.

407. Alan Feuer, "Texas Man Convicted in First Jan. 6 Trial," *New York Times*, March 8, 2022.

408. Chris Cameron, "These Are the People Who Died in Connection With the Capitol Riot," *New York Times*, January 5, 2022.

409. Ellen Barry, Nicholas Bogel-Burroughs, and Dave Philipps, "Woman Killed in Capitol Embraced Trump and QAnon After 14 Years in the Military,"

New York Times, January 7, 2021 (updated August 23, 2021); Rich Schapiro, Anna Schecter and Chelsea Damberg, "Officer who shot Ashli Babbitt during Capitol riot breaks silence: 'I saved countless lives,'" *NBC News*, August 26, 2021.

410. Masood Farivar, "Researchers: More Than a Dozen Extremist Groups Took Part in Capitol Riots," VOA, January 16, 2021; Alan Feuer, "Another Far-Right Group Is Scrutinized About Its Efforts to Aid Trump," *New York Times*, January 3, 2022.

411. Alan Feuer and Adam Goldman, "Oath Keepers Leader Charged with Seditious Conspiracy in Jan. 6 Investigation," *New York Times*, January 13, 2022.

412. Denise Lu and Eleanor Lutz, "How Oath Keepers Are Accused of Plotting to Storm the Capitol," *New York Times*, January 19, 2022.

413. See copy of the indictment: www.justice.gov/usao-dc/press-release/file/1462346/download.

414. Feuer and Goldman, ibid.

415. Matthew Rosenberg and Ainara Tiefenthäler, "Decoding the Far-Right Symbols at the Capitol Riot," *New York Times*, January 13, 2021.

416. Washington Post staff, "Identifying far-right symbols that appeared at the U.S. Capitol riot," *Washington Post*, January 15, 2021.

417. See www.youtube.com/watch?v=qBQN1321_sI.

418. Emmanuel Felton, "Black Police Officers Describe the Racist Attacks They Faced as They Protected the Capitol," *Buzzfeed*, January 9, 2021.

419. Alan Feuer, "Prosecutors Move Quickly on Jan. 6 Cases, but One Big Question Remains," *New York Times*, January 5, 2022.

420. Ibid.

421. Ken Dilanian and Ben Collins, "There are hundreds of posts about plans to attack the Capitol. Why hasn't this evidence been used in court?," *NBC News*, April 20 2021.

422. Ed Pilkington, "More than 1,000 US public figures aided Trump's effort to overturn election," *Guardian*, January 5, 2022.

423. Ibid.

424. Robert A. Pape, "American Face of Insurrection: Analysis of Individuals Charged for Storming the US Capitol on January 6, 2021," Chicago Project on Security and Threats, University of Chicago, January 5, 2022.

425. Feuer, "Prosecutors Move Quickly," ibid.

426. Luke Broadwater and Alan Feuer, "Jan. 6 Committee Subpoenas Fake Trump Electors," *New York Times*, January 28, 2022; Alan Feuer, Maggie Haberman, Michael S. Schmidt, and Luke Broadwater, "Trump Had Role in Weighing Proposals to Seize Voting Machines," *New York Times*, January 31, 2022; Amy B. Wang and John Wagner, "Georgia prosecutor granted special

grand jury in probe of Trump's efforts to overturn state's election results," *Washington Post*, January 24, 2022.

427. Kate Clifford Larson, *Bound for the Promised Land: Harriet Tubman, Portrait of an American Hero* (New York: Ballantine Books, 2004), 43.

428. Beverly Lowry, *Harriet Tubman: Imaging a Life* (New York: Anchor Books, 2007), 89.

429. Ibid., 91.

430. Ibid., 91.

431. Harriet Washington, *Medical Apartheid: The Dark History of Medical Experimentation on Black Americans from Colonial Times to the Present* (New York: Harlem Moon, 2006), 9.

432. Fred D. Gray, *The Tuskegee Syphilis Study: An Insiders' Account of the Shocking Medical Experiment Conducted by Government Doctors Against African American Men* (Montgomery, AL: NewSouth Books, 1998); and James H. Jones, *Bad Blood: The Tuskegee Syphilis Experiment* (New York: Free Press, 1981).

433. Mariah Cooper, "Tuskegee study descendants encourage COVID-19 vaccination," Campaign.us, June 30, 2021.

434. Oliver T. Brooks, "COVID-19 Underscores Wealth and Health Disparities in the African American Community," press release, National Medical Association, April 8, 2020.

435. Larson, ibid., 285; and Lowry, ibid., 373.

436. Jeffery K. Taubenberger and David M. Morens, "1918 Influenza: The Mother of All Pandemics," *Emerging Infectious Diseases*, vol. 12, no. 1 (January 2006): 15; and Soraya Nadia McDonald, "In 1918 and 2020, Race Colors America's Response to Epidemics," *The Undefeated*, April 1, 2020.

437. William Robin, "The 1918 Pandemic's Impact on Music? Surprisingly Little," *New York Times*, May 6, 2020; Shalom Goldman, "Blues in the time of Pandemic, 1919—'In a few days influenza would be controlled,'" *Informed Comment*, March 19, 2020.

438. See www.protestsonglyrics.net/Medical_Songs/1919-Influenza-Blues .phtml.

439. Ibid.

440. See Evan Andrews, "Why Was It Called the 'Spanish Flu'?", History .com, March 27, 2020.

441. McDonald, ibid.

442. Ibid.

443. See W. E. B. Du Bois, *The Health and Physique of the Negro American* (Atlanta: Atlanta University Press, 1906).

444. Frederick L. Hoffman, *Race Traits and Tendencies of the American Negro* (New York: American Economic Association, 1896), 312.

ENDNOTES

445. National Center for Health Statistics, "Health Insurance Coverage: Early Release of Estimates From the National Health Interview Survey, 2020," CDC, 2020.

446. Vicente Navarro, "The Consequences of Neoliberalism in the Current Pandemic," *International Journal of Health Service*, May 7, 2020.

447. Michelle L. Holshue et al., "First Case of 2019 Novel Coronavirus in the United States," *New England Journal of Medicine*, March 5, 2020.

448. Matthew J. Belvedere, "Trump says he trusts China's Xi on coronavirus and the US has it 'totally under control,'" *CNBC*, January 22, 2020.

449. Donald Trump, "Remarks by President Trump, Vice President Pence, and Members of the Coronavirus Task Force," press conference, White House, Washington, DC, February 27, 2020.

450. The data from this section is from the CDC's online "COVID Data Tracker".

451. Ibid.

452. Christian Spencer, "New study finds 1 in 3 Americans were infected with coronavirus by the end of 2020," *The Hill*, August 26, 2021; Carolyn Crist, "U.S. COVID-19 Deaths in 2021 Surpass 2020," WebMD, November 22, 2021.

453. The CDC's online "COVID Data Tracker" provides continuous updates in real time.

454. Sharon Weinberger and Jana Winter, "Internal CDC Report Says Racism Is Making COVID-19 Deadlier for Black Americans," *Yahoo News*, December 10, 2020.

455. See covidtracking.com/race.

456. Guardian Staff, "More than 150,000 Americans have died from COVID-19. Here is that tragic story in figures," *Guardian*, July 29, 2020.

457. APM Research Lab Staff, "The Color Of Coronavirus: Covid-19 Deaths By Race and Ethnicity in the U.S.," *APM Research*, March 5, 2021.

458. Amy Goldstein and Emily Guskin, "Almost one-third of black Americans know someone who died of COVID-19, survey shows," *Washington Post*, June 26, 2020.

459. *All In With Chris Hayes*, August 4, 2021. See Sarah Miller, Laura R. Wherry, and Bhashkar Mazumder, "Estimated Mortality Increases During the COVID-19 Pandemic by Socioeconomic Status, Race, And Ethnicity," *Health Affairs*, vol. 40, no. 8, July 21, 2021.

460. See www.apmresearchlab.org/covid/deaths-by-race.

461. Ibid.

462. See www.apmresearchlab.org/covid/deaths-by-race.

463. Leslie Perrot, "Navajo Nation Surpasses New York State for the Highest Covid-19 Infection Rate in the US," *CNN*, May 18, 2020.

464. Executive Order No. 008-20, Sixth Executive Order Related to

Extending the Declaration of a State of Emergency Due to the COVID-19 Virus on the Navajo Nation; Further Extending the Closure of Navajo Nation Government Offices and Related Entities, Navajo Nation Office of the President and Vice President, July 22, 2020.

465. Erica Gies, "The Navajo Are Fighting to Get Their Water Back," *Take Part*, April 22, 2016.

466. Reis Thebault and Alyssa Fowers, "Pandemic's weight falls on Hispanics and Native Americans, as deaths pass 150,000," *Washington Post*, July 31, 2020.

467. Aaron Sanchez-Guerra and Paola Jaramillo, "'An alley without exit.' Experts worry COVID-19 among Latinos will get dire without support," *News & Observer*, July 13, 2020; and Maria Godoy and Daniel Wood, "What Do Coronavirus Racial Disparities Look Like State By State?," NPR, May 30, 2020.

468. Elizabeth Cooney, "In another Covid-19 disparity, Black and Hispanic Americans are dying at younger ages than white Americans," *Stat*, July 10, 2020.

469. Catherine Pearson, "The First Data on Kids, COVID-19 and Race Is Here—And It's Not Good," *Huffington Post*, August 5, 2020.

470. Mary Papenfuss, "Children's COVID Hospital Admissions Hit Record High in U.S.," *Huffington Post*, December 31, 2021.

471. Denise Lu and Albert Sun, "Why COVID Death Rates Are Rising for Some Groups," *New York Times*, December 28, 2021.

472. Abby Goodnough and Jan Hoffman, "The Wealthy Are Getting More Vaccinations, Even in Poorer Neighborhoods," *New York Times*, March 4, 2021.

473. Amy Schoenfeld Walker, Anjali Singhvi, Josh Holder, Robert Gebeloff, and Yuriria Avila, "Pandemic's Racial Disparities Persist in Vaccine Rollout," *New York Times*, March 5, 2021.

474. Nambi Ndugga, Latoya Hill, Samantha Artiga, and Sweta Haldar, "Latest Data on COVID-19 Vaccinations by Race/Ethnicity," Kaiser Family Foundation, November 3, 2021.

475. Caleb Carma, "Fox News' Anti-Vax Mandate Messaging Is Out of Step With Its Own Strict Policies," *Vanity Fair*, October 7, 2021.

476. Tyler Monroe and Rob Savillo, "Fox has undermined vaccines nearly every day in the last six months," Media Matters for America, October 5, 2021.

477. Nicki Minaj, tweet, September 13, 2021.

478. "Nicki Minaj: Trinidad minister criticises rapper's vaccine tweet," *BBC*, September 16, 2021.

479. Bob Golliver, "Kyrie Irving breaks silence on decision to remain unvaccinated: 'It's bigger than the game,'" *Washington Post*, October 14, 2021.

480. Davey Alba, "Twitter Permanently Suspends Marjorie Taylor Greene's

Account," *New York Times*, January 2, 2022.

481. Ibid.

482. Ibid.

483. Emily Sullivan, "Laura Ingraham Told LeBron James to Shut Up and Dribble; He Went to the Hoop," NPR, February 19, 2018.

484. Kareem Abdul Jabbar, "On Kyrie Irving's Vaccine Refusal," *Jacobin*, October 6, 2021.

485. Ibid.

486. Jack Baer, "Ted Cruz: 'You know damn well I ain't rockin' with you,'" *Yahoo!Sports*, November 6, 2021.

487. Gil Kaufman, "Watch Dax Go In on COVID-19 in Hard-Hitting 'Coronavirus' Rap," *Billboard*, April 15, 2020.

488. See www.youtube.com/watch?v=EcLu2etbx6w

489. Claire Sterne, "Cardi B Tried To Warn Us About COVID. Now She's Ready To Party," *Elle*, December 6, 2021.

490. Ibid.

491. "Examining Options to Boost Essential Worker Wages during the Pandemic," The Hamilton Project, June 4, 2020.

492. Ibid.

493. Jeffry Bartash, "Black Americans, their lives and livelihoods on the line, suffer most from the pandemic," *Market Watch*, June 6, 2020.

494. Rakesh Kochhar, "Hispanic women, immigrants, young adults, those with less education hit hardest by COVID-19 job losses," *Fact Tank*, Pew Research, June 9, 2020.

495. "Minority small business owners harder hit by pandemic closures: 'A total nightmare,'" *CBS This Morning*, June 22, 2020.

496. Claire Kramer Mills and Jessica Battisto, *Double Jeopardy: Covid-19's Concentrated Health and Wealth Effects in Black Communities* (New York: Federal Reserve Bank of New York, 2020), 1.

497. Khristopher J. Brooks, "40% of Black-owned businesses not expected to survive Coronavirus," *CBS News*, June 22, 2020.

498. Khristopher, J. Brooks, "Black-owned small businesses hit harder by pandemic than White-owned firms," *CBS News*, February 23, 2021.

499. Justin Hansford and Tasnim Motala, "The Contradiction of Color-Blind Covid-19 Relief: Black America in the Age of the Pandemic," Criminal Justice Policy Program and Thurgood Marshall Civil Rights Center, Howard University Law School, Washington, DC, June 2020.

500. Imani Moise, "Predominately black congressional districts got fewer PPP loans: study," *Reuters*, July 30, 2020.

501. Emily Flitter, "Few Minority-Owned Businesses Got Relief Loans

They Asked For," *New York Times*, May 18, 2020.

502. Ibid.

503. "Small Business Support Must Extend to Businesses of Color," Center for Responsible Lending, May 5, 2020.

504. Robert Frank, "The billionaires and country clubs that received small business loans from the government," *CNBC*, July 7, 2020.

505. Roger Sollenberger and William Bredderman, "Kanye West's 'Independent' Campaign Was Secretly Run by GOP Elites," *Daily Beast*, December 17, 2021.

506. Gil Kaufman, "So What Was the Point of Kanye West's Presidential Run?," *Billboard*, November 6, 2020.

507. Sissi Cao, "Kanye, Reese Witherspoon Among the Celebs Who Got PPP Loans Meant for Small Business," *Observer*, July 9, 2020.

508. Alex Kotch, Hate Groups Rake in PPP Loans as Racial Justice Movement Expands, *PR Watch*, July 9, 2020; JakeThomas, "'Hate Groups' Received Millions in Aid from Small Business Relief Fund," *The Intellectualist*, July 10, 2020; and Roger Sollenberger, "Hate groups cashed in on pandemic relief before millions of Americans protested for social change," *Salon*, July 10, 2020.

509. "A State-by-State Look at Coronavirus in Prisons," The Marshall Project, August 13, 2020.

510. Ballotpedia, "Prison inmate release responses in response to the coronavirus (COVID-19) pandemic 2020," updated July 1, 2020.

511. Emily Widra, "Data update: As the Delta variant ravages the country, correctional systems are dropping the ball (again)," Prison Policy Initiative, October 21, 2021.

512. Ibid.

513. Beth Schwartzapfel and Keri Blakinger, "Omicron Has Arrived. Many Prisons and Jails Are Not Ready," The Marshall Project, December 22 2021.

514. See COVID Prison Project, covidprisonproject.com.

515. Ibid.

516. Patrice Gaines, "Coronavirus inside prisons doesn't just affect inmates. It affects communities of color," *NBC News*, July 8, 2020.

517. "African Americans Are More Likely to Develop High Blood Pressure by Middle Age," *CardioSmart*, American College of Cardiology, August 9, 2018.

518. "Heart Disease and African Americans," Office of Minority Health, U.S. Department of Health and Human Services, Washington, DC.

519. *National Diabetes Statistics Report 2020: Estimates of Diabetes and Its Burden in the United States*, Center for Disease Control and Prevention, U.S. Department of Health and Human Services, Washington, DC, 2020, 2.

520. Elias K. Spanakis and Sherita Hill Golden, "Race/Ethnic Differences in Diabetes and Diabetic Complications," *Current Diabetes Reports*, December 2013.

521. Ibram X. Kendi, "Stop Blaming Black People for Dying of the Coronavirus," *The Atlantic*, April 14, 2020.

522. Sabrina Strings, "It's Not Obesity. It's Slavery," *New York Times*, May 25, 2020.

523. Christine Byrne, "The BMI is Racist and Useless. Here's How to Measure Health Instead," *Huffington Post*, July 20, 2020.

524. Blake Farmer, "Long-standing Racial and Income Disparities Seen Creeping into Covid-19 Care," Nashville Public Radio, April 6, 2020.

525. Farmer, ibid.; and "Health Data in the COVID-19 Crisis: How racial equity is widening for patients to gain access to treatment," Rubix Life Sciences, rubixls.com/2020/04/01/health-data-in-the-covid-19-crisis-how-racial-equity-is-widening-for-patients-to-gain-access-to-treatment/.

526. Kelly M. Hoffmana, Sophie Trawaltera, Jordan R. Axta, and M. Norman Oliver, "Racial bias in pain assessment and treatment recommendations, and false beliefs about biological differences between blacks and whites," *Proceedings of the National Academy of Sciences* (PNAS), National Academy of Sciences (NAS), April 19, 2016, 4298.

527. Ibid., 4299.

528. Ibid., 4299–4300.

529. "Doctors Still Believe Black People Don't Feel Pain; and It's Being Taught in Medical School," blackdoctor.org/black-people-pain-bias-being-taught-in-med-school/2/.

530. Ibid.

531. "Chart Book: Accomplishments of Affordable Care Act," Center for Budget and Policy Priorities, Washington, DC, March 19, 2019.

532. Healthcare.gov, "Marketplace coverage & Coronavirus," healthcare.gov/coronavirus.

533. Peggy Bailey, Matt Broaddus, Shelby Gonzales, and Kyle Hayes, "African American Uninsured Rate Dropped by More Than a Third Under Affordable Care Act," Center on Budget and Policy Priorities, June 1, 2017; and Jenny Yang, "Percentage of people in the U.S. without health insurance by ethnicity 2010-2021," Statista, November 17, 2021.

534. Yang, ibid.

535. Ibid.

536. Beth LeBlanc, "Whitmer signs order calling racism a public health crisis," *Detroit News*, August 5, 2020; and Executive Order 2020-163: Black Leadership Advisory Council, www.michigan.gov/whitmer/news/state-orders-and-directives/2020/08/05/executive-order-2020-163.

537. Michigan.gov, Coronavirus, Michigan Data.

538. Ibid.

539. Amy Schoenfeld Walker, Anjali Singhvi, Josh Holder, Robert Gebeloff, and Yuriria Avila, "Pandemic's Racial Disparities Persist in Vaccine Rollout," *New York Times*, March 5, 2021.

540. Ibid.

541. Brandi Collins-Dexter, "Canaries in the Coal Mine: COVID-19 Misinformation and Black Communities," Harvard Kennedy School's Shorenstein Center on Media, Politics and Public, 2020.

542. Myah Ward, "15 times Trump praised China as coronavirus was spreading across the globe," *Politico*, April 15, 2020.

543. Ibid.

544. Ibid.

545. Donald G. McNeil Jr. and Andrew Jacobs, "Blaming China for Pandemic, Trump Says U.S. Will Leave the W.H.O.," *New York Times*, May 29, 2020.

546. Justine Coleman, "Photo of Trump's notes shows 'Chinese' virus written over 'coronavirus,'" *The Hill*, March 19, 2020.

547. See Richard Reeves, *Infamy: The Shocking Story of the Japanese American Internment in World War II* (New York: Henry Holt and Company, 2015); Lawson Fusao Inada, *Only What We Could Carry: The Japanese American Internment Experience* (Berkeley, CA: Heyday Books, 2000.); Rachel A. Bailey, *The Japanese Internment Camps: A History Perspectives Book* (Ann Arbor, MI: Cherry Lake Publishing, 2014); and Lynn Thiesmeyer, "The Discourse of Official Violence: Anti-Japanese North American Discourse and the American Internment Camps," *Discourse & Society*, vol. 6, no. 3 (July 1, 1995).

548. Michael Moore, "The Man Who Killed Vincent Chin," *Detroit Free Press*, August 30, 1987; and "35 Years After Vincent Chin's Murder, How Has America Changed?," *Asia Society*, June 16, 2017.

549. Niraj Warikoo, "Vincent Chin Murder 35 Years Later: History Repeating Itself?," *Detroit Free Press*, June 23, 2017.

550. Moore, ibid.

551. Helier Cheung, Zhaoyin Feng, and Boer Deng, "Coronavirus: What attacks on Asians reveal about American identity," *BBC News*, May 27, 2020.

552. Sheldon Ingram, "COVID-19 creates another level of fear for Pittsburgh's Asian Americans: ethnic intimidation," Pittsburgh Action News, April 8, 2020; Matthew Tom, "San Leandro woman arrested for posting xenophobic letters on homes, police say," *SFGATE*, May 23, 2020; Thomas Tracy, "Cops arrest subway bigot wanted for spitting at Asian woman on Bronx train and blaming her for COVID-19 pandemic," *New York Daily News*, August 7, 2020; and Bryan Ke, "Asian American Restaurant Owner Attacked on Video

by Alleged Racist in Sacramento," *NextShark*, July 21, 2020.

553. Cheung, Feng, and Deng, ibid.

554. House Resolution 908: Condemning all forms of anti-Asian sentiment as related to COVID-19. See www.congress.gov/bill/116th-congress/house-resolution/908/text.

555. Joe Biden, "Memorandum Condemning and Combating Racism, Xenophobia, and Intolerance Against Asian Americans and Pacific Islanders in the United States," The White House, Washington, DC, January 26, 2021.

556. Matthew Choi, "McConnell says he was wrong on Obama pandemic playbook," *Politico*, May 14, 2020.

557. Stephanie Booth, "Medicare for All: What Is It and How Will It Work?," *Healthline*, February 20, 2020.

558. Equal Justice Initiative, "Lynching in America: Confronting the Legacy of Racial Terror, Third Edition" 37.

559. Nelson George, "Angela Davis Still Believes America Can Change," *New York Times*, October 19, 2020; MrDaveyD, "Angela Davis Looks Back at the 16th Street Church Bombings 50 Years Ago," *Portside*, September 15, 2003.

560. Keeanga-Yamahtta Taylor, *From #BlackLivesMatter to Black Liberation* (Chicago: Haymarket Books, 2021), 153.

561. Devon M. Sayers and Pamela Kirkland, "Prosecutors play 911 calls Travis McMichael made weeks before Arbery's killing," CNN, November 12, 2021.

562. Patricia Murphy, "The Ugly Past of Georgia's Citizen's Arrest Law," *Atlanta Journal-Constitution*, February 17, 2021; and Sayers and Kirkland, ibid.

563. Murphy, ibid.

564. Richard Fausset, "What We Know About the Shooting Death of Ahmaud Arbery," *New York Times*, June 24, 2020; and Richard Fausset, "Suspects in Ahmaud Arbery's Killing Are Indicted on Murder Charges," *New York Times*, June 24, 2020.

565. Russ Bynum, "Prosecutors describe use of racial slur as Ahmaud Arbery lay dying," Associated Press, June 4, 2020.

566. Alexis Stevens and Bill Rankin, "Judge Denies Bond to One of the Three Men Charged in Arbery Killing," *Atlanta Journal-Constitution*, July 17, 2020.

567. Daniel Victor, "Georgia Added a Hate-Crimes Law Last Year After the Death of Ahmaud Arbery," *New York Times*, March 18, 2021.

568. Fausset, ibid.; and Rick Rojas, Richard Fausset and Serge F. Kovaleski, "Georgia Killing Puts Spotlight on a Police Force's Troubled History," *New York Times*, May 8, 2020.

569. Pilar Melendez, "All the Lawyers Who Stood Between Ahmaud

Arbery and Justice," *Daily Beast*, November 24, 2021.

570. United States District Court, Southern District of Georgia, Brunswick Division, *United States of America v. Travis McMichael, Gregory McMichael, and William "Roddie" Bryan*, April 28, 2021.

571. Richard Fausset, "How a Prosecutor Addressed a Mostly White Jury and Won a Conviction in the Arbery Case," *New York Times*, November 29, 2021.

572. Bill Chappell, Joe Hernandez, and Jaclyn Diaz, "All 3 white men convicted of murdering Ahmaud Arbery are sentenced to life in prison," NPR, January 7, 2022.

573. Richard A. Oppel Jr., Derrick Bryson Taylor and Nicholas Bogel-Burroughs, "What to Know About Breonna Taylor's Death," *New York Times*, April 26, 2021.

574. Ivan Pereira, "Kenneth Walker, boyfriend of Breonna Taylor, sues police and city of Louisville for immunity," ABC News, September 1, 2020.

575. Morgan Leads, "Years before Breonna Taylor's death, LMPD officer's Lexington supervisor saw issues," *Lexington Herald Leader*, July 14, 2020.

576. Richard A. Oppel Jr. and Derrick Bryson Taylor, "Here's What You Need to Know About Breonna Taylor's Death," *New York Times*, July 9, 2020.

577. Kevin Williams, Tim Craig, and Marisa Iati, "Kentucky grand jury declines to file homicide charges in death of Breonna Taylor," *Washington Post*, September 23, 2020.

578. Roberto Ferdman, Juanita Ceballos, and Nicole Bozorgmir, "5 Cops Involved in Breonna Taylor's Case Were Also Part of a Botched Raid in 2018," *Vice*, August 24, 2020.

579. Radley Balko, "Correcting the misinformation about Breonna Taylor," *Washington Post*, September 24, 2020.

580. Teo Armus and Hannah Knowles, "Breonna Taylor's ex was offered a plea deal that said she was part of a 'crime syndicate,' family's attorney says," *Washington Post*, September 1, 2020.

581. Marty Johnson, "Breonna Taylor grand jury recordings released," *The Hill*, October 2, 2020; and Aysha Qamar, "Release of grand jury transcripts raises more questions about Breonna Taylor case, Kentucky AG," *Daily Kos*, October 2, 2020.

582. Tim Craig and Marisa Iati, "Louisville agrees to $12 million payout and policing changes in pact with family of Breonna Taylor, killed in police raid," *Washington Post*, September 16, 2020.

583. Oppel Jr., Taylor and Bogel-Burroughs, ibid.; and Tessa Duvall, "Grievances abound in ex-Louisville cop's tell-all book on the Breonna Taylor shooting," *Louisville Courier Journal*, April 16, 2021.

584. Alisha Haridasani Gupta and Christine Hauser, "New Breonna Taylor Law Will Ban No-Knock Warrants in Louisville, Ky.," *New York Times*, June 19, 2020.

585. Austin Horn, "George Floyd and Derek Chauvin Were Once Co-Workers, Ex-Club Owner Tells TV Station," NPR, May 29, 2020.

586. Bill Campbell, "Cashier Says He Offered to Pay After Realizing Floyd's $20 Bill Was Fake," NPR, March 31, 2021.

587. Angelina Chapin, "'If I Would Have Been Here, George Floyd May Still Be Alive," *The Cut*, June 2, 2020.

588. Ibid.; and Thomas Lane police camera transcript, filed in State of Minnesota District Court, July 7, 2020, 11:00 a.m.

589. Al Baker, J. David Goodman and Benjamin Mueller, "Beyond the Chokehold: The Path to Eric Garner's Death," *New York Times*, June 13, 2015; and Ashley Southall, "Daniel Pantaleo, Officer Who Held Eric Garner in Chokehold, Is Fired," *New York Times*, August 19, 2019.

590. Thomas Lane police cam transcript, ibid.

591. Richard A. Oppel Jr. and Kim Barker, "New Transcripts Detail Last Moments for George Floyd," *New York Times*, July 8, 2020.

592. Ibid.

593. Audra D. S. Burch and John Eligon, "Bystander Videos of George Floyd and Others Are Policing the Police," *New York Times*, May 26, 2020; and Minneapolis Police Department, General Offense Public Information Report, May 26, 2020.

594. "George Floyd Death Homicide, Official Post-Mortem Declares," *BBC News*, June 2, 2020.

595. Brian Dakss, "Video shows Minneapolis cop with knee on neck of motionless, moaning man who later died," *CBS News*, May 27, 2020.

596. Elizabeth Alexander, "The Trayvon Generation," *The New Yorker*, June 15, 2020.

597. Christopher Wilson and Caitlin Dickson, "'Man Dies After Medical Incident During Police Interaction': How police originally described George Floyd's death," *Yahoo News*, April 20, 2021; Joshua Nevett, "George Floyd: The personal cost of filming police brutality," *BBC News*, June 11, 2020.

598. Derek Hawkins, "Officer charged in George Floyd's death used fatal force before and had history of complaints," *Washington Post*, May 29, 2020; Richard Read, "Derek Chauvin, officer arrested in George Floyd's death, has a record of shootings and complaints," *Los Angeles Times*, May 29, 2020.

599. Kim Barker, "The Black Officer Who Detained George Floyd Had Pledged to Fix the Police," *New York Times*, June 27, 2020.

600. Derrick Bryson Taylor, "George Floyd Protests: A Timeline," *New*

York Times, November 5, 2021.

601. Caroline Fairchild, "Occupy Arrests Near 8,000 as Wall Street Eludes Prosecution," *Huffington Post*, May 23, 2013.

602. The Crowd Counting Consortium project created a spreadsheet and called for crowdsourced information regarding location and participant number at marches and protests. The researchers carefully vetted each report and, where necessary due to differing estimates, erred on the conservative side. See Erica Chenoweth and Jeremy Pressman, "This is what we learned by counting the women's marches," *Washington Post*, February 7, 2017; and Erica Chenoweth, Tommy Leung, Nathan Perkins, Jeremy Pressman, and Jay Ulfelder, "The Trump years launched the biggest sustained protest movement in U.S. history. It's not over," *Washington Post*, February 8 2021.

603. The Crowd Counting Consortium, ibid.

604. Larry Buchanan, Quoctrung Bui and Jugal K. Patel, "Black Lives Matter May Be the Largest Movement in U.S. History," *New York Times*, July 3, 2020.

605. Ibid.

606. Ibid.

607. Rosa Cartagena, "Here Are the Fourth of July Protests and Marches in DC Happening on Saturday," *Washingtonian*, July 2, 2020.

608. *Demonstrations & Political Violence in America: New Data for Summer 2020*, Armed Conflict Location & Event Data Project, September 2020, 3.

609. Ibid.

610. The Major Cities Chiefs Association, Intelligence Commanders Group, "Report on the 2020 Protests and Civil Unrest," October 2020.

611. Rudy Chinchilla, Joe Brandt, "At Least 9 Fires Set, 109 Arrested as Shops Are Looted in Philly Protests," *NBC 10 Philadelphia*, May 30, 2020.

612. Lois Beckett, "At least 25 Americans were killed during protests and political unrest in 2020," *Guardian*, October 31, 2020.

613. Tobi Thomas, Adam Gabbatt and Caelainn Barr, "Nearly 1,000 instances of police brutality recorded in US anti-racism protests," *Guardian*, October 29, 2020.

614. Physicians for Human Rights, "U.S. Law Enforcement Shot at Least 115 People in the Head with Crowd-Control Weapons During the First Two Months of George Floyd Protests," September 14, 2020.

615. Melissa Chan, "'My Faith in This World Is Gone.' For Protesters Injured by Police, There's No Real Recovery," *Time*, October 9, 2020.

616. Frances Robles, "A Reporter's Cry on Live TV: 'I'm Getting Shot! I'm Getting Shot!,'" *New York Times*, May 30, 2020.

617. Ibid.; and Tom Scocca, "Crowd Cheers as the President Gloats About This One Time the Cops Shot a Reporter with a Rubber Bullet for No Reason," *Slate*, September 20, 2020.

618. "US: Fueled by years of Trump's demonization of the media, unprecedented violence breaks out against journalists covering protests," Reporters Without Borders, June 1, 2020.

619. Nitish Pahwa, "Why Republicans Are Passing Laws Protecting Drivers Who Hit Protesters," *Slate*, April 25, 2021.

620. The Armed Conflict Location & Event Data Project, "DEMONSTRATIONS & POLITICAL VIOLENCE IN AMERICA: NEW DATA FOR SUMMER 2020," September 2020.

621. Grace Hauck, "Cars have hit demonstrators 104 times since George Floyd protests began," *USA Today*, September 27, 2020.

622. Pahwa, ibid.

623. Elisha Fieldstadt, "James Alex Fields, Driver in Deadly Car Attack at Charlottesville Rally, Sentenced to Life in Prison," *NBC News*, June 28, 2019.

624. The International Center for Not-for-Profit Law, "US Protest Law Tracker," www.icnl.org/usprotestlawtracker/.

625. Ibid.

626. Richard Pérez-Peña, "Woman Linked to 1955 Emmett Till Murder Tells Historian Her Claims Were False," *New York Times*, January 27, 2017.

627. Alicia Garza, "A Herstory of the #BlackLivesMatter Movement," *The Feminist Wire*, October 7, 2014; Kevin Crosby, Joong-Oh Rhee, and Jimmie Holland, "Suicide By Fire: a Contemporary Method of Political Protest," *International Journal of Social Psychiatry*, vol. 23, no. 1, 60–69; Brian Cathcart, *Case of Stephen Lawrence* (London: Viking, 1999); and Tahar Ben Jelloun, *By Fire: Writings on the Arab Spring* (Evanston, IL: Curbstone Books/Northwestern University Press, 2016).

628. *Washington Post*, "Police Shootings Database 2015–2022."

629. Ibid.

630. Ibid.

631. N. Jamiyla Chisholm, "Reform, Abolish or Defund the Police—Explained," Color of Change, August 3, 2020.

632. Mapping Police Violence, mappingpoliceviolence.org/.

633. Alicia Garza, "A Herstory of the #BlackLivesMatter Movement," *Feminist Wire*, October 7, 2014.

634. Ibid.

635. "Comments by Barbara Ransby at Socialism 2017 Conference Panel on the Fortieth Anniversary of the Combahee River Collective, in Keeanga-Yamahtta Taylor, ed., *How We Get Free: Black Feminism and the Combahee River Collective* (Chicago: Haymarket Books, 2017), 181.

636. Jim Milliot, "PW's Person of the Year: Ellen Adler," *Publishers Weekly*, December 17, 2021.

637. Kim Parker, Juliana Menasce Horowitz and Monica Anderson, "Amid

Protests, Majorities Across Racial and Ethnic Groups Express Support for the Black Lives Matter Movement," Pew Research Center, June 12, 2020.

638. "Police: Richmond riots instigated by white supremacists disguised as Black Lives Matter," 10 News, July 27, 2020.

639. J. Edward Moreno, "Minneapolis 'Umbrella Man' seen in viral video believed to be white supremacist trying to incite violence," *The Hill*, July 28, 2020.

640. Aaron Holmes, "An 'ANTIFA' Twitter account that called for looting 'white hoods' was actually run by white nationalist group Identity Evropa," *Business Insider*, June 2, 2020.

641. Southern Poverty Law Center, "Identity Evropa/American Identity Movement."

642. Southern Poverty Law Center, "White Nationalist Group Identity Evropa Rebrands Following Private Chat Leaks, Launches 'American Identity Movement,'" March 12, 2019.

643. Annie Karni, Maggie Haberman, and Sydney Ember, "Trump Plays on Racist Fears of Terrorized Suburbs to Court White Voters," *New York Times*, January 20, 2021.

644. Abdullah Hasan, "The Law Enforcement Violence Trump Won't Talk About," ACLU, September 1, 2020.

645. Casye Harden, "How 3 of Donald Trump's Executive Orders Target Communities of Color," *Time*, February 27, 2017; Matthew Choi, "Trump issues executive order warning cities, protesters over destruction of monuments," *Politico*, June 26, 2020.

646. Tweet, Donald Trump, May 29, 2020.

647. Michael Rosenwald, "'When the looting starts, the shooting starts': Trump quotes Miami police chief's notorious 1967 warning," *Washington Post*, May 29, 2020.

648. Ibid.

649. Katelyn Burns, "The racist history of Trump's 'When the looting starts, the shooting starts' tweet," *Vox*, May 29, 2020; Barbara Sprunt, "The History Behind 'When The Looting Starts, The Shooting Starts,'" NPR, May 29, 2020.

650. Oxfam, "Inequality Kills: The unparalleled action needed to combat unprecedented inequality in the wake of COVID-19," January 17, 2022.

651. Carol Leonnig, "Protesters' breach of temporary fences near White House complex prompted Secret Service to move Trump to secure bunker," *Washington Post*, June 4, 2020.

652. J.M. Rieger, "Trump team's effort to explain away Lafayette Square hits yet another snag, one year later," *Washington Post*, June 10, 2021.

653. Nathan Baca and Becca Knier, "MPD admits it used tear gas on Lafayette Park protesters in June 2020," *WUSA 9*, June 1, 2021.

654. Tom Jackman and Carol D. Leonnig, "National Guard officer says police suddenly moved on Lafayette Square protesters, used 'excessive force' before Trump visit," *Washington Post*, July 27, 2020; and Marissa J. Lang, "Federal officials stockpiled munitions, sought 'heat ray,'" *Washington Post*, September 17, 2020.

655. Ibid.

656. Ibid.

657. Ibid., and "Trump had allegedly been suspicious of Nielsen because she'd worked for former President George W. Bush in the past," *Market Watch*, April 8, 2019.

658. Radley Balko, "The Mystery Around What Happened in Lafayette Square," *Washington Post*, July 14, 2021.

659. "President Trump's call with US governors over protests," CNN, June 1, 2020.

660. David Nakamura and Fenit Nirappil, "As protests grip Washington, President Trump and D.C. Mayor Bowser clash in contest over control of city streets," *Washington Post*, June 4, 2020.

661. Tweet, Muriel Bowser, May 30, 2020.

662. Tweet, Black Lives Matter DC, June 5, 2020.

663. Roudabeh Kishi and Sam Jones, "Demonstrations & Political Violence in America: New Data for Summer 2020," the Armed Conflict Location & Event Data Project, September 2020,16.

664. Iman Amrani and Angelique Chrisafis, "Adama Traoré's death in police custody casts long shadow over French society," *Guardian*, February 17, 2017.

665. Associated Press in Beaumont-sur-Oise, "Paris protesters mark fourth anniversary of Adama Traoré's death," *Guardian*, July 18, 2020.

666. Brendan Cole, "Paris Protests Erupt over Adama Traoré, Young Black Man Who Died Like 'Our Brother' George Floyd in Police Custody," *Newsweek*, June 3, 2020.

667. Myriam François, "Adama Traoré: How George Floyd's Death Energised French Protests," *BBC News*, May 19, 2021; and Aurelien Breeden, "'I'm Suffocating': Details of Chokehold Death in Paris Renew Scrutiny of Police," *New York Times*, June 23, 2020.

668. Ali Gostanian, "New Zealanders perform haka dance outside U.S. Embassy during protest, *NBC News*, June 1, 2020; Daniel Villarreal, "U.S. Embassy in Mexico City Locked Down Due to George Floyd Protests," *Newsweek*, June 5, 2020; and "Protest against racism and police violence in front of US embassy in Warsaw," TVN24, June 4, 2020.

669. Amnesty International, "'Don't bother, just let him die': Killing with impunity in Papua," 2018, 17–18; and David Pierson, "George Floyd's death

inspires an unlikely movement in Indonesia: Papuan Lives Matter," *Los Angeles Times*, July 2, 2020.

670. Peterson, ibid.

671. Ibid.

672. Febriana Firdaus, "Seven Papuan Activists Convicted of Treason After Anti-Racism Protests," *Guardian*, June 17, 2020; and "'Balikpapan 7' political prisoners released from jail," Free West Papua Campaign, August 23, 2020.

673. Conor Friedersdorf, "Ferguson's Conspiracy Against Black Citizens," *The Atlantic*, March 5, 2015.

674. Angela Y. Davis, *Are Prisons Obsolete?* (New York: Seven Stories Press, Open Media Series, 2003); Michelle Alexander, *The New Jim Crow: Mass Incarceration in the Age of Colorblindness* (New York: New Press, 2010); Paul Butler, *Chokehold: Policing Black Men* (New York: New Press, 2017); Angela Y. Davis, ed., *Policing the Black Man: Arrest, Prosecution and Imprisonment* (New York: Pantheon Books, 2017); Angela J. Hattery, *Policing Black Bodies: How Black Lives Are Surveilled and How to Work for Change* (Lanham, MD: Rowman & Littlefield, 2018); Jamie Thompson, *Standoff: Race, Policing, Deadly Assault That Gripped a Nation* (New York: Henry Holt and Company, 2020); and Alex S. Vitale, *The End of Policing* (New York: Verso, 2017).

675. Derecka Purnell, "How I Became a Police Abolitionist," *The Atlantic*, July 6, 2020.

676. Ibid.

677. Mariame Kaba, "Yes, We Mean Literally Abolish the Police," *New York Times*, June 12, 2020.

678. Michael Wilson, Jesse McKinley, Luis Ferré-Sadurní, Troy Closson, and Sarah Maslin Nir, "Daniel Prude's Death: Police Silence and Accusations of a Cover-Up," *New York Times*, September 10, 2020; and Steve Orr, "A Black man pinned to the ground by NY police died two months before George Floyd," *USA Today*, September 3, 2020.

679. "Metro Council passes Breonna's Law, 'No-Knock' warrants are banned for LMPD," Louisvilleky.gov, June 11, 2020.

680. Ibid.

681. Ibid.

682. Dionne Searcey and John Eligon, "Minneapolis Will Dismantle Its Police Force, Council Members Pledge," *New York Times*, June 7, 2020.

683. Kimberly Kindy, Kevin Schaul, and Ted Mellnik, "Half of the nation's largest police departments have banned or limited neck restraints since June," *Washington Post*, September 6, 2021.

684. "Final Vote Results for Roll Call 119: Question: On Passage: George Floyd Justice in Policing Act," Office of the Clerk of the House of Representatives, June 25, 2020; and "Roll Call 60: H.R. 1280," Office of the Clerk, U.S. House of Representatives, March 3, 2021.

ENDNOTES

685. Congressional Black Caucus Leads House Democrats and Senators to Introduce the Justice in Policing Act, https://cbc.house.gov/news/documents ingle.aspx?DocumentID=2195.

686. House Judiciary Committee, CBC, "Fact Sheet: George Floyd Justice in Policing Act of 2020".

687. See breatheact.org

688. Ibid.

689. "Movement for Black Lives Opposes George Floyd Justice in Policing Act," AP, March 17, 2021; and Zack Linly, "The Movement for Black Lives Opposes the George Floyd Justice in Policing Act. Here's Why the Movement Has a Point," *The Root*, March 17, 2021.

690. Emma Tucker, Mark Morales, and Priya Krishnakumar, "Why it's rare for police officers to be convicted of murder," CNN, April 21, 2021. See Henry A. Wallace Police Crime Database: policecrime.bgsu.edu/.

691. Tim Arango, Nicholas Bogel-Burroughs, and Jay Senter, "3 Former Officers Are Convicted of Violating George Floyd's Civil Rights," *New York Times*, February 24, 2022.

692. David K. Li and Janelle Griffith, "Tearful witness regrets not doing more to possibly save George Floyd's life," *NBC News*, March 30, 2021.

693. Timothy Bella, "Darnella Frazier says her uncle was killed by a police car that was chasing a robbery suspect," *Washington Post*, July 7, 2021.

694. Fox 9 Staff, "Minneapolis police officer Brian Cummings charged in crash that killed Leneal Frazier," *Fox 9.com*, October 22, 2021.

695. Joe Hernandez, "Read This Powerful Statement From Darnella Frazier, Who Filmed George Floyd's Murder," NPR, May 26, 2021.

696. N'dea Yancey-Bragg, "Minneapolis teen who recorded death of George Floyd honored with PEN America award for courage," *USA Today*, December 9, 2020.

697. See www.pulitzer.org/winners/darnella-frazier.

698. *Washington Post*, "Police Shootings Database 2015–2022."

699. Fabiola Cineas, "Why they're not saying Ma'Khia Bryant's name," *Vox*, May 1, 2021; and Nicholas Bogel-Burroughs, Ellen Barry and Will Wright, "Ma'Khia Bryant's Journey Through Foster Care Ended With an Officer's Bullet," *New York Times*, May 8, 2021.

700. Marisa Iati, Steven Rich, and Jennifer Jenkins, "Fatal police shootings in 2021 set record since The Post began tracking, despite public outcry," *Washington Post*, February 9, 2022.

701. Elizabeth Hinton, *America on Fire: The Untold History of Police Violence and Black Rebellion Since the 1960s* (New York: W.W. Norton, 2021), 313–338.

702. N. Jamiyla Chisholm, "Reform, Abolish or Defund the

ENDNOTES

Police—Explained," Color of Change, August 3, 2020.

703. Keeanga-Yamahtta Taylor, *From #BlackLivesMatter to Black Liberation* (Chicago: Haymarket Books, 2021), 237.

704. Hank Tucker, "'An impossible dream': Duke's first black scholarship football players reflect 50 years later," *The Duke Chronicle*, September 26, 2018.

705. Nadia Prupis, "'We Can't Wait Any Longer': Activist Removes Confederate Flag from SC Courthouse," *Common Dreams*, June 27, 2015.

706. Justin Worland, "This Is Why South Carolina Raised the Confederate Flag in the First Place," *Time*, June 22, 2015.

707. Ibid.

708. See John Lofton, *Denmark Vesey's Revolt: The Slave Plot that Lit a Fuse to Fort Sumter* (Kent, OH: Kent State University Press, 1983); David Robertson, *Denmark Vesey: The Buried Story of America's Largest Slave Rebellion and the Man Who Led It* (New York: Alfred A. Knopf, 1999); and Robert S. Starobin, ed., *Denmark Vesey: The Slave Conspiracy of 1822* (Englewood Cliffs, NJ: Prentice-Hall,1970).

709. U.S. National Park Service, "South Carolina: Mother Emanuel AME Church," www.nps.gov/places/south-carolina-mother-emanuel-ame-church.htm.

710. Ibid.

711. Abby Phillip and DeNeen L. Brown, "3 survivors of the Charleston church shooting grapple with their grief," *Washington Post*, June 25, 2015.

712. Doug Stanglin, and Melanie Eversley, "Suspect in Charleston church rampage returns to South Carolina," *USA Today*, June 18, 2015.

713. "Dylann Roof's and Michael Slager's cells are right next to each other," *USA Today*, June 19, 2015.

714. Alan Blinder and Kevin Sack, "Dylann Roof, Addressing Court, Offers No Apology or Explanation for Massacre," *New York Times*, January 4, 2017.

715. "Charleston shooting trial: Dylann Roof had list of other local black churches," AP, December 12, 2016.

716. Alan Blinder and Kevin Sack, "Dylann Roof Is Sentenced to Death in Charleston Church Massacre," *New York Times*, January 10, 2017.

717. See https://sign.moveon.org/petitions/remove-the-confederate-3.

718. "Statement by the President on the Shooting in Charleston, South Carolina," press statement, White House, Washington, DC, June 18, 2015.

719. See https://obamawhitehouse.archives.gov/the-press-office/2015/06/26/remarks-president-eulogy-honorable-reverend-clementa-pinckney.

720. Lottie Joiner, "Bree Newsome reflects on taking down South Carolina's Confederate flag 2 years ago," *Vox*, June 27, 2017.

721. Ibid.

722. BBC Trending, "Bree Newsome: Flag activist becomes online folk hero," *BBC News*, June 30 2015.

723. Nikki Haley, speech, Republican National Convention, August 24, 2020, www.cnn.com/2020/08/24/politics/nikki-haley-speech-transcript/index.html.

724. Mother Jones News Team, "Bree Newsome Explains Why She Tore Down the Confederate Flag in South Carolina," *Mother Jones*, June 29, 2015.

725. Vincent Right, "The Make It Right Project cultivates community in the shadow of Confederate monuments," *Charleston City Paper*, May 15, 2019.

726. Kali Holloway speech, Literary and Debating Society at the University of Virginia, October 23, 2020.

727. DeNeen L. Brown, "Frederick Douglass delivered a Lincoln reality check at Emancipation Memorial unveiling," *Washington Post*, June 27, 2020; and Hannah Natanson, Joe Heim, Michael E. Miller, and Peter Jamison, "Protesters denounce Abraham Lincoln statue in D.C., urge removal of Emancipation Memorial," *Washington Post*, June 26, 2020.

728. Jonathan W. White and Scott Sandage, "What Frederick Douglass Had to Say About Monuments," *Smithsonian Magazine*, June 30, 2020.

729. Natanson et al., ibid.

730. Ibid.

731. DeNeen L. Brown, ibid. See also full text of speech: teachingamerican history.org/document/oration-in-memory-of-abraham-lincoln/

732. Ibid.

733. Daniella Cheslow and Elliot C. Williams, "New Fences Go Up Near Lafayette Square As Protesters Stand Off With Police," WAMU American University Radio, June 23, 2020.

734. Ibid.

735. Loretta Ross, "Fighting White Supremacy and White Privilege to Build a Human Rights Movement," *Understanding and Dismantling Privilege*, April 1, 2016.

736. Yair Rosenberg, "'Jews will not replace us': Why white supremacists go after Jews," *Washington Post*, August 14, 2017.

737. Angie Drobnic Holan, "In Context: Donald Trump's 'very fine people on both sides' remarks (transcript)," *Politifact*, April 26, 2019.

738. Ellie Silverman, Ian Shapira, Tom Jackman and John Woodrow Cox, "Spencer, Kessler, Cantwell and other white supremacists found liable in deadly Unite the Right rally," *Washington Post*, November 23, 2021.

739. Ben Paviour, "Charlottesville Removes Robert E. Lee Statue That Sparked a Deadly Rally," NPR, July 10, 2021.

740. Teo Armus, "Charlottesville's Robert E. Lee statue will be melted down by city's African American history museum," *Washington Post*, December 7, 2021.

741. Booth Gunter and Jamie Kizzire, *Whose Heritage: Public Symbols*

of the Confederacy, Southern Poverty Law Center, Atlanta, GA, February 1, 2019, 9.

742. Stephanie McCurry, "The Confederacy Was an Antidemocratic, Centralized State," *The Atlantic,* June 21, 2020.

743. Ibid.

744. James W. Loewen and Edward H. Sebesta, eds., *The Confederate and Neo-Confederate Reader: The "Great Truth" about the "Lost Cause"* (Jackson: University Press of Mississippi, 2010), 127, 130, 137, 146, and 147.

745. Ibid., 185.

746. Ibid., 186.

747. Ibid., 131.

748. William F. Buckley Jr., "Why the South Must Prevail," *National Review,* August 24, 1957.

749. Ibid.

750. Laura Vozzella and Jenna Portnoy, "Virginia's McAuliffe plans to phase out Confederate flag license plate," *Washington Post,* June 23, 2015.

751. "Governor Pat McCrory says it's time to end North Carolina Confederate car tags," ABC.11, June 23, 2015.

752. Josh Hicks, "Hogan: No Further Review of Confederate Symbols," *Washington Post,* July 9, 2015.

753. Ron Cassie, "Raising a Controversy," *Baltimore Magazine,* March 2018.

754. Ibid.

755. Emanuella Grinberg, "Battle over Confederate symbols continues with Mississippi state flag," CNN, June 19, 2016.

756. Steve Almasy, "Mississippi governor defends Confederate Heritage Month decree," CNN, February 25, 2016; and Anagha Srikanth, "Mississippi declares April Confederate Heritage Month during coronavirus pandemic," *The Hill,* April 6, 2020.

757. James Tennent, "What Is Confederate Memorial Day? Mississippi Observes Controversial State Holiday," *Newsweek,* April 30, 2018.

758. Byron D'Andra Orey, "Here's How Black Power Finally Prevailed in Mississippi State Flag Fight," *Daily Beast,* July 12, 2020.

759. See https://mississippiencyclopedia.org/entries/henry-kirksey/.

760. Paul LeBlanc, "Mississippi state legislature passes bill to remove Confederate symbol from state flag in historic vote," CNN, June 29, 2020.

761. Rick Rojas, "Mississippi Lawmakers Vote to Retire State Flag Rooted in the Confederacy," *New York Times,* June 28, 2020; and Barbie Latza Nadeau and Madeline Charbonneau, "Mississippi Lawmakers Vote to Remove Confederate Symbol from State Flag," *Daily Beast,* June 28, 2020.

762. Godwin Kelly, "NASCAR and the Confederate flag share a long history. A split has been in the works for decades," *Daytona Beach News-Journal,*

June 12, 2020.

763. "NASCAR backs moves to remove Confederate flag," *Sports Illustrated,* June 23, 2015.

764. Ryan McGee, "How Bubba Wallace pushed NASCAR to evolve," ESPN, December 14, 2021.

765. Joseph Goodman, "NASCAR can't be allowed to whitewash history so easily," AL.com, June 11, 2020.

766. Ibid.

767. George Diaz, "Brian France Trump endorsement puts NASCAR in hypocritical crosshairs," *Orlando Sentinel,* March 1, 2016.

768. See www.opensecrets.org/orgs/nascar/summary?id=D000036094.

769. Statement from NASCAR Industry Members on Confederate flag, July 2, 2015, www.nascar.com/news-media/2015/07/02/statement-from-nascar-industry-members-on-confederate-flag/.

770. McGee, ibid.

771. "President Donald Trump calls out Bubba Wallace, NASCAR in tweet," ESPN, July 6, 2020.

772. NASCAR statement on Confederate flag, June 10, 2020, www.nascar.com/news-media/2020/06/10/nascar-statement-on-confederate-flag/.

773. Barbara Sprunt, "The House Votes to Remove Confederate Statues in the U.S. Capitol," NPR, June 29, 2021.

774. See www.congress.gov/bill/117th-congress/house-bill/3005

775. Sprunt, ibid.

776. bell hooks, *Outlaw Culture* (New York: Routledge, 1994), 236–237.

777. Christopher Brito, "Dozens of Christopher Columbus statues have been removed since June," CBC News, September 25, 2020.

778. Colin Campbell and Emily Opilo, "Christopher Columbus statue near Little Italy brought down, tossed into Baltimore's Inner Harbor," *Baltimore Sun,* July 4, 2020.

779. Andrew Lawler, "Pulling down statues? It's a tradition that dates back to U.S. independence," *National Geographic,* July 1, 2020.

780. Tim Elfrink, "Britons toppled an enslaver's statue. A guerrilla artist replaced it with a Black Lives Matter protester," *Washington Post,* July 15, 2020.

781. "Edward Colston: Bristol slave trader statue 'was an affront,'" *BBC News,* June 8, 2020.

782. Ibid.

783. Brian Saunders, "Harriet Tubman statue unveiled at City Hall," *Philadelphia Tribune,* January 12, 2022.

784. Ernie Suggs, "John Lewis Statue Rises in Vine City's New Park," *Atlanta Journal-Constitution,* July 7, 2021; Rob Moore, "Ida B. Wells Monument and Plaza Will Stand at Beale and Fourth," *Daily Memphian,* June 8, 2021; and

Christine Fernando, "New Jersey city is replacing its Christopher Columbus statue with one honoring Harriet Tubman," *USA Today*, June 22, 2021.

785. Michael Hill, "Creating a monument to Harriet Tubman 'rooted in community' in Newark," *PBS News Hour*, January 2, 2022.

786. Eric Kelderman, "Georgia's Campuses Will Continue to Honor People Who Had Ties to Slavery and Racism," *The Chronicle for Higher Education*, November 22, 2021.

787. See www.usg.edu/assets/usg/docs/Final_Naming_Advisory_Group_Report_A_to_Z.pdf

788. Ibid.

789. Government of the District of Columbiam Washington, DC, *DCFACES Working Group Report*.

790. Ibid., 6.

791. Ibid., 16.

792. Julie Zauzmer and Michael Brice-Saddler, "In latest Trump-Bowser fight, Republicans accuse D.C. of wanting to relocate the Jefferson Memorial," *Washington Post*, September 2, 2020.

793. Ibid, 7.

794. Connor O'Brian, "Senate clears bill removing Confederate names from military bases, setting up clash with Trump," *Politico*, July 23, 2020.

795. Matthew Daly, "In a First, Congress Overrides Trump Veto of Defense Bill," AP, January 1, 2021.

796. Corey Mitchell, "The Schools Named After Confederate Figures," *Education Week*, November 23, 2020.

797. Corey Mitchell, "Schools Named for Confederate Leaders: The Renaming Debate, Explained," *Education Week*, April 13, 2018.

798. Mitchell, ibid., November 23, 2020.

799. Margaret Renkl, "America's Ugliest Confederate Statue Is Gone. Racism Isn't," *New York Times*, January 17, 2022.

800. Ibid.

801. See www.thirteen.org/wnet/supremecourt/rights/sources_document2.html.

802. "Schools with Segregationists' Names: Where They Are and Who They're Named For," *Education Week*, January 23, 2019.

803. April C. Armstrong, "Erased Pasts and Altered Legacies: Princeton's First African American Students," *Princeton & Slavery Project*, slavery.princeton.edu/stories/runaways.

804. Woodrow Wilson, draft of a letter to G. McArthur Sullivan, 3 December 1909, in *The Papers of Woodrow Wilson vol. 15*, ed. Arthur S. Link (Princeton, NJ: Princeton University Press, 1973), 550.

805. See Richard Rothstein, "On renaming the Woodrow Wilson School," Economic Policy Institute, April 14, 2016; and Kathleen L. Wolgemuth,

"Woodrow Wilson and Federal Segregation," *The Journal of Negro History,* April 1959, 158–173.

806. See Zachary Shevin, Evelyn Doskoch, and Sam Kagan, "U. renames Woodrow Wilson School and Wilson College," *Daily Princetonian,* June 27, 2020; Rebecca Ngu, "BJL members reflect on successes, seek greater engagement," *Daily Princetonian,* June 1, 2017; Benjamin Ball, "U. inaugurates installation on Woodrow Wilson's legacy with discussion, dedication," *Daily Princetonian,* October 6, 2019; and Letter to Princeton President Christopher Eisgruber, et al., from Change WWS, June 22, 2020.

807. Rothstein, ibid.

808. President Eisgruber's message to the community on removal of Woodrow Wilson's name from public policy school and Wilson College, Office of Communications, Princeton University, June 27, 2020.

809. Michael Brice-Saddler, "D.C. Council votes to rename Woodrow Wilson High School to Jackson-Reed High School," *Washington Post,* December 7, 2021.

810. Ian Shapira, "A brief history of the word 'redskin' and how it became a source of controversy," *Washington Post,* July 3, 2020.

811. Ibid.

812. Guy Gugliotta, "A Linguist's Alternative History of 'Redskin,'" *Washington Post,* October 3, 2005; and James V. Fenelon, *Redskins?: Sport Mascots, Indian Nations and White Racism* (New York: Routledge, 2016), 40–41.

813. *Enduring the Legacy of Racism in Sports & the Era of Harmful "Indian" Sports Mascots,* National Congress of American Indians, Washington, DC, October 2013, p. 10.

814. Shapira, ibid.

815. *Ending the Legacy of Racism in Sports & the Era of Harmful "Indian" Sports Mascots,* ibid., 12.

816. Shapira, ibid.

817. Kenneth Carroll, "Keeping It Real," unpublished, 1992.

818. Nick Martin, "Native American Imposters Keep Corrupting the 'Redskins' Debate," *The New Republic,* August 13, 2019.

819. See "Preserving Native Legacy," www.nagaeducation.org/preserving-native-legacy.

820. Dan Steinberg, "Redskins owner Daniel Snyder donated $1 million to Trump's inaugural festivities," *Washington Post,* April 19, 2017; and Mark Hensch, "Trump: Some Indians 'extremely proud' of the Redskins," *The Hill,* October 5, 2015.

821. Kevin B. Blackistone, "Activist Suzan Shown Harjo is still winning her fight against Native American mascots," *Washington Post,* September 23, 2019.

822. Ibid.

823. Les Carpenter, "Washington's NFL team to retire Redskins name, following sponsor pressure and calls for change," *Washington Post*, July 13, 2020.

824. Statement from the Washington Redskins Football Team, July 13, 2020. See https://twitter.com/WashingtonNFL/status/1282661063943651328/photo/1.

825. Trish Bendix, "Late Night Comments on the Washington Commanders," *New York Times*, February 3, 2022.

826. Roman Stubbs and Scott Allen, "Activists, politicians, players weigh in on Redskins name change: 'Start of the new era,'" *Washington Post*, July 13, 2020.

827. David Waldstein and Michael S. Schmidt, "Cleveland's Baseball Team Will Drop Its Indians Team Name," *New York Times*, December 13, 2020; and David Waldstein, "With Guardians, Cleveland Steps away from an Offensive Name," *New York Times*, July 23, 2021.

828. Matt Bonesteel, "The Braves have resisted a name change, but Hank Aaron's death renews calls for 'the Hammers,'" *Washington Post*, January 22, 2021; Luke X. Martin, "Kansas City Chiefs Removed Their Offensive Mascot, But Have No Plans To Change Name," NPR, July 27, 2021; and Allen Kim, "The Chicago Blackhawks won't change nickname because it honors the life of an actual Native American," CNN, July 8, 2020.

829. Suzan Shown Harjo, "The R-Word Is Even Worse Than You Think," *Politico*, June 23, 2014.

830. Loretta Ross, "Fighting White Supremacy and White Privilege to Build a Human Rights Movement," *WPC Journal*, vol. 6, no. 1 (Understanding and Dismantling Privilege) April 1, 2016, www.wpcjournal.com/article/view/16080.

831. See www.youtube.com/watch?v=yfQ_JGSobMI

832. Mike Mills, "Gov. Whitmer got it right: Lewis Cass is link to a sordid history, *Detroit Free Press*, July 2, 2020.

833. Ibid.

834. Karolyn Smardz Frost, "Thornton and Lucie Blackburn," *The Canadian Encyclopedia*, May 6, 2021, www.thecanadianencyclopedia.ca/en/article/thornton-and-lucie-blackburn.

835. John Mogk, "Reconsider honors to Lewis Cass, do more to honor abolitionist Jacob Howard," *Detroit Free Press*, January 21, 2018; and Herb Boyd, *Black Detroit: A People's History of Self-Determination* (New York: Amistad, 2017), 27–34.

836. Mogk, ibid.

837. Bryce Huffman, "Detroit's Cass Tech was named for a slave owner. Should this name change too?," *Bridge*, June 24, 2020.

838. Semaj Brown, "Poet and Cass Tech alumna Semaj Brown calls on school to live up to its ideals and change its name," michiganradio.co, July 9, 2020.

839. See https://twitter.com/BreeNewsome/status/1463601456318144528

840. Guardian staff and agencies, "John Lewis crosses Edmund Pettus Bridge in Selma for final time," *Guardian*, July 26, 2020; and The John Lewis Bridge Project, "Who Was Edmund Pettus?," johnlewisbridge.com.

841. Seth Holloway, "Civil Rights Foot Soldier Celebrates Birthday," *Western Star*, September, 2013.

842. See www.congress.gov/bill/117th-congress/house-bill/323/titles?r=2 &s=1.

843. A number of scholars and activists have used the framework of a "third Reconstruction" to describe both the rollback of the gains of the Civil Rights and Black Power eras and the progressive public policies that will define a new period of social, racial, and economic progress. See William J. Barber, *The Third Reconstruction: Moral Mondays, Fusion Politics, and the Rise of a New Justice Movement* (Boston: Beacon Press, 2016); Manning Marable, *Race, Reform and Rebellion: The Second Reconstruction and Beyond in Black America, 1945–2006* (Jackson: University Press of Mississippi, 2007); and Bob Wing, *Toward Racial Justice and a Third Reconstruction: Essays on Politics, Theory & Strategy* (Lulu.com, 2018).

844. Michael Wines, "Harassed and Harangued, Poll Workers Now Have a New Form of Defense," *New York Times*, September 18, 2021.

845. Barton Gellman, "TRUMP'S NEXT COUP HAS ALREADY BEGUN," *The Atlantic*, December 6 2021.

846. Jonathan Lemire, Eric Tucker, Jill Colvin, "Trump pardons ex-strategist Steve Bannon, dozens of others," AP, January 20, 2021; Alan Feuer William K. Rashbaum and Maggie Haberman, "Steve Bannon Is Charged With Fraud in We Build the Wall Campaign," *New York Times*, August 20 2020.

847. Isaac Arnsdorf, Doug Bock Clark, Alexandra Berzon and Anjeanette Damon, "Heeding Steve Bannon's Call, Election Deniers Organize to Seize Control of the GOP—and Reshape America's Elections," *ProPublica*, September 2, 2021.

848. James Oliphant and Nathan Layne, "Georgia Republicans purge Black Democrats from county election boards," Reuters, December 9, 2021.

849. Amy Gardner, Tom Hamburger, and Josh Dawsey, "Trump allies work to place supporters in key election posts across the country, spurring fears about future vote challenges," *Washington Post*, November 29, 2021.

850. Ibid.

851. Nick Corasaniti and Reid J. Epstein, "How Republican States Are Expanding Their Power Over Elections," *New York Times*, July 1, 2021.

852. "Voting Laws Roundup: December 2021," Brennan Center for Justice, December 21, 2021.

853. Amy Gardner, Emma Brown, and Josh Dawsey, "Inside the nonstop pressure campaign by Trump allies to get election officials to revisit the 2020 vote," *Washington Post*, December 22, 2021.

854. Ibid.

855. Ibid.

856. Carol Anderson, *One Person, No Vote: How Voter Suppression Is Destroying Our Democracy* (New York: Bloomsbury Publishing, 2018), xiv.

857. Ronald G. Shafer, "The 'Mississippi Plan' to keep Blacks from voting in 1890: 'We came here to exclude the Negro,'" *Washington Post*, May 1, 2021; and Sam Levine, "The racist 1890 law that's still blocking thousands of African Americans from voting," *Guardian*, January 8, 2022.

858. Ibid.

859. Anderson, ibid.

860. Tyler Stovall, *White Freedom: The Racial History of an Idea* (Princeton, NJ: Princeton University Press, 2021), 7.

861. Michelle Alexander, *The New Jim Crow: Mass Incarceration in the Age of Colorblindness* (New York: New Press, 2010), 20.

862. Christopher Z. Mooney, "Unrepresentative Body," NPR Illinois, February 9, 2021.

863. Ibid.

864. Martha S. Jones, "What the 19th Amendment Meant for Black Women," *Politico*, August 26, 2020.

865. Ibid.

866. Patricia Mazzei and Michael Wines, "How Republicans Undermined Ex-Felon Voting Rights in Florida," *New York Times*, September 17, 2020.

867. The Sentencing Project, "Locked Out 2020: Estimates of People Denied Voting Rights Due to a Felony Conviction," October 30, 2020.

868. Vishal Agraharkar, "50 Years Later, Voting Rights Act Under Unprecedented Assault," Brennan Center for Justice, August 2, 2015.

869. See "Women Holding State Public Offices by Office and State: 2009," www2.census.gov/library/publications/2010/compendia/statab/130ed/tables/11s0413.pdf.

870. Anna Brown and Sara Atske, "Black Americans have made gains in U.S. political leadership, but gaps remain," Pew Research Center, January 22, 2021.

871. Eliza Sweren-Becker, "Filling the Voting Rights Hole Left by SCOTUS in Shelby Country v. Holder," Brennan Center for Justice, June 22, 2021.

872. Ibid.

873. Ashley Southall, "Statue of Rosa Parks Is Unveiled at the Capitol," *New*

York Times, February 27, 2013.

874. U.S. Supreme Court, *Shelby County v. Holder,* 570 U.S. 529 (2013).

875. See Brief of Political Science and Law Professors as Amici Curiae in Support of Respondents, Brennan Center for Justice.

876. Whereas gerrymandering involves cutting up the electoral pie in favorable ways, annexing involves adding to the pie, i.e., incorporating nearby or adjacent areas. They are often both done at the same time.

877. Ibid.

878. "The Effects of Shelby County v. Holder," Brennan Center for Justice, August 6, 2018.

879. Guy-Uriel E. Charles and Luis E. Fuentes-Rohwer, "The Court's Voting-Rights Decision Was Worse Than People Think," *The Atlantic,* July 8, 2021.

880. Ari Berman and Nick Surgey, "Leaked Video: Dark Money Group Brags About Writing GOP Voter Suppression Bills Across the Country," *Mother Jones,* May 13, 2021.

881. Tomas Lopez and Jennifer L. Clark, "Uncovering Kris Kobach's Anti-Voting History," Brennan Center for Justice, May 11, 2017.

882. Stephen Koranda, "Kansas Secretary of State Supports Trump's Unsubstantiated Claim of Illegal Voting," KCUR/NPR, December 1, 2016.

883. Greg Palast, "The GOP's Stealth War Against Voters," *Rolling Stone,* August 24, 2016.

884. Roxana Hegelman, "Judge Fines Kobach Over Document He Took to Trump Meeting," AP, June 23, 2017.

885. "Ken Blackwell's 'Greatest' Hits: Voting Edition," ACLU, May 25, 2017.

886. "Former Ohio Elections Chief Blackwell Brings a Troubled Record on Elections to Fraud Commission," Brennan Center for Justice, undated.

887. James Dao, Ford Fessenden, and Tom Zeller Jr., "Voting Problems in Ohio Spur Call for Overhaul," *New York Times,* December 24, 2004.

888. Jane Mayer, "The Voter-Fraud Myth," *The New Yorker,* October 22, 2012.

889. Ibid.

890. Berman and Surgey, ibid.

891. Ari Berman, "A Dark Money Group Faces an Ethics Probe After Boasting of Drafting Voter Suppression Laws," *Mother Jones,* May 18, 2021.

892. Jessica Taylor, "Trump Dissolves Controversial Election Commission," NPR, January 3, 2018.

893. "Trump Administration Civil and Human Rights Rollbacks," Leadership Conference on Civil and Human Rights, January 2021.

894. Justin Levitt, "A comprehensive investigation of voter impersonation finds 31 credible incidents out of one billion ballots cast," *Washington Post,*

August 6, 2014.

895. Natasha Khan and Corbin Carson, "Comprehensive Database of U.S. Voter Fraud Uncovers No Evidence That Photo ID Is Needed," News21, August 2, 2012; and Sami Edge and Sean Holstege, "Voter fraud is not a persistent problem," News21, August 20, 2016.

896. David Cottrell, Michael C. Herron, and Sean J. Westwood, "An exploration of Donald Trump's allegations of massive voter fraud in the 2016 General Election," *Electoral Studies*, vol. 51, February 2018: 123–142; and Phillip Bump, "There have been just four documented cases of voter fraud in the 2016 election," *Washington Post*, December 1, 2016.

897. Bump, ibid.

898. See "Debunking the Voter Fraud Myth," Brennan Center for Justice, January 31, 2017.

899. Jeremy Duda and Jim Small, "Arizona Senate Hires a 'Stop the Steal' Advocate to Lead 2020 Election Audit," *AZ Mirror*, March 31, 2021.

900. David Schwartz and Nathan Layne, "'Truth is truth': Trump dealt blow as Republican-led Arizona audit reaffirms Biden win," Reuters, September 27, 2021.

901. Darragh Rouche, "Arizona Governor Hits Back at Donald Trump Over Audit: 'No Decertification,'" *Newsweek*, September 25, 2021.

902. Michael Wines, "Cyber Ninjas, Derided for Arizona Vote Review, Says It Is Shutting Down," *New York Times*, January 7, 2022.

903. Ibid.

904. Craig Silverman, Craig Timberg, Jeff Kao, and Jeremy B. Merrill, "Facebook groups topped 10,000 daily attacks on election before Jan. 6, analysis shows," *Washington Post*, January 4, 2022.

905. Stuart A. Thompson, "Election Falsehoods Surged on Podcasts Before Capitol Riots, Researchers Find," *New York Times*, January 4, 2022; Media Matters Staff, "Steve Bannon and his co-host discuss beheading Dr. Anthony Fauci and FBI Director Christopher Wray," Media Matters, November 5, 2020.

906. Thompson, ibid.

907. Aaron Blake, "Birtherism paved the way for the 'big lie.' The latter is proving more pervasive and stubborn,'" *Washington Post*, January 3, 2022.

908. Gaby Goldstein and David Daley, "Beware the 'Independent State Legislatures doctrine' — it could checkmate democracy," *Slate*, September 27, 2021.

909. Hayward H. Smith, "History of the Article II Independent State Doctrine," *Florida State University Law Review*, vol. 29, no. 2 (Winter 2001): 736.

910. Ari Berman And Nick Surgey, "Leaked Video: Dark Money Group Brags About Writing GOP Voter Suppression Bills Across the Country," *Mother Jones*, May 13, 2021; and Ari Berman, "A Dark Money Group Faces

an Ethics Probe After Boasting of Drafting Voter Suppression Laws," *Mother Jones*, May 18, 2021.

911. Christopher Ingraham, "In at least three states, Republicans lost the popular vote but won the House," *Washington Post*, November 13, 2018.

912. Susan Tebben, "Republican majority gerrymanders Ohio for another four years," *Ohio Capital Journal*, September 16, 2021.

913. Christian R. Grose, Jordan Carr Peterson, Matthew Nelson, and Sara Sadhwani, *The Worst Partisan Gerrymanders in U.S. State Legislatures*, USC Schwarzenegger Institute for State and Global Policy, September 5, 2019: i.

914. Ibid., 3.

915. Ibid.

916. Nick Corasaniti, "Let the Gerrymandering (and the Legal Battles) Begin," *New York Times*, November 17, 2021.

917. "Voting Laws Roundup: December 2021," Brennan Center for Justice, December 21, 2021.

918. Colby Itkowitz, "House MAGA squad seeks to expand by boosting challengers to fellow Republicans," *Washington Post*, December 26, 2021.

919. Ibid.

920. Jane Mayer, "The Big Money Behind the Big Lie," *The New Yorker*, August 9, 2021.

921. Nick Corasaniti, "Republicans Aim to Seize More Power Over How Elections Are Run," *New York Times*, March 24, 2021.

922. Ashley Parker, Amy Gardner and Josh Dawsey, "How Republicans became the party of Trump's election lie after Jan. 6," *Washington Post*, January 5, 2022.

923. Amy Gardner, Tom Hamburger, and Josh Dawsey, "Trump allies work to place supporters in key election posts across the country, spurring fears about future vote challenges," *Washington Post*, November 29, 2021.

924. Ibid.

925. Amber Phillip, "How Trump-backed secretary of state candidates would change elections in the United States," *Washington Post*, December 1, 2021.

926. Max Greenwood, "Stacey Abrams backs Senate Democrats' voting rights compromise," *The Hill*, September 14, 2021.

927. Sarah A. Binder, "The History of the Filibuster," Brookings Institution, April 22, 2010.

928. Magdalene Zier and John Fabian Witt, "For 100 Years, the Filibuster Has Been Used to Deny Black Rights," *Washington Post*, March 18, 2021.

929. Ibid.

930. See "Voting Laws Roundup: February 2022," Brennan Center for Justice, February 9, 2022.

931. Ibid.

932. Ibid.

933. *Lynching in America: Confronting the Legacy of Racial Terror* (Montgomery, AL: Equal Justice Initiative, 2017), 3rd ed.

934. Jamelle Bouie, "What Does 'White Freedom' Really Mean?," *New York Times*, December 17, 2001.

935. Martin Luther King Jr., *Why We Can't Wait* (New York: Penguin Books, 1964), 43.

936. Charles Marsh, *God's Long Summer: Stories of Faith and Civil Rights* (Princeton, NJ: Princeton University Press, 1997), 24.

INDEX

"Passim" (literally "scattered") indicates intermittent discussion of a topic over a cluster of pages.

Abbott, Greg, 317–18
Abrams, Stacey, 314, 316, 318
ACLU. *See* American Civil Liberties Union (ACLU)
Adams, Chanelle, 106
Adams, John Quincy, 76
Advanced Counterfeit Deterrence Steering Committee (ACD), 92–93, 99
Affordable Care Act (ACA), 181, 189
Alexander, Lamar, 118
Alexander, Michelle, 295; *New Jim Crow*, 213
Altemeyer, Bob, 149
American Civil Liberties Union (ACLU), 143, 215, 304–5
American Equal Rights Association (AERA), 64
American Indians. *See* Native Americans
American Legislative Exchange Council (ALEC), 312
American Progress (Gast), *20*, 31
American Woman Suffrage Association, 64, 68
American Women Quarters Program, 6, *6*
America on Fire (Hinton), 238
Anderson, Elijah, 45
Anderson, Marian: five-dollar bill verso (proposed), 5, 98

Anderson, Osborne Perry, 45
Angelou, Maya: quarter, xix, 6, *6*
Anthony, Susan B., 63, 64, 65, 67–68; dollar coin, 5; ten-dollar bill verso (proposed), 5, 98, 116
anti-counterfeiting measures, 92–93, 99, 100, 120
anti-Muslim policies, 128, 139, 176
anti-Semitism, 152, 253, 271
Arbery, Ahmaud, 192–95
Arizona: COVID-19, 166; "show me your papers" law, 303; 2020 presidential election results, 155, 308, 315
Asia-bashing, 184–88 passim
Asian Americans: attacks on, 185–88; Black Lives Matter support, 214; COVID-19, 173, 174; diabetes, 178; health insurance, 181
ATM machines, 100
attacks by drivers. *See* car-ramming attacks

Baker, Jordan, 29
Ball, Ankeet, 94–95
Ball, Charles, 79
Balogun, Rakem, 141
Baltimore: Columbus statue toppling, 268–69; Tubman in, 53
Banks, Jim, 209
Bannon, Steven, 309

INDEX

Barr, William, 219–20
Bass, Karen, 142, 229, 266, 291
Beal, Bradley, 171
Benezet, Anthony, 45
Bernanke, Ben, 95
Biden, Joe, 187–88, 309, 319
Birmingham, Alabama, 192, 290
The Birth of a Nation (Griffith), 40, 277
Blackburn Riots of 1833, 285
"Black Identity Extremist" (BIE) label, 140–43
Blackistone, Kevin B., 281–82
Black Lives Matter, 119, 133, 171, 204–17 passim; Bristol, England, 268–69; France, 222; Mississippi, 261; NASCAR and, 265; police reforms and, 228; Princeton University, 278; Trayvon Martin murder as impetus, 211, 212; Washington, D.C., 220–21
black suffrage, 63, 296, 297; disenfranchisement, 298–99
Blackwell, J. Kenneth, 303, 304–5
Blake, Aaron, 310
Blendon, Robert, 146–47
blind and visually impaired people: paper currency and, 4, 99–100, 103
Blow, Charles, 128
blues music: 1918–1919 flu in, 160–61
body cameras, police. *See* police body cameras
Booker, Cory, 232
Bouie, Jamelle, 322
Bowser, Muriel, 220–21
Bradford, Sarah H., 55–56, 59
BREATHE Act, 232
Bristol, England: Colston statue toppling, 269–70
Brnovich v. Democratic National Committee, 302

Brodess family, 49
Brooks, Oliver T., 159–60
Brown, John, xvi–xvii, 57, 61, 160
Brown, Joseph Mackey, 271
Brown, Semaj, 287
Brown v. Board of Education, 242–43, 276
Bryan, William, 193–95
Buckley, William F., Jr., 257–58
building renaming, 265, 271, 278
Bunch, Lonnie G., III, 108
Bush, George W., 131, 305–6, 310–11
Bush v. Gore, 310–11
Butterfield, G. K., 106–7

Calhoun, John C., 28; Confederate hundred-dollar bill, 28, *28*; statues, xvi–xvii, 266
Calvert family (Maryland), 259–60
Cameron, Daniel, 198–99
"cancel culture," 116–17, 273
Capitol insurrection, January 6, 2021. *See* U.S. Capitol insurrection, January 6, 2021
Cardi B., 172
CARES Act. *See* Coronavirus Aid, Relief, and Economy Security (CARES) Act
Carlson, Tucker, 129, 130–31, 137
car-ramming attacks, 208, 209, 254
Carson, Ben, 115, 116, 119
Cary, Mary Ann Shadd, 67–68
Cass, Lewis, 284–86
Cassie, Ron, 259–60
Cass Technical High School, Detroit, 283–87 passim
Catt, Carrie Chapman, 65–66
censorship of mail. *See* mail censorship
Census, U.S. *See* U.S. Census
Chapman, John Gadsby, 33

Charles, Guy-Uriel E., 303
Charleston, South Carolina: Calhoun statue, xvi–xvii; Emanuel AME Church, 243–46, 252, 259
Charlottesville, Virginia: Confederate monuments, 254–55; United the Right rally, 209, 252–54
Chauvin, Derek, 201–3, 210, 233–37 passim
Cheathem, Mark R., 82
Cherokees, 83–86 passim
child COVID-19 cases, 167–68
Chin, Vincent, 185–86
China-bashing, 184–85
Choudhury, Nusrat, 143
Chouviat, Cédric, 222
"citizen's arrest" laws, 193
Civil Rights Acts of 1964, 288, 317
civil rights movement, xvii–xviii, 133, 243, 289–91
Civil War, Tubman participation in, 1–4
Clarke, Kristen, 142–43
Cleveland: Major League Baseball team, 282–83
Cleveland, Grover, 37, 39
Clinton, Bill, 7
Clinton, Hillary, 98
Cobb, Thomas R. R., 193
coinage, 25. See also dollar coin; quarter (U.S. coin)
Colberg, Jake, 31
Collins, Kaitlan, 145
Collins-Dexter, Brandi, 183
Colston, Edward: Bristol monument, 269–70
Columbia (U.S. symbol), 29–31; in art, 20, 31; on currency, 28, 29, 32, 36, 36
Columbia, South Carolina: Columbus statue, 268;

Confederate flag removal, 240, 241–48 passim, 252
Columbus, Christopher, 29; monuments, 265, 267–69
Combahee Ferry Raid, 1863, 1, 4, 57–62, 58, 70–71
Confederate flag, 240, 241–48 passim, 252, 258–59, 265; NASCAR, 262, 263, 265
Confederate monuments/memorials, xviii–xix, 253, 254–55, 265–66, 275, 289; U.S. military site names, 273–74
Confederate States of America (CSA), xv–xvi, 255–56, 259; constitution, 256; currency, 26–32 passim; symbols, 255–59 passim. See also Confederate flag; Confederate mounuments/memorials
Congressional Black Caucus (CBC), 106–7, 142
Constitution, U.S. See U.S. Constitution
"continentals" (first U.S. currency), 25
Cooper, Anna J., 68–69
Cooper, Brittney, 10, 112
Coronavirus Aid, Relief, and Economy Security (CARES) Act, 174, 209
Counterfeit Deterrence Steering Committee. See Advanced Counterfeit Deterrence Steering Committee (ACD)
COVID-19 pandemic, 147, 159–89 passim; children and, 167–68; denial of aid, 209; economic impact, 172–76; George Floyd, 201; impact on incarcerated, 176–78

Craig, Maureen A., 131
Creek Indians, 83–87 passim
Crenshaw, Kimberlé, 14, 133
Criqui, Alex, *xiv, 190*
critical race theory (CRT), 133–34
Crockett, Davy, 83
Crusius, Patrick Wood, 131
Cruz, Ted, 115, 116, 172
Cullors, Patrisse, 212
Cummings, Elijah, 101, 107
currency, paper, 21–40, 62. *See also*
    ten-dollar bill; twenty-dollar bill
Curtis, Mary C., 108–9, 113
Cyber Ninjas, 308–9

Daley, David, 310
Dallas: policing policy, 229; Rakem
    Balogun, 141
Dassonneville, Ruth, 145
Davis, Angela Y., 46, 50, 64, 192; *Are
    Prisons Obsolete?*, 213
Davis, Jefferson, xix; Confederate
    currency, 31; great-great-
    grandson, 261; in school names,
    275; U.S. Capitol statue, 266
Davis, Nelson, 3, 4
Dax, 172
Dean, John, 149
Declaration of Independence, 269
Deere, Judd, 220
Deloire, Christophe, 207
DeMarco, Adam D., 219
demographic fears, racial. *See*
    "majority-minority": white fears
    and data
demonstrations and protests. *See*
    protests and demonstrations
DeSantis, Ron, 133, 208, 298
disenfranchisement, 46, 231–32,
    294–99 passim, 304, 307, 311.
    See also voter suppression

disinformation: COVID-19, 171,
    183; elections, 303, 304
"dollar" (word), 24–25
dollar bill: in "E Pluribus Unum"
    (Last Poets), 21–23
dollar coin, 5, 25
Donnelly, Paul, 58
Douglass, Frederick, 62–64, 65,
    249–51
Dred Scott v. Sandford, 266
Du Bois, W. E. B., xvi–xvii, 12,
    323–24; *Health and Physique of
    the American Negro*, 162
Duke, David, 129
Dunbar-Ortiz, Roxanne, 74, 85
Dunn, Harry, 153
Durbin, Dick, 294–95
DuRoss, Michelle, 95

Ebens, Ronald, 185–86
election administration, 314–15
elections, presidential. *See*
    presidential elections
electoral college, 76, 131, 296, 297
Emanuel AME Church, Charleston,
    South Carolina, 243–46, 252, 259
England, 260, 269–70
"E Pluribus Unum" (Last Poets),
    21–23
Estes, Adam Clark, 24–25

false beliefs about African
    Americans, 180–81
FBI, 137–43 passim
Federal Reserve, 25, 37
felons and ex-felons: voting rights,
    231–32, 294, 298
Fenelon, James V., 279
Ferguson, Missouri: Michael Brown
    murder, 140, 192, 211
Fields, Mamie Garvin, xvi, xvii

filibuster (U.S. Senate), 230, 316–17
Fiorina, Carly, 115, 116, 122
five-dollar bill, 37, 39; proposed change, 5, 97, 98, 106; Running Antelope, 35–36, *35*
five-dollar bill (Confederate States of America), 27, *27*
Florida: anti-black legislation, 133, 134, 298; immunity to drivers who injure protesters, 208; presidential election of 2016, 310–11; presidential election of 2020, 298; Walter Headley, 216
flu pandemic, COVID-19. *See* COVID-19 pandemic
flu pandemic of 1918–1919, 160–63
Floyd, George, 11, 150, *190*, 192, 200–206 passim, 210, 213, 252; Chauvin murder trial, 233–34; Darnella Frazier and, 202–3, 210, 233–36; post-murder protests, 204–10 passim, 215–24 passim; Trump and, 215, 216
Forrest, Nathan Bedford: in school names, 275
Forten family, 67
For the People Act, 315, 316
Foster, Glenn, 251
Fox News, 119–20, 129, 130, 137; COVID-19, 170
France: police brutality, 222
Frank, Douglas, 294
Franklin, Benjamin, 45, 333–34n84; hundred-dollar bill, 39
Frazier, Darnella, 233–36
Freedom to Vote Act, 316
French, Bill, Sr., 262, 263
French, Brian, 263
Fuentes-Rohwer, Luis E., 302
Fugitive Slave Act of 1793, 51, 285, 286
Fugitive Slave Act of 1850, 48, 51, 67

Garner, Eric, 201
Garza, Alicia, 14, 212, 217
Gast, John: *American Progress, 20*, 31
Gellman, Barton, 292
gerrymandering, 301, 312–14
George Floyd Justice in Policing Act, 229–31
George III, King, 269
Gieswein, Robert, 153
Ginsburg, Ruth Bader, 301–2
Glover, Jamarcus, 198–99
Goddard, Yves, 279
gold standard, 37
Goldstein, Gaby, 310
Goodman, Joseph, 262
Graham, Lindsey, 130, 245
Grant, Ulysses, 251; fifty-dollar bill, 39
"great replacement theory." *See* white replacement anxiety
Green, Marjorie Taylor, 171
"greenbacks," 32
Greenblatt, Jonathan, 130–31
"greybacks." *See* Confederate States of America: currency
Grimké family, 67
Griswold, Jena, 314–15

Haley, Nikki, 245, 247
Hamer, Fannie Lou, 326
Hamilton (Miranda), 95–96
Hamilton, Alexander: First Bank, 25; ten-dollar bill, 39, 93, 94, 97–98, 115–16; twenty-dollar bill, 36
Hankison, Brett, 196–99 passim
Hannah, John, 308–9
Harjo, Suzan Shown, 281–82, 283
Harper, Frances Ellen Watkins, 68
Harriet Tubman Underground Railroad Visitor Center, Church Creek, Maryland, xxiii

hate crimes, 130, 131; Ahmaud
  Arbery murder, 192–95;
  COVID-19 Hate Crimes Act,
  188; Dylann Roof, 244–45, 248,
  252; Heather Heyer killing,
  209, 254; Vincent Chin murder,
  185–86
*The Haunting of Lin-Manuel
  Miranda* (Reed), 96
Hay, Robert P., 79
Health and Economic Recovery
  Omnibus Emergency Solutions
  (HEROES) Act, 174
health and health care, 157–89. *See
  also* COVID-19 pandemic
health insurance, 163, 181, 189
*Health and Physique of the American
  Negro* (Du Bois), 162
Henry, Aaron, 261
Heritage Foundation, 306, 312
Hermitage (Andrew Jackson home),
  77–78, 98
HEROES Act. *See* Health and
  Economic Recovery Omnibus
  Emergency Solutions (HEROES)
  Act
Heyer, Heather, 209, 254
Higham, John, 29–30
Hinton, Elizabeth: *America on Fire*,
  238
historical monuments. *See*
  monuments
Hoffman, Frederick L.: *Race Traits
  and Tendencies of the American
  Negro*, 162–63
Hogan, Larry, 99, 259, 269
holidays, 260, 267–68
Holloway, Kali, 123, 249, 284
Homeland Security Department. *See*
  U.S. Department of Homeland
  Security

Hooghe, Marc, 145
Horn, Werner, 136
hundred-dollar bill: Confederate
  States of America, 28, *28*; United
  States, 39
*Husted v. A. Philip Randolph
  Institute*, 307
Hynes, Dan, 136

Illges, John Paul, Sr., 271
immigrants and immigration, 128,
  129–30, 145
Indian Removal Act, 82, 284
Indigenous Americans. *See* Native
  Americans
Indigenous Peoples Day, 267–68
Indonesia, 223–24
Ingraham. Laura, 129, 170, 171
insurance, health. *See* health
  insurance
intersectionality, 14, 62, 70, 212, 252
Irving, Kylie, 170–71

Jabbar, Kareem Abdul, 177
Jackson, Andrew, 9–10, 11, 28,
  38, 40, 71, 73–89; Confederate
  currency, 31; Native Americans
  and, 74–75, 82–89; postage
  stamp, *40*; slavery and, 71, 77–82,
  95; ten-dollar bill, 38; thousand-
  dollar bill (proposed), 39; Trump
  and, 98; twenty-dollar bill, 4–5,
  38–39, 92, 97, 101, 117–20
  passim, 127–28, 248, 322; Webb
  on, 120–21
Jackson, Maurice, 45
Jackson, Stonewall: in school names,
  274, 275; statue, 254
Jackson Lee, Sheila, 232
jails and prisons. *See* prisons and
  jails

Jefferson, Thomas, 82–83, 296; First
  Bank, 25; two-dollar bill, 39
John Lewis Voting Rights
  Amendment Act, 315–16
Johnson, Derrick, 102–3
Johnson, Jackie L., 194
Jones, Daniel, 154
Jones, Feminista, 110–11
Jones, Martha S., 297
Jones, Shevrin, 134
Judge, Oney, 34–35
Justice Department. *See* U.S.
  Department of Justice

Kaba, Mariame, 226
Katko, John, 10, 101, 340n234
Kendall, Amos, 81–82
Kendi, Ibram X., 178
Kerner Commission, 238
Kessler, Jason, 253
Kimberley, Margaret, 111–12
King, Martin Luther, Jr., *288*,
  290, 324; five-dollar bill verso
  (proposed), 98; Washington,
  D.C., memorial, 7
King, Rodney, 211
King, Steve, 118
King George III. *See* George III,
  King
Klein, Dustin, *xiv*, *190*
Klein, Ezra, 131
Klein, Naomi, 13
Kobach, Kris, 303–4
Ku Klux Klan (KKK), 258, 275, 277,
  289

La Bella, Donavan, 207
Lankford, James, 10, 101
Larson, Kate Clifford, 50, 65–66, 100
Last Poets: "E Pluribus Unum,"
  21–23

Latinx people: Black Lives Matter
  support, 214; COVID-19 and,
  165–69 passim, 173, 174, 175;
  diabetes, 178; health insurance,
  181; killed by police, 211; pain
  medication, 181
lawsuits: American Council of the
  Blind, 99; Japanese Americans,
  185; against Proud Boys and
  Oath Keepers, 152; Tuskegee
  Syphilis Study, 159
Lee, Barbara, 107
Lee, Robert E.: in school names,
  274, 275; statues, *xiv*, *190*, 253,
  254
Levy, Alba Morris, 132
Lew, Jacob J., 93–98 passim
Lewis, John, 18, 107, 289–90,
  300, 305; Atlanta statue, 270;
  namesake voting act, 315–16
license plates: Confederate symbols
  on, 259
Lincoln, Abraham, 48, 57–58, 257;
  Emancipation Memorial, 249–
  51, *250*; five-dollar bill, 37, 39
Lindell, Mike, 294
Little, Maya, xviii
Loewen, James, 26
Logan, Doug, 308
Lolos, John, 155
Lost Cause mythology, xv–xvi, 257,
  263
Louisiana Purchase, 83
lynching and lynchings, 152–53,
  191–92, 193, 317; Ahmaud
  Arbery, 192–95; Emmett Till,
  201–11; George Floyd murder as,
  203; Leo Frank, 271

Madison, James, 25, 39, 73–74
mail censorship, 81–82

"majority-minority": white fears and
data, 128–32 passim, 144, 147
Malcolm X, 291
Mankiller, Wilma, 6, 92
maroon communities, 43–44, 73
Marshall, George Preston, 280
Marshall, Thurgood, 266, 267
Martin, Trayvon, 211, 242
Martin Luther King Jr. Memorial,
Washington, D.C., 7
mass shootings, 130, 131;
Charleston, S.C., 244–45, 248,
252
Mattingly, Jonathan, 196, 197, 199
May-Pittman, Ineva, 261
McAuliffe, Terry, 258–59
McConnell, Mitch, 199, 229, 266,
300
McCrory, Pat, 258–59
McCurry, Stephanie, 255
McDougall, Clinton Dugald, 2–3
McMichael, Gregory and Travis,
193–95
Medical Apartheid (Washington),
158–59
medical experimentation,
nonconsensual. See
nonconsensual medical
experimentation
Mehta, Amit P., 155
Mellon, Andrew, 39, 94
memorial statues and markers,
xvi–xvii, 40; Columbus, 265,
267–69; Lincoln, 249–51, 250;
defacement of, xvii. See also
Confederate monuments/
memorials
Mexico: Mexican-American War, 33;
police killings, 223
Michigan: COVID-19 response, 182;
election canvassing boards, 293

military site names, 273–74
Milley, Mark A., 218, 219
Minaj, Nicki, 170
Minneapolis: George Floyd murder
and uprising, 200–207 passim,
216, 228–29, 233–36; Leneal
Frazier death, 234
Miranda, Lin-Manuel: Hamilton,
95–96
Mississippi: photo ID laws, 302; state
flag, 260–61
Mississippi Plan, 294–95
Mnuchin, Steven, 99, 100, 122
Mogk, John, 286
Montgomery, James, 57–61
monuments. See memorial statues
and markers
Mooney, Christopher Z., 296
Mooney, James, 86
Moore, Gwen, 107
Morrison, Toni, 41, 96
"motor voter" law. See National
Voter Registration Act
Mott, Lucretia: ten-dollar bill verso
(proposed), 5, 98
Movement for Black Lives, 232
Murray, Freeman Henry Morris, 251
Muscogee Nation. See Creek Indians
Muslims, political attacks on. See
anti-Muslim policies
Myers, Dowell, 132

NAACP, xvi–xvii, 102–3, 247
Nadler, Jerry, 232
Nalle, Charles, 54–57
names, new. See renaming of
schools, buildings, etc.
names of schools. See school names
NASCAR, 262–65
National American Woman Suffrage
Association, 64

National Association of Colored
Women, 68
National Association for Stock Car
Auto Racing. *See* NASCAR
National Association for the
Advancement of Colored People.
See NAACP
National Association of Colored
Women's Clubs (NACWC), 66,
69
National Museum of African
American History and Culture,
7–9
National Voter Registration Act,
304, 305
National Women's Party, 297
National Woman Suffrage
Association, 64, 67
Native Americans, *34*, 44; American
Revolution, 29; Cass and, 284–
85; on coins, 5, 6; COVID-19,
165, 166–67; diabetes, 178;
Indian Removal Act, 82, 284;
Jackson and, 74–75, 82–89;
massacres and atrocities, 84–85,
87; Negro Fort, 74; on paper
money, 5, *32*, 33, 35–36, *35*; and
sports team names, 279–83; Trail
of Tears, 85–89; treaties, 85
Native American's Guardian
Association (NAGA), 281
Navajo Nation: COVID-19, 166–67
Negro Fort, 73–74
Newark, New Jersey: Tubman statue,
270
The New Jim Crow (Alexander), 213
Newman, Omarosa Manigault, 122
Newsome, Clarence G., 242
Newsome Bass, Bree, *240*, 241–48
passim, 287
New Zealand, 222

Nielsen, Kirstjen, 219
Nitz, Michael, 185–86
Nixon, Richard, 258, 263
no-knock warrants, 199, 228, 230
nonconsensual medical
experimentation, 159
Norton, Michael I., 146, 150
Nossel, Suzanne, 236
Nunez-Smith, Marcella, 183

Oath Keepers, 152
Obama, Barack, 7–9, 91, 92, 300;
Emanuel AME Church and,
245–46; pandemic planning, 188;
Trump and, 135
Obamacare. *See* Affordable Care Act
(ACA)
Ocasio-Cortez, Alexandria, 135, 151
Oklahoma: immunity to drivers who
injure protesters, 208; Native
American population, 101
Oluo, Ijeoma, 112
Omar, Ilhan, 135
one-dollar bill. *See* dollar bill
Onion, Rebecca, 87
Orey, Delores, 261
Ortiz Howard, Barbara, 92, 97

Pacific Islanders: COVID-19, 165.
See also Papuans
paintings, *20*, 31, 33
pandemics, flu. *See* COVID-19
pandemic; flu pandemic of
1918–1919
paper money. *See* currency, paper
Papuans, 223–24
Pardlo, Gregory, 134
Parks, Rosa, 91, 92, 115, 116, 122;
U.S. Capitol statue, 300
Paul, Alice: ten-dollar bill verso
(proposed), 5, 98
Pelosi, Nancy, 98, 152, 269, 300

Pence, Mike, 151
Pettus, Edmund, 289
photo ID laws for voters. *See* voter
    ID laws
Pickens, Lucy Holcombe, 31
Pinckney, Clementa C., 243, 244
Plessy v. Ferguson, 37
Pocahontas, 33; twenty-dollar bill
    (1865), 5, *32*, 33
podcasts, 309–10
police body cameras, 197, 201, 228,
    229, 230, 237
police killings, 233, 236–37; Breonna
    Taylor, 195–99; David Prude,
    227; Eric Garner, 201; France,
    222; George Floyd, 200–206
    passim, 233–36; Mexico, 223;
    Walter Scott, 244, 245
police no-knock warrants. *See* no-
    knock warrants
police rape and sexual assault, 231
police violence against people of
    color, 211, 238; France, 222. *See
    also* police killings
police violence against protesters,
    206–7, 215, 218
polls, public opinion. *See* public
    opinion polls
poll taxes, 294, 297, 298
Portland, Oregon: Black Lives
    Matter protests, 207
poverty, xix; COVID-19 and, 166
Presidential Advisory Commission
    on Election Integrity, 303, 306–7
presidential elections, 131, 150;
    D.C. citizens' right to vote, 297;
    1824, 76; 2000, 131, 150, 310;
    2008, 131, 300; 2016, 131, 145,
    147, 150, 303, 304; 2020, 150–56
    passim, 292, 298, 308–10 passim,
    315, 319, 325

Pressley, Ayanna, 108, 135, 232
Princeton University, 278
prisons and jails: COVID-19,
    176–78
protests and demonstrations: anti-
    protest legislation, 209; car-
    ramming attacks on, 208, 209;
    civil rights movement, 289–90;
    post–George Floyd murder, 204–
    10 passim, 215–24 passim
Proud Boys, 138, 152
Prude, David, 227
Psaki, Jen, 102
pseudoscience, 162–63
public opinion polls, 137, 146–49
    passim, 310; on currency
    redesign, 102
Purnell, Derecka, 226

quarter (U.S. coin), xix, 5, 6, *6*

*Race Traits and Tendencies of the
    American Negro* (Hoffman),
    162–63
racism, reverse. *See* "reverse racism"
Ransby, Barbara, 212
rape by police. *See* police rape and
    sexual assault
Reagan, Ronald, 258, 263
"Redskins" (pro football team
    name), 279–83
Reed, Ishmael: *Haunting of Lin-
    Manuel Miranda*, 96
Reeves, Tate, 260, 261
Rehnquist, William, 310–11
Remini, Robert V., 75, 121
renaming of schools, buildings, etc.,
    270–79
Renderos, Steven, 143
replacement theory. *See* white
    replacement anxiety

Restall, Matthew, 33
"reverse racism," 146, 147, 148
Rhodes, Stewart, 152
Richmond, Cedric, 107
Richmond, Virginia: Black Lives
    Matter protest, 214; Columbus
    statue, 268; Robert E. Lee statue,
    xiv, *190*
"right-wing authoritarian scale," 149
right-wing mass shootings, 130, 131
Roberts, John, 301
Robinson, Rashad, 175
Roof, Dylann, 244–45
Roosevelt, Eleanor, 91, 92, 98
Roosevelt, Franklin D., 185;
    Executive Order 9066, 185
Rosato, Michael, *104*
Ross, Harriet and Ben, 1, 49, 50
Ross, Loretta, 252, 283–84
Rothstein, Richard, 277–78
rubber stamps, *101*, 102

Sacagawea: dollar coin, 5
Sager, Carrie Beatrice "Mudear,"
    290–91
Savali, Kirsten West, 109–10
Scalia, Antonin, 310–11
school names, 255, 270–79 passim
Schumer, Chuck, 99
Scott, Dred, 266
Scott, Tim, 230, 245
Scott, Walter, 244, 245
Second Bank of the United States, 28
Seneca Falls Convention, 1848,
    62–63, 65
Sessions, Jeff, 140, 142, 307
Sewell, Samuel, 29
Seward, Frances, 1, 2, 65
Seward, William H., 1–2
Shaheen, Jeanne, 98, 99, 101
Shelby v. Holder, 300, 315

Shirley, Ollye, 261
silver dollar, 25
Slager, Michael, 244, 245
Smith, Barbara, 69–71
Snyder, Daniel, 280–83 passim
social media: George Floyd
    murder, 203; misinformation
    and disinformation, 309; white
    supremacists, 214–15
Sommers, Samuel R., 146, 150
Southern Manifesto, 276
sports team nicknames and mascots,
    279–83
Stanton, Elizabeth Cady, 64
slave revolts, 44, 57, 160, 243, 245
slavery, 11–13 passim, 179;
    Confederate States, 255–56;
    Dred Scott case and, 267;
    Emancipation Memorial
    (Washington, D.C.), 249–51,
    250; Jackson and, 71, 77–82,
    95; health of enslaved people,
    158–59, 193; Martha Washington
    and, 34–35; Tubman and,
    43–57; U.S. Constitution, 256.
    See also Fugitive Slave Act of
    1793; Fugitive Slave Act of 1850;
    Underground Railroad
Stanton, Elizabeth Cady, 67–68; ten-
    dollar bill verso (proposed), 5, 98
statues: African American heroes,
    270, 300; Calhoun, xvi–xvii;
    Colston, 269–70; Columbus, 265,
    267–69; Jackson, 40; Lincoln,
    249–51, *250*; Robert E. Lee, *xiv*,
    190, 253, 254
Stein, Jeff, 99
Stern, Claire, 172
Stokesbury, James, 32
Stoller, Matt, 94
Stone, Susan Ades, 94

Stop W.O.K.E. Act (Florida), 133
Stovall, Tyler: *White Freedom*, 295, 322
Strings, Sabrina, 179
student activism, xviii, 251, 278
Supreme Court, U.S. *See* U.S. Supreme Court

Takaki, Ronald, 75, 84
Taney, Roger B., 266, 267
Taylor, Breonna, 195–99; "Breonna's Law," 227–28
Taylor, Keeanga-Yamahtta, 192, 239
taxation, 217; estate taxes, 49; Federal Reserve, 25. *See also* poll taxes
tear gas, 206, 218, 219, 229
ten-dollar bill: Jackson (1914), 38; proposed change, 5, 92–93, 94, 96, 97, 106, 108, 115–16
Texas: car-ramming attacks, 208; Columbus monuments, 268; mass shootings, 130, 131; police killings, 236–37; school names, 274, 275; voter suppression laws, 302, 306, 307, 317–18. *See also* Dallas
Thomas, Clarence, 310–11
Thompson, Bennie, 107
Thurmond, Strom, 262
Till, Emmett, 210–11
Tlaib, Rashida, 135, 232
Tometi, Opal, 212
Traoré, Adama, 222
Treasury Department. *See* U.S. Department of the Treasury
Trinidad and Tobago: COVID-19, 170
Trump, Donald, xxiv, 98–99, 116–22 passim, 127–55 passim, 171, 215–21 passim; Advisory
Commission on Election Integrity, 303, 306–7; Black Lives Matter and, 215; black supporters, 175, 199; COVID-19 and, 163–64; D.C. protests and, 218, 219, 220; on D.C. mayor Bowser, 273; George Floyd and, 215–16; Haley and, 247; judicial appointments, 317; name-changing and, 273, 274; NASCAR relations, 263; pardons, 292; presidential election of 2016, 131, 145, 147, 150, 303, 304; presidential election of 2020, 150–56 passim, 292, 298, 308–11 passim, 315, 219, 325; Unite the Right rally, 254; U.S. Capitol insurrection, 150–151, 155, 247; Washington Redskins and, 281
Trump, Ivanka, 121–22, 218
Trump, Mary L., 149
Truth, Sojourner, 2, 47–48; ten-dollar bill verso (proposed), 5, 98, 108
Tubman, Harriet, 46–48, 69–71, 321–25 passim; Auburn, N.Y., 160; Charles Nalle liberation, 54–57; Civil War pension, 1–4; Combahee Ferry Raid, 1, 4, 57–62; death, 71, 160; in *Haunting of Lin-Manuel Miranda*, 96; health, 158; husbands, 3, 4, 50; Newark statue, 270; photos, *xxvi*, *42*; post-slavery activism, 62–69; Rosato mural, *104*; self-emancipation, 48–54, 102–3; siblings, 48–52 passim; Tubman Home for Aged and Infirm Negroes, 160; twenty-dollar bill, 4–11 passim, 15, *90*,

97–128 passim, 323; U.S. Army
recognition (2021), 61–62
Tubman, John, 50
Tuskegee, Alabama: Sammy Younge
Jr., xvii–xviii
Tuskegee Experiment (syphilis
study), 159, 169
Turner, Nat, 44
twenty-dollar bill, 36–39; first, 36;
Cleveland, 37; Jackson, 4–5, 38–
39, 92, 97, 101, 117–20 passim,
127–28, 248, 322; Pocahontas,
5, *32*, 33; redesign, 96; redesign
with Tubman (proposed), 4–11
passim, 15, *90*, 97–128 passim,
248, 323
twenty-five dollar bill (proposed),
96, 119
Tyson, James,. 246–47

Underground Railroad, 45, 49, 53,
54
United Daughters of the
Confederacy, xvi–xvii
Unite the Right rally, Charlottesville,
Virginia, 2017, 209, 252–54
University of Georgia, 271
University of North Carolina, xviii
uprisings, slave. *See* slave revolts
U.S. Capitol: Statuary Hall, 266, 267,
300
U.S. Capitol insurrection, January 6,
2021, 150–56 passim, 247, 319
U.S. Census: demographic data,
143–44
U.S. Constitution: Buckley view,
258; *Bush v. Gore*, 310–11; 14th
Amendment, 63, 296, 311;
15th Amendment, 63, 64, 296;
19th Amendment, 297; slavery
and 256; 13th Amendment,

296; 12th Amendment, 296;
24th Amendment, 298; 26th
Amendment, 299; 23rd
Amendment, 297; voting rights
in, 296–99
U.S. Department of Homeland
Security, 138–40, 219, 307
U.S. Department of Justice, 139,
188, 231, 290, 315; Biden
administration, 188; Civil
Rights Division, 231; Trump
administration, 140, 142, 305–6,
307
U.S. Department of the Treasury,
91, 102, 108, 118–19, 218; ACD,
93; American Council of the
Blind lawsuit, 99–100; Biden
administration, 17; Hamilton,
25, 36, 94; Mellon, 39, 94;
Obama administration, xxiv, 4,
15, 38, 93, 97–98, 115; Trump
administration, 98–103 passim,
122
U.S. presidential elections. *See*
presidential elections
U.S. Supreme Court: *Arizona v.
United States*, 303; *Brnovich*,
302; *Brown*, 242–43, 276; *Bush
v. Gore*, 310–11; *Dred Scott*,
266–67; *Guinn*, 298; *Husted*, 307;
Shelby, 300–302, 315
U.S. Trademark Trial and Appeal
Board, 281

vaccines and vaccination, 168–72
passim, 183
Van Susteren, Greta, 119
Vesey, Denmark, 243, 245
Von Spakovsky, Hans, 303, 305–6
vote, blacks' right to. *See* black
suffrage

vote, women's right to. *See* women's suffrage
voter fraud, 307–8
voter ID laws, 302, 306
Voter Registration Act. *See* National Voter Registration Act
voter suppression, 290–319 passim
voting age, 299
Voting Rights Act of 1965, 290, 299, 315; preclearance provision, 300, 301

Walker, Nikuyah, 254
Wall, Dano, *101*, 102
Wallace, Darrell "Bubba," 262, 263–65, *264*
Wallace, George, 150, 216, 262–63
Washington, A. Shuanise, 107–8
Washington, D.C.: black history museum, 7–9; citizens' right to vote, 297; post–George Floyd murder protests, 217–21; King Memorial, 7; Lincoln statue (Emancipation Memorial), 249–51, *250*; NFL team, 279–83; renaming of public properties, 271–73, 279
Washington, George, 269; dollar bill, 23, 39; Confederate five-dollar bill, 27, *27*; First Bank, 25; quarter, 6; twenty-dollar bill (1905), 37
Washington, Harriet: *Medical Apartheid*, 158–59
Washington, Martha, 34–35; dollar bill (1886), 5, 34

Waters, Maxine, 107
Webb, Jim, 120–21
Wells, Ida B., 236, 270
West, Kanye, 175–76
Wheatley, Phillis, 30–31
Whiskey Rebellion, 26–27
whistle-blowers, 159–60
White Freedom (Stovall), 295, 322
white replacement anxiety, 128–32 passim, 144, 147
white supremacist violence, 130, 131, 137–40 passim, 186–87, 192–95, 209, 244–46
Whitmer, Gretchen, 182, 286
Wickenden, Dorothy, 47, 49, 65
Wilson, Rick, 314
Wilson, Woodrow, 276–79
Women on 20s, 92–98 passim, 102, 103, 110–11
Women Quarters Program. *See* American Women Quarters Program
women's movement (nineteenth century), 62–69
women's suffrage, 62–69 passim, 297
Woods, Charles, 2
Wray, Christopher A., 137–38, 142
Wright, Crystal, 119–20
Wright, Martha Coffin, 65

X, Malcolm. *See* Malcolm X

Zia, Helen, 186
Zimmerman, George, 212
Zinn, Howard, 82

ABOUT THE AUTHOR

 Dr. Clarence Lusane is a professor, the director of the International Affairs program, and former chair of the Political Science Department at Howard University. He earned his B.A. from Wayne State University, and both his Masters and PhD from Howard University in political science. His research focuses on the intersection of race and politics in the United States and globally, ranging from human rights and racial equality to social movements and public policy. That research has included fieldwork in Brazil, Japan, Cuba, South Korea, Cambodia, New Zealand, Bosnia-Herzegovina, Rwanda, France, South Africa, and Ukraine, among others. In addition to his scholarship on global relations, Dr. Lusane has been an official international election observer in Haiti and the Democratic Republic of the Congo. His most recent books include *The Black History of the White House*; *Colin Powell and Condoleezza Rice: Foreign Policy, Race, and the New American Century*, and *Hitler's Black Victims: The Historical Experiences of Afro-Germans, European Blacks, Africans, and African Americans in the Nazi Era*. He currently lives in the Washington, D.C., area.

ALSO AVAILABLE IN THE OPEN MEDIA SERIES

Build Bridges, Not Walls
By Todd Miller

Dispatches from the Race War
By Tim Wise

No Fascist USA!
The John Brown Anti-Klan Committee
and Lessons for Today's Movements
By Hilary Moore and James Tracy, Foreword by Robin D. G. Kelley

Loaded
A Disarming History of the Second Amendment
By Roxanne Dunbar-Ortiz

Have Black Lives Ever Mattered?
By Mumia Abu-Jamal

American Nightmare
Facing the Challenge of Fascism
By Henry A. Giroux

The Black History of the White House
By Clarence Lusane

Narrative of the Life of Frederick Douglass,
an American Slave, Written by Himself
A New Critical Edition
By Angela Y. Davis

CITY LIGHTS BOOKS | OPEN MEDIA SERIES
Arm Yourself With Information